AMERICAN THOUGHT BEFORE 1900

American Thought Before 1900, and its companion volume *American Philosophy in the Twentieth Century*, are part of a series, Classics in the History of Thought, prepared under the general editorship of Crane Brinton and Paul Edwards.

American Thought Before 1900

A Sourcebook

FROM PURITANISM TO DARWINISM

Edited, with an Introductory Survey, Notes,

and Bibliographies, by **PAUL KURTZ**

THE MACMILLAN COMPANY, NEW YORK

COLLIER-MACMILLAN LTD., LONDON

The Macmillan Company, New York

Collier-Macmillan Canada Ltd., Toronto, Ontario

Printed in the United States of America

The author wishes to acknowledge the kind cooperation of the following for permission to reprint material in this book:

From *Samuel Johnson, President of King's College*, Vol. II, by H. W. and C. Schneider. Copyright 1929. Used by permission of Columbia University Press.

From *A Summary of the Principles of Action* by Cadwallader Colden. Used by permission of The New York Historical Society.

From "Darwin's Influence Upon Philosophy," by John Dewey, in *Popular Science Monthly*, Vol. LXXV (July, 1909). Reprinted courtesy of *Popular Science Monthly*, © 1962 by Popular Science Publishing Company, Inc., and courtesy of Mrs. John Dewey.

191

K

for Herbert W. Schneider

Contents

PART THREE: CONSERVATISM IN POLITICAL THEORY AND PHILOSOPHY (1800–1850)

PART FOUR: TRANSCENDENTALISM (1820–1860)

PART FIVE: SPECULATIVE AND ABSOLUTE
IDEALISM (1860–1900)

PART SIX: EVOLUTION AND DARWINISM (1859–1900)

Preface

American Thought Before 1900: A Sourcebook from Puritanism to Darwinism and *American Philosophy in the Twentieth Century: A Sourcebook from Pragmatism to Philosophical Analysis* are companion volumes, which may be used separately or together. *American Thought Before 1900* is designed for a wide range of readers in the fields of American studies and American philosophy. Inasmuch as the kind of intellectual interests expressed in the United States before the twentieth century is continuous with the social context, the term "thought" rather than "philosophy" perhaps better applies, and readers of history, literature, religion, and politics, as well as those interested in philosophy, will find this volume useful. *American Philosophy in the Twentieth Century* is more specifically devoted to the tracing of the development of philosophical ideas in the United States from the latter part of the nineteenth century until the present day. It too, however, should be of use to students in American studies programs and to the general reader interested in recent and current philosophical thinking.

My special thanks in preparing these volumes go to Paul Edwards for his wise counsel and assistance. I also wish to acknowledge my appreciations to Herbert W. Schneider and Harold Larrabee for their valuable suggestions, especially in the preparation of *American Thought Before 1900*. The following people were also helpful in selecting appropriate pieces or in providing important information, especially for *American Philosophy in the Twentieth Century:* Sidney Hook, Brand Blanshard, C. I. Lewis, Rudolf Carnap, Paul Tillich, Max Black, Horace L. Friess, Bernard Perry, and Edward Boring. I wish to thank those of my students on whom I have tested portions of this manuscript and the library staffs of Union College and Vassar College for bibliographical assistance. The Ford Foundation Public Affairs Program and the Union College Social Science Research Center are responsible for providing a grant to defray some of the costs involved in research for these books. I am grateful to my wife for her constant inspiration and devotion.

PAUL KURTZ

Introduction

Prior to 1900, European reaction to American thought was generally disdainful. Alexis de Tocqueville observed in 1835 that: ". . . in no country in the civilized world is less attention paid to philosophy than in the United States. The Americans have no philosophical school of their own; and they care but little for all the schools into which Europe is divided . . ." [1] America, it was widely held, was the receiving port for European men and ideas, but contributed little that was original to philosophical thought.

This indictment of American thought, though overstated, was justifiable if one took as the standard of excellence the kind of academic philosophy practiced in Europe. For academic philosophy did not fully develop in America until the mid and late nineteenth century; and America produced few, if any, outstanding technical philosophers. Yet America was far from being an intellectual wasteland; creative thought was present, though it was usually related to practical interests.

Is there any quality of "American" thought which distinguishes it from that developed elsewhere?

One peculiar and all-pervasive characteristic is its pluralism. For any single generalization about it, a countergeneralization is usually possible. Thought in America has developed in response to external influences and to internal problems and challenges. America has been receptive to many cultures and to a variety of intellectual themes. There is, for example, both a liberal and a conservative tradition throughout American history. There is the America of radical democratic individualism and equalitarianism of Thomas Jefferson, Thomas Paine, Ethan Allen, Benjamin Rush, Henry Thoreau, Abraham Lincoln and John Dewey—an America in which liberal causes are espoused or in which a dominant secular and naturalistic outlook prevails. But there is also a conservative stream in American history, represented in the religious interests of the Puritans, Jonathan Edwards, and Samuel Johnson, in the defense of orthodoxy by the Scottish realists and speculative idealists, and in the conservative politics of Cadwallader Colden, Alexander Hamilton, John C. Calhoun, and even George Santayana. America is thus the meeting place of divergent ideas and movements: Puritanism, deism, materialism, Unitarianism, transcendentalism, ideal-

[1] Alexis de Tocqueville, *Democracy in America*, New York, 1845, Vol. II, p. 1.

ism, realism, and pragmatism—and most recently of naturalism, positivism, analytic philosophy, Marxism, Thomism, phenomenology, Zen Buddhism, and existentialism. Any simple formulas designed to reduce these diverse elements into a uniform tradition are bound to be distorted.

Nevertheless, one characteristic theme seems to distinguish the American tradition: *ideas are evaluated pragmatically, and their significance is most frequently determined by reference to their practical contexts, their political, religious, moral or social purposes. Thinking is a form of activity; and there is great confidence and optimism in the ability of knowledge to solve the problems of men.*

Philosophical thought may be approached in either of two ways: (1) as technical philosophy, abstracted from its broader contexts of origin and application, or (2) as it is related to the actual problems encountered within the sociological and cultural setting. The relationship between (1) and (2) is not always clear, and we do not know with any accuracy what kind of philosophy a given set of historic conditions will produce. Does philosophy reflect the culture as we generally assume? Or is it at times an escape from it? Although philosophy is related to socio-cultural conditions, it claims not to be solely a local or temporal affair. In American thought prior to 1900, at least, there was not much philosophizing in the first, strict, sense. Hence American ideas must be examined primarily—although not exclusively—in terms of their institutional contexts. But this does not mean that these ideas are without philosophical content; only that they are embedded in the very way of life. Indeed, de Tocqueville himself notes ". . . almost all the inhabitants of the United States use their minds in the same manner, and direct them according to the same rules; that is to say, without ever having taken the trouble to define the rules, they have a philosophical method common to the whole people."[2] There is a national bias, according to Ralph Barton Perry, which is hidden underneath the level of formal expression, an unarticulated set of premises which govern not only the judgments of everyday life, but to some extent color scientific, literary, and philosophic expression, in the problems considered and in the solutions accepted.

Rather than pre-twentieth-century America be judged harshly for its failure to develop technical philosophy, let it be noted that what happened here is perhaps inevitable in a frontier community. It is rare that colonial or virgin territories equal mature and settled lands in their creative cultural expression.

However, the problems which confronted young America did raise fundamental issues—metaphysical, religious, political and ethical—that were philosophical in character. And the origins of American thought

[2] *Ibid.*

show that the roots of the pragmatic method lie deep within the American experience. Pragmatism as a philosophic doctrine was not formally enunciated and explicitly defended until the end of the nineteenth century, by Charles Peirce (1839–1914), William James (1848–1910) and John Dewey (1859–1952)—long after it had been unconsciously practiced. According to the pragmatists, the meaning of an idea is to be discovered by reference to its bearing on practice and conduct. Ideas are inextricably connected to their consequences in behavior, and they are to be judged by the differences they make in concrete contexts. With Peirce, James, and Dewey, pragmatic philosophy was heralded as the unique American contribution to the history of philosophy, although it seemed to many foreign critics to be merely the rationalization of a way of life, a philosophical expression of the American inclination to judge ideas by their uses and functions.

The history of American thought shows that although there has been extensive borrowing of foreign ideas (primarily European), these have been transformed in the light of American needs. European critics have attacked this adaptation of ideas to practical ends as crudely "materialistic." But America not only conquered a vast unknown land and developed an advanced technological society, it also assimilated countless immigrants from all over the world, and created a democratic social order. And the energies which made this enormous achievement possible have their sources in certain philosophical and psychological beliefs, attitudes and values. These can be seen in the pioneer spirit of the first settlers, in the radical democracy of the Age of Reason and Revolution, in the continuing journey westward, in the renaissance that followed the Civil War, and finally, in the twentieth century, in the elaboration of a distinctive pragmatic philosophy.

I. THE COLONIAL PERIOD (1620-1776)

A continuing challenge to the American intellectual scene has been provided by the successive waves of immigration, and the resulting infusions of divergent ideas. No sooner did one wave begin to be assimilated than a new force appeared. Thus America constantly added the experience and thought of older traditions to its shore; yet at the same time these traditions were themselves profoundly altered by the new habitat. The settlements in America were established by European colonists: the Puritans of Plymouth, the Anglicans of Jamestown and Charleston, the Dutch of New York, the Quakers and Germans of Pennsylvania, the French of New Orleans, the Scotch-Irish of the advancing frontier communities, to mention only a few—and later the Negroes, Irish, Jews, Poles, Italians, and others exerted a significant influence.

The British influence on our institutions has been the strongest, however; perhaps the fact that we possess a common tongue is the chief reason for this. Thus the colonies of New England, particularly the Massachusetts Bay area, seem to have left the strongest impression; at least, historians have been particularly concerned with their influence and have emphasized our Puritan heritage. Curiously, America, partly Puritan in origin, has been strongly concerned with rejecting its Puritanism; but the mark left on American character still remains.

The Puritans (1620–1700)

The Puritans were united and motivated by religious conviction. Initially members of the Church of England, they wished to purge it of "Popish practices." Dissatisfied with the meager reforms enacted by the Anglican Church, they settled in the unknown wilderness, hoping to build a New Zion. The Puritans were thoroughly British in culture and conventions; they differed from their contemporaries primarily in the degree of their religious dissent.

The New England Puritans were particularly characterized by their agreement with the principles of Calvinism. Even though they did not consider themselves to be literal disciples of John Calvin, they shared with him the belief in the absolute sovereignty of God and of the utter dependence of man upon Him. They believed that God was an all-powerful and arbitrary being whose ways were inscrutable to man. He had originally made a covenant with Adam, for which man was to receive immortal life. But Adam disobeyed God, and as a consequence merited damnation. All of Adam's descendants inherited the curse of "original sin," and were irresistibly given over to evil. But God made a second covenant enabling man to receive salvation through the intermediary of his Son, Jesus Christ. However, this salvation could not be earned by good works or moral excellence, for it was entirely foreordained by God's will, and the elect (a "Society of Saints") were totally dependent upon His grace. Man must offer God faith and obedience, but such devotion (seen in conversion and regeneration) was in response to God's gift of grace and not possible without it. The Puritans, like Saint Augustine and Calvin, thus faced a dilemma between the doctrines of determinism and free will. It was this dilemma which Jonathan Edwards, in his book *Freedom of the Will* (1754), attempted to resolve.

For the Puritans, life was a moral process originating in sin, dedicated to faith, and culminating in the hope that ultimate salvation might be achieved. Certain moral virtues were typically emphasized: discipline, devotion, honesty, moderation, temperance, frugality, industry, simplicity. Theirs was an ethic of serious and hard work, an ethic of practical activity and enterprise—although one might expect that philosophical predestinationism would lead to passive inaction. Perhaps the dynamic activism of the American Puritan might better be explained, not by his religion or his philosophy, which he brought with him, but by the new geographical and economic necessities; here was a frontier to claim, a wilderness to conquer, a future to forge.

Much has been written about the fact that a form of individualism was implicit in the Puritan rejection of the authority of the medieval Church and in the claim that man's relation to God was private. Yet New England Puritanism was intolerant of dissent and heresy, and the Massachusetts Bay Colony in particular was organized along theocratic lines. Increase Mather and Cotton Mather were both prone to authoritarian attitudes; and Anne Hutchinson, Roger Williams, the "witches" of Salem among others, encountered innumerable difficulties with the religious intolerance of the new establishment. The covenant with God seemed to be more of a corporate arrangement between the whole community and God rather than a private affair. Moreover, the earliest settlements did not espouse a doctrine of the separation of church and state. The Congregational Churches, being organized as autonomous bodies, perhaps contained the seeds of democracy. But it was only after new sects began arriving, such as the Quakers, Baptists, antinomists, and others, that separate and freer communities were established in Rhode Island, Baltimore and the middle Colonies; for toleration seemed the only way to cope with the plethora of denominations. It was during the Age of Reason—when secularism prevailed—that the separation of church and state, and religious toleration, as fundamental American principles were finally and clearly enunciated.

Colonial Materialism and Immaterialism (1700–1776)

By and large, seventeenth-century America was so dominated by practical pursuits and religious interests that little time was devoted to theoretical philosophy or science (with some exceptions, such as the work of the astronomer, William Brattle, at Harvard). It was not until the eighteenth century that intellectual philosophic and scientific interests were more directly nourished. Jonathan Edwards (1703–1758) represents the most thoroughgoing use of philosophical idealism in an attempt to provide a rational philosophical vindication of the Calvinistic system against its critics. But he arrived on the scene virtually at the end of the period in which Calvinism was influential. Samuel Johnson (1696–1772), an Anglican, shared Edwards' desire to use philosophical immaterialism to combat materialism; and his work was deeply influenced by George Berkeley of Great Britain. But despite intermittent periods of religious revival, neither Edwards

nor Johnson could stem the tide of new forces, especially the development of modern science and modern philosophy, which had begun to
emerge in Europe. The early Puritans were inspired by the Reformation; but by the eighteenth century, Newton, Locke, and the materialists provided a more powerful source of influence.

Within the Colonies there emerged American counterparts of European materialism and deism. Both Cadwallader Colden (1688-1776)
and Benjamin Franklin (1706-1790) represented these modern tendencies. Colden was a serious student of Newtonian science, and he
offered a major defense and elaboration of materialistic philosophy.
Franklin experimentally applied and extended the concepts of Newtonian physics to electrical phenomena. Franklin is a transitional
figure. Although he came early under the influence of Calvinism, he
proceeded to naturalize moral values, retaining Calvinism's practical
code of hard work, but making happiness rather than faith its chief
aim. Thus, the revealed religion of the early settlers was gradually
supplanted by a religion of reason.

II. REASON AND REVOLUTION (1776-1800)

With the outbreak of the War for Independence in 1776, interest
in the ideals of the Age of Reason became pre-eminent. The Enlightenment had a correlative impact in America. Many of the colonists were
inspired by the English Deists such as Blount, Clarke, Bolingbroke,
Collins, Shaftesbury, and Wollaston, and by French writers such as
Condillac, Diderot, Condorcet, Cabanis, Holbach, Volney, La Mettrie,
and Voltaire. However, it was the empiricism and liberalism of the
British philosopher John Locke that had the most important and direct
influence on American thought—though once again his major impact
was practical.

The Age of Reason in America assumed three forms: first, it contributed to the development of materialism and deism in metaphysics
and religion; second, it helped to emphasize the values of a secular
and naturalistic morality; and third, and most dramatically, it made
meaningful the ideals of republicanism and revolution.

Materialism

The Newtonian materialism of the colonial period came to full
maturity in the latter part of the eighteenth century. Many of its proponents were medical men, such as Benjamin Rush (1745-1813) of
Philadelphia. Among other materialists were Joseph Priestley, the
noted discoverer of oxygen who fled from England to America in
1794, Thomas Cooper, Southern exponent of progressive thought,

and Joseph Buchanan, leader of a remarkable renaissance in secular naturalism at Transylvania University in Kentucky. The materialists had strong interests in science and they attempted to extend what they considered to be the legitimate aims of science to other areas of the cosmos, including man. Thus, they consistently attempted to apply physical and mechanistic explanations to mind and morality.

Deism

Deism as a religious philosophy was widely espoused by many of the advanced leaders of the new republic, such as Jefferson and Washington. Its most forceful and persistent defenders, however, were Thomas Paine (1737–1809), Ethan Allen (1737–1789), and Elihu Palmer (1764–1806). The deists affirmed the supremacy of reason, and denied the claims of revelation, prophecies, and miracles. They were bitter critics of the established church and clerical authority, defending the principles of religious freedom, toleration, and the separation of church and state. Paine and Allen in particular submitted the Old and New Testaments to scathing criticism and denunciation. Their religious radicalism was perhaps atypical in its extremism, but it did express a widely-shared point of view in the age.

For the deist, all events in nature were determined by natural laws. God, as the first cause, designed the natural order. Most deists looked upon nature, including man, as a manifestation of the goodness of God. This belief in the basic goodness of man was incompatible with the Calvinist conceptions of human depravity and original sin. Moreover, the deists held that man, as a rational being, was capable of achieving the good life on earth, and did not need to wait for the heavenly kingdom to come. Their morality was humanistic, and relative to human aims and goals—a marked contrast to the religious morality of the first settlers. Happiness and pleasure, not faith and humility, were the standards of choice. The Enlightenment manifested an optimistic faith in science, in reason, and in education, as the instruments of human progress. Following Lockian empiricism, all knowledge was reduced to original sensations. Man was held to be the product of conditioning forces in his environment and there was, therefore, a great interest in achieving social justice and welfare; for it was held that if one improved the social environment, one might change man for the better.

Political Ideas

If America contributed anything original in this period, it was the practical development of new political and social ideals. The ideas which inspired the Revolution had their origins in the writings of

Locke and Montesquieu, but their experimental application in a new context was a significant innovation. The application of the general ideas of liberalism to the Revolutionary situation involved difficult problems and required serious thought. Thomas Jefferson (1743–1826), Thomas Paine (1737–1809), and others maintained that justice is related to the doctrine of "natural rights" ("life, liberty, and the pursuit of happiness") and not to the divine right of kings, hereditary rights, or the conserving of established institutions. Governments are artificial contracts made by men, to be overthrown and changed by men if they do not fulfill their original purposes or if they violate inalienable human rights. Thus republican institutions and democratic attitudes were tested in action, and the principles of democracy became an essential element in American life.

This does not mean that there was unanimity among the colonists. And indeed, after the Revolutionary cause was gained, there was need to reason out and build a new system of government. *The Federalist* papers (1787–88) were written by Alexander Hamilton (1757–1804) the conservative, James Madison (1751–1836) the liberal, and John Jay (1745–1829) in order to explain and justify the Federal Constitution. These papers raised profound issues in areas relating to political science and philosophy, issues that were especially troubling in that period: what are the claims to power of the various factions and classes of society? how does one reconcile the claims of the democratic with the oligarchical principle? which is more important, liberty or equality? and many others. Some American thinkers, such as Jefferson, considered agrarian society as the ideal, but others, such as Hamilton, favored a commercial or industrial society. Some wished to defend sectional interests and state governments, but Hamilton defended the necessity of strong centralized government. The problem of how to safeguard human liberties against the encroachments of a tyrannical government was dealt with by the development of a system of checks and balances among the three branches of government.

Impressive and unique in the origin of the new republic was the attempt of the colonists, unencumbered by tradition, to apply a vigorous and fresh outlook to political and social problems. If their ideas were not original in genesis they were original in the pragmatic uses to which they were put.

III. CONSERVATISM IN POLITICAL THEORY AND PHILOSOPHY (1800–1850)

No sooner had America reached its apogee in brilliance than a conservative reaction set in—political, religious, moral, and philosophic. The liberal stream of the Enlightenment was overwhelmed by a conservative undercurrent, which now rose to the surface. This seems to be a fairly recurrent phenomenon in American history, where liberal free thought has at various times been subjected to suppression by evangelical revivalist movements or by reactionary pressures. Yet a good case can be made for the counter-thesis that, in spite of periods of conservative reaction, the dominant theme of American life is one of changing, hence liberal, social values. Nonetheless, the period between the American Revolution and the Civil War, with the exception of transcendentalism, was peculiarly lacking in intellectual distinction. There were profound social and political problems that the United States faced in consolidating the gains of the Revolution and in coming to terms with slavery. But this had little effect in creating a new or vigorous philosophical point of view.

Southern Racial Aristocracy (1800–1860)

In political theory, an immediate reaction against the Declaration of Independence was stimulated by a fear of "the mob" inspired to some extent by the Jacobin excesses of the French Revolution. The South was unable to reconcile itself to Jeffersonian democracy. Is the principle "all men are created equal" defensible, or does it rest on untenable metaphysical grounds? And if it is acceptable, does it apply to Negroes? Virginia was at first under the influence of Jeffersonian ideals. But the black belt, with its center in Charleston and extending to the southwest, and later Virginia itself, came to defend an ideal of "Greek democracy" in which only the white "citizens," not the slaves, were to be properly considered. People like John Taylor, George Tucker, Thomas Dew, Alexander H. Stephens, Albert Bledsoe, and John C. Calhoun attempted to provide a defense of the *status quo*, which included the institution of slavery and the economic interests that it supported. Variously attacked were the notions of liberty, equality, natural rights, democracy, and strong federal government. Some southerners based their defense on racial superiority, on custom, or passion, or even Biblical authority; some held, too, that slavery was a good, since it strengthened the character of the masters! John C. Calhoun (1782-1850), the most serious southern philosophical writer of this period, denied that there were natural rights prior to society—such rights were metaphysical abstractions—and he attempted to defend a hierarchical and organic conception of society. Order and security, rather than scientific reason or democratic reform, were to be valued and preserved.

There were times, of course, when the liberals were ascendant, as during the election of Jefferson to the Presidency (1801–09) and during the Jacksonian period (1829–37), when western frontier individualism and egalitarianism returned in full force. But in the nineteenth century, these political differences represented a fundamental division between the States, which was sealed, finally, only through war and by force. Lincoln gave renewed expression to the ideals of Jeffersonian democracy and, victorious in the Civil War, was able to preserve the Union.

Academic Philosophy: Scottish Realism (1800–1850)

A similar conservatism was evident in religion in the early nineteenth century. The radical deistic spirit of the Age of Reason was lost in the general subservience of science to religion. The earlier confidence in the powers of human intelligence was replaced by a failure of courage and a sense of human dependence. Remarkable during this period were the numerous scholarly attempts to rationalize received traditions and values. Many national religious denominations were established— Methodists, Presbyterians, Episcopalians, Baptists, Mormons, etc.— and many colleges were founded under religious auspices. When Union College (Schenectady) was founded in 1795 as a nondenominational college its motto—*Fraternité*—was taken from the French Revolution; Trinity College (Hartford), on the other hand, was chartered by Episcopalians in 1823, and its motto was *Pro ecclesia et patria*. During the colonial period philosophy had no special place in the colleges, which were looked upon at first as a training ground for the ministry, and later for the learned professions, such as medicine and law. But, with the founding of many liberal arts colleges in the nineteenth century, philosophy was widely taught as a subject having an important place in the curriculum. It was generally divided into three parts: natural, mental, and moral philosophy. Frequently, the college president was a clergyman who taught an "edifying" course in philosophy, that is, a course that was safe, respectable, and designed to indoctrinate. The purpose of many or most of these institutions of higher learning was to provide moral discipline and an ordered conception of the universe. The college thus had the conservative function of preserving a cultural tradition and, in effect, of justifying the *status quo*. The early nineteenth century was the heyday of the writer of philosophy textbooks—equaled perhaps only in our day. In 1835, for example, Francis Wayland, President of Brown University, published *Elements of Moral Science*, which eventually sold two hundred thousand copies. The key to its popularity lay, perhaps, in the fact that two-thirds of the text was devoted to "practical ethics." Wilson Smith has observed that between 1830 and 1860 a high percentage of professors of moral philosophy were personally involved in public affairs. Most of the books published in philosophy were works intended for either moral or religious application. Indeed, Noah Porter, President of Yale, maintained that philosophy in America had been prosecuted chiefly as an "applied science" and in its special connection to theology, morals, and politics.

There were at least two dominant philosophical influences apparent in this period: Scottish realism, and philosophical idealism, with the latter finally prevailing toward the end of the century (see Part V, below). The Scottish philosophers, Thomas Reid, Dugald Stewart, Adam Ferguson, and others, seemed to many in America to offer a powerful answer to Hume's skepticism.

Scottish realism was first introduced at Princeton before 1800 by John Witherspoon and Samuel Stanhope Smith. It was espoused later in one form or another by Francis Bowen, Joseph Haven, Noah Porter, and James McCosh, among others. James McCosh (1811–1894), a late arrival to American shores, was able to summarize the significance of the movement more effectively than his predecessors. McCosh thought that ". . . Yankees are distinguished from most others by their practical observation and invention," and that realism might very well be the "distinctive" American philosophy. The return to "common sense" implicit in realism no doubt appealed to native American practicalism.

Realism was based on the doctrine that "real objects" existed independently of man and were perceivable as such. Real objects were neither unknowable nor reducible to phenomena or ideas. All of this seemed "self-evident" and "given" to inductive intuition. But the realists also thought that such intuition might establish moral, political and religious truths. Indeed, all "first and fundamental truths" could be known in the same way. There were self-evident certitudes of right and wrong, standards of justice and injustice, truth of God's existence and of immortality of the soul, mathematical objects, and basic scientific universals. This method could be extended indefinitely, and Edinburgh philosophy was conveniently used to instate a whole set of orthodox ideas and values, giving them the sanction of philosophical necessity. Thus, what at first appeared as a solution to knotty philosophical problems became a means of rationalizing the unquestioning acceptance of traditional values which appealed to "common sense."

IV. TRANSCENDENTALISM (1820–1860)

Many literary historians consider transcendentalism the distinctive development in American letters of the nineteenth century. It was largely a pre-Civil War movement, although many of its adherents lived well beyond that period, and it attempted to establish Boston as the cultural center of America. Among its proponents were Ralph Waldo Emerson, Henry David Thoreau, William Ellery Channing, Theodore Parker, Bronson Alcott, James Freeman Clarke, James Marsh, Frederick Henry Hedge, Margaret Fuller, and Caleb Sprague Henry. Henry James the elder, a Swedenborgian mystic, might also be classed as a transcendentalist of sorts.

The movement was rather conservative in its metaphysics and epistemology, but it was decidedly liberal in its morals and politics. It was a fairly inchoate movement—literary, religious, political, and philosophical—distinguishable more perhaps by what it opposed than by what it supported.

Initially the transcendentalists were Unitarians, in particular William Ellery Channing (1780–1842), Ralph Waldo Emerson (1803–1882), and Theodore Parker (1810–1860). Liberal in sentiment, the Unitarian transcendentalists transformed Calvinistic pessimism to optimism; God was loving and just, not arbitrary or vindictive; man was not necessarily sinful but capable of moral virtue and goodness. The Unitarians also reacted against the mechanistic universe and rational religion of the deists. Nature manifested divine purpose, and man might know and appreciate its full beauty. But man must transcend ordinary understanding or experience, and his soul must have direct contact with divinity; this might be done largely without benefit of clergy. The Unitarians, like the deists, wished to use reason to interpret the Bible but, unlike the deists, many, such as Channing, accepted revelation and Biblical miracles as true.

The transcendentalists were reacting against what they considered to be the limitations of the Lockian conception of experience, but they went somewhat beyond rational Unitarianism. Many rejected Biblical religion. Influenced by the romantic idealists, Coleridge, Kant, Schelling, and Cousin, by Platonism, and by Indian mysticism, they attempted to expand the categories of the Enlightenment. The universe was richer and deeper, they claimed, than the empiricists had allowed. There was a "transcendental realm" over and beyond the world of phenomenal appearances, an "ultimate reality" which only reason and intuition could penetrate. The transcendentalists gave free play to subjective and mystical insight. Transcendentalists, such as Theodore Parker, criticized the dependence upon empirical and scientific facts and understanding; knowledge based on such evidence was no more than probable, and ended in skepticism. Parker claimed that there was an "ultimate truth" which was certain and absolute, and this provided a basis, not only for metaphysics, but for morals and politics as well. In general, the transcendentalists were poets and seers who proclaimed the truth as they saw it and were not interested in rational proofs. Transcendental epistemology thus seemed impervious to the rules of scientific verification or logical consistency: it was tested by intuition and sentiment.

The transcendentalists were idealists in metaphysics. They postulated two realms: the unreal world of sensations, which was the object of physical science; and the unseen world, a religious, moral, and aesthetic universe, which only poetry and philosophy could discover. The universe, according to Ralph Waldo Emerson, was at root one in which "mind," the "over-soul," and the "spirit" ultimately prevailed. In spite of Emerson's idealism, many have recognized a core of Yankee pragmatism even in transcendentalism. Emerson himself distinguished three stages of idealism: the academic, the poetic, and the practical, by which man relates to nature. And his late work, *The Conduct of Life*, is concerned with the ". . . practical question of the conduct of life. How shall I live?"

Transcendentalism was, therefore, not limited to metaphysical speculation, but sought to provide a fulfilling way of life. It was a movement stimulated by moral idealism. Transcendentalists attempted to liberate the individual and to free him from the blind hold of custom and convention. Henry David Thoreau (1817–1862), whom Herbert W. Schneider describes as a "pagan" and the "Nietzsche of New England," best illustrates the model of the nonconforming individual. Thoreau insisted that the individual must be free to consult his inner light, and he opposed institutions when they imposed on an individual's intuition. Thus civil disobedience was man's highest obligation, if society contradicted his moral conscience. This was a continuation of the radical individualism and anarchism implicit in the spirit of the frontier. Even the genteel Emerson, in his essay *Self-Reliance*, hails the nonconforming individual and defends his independence from tradition. Emerson, whose very name later became synonymous with respectability, was himself a rebel of sorts. Indeed, an early theological address he delivered at the Harvard Divinity School was considered too radical and was likely one of the reasons why he was, for many years, ostracized from the Harvard Yard.

The transcendentalists were humanitarians deeply concerned with moral progress, with political and social justice and equality. Each individual possessed an implicit dignity, which was also a claim to equality, for each person had both the ability and the right to consult his private intuition. From the dignity of each man and his inalienable natural rights it followed that slavery was an unpardonable moral crime. Many of the transcendentalists were leaders in the abolitionists' cause. Some defended women's rights, others espoused the building of ideal Utopian communities (such as Brook Farm). They fought against acquiescence to injustice and defended liberalism in social action.

V. SPECULATIVE AND ABSOLUTE IDEALISM (1860–1900)

Transcendentalism was sympathetic to philosophical idealism, but it seemed primarily to offer a literary and romantic rather than a technical approach to philosophy. European philosophical idealism had taken root in American thought, and it reappeared after the Civil War as the dominant academic tradition. But it was transformed into pure and technical speculative philosophy. A group known as the St. Louis Hegelians was especially influential in the development of this kind of speculative idealism. Its members included William T. Harris, Henry C. Brokmeyer, Thomas Davidson, George H. Howison, Denton J. Snider, J. E. Woerner, Joseph Pulitzer, and Carl Schurz. Many of these men were immigrants who fled Germany after the failure of the 1848 revolution. The teaching of this group became known throughout the midwest from Milwaukee to Chicago, and later in California; eventually it even penetrated New England, the heartland of transcendentalism.

The St. Louis Hegelians published two major journals: *The Journal of Speculative Philosophy,* the first of its kind in America, and *The Western,* a review of education, science, literature, and art. The movement was initiated (about 1858) by the "Kant Club" through the serious study of German absolute idealism: Hegel, Kant, Fichte, Schelling, and later of lesser scholars, such as Erdmann, Trendelenburg and Lotze. The transcendentalists had received their idealism from secondary sources; the speculative idealists went to primary sources, translating and studying directly the works of absolute idealists, especially Hegel's *Logic.* Hegelian philosophers offered a coherent world view and applied it in many different areas: metaphysics, religion, art, morals, politics, law, and education. The German influence continued later, though in a different form, as American scholars, Henry James, George Bancroft, Horace Mann, Henry Barnard, George Ticknor, Edward Everett, and others, studied abroad in German universities. The net result was that Germanic methods of scholarship and philosophy were imported into America.

The speculative idealists argued single-mindedly for the speculative method: they attacked the positivism, empiricism, and agnosticism of Comte, Mill and Spencer, and defended "abstract philosophy." Reason, they believed, could achieve knowledge of "ultimate reality."

William T. Harris (1835–1919), influential editor of *The Journal of Speculative Philosophy,* thought that before America could develop a philosophy of its own it must study the great masters; and Hegel seemed the most promising. Harris observed, however, that for the St. Louis Hegelians philosophy came to mean "the most practical of all species of knowledge," which suggests that even for those theoretical philosophers, some pragmatic element was present. Laurens Perseus Hickok (1798–1888) was also among the first to become a full-fledged advocate of German idealism. Well-grounded in the work of Kant and Hegel, he attempted to build a systematic theory of the universe based on absolute reason.

As philosophy became increasingly professionalized and institutionalized in the colleges and universities, idealism became the foremost doctrine of the schools. Many academic professors, like the earlier Scottish realists, were thoroughly orthodox. They used idealism as a support for the "eternal verities" and supernatural religion.

Other noteworthy idealists in the nineteenth century were George T. Ladd, Paul Carus, and the personalists, George H. Howison and Borden Parker Bowne, who claimed that persons or selves are the principal reality. Felix Adler, a Kantian, in 1876 founded the liberal religious Society for Ethical Culture. At Cornell, idealism was strong; and the founding of the *Philosophical Review* by Jacob Gould Schurman in 1892 may be considered the high point of idealism in America.

In a symposium in 1895, George H. Howison summed up the dominant temper of American academic idealism when he said: "We are all agreed" in one "great tenet," which is "the entire foundation of philosophy itself: that explanation of the world which maintains that the only thing absolutely real is mind; that all material and all temporal existences take their being from consciousness that thinks and experiences; that out of consciousness they all issue, to consciousness they are presented, and that presence to consciousness constitutes their entire reality." [3]

The kind of idealism which generally prevailed, however, was neo-Hegelian absolute or objective idealism. This kind of idealism, unlike mentalistic or subjective idealism (such as the idealism of Berkeley and Johnson), did not simply reduce reality to ideas. Mind was held to be central to the universe; but the universe was thought to be a systematic or organic whole, encompassing the experience of individual men, social mind, and culminating in an objective intelligible order. The order of the universe was not only a logical or causal order, but value and purpose were also said to have an ontological basis in reality. Metaphysical idealism, both in England and America, enjoyed its greatest influence in the nineteenth century, although many important idealists lived on into the twentieth century. Among these were Frank Thilly, George S. Fullerton, Mary W. Calkins, Hugo Munsterberg, George H. Palmer, and James E. Creighton.

Perhaps the greatest representative of idealism in America was

[3] Quoted from Arthur O. Lovejoy, in *Contemporary American Philosophy. Personal Statements*, Vol. II, New York: Macmillan, 1930, p. 85.

Josiah Royce (1855–1916). Royce defended the great tradition of perennial philosophy. Although of the twentieth century and a major influence during the "Golden Age of American Philosophy" on James, Santayana and others at Harvard, Royce is really heir to the nineteenth century. He made a persistent attempt to discover the Absolute in the universe. From fragmentary experience he was led to "the larger self," from the possibility of error to a standard of Absolute truth, and from logic to a theory of order.

Absolute idealism was far removed from pragmatic and experimental naturalism, and was, thus, plainly alien to the native American practical temper. Yet even Royce considered himself to be under the influence of pragmatism, and he called himself an "absolute pragmatist"; for though truth was eternal and timeless, it was nonetheless related to purpose. Royce was doubtless attempting to accommodate some of the newer intellectual influences building in the late nineteenth century. In particular, the Darwinian revolution in biology had such a profound effect upon American thought that by the beginning of the twentieth century the death of absolute idealism seemed a foregone conclusion. The idealists that remained appeared to be, especially in the light of later developments, an anachronistic residue of things past, part of the "cultural lag."

VI. EVOLUTION AND DARWINISM (1859–1900)

The Civil War marks a turning point in American culture. During the war, the energies of the nation were spent in resolving internal discord. With its termination, men were free to turn some of their energies to the creation of new worlds of imagination and thought. There was an enormous release of creative talent—in the arts, science, literature, and philosophy. The growth of American industrial and technological power and its increasing influence on the world scene was accompanied by correlative intellectual and cultural achievements.

The impact of the scientific revolution on the modern world took on significant proportions with the introduction of Darwin's theory of evolution. This theory stimulated new and bold philosophical discussion, and led to deep conflict, in both Europe and the United States, between science and traditional religion, metaphysics, and ethics. There were two outstanding questions in this dispute: first, was Darwin's scientific hypothesis true? And second, what were the broader philosophical implications of the theory?

The first question was rapidly resolved. Evolutionary ideas in one form or another had been in circulation for almost a century. In biology, Buffon and Lamarck had suggested evolutionary explanations for the variety of life; similarly, geologists had used evolution to account for changes on the earth's surface. Even in America, Jefferson, Benjamin Rush, Samuel Stanhope Smith, and others had observed fossils and were generally aware of the existence of evolutionary processes. Moreover, evolutionary ideas featured prominently in philosophy: Hegelianism took historical development seriously; and Auguste Comte's positivism predicated three stages of social evolution. But it was with the publication of Darwin's *Origin of Species* in 1859 and of *The Descent of Man* in 1871 that evolution, for the first time, seemed to be taken out of the range of speculation and to be given fairly definite factual confirmation. In America, Asa Gray, a botanist at Harvard, became an immediate proponent of the theory. On the other hand, Jean Louis Agassiz, noted Harvard geologist and paleontologist, opposed evolution and defended instead "preformationism"—the idea that each type was fixed and not capable of evolving from one species to another. In scientific circles generally, however, opposition to Darwin was soon dissipated, and most scientists came to accept his theory of evolution.

Behind much of the determined opposition to Darwin lay the strong religious, metaphysical and moral antipathies his theory provoked. Thus Agassiz rejected Darwin on theological grounds. And religious fundamentalists opposed evolution because it conflicted with literal interpretation of the Bible. Religious liberals, on the other hand, welcomed Darwinism, for it provided a basis for free symbolic interpretation. Many thinkers, like James McCosh, made room for evolution in their philosophical positions, yet maintained that God had created the universe and was its first cause. One basic problem, however, was whether and to what extent divine design could be reconciled with evolution. Critics of traditional theology held that natural selection undermined purpose, that chance replaced fixed entelechies, and that scientific law did not imply design. Darwinism challenged many traditional concepts: the notion of a teleological universe, of fixed species, and of man as separate from nature and the product of a special act of divine creation.

All of this led to drastic attempts to adjust philosophy to scientific discovery by the construction of new metaphysical and moral theories. In England, Spencer and Huxley defended Darwinism, and Spencer developed a new metaphysical world view. In America, John Fiske (1842–1901) propounded a cosmic theism, and attempted to explain through evolution the origin of all human capacities, including moral sympathy and intellectual ability. Francis Ellingwood Abbot (1836–1903) attempted to develop the broader implications of Darwin for philosophy. Chauncey Wright (1830–1875) accepted Darwin's explanations within biology and used them to account for self-consciousness and the growth of language, but he resisted the attempt to extend the

evolutionary process into a cosmic metaphysic. The major effect of Darwin on metaphysics in America, however, was that nature was now seen as a state of dynamic flux or change, not a fixed system of eternal reality. The classical category of substance or essence thus was transformed into the category of process or event.

Darwinism also encouraged the extension of scientific explanations beyond the physical sciences to the psychological and social sciences. As John Dewey later observed, Darwinism helped break down the dualism between man and nature, mind and body, and it made possible the study of "consciousness" in an objective scientific way. Social scientists such as Lewis Henry Morgan, Lester Ward, and William Graham Sumner early introduced Darwinism into their thinking, a trend which was continued in the twentieth century by George H. Mead and others. Indeed, behaviorism as a psychological method was stimulated in no small part by the Darwinian revolution; and the contemporary behavioral sciences may be said to have the same inspiration.

Within philosophy there was an attempt to naturalize morality by relating it to the natural conditions of human life; and various philosophers tried to apply reason to ethics and to develop a science of valuation and value. Values were not considered as external verities unavailable to scientific treatment and control, but as amenable to careful scientific investigation. American philosophers displayed great confidence in human powers, in the ability of man to know nature and to control it for his own purposes. This confidence, moreover, was extended to politics and society, and there was great emphasis on the potentialities of intelligence for creating a good society. The values emphasized were those of democracy, freedom, art, and education. Some philosophers suggested a "rational" approach to religion, a common faith in naturalistic humanism, justified by its functional value to the individual and the society.

Perhaps the most important fundamental consequence of Darwinism was that it undermined the classical edifice and made possible an experimental and naturalistic philosophy. Chauncey Wright was among the first to defend this kind of thought. Concurrent with the development of philosophic pragmatism and naturalism was a profound interest in problems of logic, semantics, language, and meaning. There was also strong interest in the philosophy of science; scientific method was taken as the key to knowledge. Human behavior was now considered to be continuous with other natural processes and an appropriate subject for science. Thus, the ideals of the Age of Reason which prevailed at the birth of the American republic became dominant again at the beginning of the twentieth century.

Editor's Note

A perennial problem in editing a book of this kind is that of selection within limitations of space. Accordingly, there are important philosophers or philosophical pieces that might have been included, but had necessarily to be omitted. Another recurrent question is whether a given selection or group of selections should be (1) representative of the entire work of a philosopher, or whether (2) a given piece of high philosophical merit should be reprinted, even though it may not entirely represent the complete point of view of the writer. Generally I have sought a compromise between these two principles of selection—though the first consideration has more often been the deciding factor (as with Jonathan Edwards and Thomas Paine). However, in an effort to provide some contrast among the different schools I have at times used a piece which, although not fully representative in itself, has high intrinsic philosophical interest. (This is the rationale, for example, for choosing William Ellery Channing's *The Evidences of Revealed Religion* rather than his more influential, though less philosophical, *Unitarian Christianity*.)

Another besetting problem encountered in American philosophy concerns the definition of an "American" philosopher. Immigration is a special problem for American letters. In some instances when a philosopher arrived in this country late in life, or spent only a few years here (Thomas Paine and James McCosh, for instance), I have—if he typifies or expresses an important trend of thought in America—chosen to consider him "American."

Where it has been possible to modernize spellings and grammar without distorting or changing meaning, I have done so. Excessive capitalizations, italics, and archaic usages have generally been amended.

PART ONE

The Colonial Period
(1620-1776)

Jonathan Edwards

[1703–1758]

Jonathan Edwards was the first American philosopher-theologian and the ablest thinker the early Colonies produced. Although he wrote for a special religious purpose and addressed himself to a narrow circle, the character of his mind was thoroughly deductive and logical. He was born in East Windsor, Connecticut, in 1703, and educated at Yale College. In 1729 he became minister of the Congregational Church in Northampton, Massachusetts. A powerful preacher as well as writer, he lived through the "Great Awakening," a popular religious revival movement in the Colonies of the seventeen-thirties and -forties. The spirit and tone of his philosophy was Calvinistic, and he accepted the general philosophical background of Augustinianism and the values of evangelical Puritanism. His severe attitude and his strict insistence that the qualification for membership in the church must be uncompromising piety and devotion caused his congregation to dismiss him in 1750. He moved to Stockbridge, Massachusetts, to serve as a missionary to the Indians. There many of his mature works were written. In 1757 he was appointed president of the College of New Jersey (later Princeton). A smallpox inoculation led to his premature death in 1758.

Edwards' collected writings contain many important sermons, such as "God Glorified in Man's Depend-ence" (1731) and "A Divine and Supernatural Light" (1734). His famous sermon, "Sinners in the Hands of an Angry God" (1741), preached during the religious revival, with its terrifying pronouncement that God ". . . holds you over the pit of hell, much as one holds a spider, or some loathsome insect over the fire, abhors you, and is dreadfully provoked, . . ." is reprinted here because it represents an important aspect of Edwards' preaching and is indicative of the Calvinistic culture at the time. However, it should not be emphasized disproportionately among his writings. Underlying Edwards' primary religious motivation was a remarkable capacity for philosophic reflection.

His most philosophical work, *Freedom of the Will* (1754), a portion of which is reprinted below, puts forth a deductive defense of Calvinistic determinism against the arguments for free will, which Edwards called "Arminianism." This term was originally applied to the teachings of the Dutch theologian, Jacobus Arminius (1560–1609), but it was also loosely applied to that of others who criticized Calvinistic determinism and defended moral freedom and responsibility as essential to salvation. Edwards argued that "every event has a cause," but that Divine Omnipotence, Foreknowledge, and Efficacious Grace, all of which are Calvinistic doctrines, are consonant with moral responsibility. Edwards' approach is interesting to the contemporary philosopher, in that he attempts to resolve the alleged paradox by careful linguistic definitions of key terms.

In *The Nature of True Virtue* (written in 1755 and published posthumously in 1765) he defended the conception of "true virtue" as being a "beauty of heart" and a religious love of being in general, that is, of God. The first and part of the last chapters are here reprinted. Edwards claimed that man is naturally incapable of true virtue, being sinful and corrupt. Yet there is the grace of God that has elected some for salvation, and one sign of this is the individual's religious affection and sense of beauty. Edwards' analysis also anticipated to some extent the recent emotive interpretation of moral judgments in claiming that such judgments rest on sentiment, not reason.

In *A Treatise Concerning Religious Affections* (1746), part of which is printed below, he maintained that belief in God has its source in the religious affections, love and joy, and that these are transmitted from a supernatural source and are not to be comprehended by the natural senses.

Of Being (in *Notes on Natural Science*) and *The Mind*, also published here, were early essays, begun probably while Edwards was at college. Here Edwards provided a metaphysical defense of philosophical idealism, holding that mind and spirit are fundamental to the universe.

SINNERS IN THE HANDS OF AN ANGRY GOD [1]

. . . "There is nothing that keeps wicked men at any one moment out of hell, but the mere pleasure of God"—By the mere pleasure of God, I mean his sovereign pleasure, his arbitrary will, restrained by no obligation, hindered by no manner of difficulty, any more than if nothing else but God's mere will had in the least degree, or in any respect whatsoever, any hand in the preservation of wicked men one moment.—The truth of this observation may appear by the following considerations.

1. There is no want of power in God to cast wicked men into hell at any moment. Men's hands cannot be strong when God rises up. The strongest have no power to resist him, nor can any deliver out of his hands. He is not only able to cast wicked men into hell, but he can most easily do it. Sometimes an earthly prince meets with a great deal of difficulty to subdue a rebel, who has found means to fortify himself, and has made himself strong by the numbers of his followers. But it is not so with God. There is no fortress that is any defense from the

[1] *The Works of Jonathan Edwards*, ed. by E. Hickman, Vol. II, edited and corrected.

power of God. Though hand join in hand, and vast multitudes of God's enemies combine and associate themselves, they are easily broken in pieces. They are as great heaps of light chaff before the whirlwind; or large quantities of dry stubble before devouring flames. We find it easy to tread on and crush a worm that we see crawling on the earth; so it is easy for us to cut or singe a slender thread that anything hangs by: thus easy is it for God, when he pleases, to cast his enemies down to hell. What are we, that we should think to stand before him, at whose rebuke the earth trembles, and before whom the rocks are thrown down?

2. They deserve to be cast into hell; so that divine justice never stands in the way, it makes no objection against God's using his power at any moment to destroy them. Yes, on the contrary, justice calls aloud for an infinite punishment of their sins. Divine justice says of the tree that brings forth such grapes of Sodom, "Cut it down, why cumbereth it the ground?" (Luke xiii. 7.) The sword of divine justice is every moment brandished over their heads, and it is nothing but the hand of arbitrary mercy, and God's mere will, that holds it back.

3. They are already under a sentence of condemnation to hell. They do not only justly deserve to be cast down thither, but the sentence of the law of God, that eternal and immutable rule of righteousness that God has fixed between him and mankind, is gone out against them, and stands against them; so that they are bound over already to hell. (John iii. 18.) "He that believeth not is condemned already." So that every unconverted man properly belongs to hell; that is his place; from thence he is. (John viii. 23.) "Ye are from beneath." And thither he is bound; it is the place that justice, and God's word, and the sentence of his unchangeable law assign to him.

4. They are now the objects of that very same anger and wrath of God, that is expressed in the torments of hell. And the reason why they do not go down to hell at each moment, is not because God, in whose power they are, is not then very angry with them; as he is with many miserable creatures now tormented in hell, who there feel and bear the fierceness of his wrath. Yes, God is a great deal more angry with great numbers that are now on earth; yes, doubtless with many that are now in this congregation, who it may be are at ease, than he is with many of those who are now in the flames of hell.

So that it is not because God is unmindful of their wickedness, and does not resent it, that he does not let loose his hand and cut them off. God is not altogether such a one as themselves, though they may imagine him to be so. The wrath of God burns against them, their damnation does not slumber; the pit is prepared, the fire is made ready, the furnace is now hot, ready to receive them; the flames do now rage and glow. The glittering sword is whet, and held over them, and the pit hath opened its mouth under them.

5. The devil stands ready to fall upon them, and seize them as his own, at what moment God shall permit him. They belong to him; he has their souls in his possession, and under his dominion. The scripture represents them as his goods. (Luke xi. 12.) The devils watch them; they are ever by them at their right hand; they stand waiting for them, like greedy hungry lions that see their prey, and expect to have it, but are for the present kept back. If God should withdraw his hand, by which they are restrained, they would in one moment fly upon their poor souls. The old serpent is gaping for them; hell opens its mouth wide to receive them; and if God should permit it, they would be hastily swallowed up and lost.

6. There are in the souls of wicked men those hellish principles reigning, that would presently kindle and flame out into hell-fire, if it were not for God's restraints. There is laid in the very nature of carnal men, a foundation for the torments of hell. There are those corrupt principles, in reigning power in them, and in full possession of them, that are seeds of hell-fire. These principles are active and powerful, exceeding violent in their nature, and if it were not for the restraining hand of God upon them, they would soon break out, they would flame out after the same manner as the same corruptions, the same enmity does in the hearts of damned souls, and would beget the same torments as they do in them. The souls of the wicked are in scripture compared to the troubled sea. (Isa. lvii. 20.) For the present, God restrains their wickedness by his mighty power, as he does the raging waves of the troubled sea, saying, "Hitherto shalt thou come, but no further"; but if God should withdraw that restraining power, it would soon carry all before it. Sin is the ruin and misery of the soul; it is destructive in its nature; and if God should leave it without restraint, there would need nothing else to make the soul perfectly miserable. The corruption of the heart of man is immoderate and boundless in its fury; and while wicked men live here, it is like fire pent up by God's restraints, whereas if it were let loose, it would set on fire the course of nature; and as the heart is now a sink of sin, so if sin was not restrained, it would immediately turn the soul into a fiery oven, or a furnace of fire and brimstone.

7. It is no security to wicked men for one moment, that there are no visible means of death at hand. It is no security to a natural man, that he is now in health, and that he does not see which way he should now immediately go out of the world by any accident, and that there is no visible danger in any respect in his circumstances. The manifold and continual experience of the world in all ages, shows this is no evidence that a man is not on the very brink of eternity, and that the

next step will not be into another world. The unseen, unthought-of ways and means of persons going suddenly out of the world are innumerable and inconceivable. Unconverted men walk over the pit of hell on a rotten covering, and there are innumerable places in this covering so weak that they will not bear their weight, and these places are not seen. The arrows of death fly unseen at noonday; the sharpest sight cannot discern them. God has so many different unsearchable ways of taking wicked men out of the world and sending them to hell, that there is nothing to make it appear, that God had need to be at the expense of a miracle, or go out of the ordinary course of his providence, to destroy any wicked man, at any moment. All the means that there are of sinners going out of the world, are so in God's hands, and so universally and absolutely subject to his power and determination, that it does not depend at all the less on the mere will of God, whether sinners shall at any moment go to hell, than if means were never made use of, or at all concerned in the case.

8. Natural men's prudence and care to preserve their own lives, or the care of others to preserve them, do not secure them a moment. To this, divine providence and universal experience do also bear testimony. There is this clear evidence that men's own wisdom is no security to them from death; that if it were otherwise we should see some difference between the wise and politic men of the world and others, with regard to their liableness to early and unexpected death: but how is it in fact? (Eccles. ii. 16.) "How dieth the wise man? even as the fool."

9. All wicked men's pains and contrivance which they use to escape hell, while they continue to reject Christ, and so remain wicked men, do not secure them from hell one moment. Almost every natural man that hears of hell, flatters himself that he shall escape it; he depends upon himself for his own security; he flatters himself in what he has done, in what he is now doing, or what he intends to do. Everyone lays out matters in his own mind how he shall avoid damnation, and flatters himself that he contrives well for himself, and that his schemes will not fail. They hear indeed that there are but few saved, and that the greater part of men that have died heretofore are gone to hell; but each one imagines that he lays out matters better for his own escape than others have done. He does not intend to come to that place of torment; he says within himself, that he intends to take effectual care, and to order matters so for himself as not to fail.

But the foolish children of men miserably delude themselves in their own schemes, and in confidence in their own strength and wisdom; they trust to nothing but a shadow. The greater part of those who heretofore have lived under the same means of grace, and are now dead, are undoubtedly gone to hell; and it was not because they were not as wise as those who are now alive: it was not because they did not lay out matters as well for themselves to secure their own escape. If we could speak with them, and inquire of them, one by one, whether they expected, when alive, and when they used to hear about hell, ever to be the subjects of that misery: we doubtless, should hear one and another reply, "No, I never intended to come here: I had laid out matters otherwise in my mind; I thought I should contrive well for myself: I thought my scheme good. I intended to take effectual care; but it came upon me unexpected; I did not look for it at that time, and in that manner; it came as a thief: death outwitted me: God's wrath was too quick for me. Oh, my cursed foolishness! I was flattering myself, and pleasing myself with vain dreams of what I would do hereafter; and when I was saying: Peace and safety, then suddenly destruction came upon me."

10. God has laid himself under no obligation, by any promise to keep any natural man out of hell one moment. God certainly has made no promises either of eternal life, or of any deliverance or preservation from eternal death, but what are contained in the covenant of grace, the promises that are given in Christ, in whom all the promises are yea and amen. But surely they have no interest in the promises of the covenant of grace who are not the children of the covenant, who do not believe in any of the promises, and have no interest in the Mediator of the covenant.

So that, whatever some have imagined and pretended about promises made to natural men's earnest seeking and knocking, it is plain and manifest that whatever pains a natural man takes in religion, whatever prayers he makes, till he believes in Christ, God is under no manner of obligation to keep him a moment from eternal destruction.

So that thus it is that natural men are held in the hand of God, over the pit of hell; they have deserved the fiery pit, and are already sentenced to it; and God is dreadfully provoked, his anger is as great toward them as to those that are actually suffering the executions of the fierceness of his wrath in hell, and they have done nothing in the least to appease or abate that anger, neither is God in the least bound by any promise to hold them up one moment; the devil is waiting for them, hell is gaping for them, the flames gather and flash about them, and would fain lay hold on them, and swallow them up; the fire bent up in their own hearts is struggling to break out: and they have no interest in any Mediator, there are no means within reach that can be any security to them. In short, they have no refuge, nothing to take hold of; all that preserves them every moment is the mere arbitrary will, and uncovenanted, unobliged forbearance of an incensed God. . . .

FREEDOM OF THE WILL [2]

PART 1: DEFINITION OF TERMS (Wherein Are Explained and Stated Various Terms and Things Belonging to the Subject of the Ensuing Discourse)

§1. Concerning the Nature of the Will

It may possibly be thought that there is no great need of going about to define or describe the *will*; this word being generally as well understood as any other words we can use to explain it: and so perhaps it would be, had not philosophers, metaphysicians and polemic divines brought the matter into obscurity by the things they have said of it. But since it is so, I think it may be of some use, and will tend to the greater clearness in the following discourse, to say a few things concerning it.

And therefore I observe, that the will (without any metaphysical refining) is plainly that by which the mind chooses anything. The faculty of the will is that faculty or power or principle of mind by which it is capable of choosing: an act of the will is the same as an act of choosing or choice.

If any think it is a more perfect definition of the will, to say, that it is that by which the soul either chooses or refuses; I am content with it: though I think that it is enough to say, it is that by which the soul chooses: for in every act of will whatsoever, the mind chooses one thing rather than another; it chooses something rather than the contrary, or rather than the want or nonexistence of that thing. So in every act of refusal, the mind chooses the absence of the thing refused; the positive and the negative are set before the mind for its choice, and it chooses the negative; and the mind's making its choice in that case is properly the act of the will: the will's determining between the two is a voluntary determining; but that is the same thing as making a choice. So that whatever names we call the act of the will, choosing, refusing, approving, disapproving, liking, disliking, embracing, rejecting, determining, directing, commanding, forbidding, inclining or being averse, a being pleased or displeased with; all may be reduced to this of choosing. For the soul to act voluntarily, is evermore to act electively.

[2] The complete title is: *A Careful and Strict Enquiry Into the Modern Prevailing Notions of That Freedom of the Will Which is Supposed to be Essential to Moral Agency, Virtue and Vice, Reward and Punishment, Praise and Blame.* Reprinted in *The Works of Jonathan Edwards*, ed. by E. Hickman, London, 1834, Vol. I, with editorial corrections and modernizations added.

§2. Concerning the Determination of the Will

By *determining the will*, if the phrase be used with any meaning, must be intended, causing that the act of the will or choice should be thus, and not otherwise: and the will is said to be determined when, in consequence of some action or influence, its choice is directed to and fixed upon a particular object. As when we speak of the determination of motion, we mean causing the motion of the body to be such a way, or in such a direction, rather than another.

The determination of the will supposes an effect, which must have a cause. If the will be determined, there is a determiner. This must be supposed to be intended even by them that say, the will determines itself. If it be so, the will is both determiner and determined; it is a cause that acts and produces effects upon itself, and is the object of its own influence and action.

With respect to that grand inquiry, what determines the will, it would be very tedious and unnecessary at present to enumerate and examine all the various opinions which have been advanced concerning this matter; nor is it needful that I should enter into a particular disquisition of all points debated in disputes on that question: whether the will always follows the last dictate of the understanding. It is sufficient to my present purpose to say, it is that motive, which, as it stands in the view of the mind, is the strongest, that determines the will. But it may be necessary that I should a little explain my meaning.

By *motive*, I mean the whole of that which moves, excites or invites the mind to volition, whether that be one thing singly, or many things conjunctly. Many particular things may concur and unite their strength to induce the mind; and when it is so, all together are as it were one complex motive. And when I speak of the *strongest motive*, I have respect to the strength of the whole that operates to induce to a particular act of volition, whether that be the strength of one thing alone, or of many together. . . .

Things that exist in the view of the mind, have their strength, tendency or advantage to move or excite its will, from many things appertaining to the nature and circumstances of the thing viewed, the nature and circumstances of the mind that views, and the degree and manner of its view; which it would perhaps be hard to make a perfect enumeration of. But so much I think may be determined in general, without room for controversy, that whatever is perceived or apprehended by an intelligent and voluntary agent, which has the nature and influence of a motive to volition or choice, is considered or viewed as good; nor has it any tendency to invite or engage the election of the soul in any further degree than it appears as such.

For to say otherwise would be to say, that things that appear have a tendency by the appearance they make, to engage the mind to elect them, some other way than by their appearing eligible to it; which is absurd. And therefore it must be true, in some sense, that the will always is as the greatest apparent good is. . . .

. . . In some sense, the will always follows the last dictate of the understanding. But then the understanding must be taken in a large sense, as including the whole faculty of perception or apprehension, and not merely what is called reason or judgment. If by the dictate of the understanding is meant what reason declares to be best or most for the person's happiness, taking in the whole of his duration, it is not true that the will always follows the last dictate of the understanding. Such a dictate of reason is quite a different matter from things appearing now most agreeable; all things being put together which pertain to the mind's present perceptions, apprehensions or ideas, in any respect. Although that dictate of reason, when it takes place, is one thing that is put into the scales, and is to be considered as a thing that has concern in the compound influence which moves and induces the will; and is one thing that is to be considered in estimating the degree of that appearance of good which the will always follows; either as having its influence added to other things, or subducted from them. When it concurs with other things, then its weight is added to them, as put into the same scale; but when it is against them, it is as a weight in the opposite scale, where it resists the influence of other things: yet its resistance is often overcome by their greater weight, and so the act of the will is determined in opposition to it. . . .

§3. Concerning the Meaning of the Terms Necessity, Impossibility, Inability, etc.; and of Contingence

The words *necessary, impossible*, etc., are abundantly used in controversies about free will and moral agency; and therefore the sense in which they are used should be clearly understood.

Here I might say, that a thing is then said to be necessary, when it must be, and cannot be otherwise. But this would not properly be a definition of necessity, or an explanation of the word, any more than if I explained the word *must* by there being a necessity. The words *must, can,* and *cannot* need explication as much as the words *necessary* and *impossible*; excepting that the former are words that children commonly use, and know something of the meaning of earlier than the latter.

The word *necessary*, as used in common speech, is a relative term; and relates to some supposed opposition made to the existence of the thing spoken of, which is overcome, or proves in vain to hinder or alter it. That is necessary, in the original and proper sense of the word, which is, or will be, notwithstanding all supposable opposition. To say, that a thing is necessary, is the same thing as to say, that it is impossible it should not be: but the word *impossible* is manifestly a relative term, and has reference to supposed power exerted to bring a thing to pass, which is insufficient for the effect; as the word *unable* is relative, and has relation to ability or endeavor which is insufficient; and as the word *irresistible* is relative, and has always reference to resistance which is made, or may be made to some force or power tending to an effect, and is insufficient to withstand the power, or hinder the effect. The common notion of necessity and impossibility implies something that frustrates endeavor or desire. . . .

. . . These terms *necessary, impossible,* etc., are often used by philosophers and metaphysicians in a sense quite diverse from their common use and original signification: for they apply them to many cases in which no opposition is supposed or supposable. Thus they use them with respect to God's existence before the creation of the world, when there was no other being but he: so with regard to many of the dispositions and acts of the Divine Being, such as his loving himself, his loving righteousness, hating sin, etc. So they apply these terms to many cases of the inclinations and actions of created intelligent beings, angels and men; wherein all opposition of the will is shut out and denied, in the very supposition of the case.

Metaphysical or philosophical necessity is nothing different from certainty. I speak not now of the certainty of knowledge, but the certainty that is in things themselves, which is the foundation of the certainty of the knowledge of them; or that wherein lies the ground of the infallibility of the proposition which affirms them.

What is sometimes given as the definition of philosophical necessity, namely, that by which a thing cannot but be, or whereby it cannot be otherwise, fails of being a proper explanation of it on two accounts: first, the words *can* or *cannot* need explanation as much as the word *necessity*; and the former may as well be explained by the latter, as the latter by the former. Thus, if anyone asked us what we mean when we say, a thing cannot but be, we might explain ourselves by saying, we mean, it must necessarily be so; as well as explain necessity by saying, it is that by which a thing cannot but be. And secondly, this definition is liable to the forementioned great inconvenience: the words *cannot* or *unable* are properly relative, and have relation to power exerted, or that may be exerted, in order to the thing spoken of; to which, as I have now observed, the word *necessity*, as used by philosophers, has no reference.

Philosophical necessity is really nothing else than the full and fixed connection between the things signified by the subject and predicate of a proposition, which affirms something to be true. When there is such a connection, then the thing affirmed in the proposition is necessary, in a philosophical sense; whether any opposition, or contrary effort be supposed, or supposable in the case, or no. When the subject and predicate of the proposition, which affirms the existence of anything, either substance, quality, act or circumstance, have a full and certain connection, then the existence or being of that thing is said to be necessary in a metaphysical sense. And in this sense I use the word *necessity*, in the following discourse, when I endeavor to prove that necessity is not inconsistent with liberty. . . .

§4. Of the Distinction of Natural and Moral Necessity, and Inability

That *necessity* which has been explained, consisting in an infallible connection of the things signified by the subject and predicate of a proposition, as intelligent beings are the subjects of it, is distinguished into moral and natural necessity.

I shall not now stand to inquire whether this distinction be a proper and perfect distinction; but shall only explain how these two sorts of necessity are understood, as the terms are sometimes used, and as they are used in the following discourse.

The phrase *moral necessity* is used variously: sometimes it is used for a necessity of moral obligation. So we say, a man is under necessity, when he is under bonds of duty and conscience, which he cannot be discharged from. So the word *necessity* is often used for great obligation in point of interest. Sometimes by *moral necessity* is meant that apparent connection of things, which is the ground of moral evidence; and so is distinguished from absolute necessity, or that sure connection of things, that is a foundation for infallible certainty. In this sense, *moral necessity* signifies much the same as that high degree of probability, which is ordinarily sufficient to satisfy, and be relied upon by mankind, in their conduct and behavior in the world, as they would consult their own safety and interest, and treat others properly as members of society. And sometimes by *moral necessity* is meant that necessity of connection and consequence, which arises from such moral causes as the strength of inclination, or motives, and the connection which there is in many cases between these, and such certain volitions and actions. And it is in this sense, that I use the phrase *moral necessity* in the following discourse.

By *natural necessity*, as applied to men, I mean such necessity as men are under through the force of natural causes; as distinguished from what are called moral causes, such as habits and dispositions of the heart, and moral motives and inducements. Thus men placed in certain circumstances are the subjects of particular sensations by necessity: they feel pain when their bodies are wounded; they see the objects presented before them in a clear light, when their eyes are opened: so they assent to the truth of certain propositions, as soon as the terms are understood; as that two and two make four, that black is not white, that two parallel lines can never cross one another: so by a natural necessity men's bodies move downward, when there is nothing to support them. . . .

§5. *Concerning the Notion of Liberty, and of Moral Agency*

The plain and obvious meaning of the words *freedom* and *liberty*, in common speech, is the power, opportunity, or advantage, that anyone has, to do as he pleases. Or in other words, his being free from hindrance or impediment in the way of doing, or conducting in any respect, as he wills.[3] And the contrary to liberty, whatever name we call that by, is a person's being hindered or unable to conduct as he will, or being necessitated to do otherwise.

If this which I have mentioned be the meaning of the word *liberty*, in the ordinary use of language; as I trust that none that has ever learned to talk, and is unprejudiced, will deny; then it will follow, that in propriety of speech, neither liberty nor its contrary can properly be ascribed to any being or thing, but that which has such a faculty, power or property, as is called *will*. For that which is possessed of no such thing as will, cannot have any power or opportunity of doing according to its will, nor be necessitated to act contrary to its will, nor be restrained from acting agreeably to it. And therefore to talk of liberty, or the contrary, as belonging to the very will itself, is not to speak good sense; if we judge of sense, and nonsense, by the original and proper signification of words. For the will itself is not an agent that has a will: the power of choosing, itself, has not a power of choosing. That which has the power of volition or choice is the man or the soul, and not the power of volition itself. And he that has the liberty of doing according to his will, is the agent or doer who is possessed of the will; and not the will which he is possessed of. We say with propriety, that a bird let loose has power and liberty to fly; but not that the bird's power of flying has a power and liberty of flying. To be free is the property of an agent, who is possessed of powers and faculties, as much as to be cunning, valiant, bountiful, or zealous. But these qualities are the properties of men or persons; and not the properties of properties.

[3] I say not only *doing*, but *conducting*; because a voluntary forbearing to do, sitting still, keeping silence, etc. are instances of persons' conduct, about which liberty is exercised; though they are not properly called *doing*.—E.

There are two things that are contrary to this which is called *liberty* in common speech. One is *constraint*; the same is otherwise called force, compulsion, and coaction; which is a person's being necessitated to do a thing *contrary* to his will. The other is *restraint*; which is his being hindered, and not having power to do *according* to his will. But that which has no will, cannot be the subject of these things.—I need say the less on this head, Mr. Locke having set the same thing forth, with so great clearness, in his *Essay on the Human Understanding*.[4]

But one thing more I would observe concerning what is vulgarly called *liberty*; namely, that power and opportunity for one to do and conduct as he will, or according to his choice, is all that is meant by it; without taking into the meaning of the word, anything of the cause or original of that choice; or at all considering how the person came to have such a volition; whether it was caused by some external motive, or internal habitual bias; whether it was determined by some internal antecedent volition, or whether it happened without a cause; whether it was necessarily connected with something foregoing, or not connected. Let the person come by his volition or choice how he will, yet, if he is able, and there is nothing in the way to hinder his pursuing and executing his will, the man is fully and perfectly free, according to the primary and common notion of freedom.

What has been said may be sufficient to show what is meant by liberty, according to the common notions of mankind, and in the usual and primary acceptation of the word: but the word, as used by Arminians, Pelagians and others, who oppose the Calvinists, has an entirely different signification. These several things belong to their notion of liberty: (1) That it consists in a self-determining power in the will, or a certain sovereignty the will has over itself, and its own acts, whereby it determines its own volitions; so as not to be dependent in its determinations, on any cause without itself, nor determined by anything prior to its own acts. (2) Indifference belongs to liberty in their notion of it, or that the mind, previous to the act of volition be, *in equilibrio*. (3) Contingence is another thing that belongs and is essential to it; not in the common acceptation of the word, as that has been already explained, but as opposed to all necessity, or any fixed and certain connection with some previous ground or reason of its existence. They suppose the essence of liberty so much to consist in these things, that unless the will of man be free in this sense, he has no real freedom, how much soever he may be at liberty to act according to his will. . . .

[4] Locke, *Essay*, Bk. II, ch. 21, nos. 14–21; *1*, 319–24.

PART 2: THE ARMINIAN NOTION OF FREEDOM. (Wherein It Is Considered, Whether There Is, or Can Be Any Such Sort of Freedom of
Will, as That Wherein Arminians Place the Essence of the Liberty
of All Moral Agents; and Whether Any Such Thing Ever Was
or Can Be Conceived of)

§1. *Showing the Manifest Inconsistence of the Arminian Notion of
Liberty of Will, Consisting in the Will's Self-Determining Power*

Having taken notice of those things which may be necessary to
be observed, concerning the meaning of the principal terms and
phrases made use of in controversies concerning human liberty, and
particularly observed what liberty is, according to the common language, and general apprehension of mankind, and what it is as
understood and maintained by Arminians; I proceed to consider the
Arminian notion of the freedom of the will, and the supposed necessity of it in order to moral agency, or in order to anyone's being
capable of virtue or vice, and properly the subject of command or
counsel, praise or blame, promises or threats, rewards or punishments; or whether that which has been described, as the thing meant
by liberty in common speech, be not sufficient, and the only liberty,
which makes, or can make anyone a moral agent, and so properly the
subject of these things. In this part, I shall consider whether any
such thing be possible or conceivable, as that freedom of will which
Arminians insist on; and shall inquire whether any such sort of liberty
be necessary to moral agency, etc., in the next part.

And first of all, I shall consider the notion of a self-determining
power in the will: wherein, according to the Arminians, does most
essentially consist the will's freedom; and shall particularly inquire,
whether it be not plainly absurd, and a manifest inconsistence, to
suppose that the will itself determines all the free acts of the will.

Here I shall not insist on the great impropriety of such phrases
and ways of speaking, as *the will's determining itself*; because actions
are to be ascribed to agents, and not properly to the powers of agents;
which improper way of speaking leads to many mistakes, and much
confusion, as Mr. Locke observes. But I shall suppose that the
Arminians, when they speak of the will's determining itself, do by
the will mean *the soul willing*. I shall take it for granted, that when
they speak of the will as the determiner, they mean the soul in the
exercise of a power of willing, or acting voluntarily. I shall suppose
this to be their meaning, because nothing else can be meant, without
the grossest and plainest absurdity. In all cases, when we speak of
the powers or principles of acting, as doing such things, we mean
that the agents which have these powers of acting, do them in the

exercise of those powers. So when we say, valor fights courageously, we mean, the man who is under the influence of valor fights courageously. When we say, love seeks the object loved, we mean, the person loving seeks that object. When we say, the understanding discerns, we mean the soul in the exercise of that faculty. So when it is said, the will decides or determines, the meaning must be, that the person in the exercise of a power of willing and choosing, or the soul acting voluntarily, determines.

Therefore, if the will determines all its own free acts, the soul determines all the free acts of the will in the exercise of a power of willing and choosing; or, which is the same thing, it determines them of choice; it determines its own acts by choosing its own acts. If the will determines the will, then choice orders and determines the choice: and acts of choice are subject to the decision, and follow the conduct of other acts of choice. And therefore if the will determines all its own free acts, then every free act of choice is determined by a preceding act of choice, choosing that act. And if that preceding act of the will or choice be also a free act, then by these principles, in this act too, the will is self-determined; that is, this, in like manner, is an act that the soul voluntarily chooses; or which is the same thing, it is an act determined still by a preceding act of the will, choosing that. And the like may again be observed of the last mentioned act. Which brings us directly to a contradiction: for it supposes an act of the will preceding the first act in the whole train, directing and determining the rest; or a free act of the will, before the first free act of the will. Or else we must come at last to an act of the will, determining the consequent acts, wherein the will is not self-determined, and so is not a free act, in this notion of freedom: but if the first act in the train, determining and fixing the rest, be not free, none of them all can be free. . . .

. . . Thus, this Arminian notion of liberty of the will, consisting in the will's self-determination, is repugnant to itself, and shuts itself wholly out of the world.

§3. *Whether Any Event Whatsoever, and Volition in Particular, Can Come to Pass Without a Cause of Its Existence*

Before I enter on any argument on this subject, I would explain how I would be understood when I use the word *cause* in this discourse: since, for want of a better word, I shall have occasion to use it in a sense which is more extensive than that in which it is sometimes used. The word is often used in so restrained a sense as to signify only that which has a positive efficiency or influence to produce a thing, or bring it to pass. But there are many things which have no such positive productive influence; which yet are causes in the respect that they have truly the nature of a ground or reason why some things are, rather than others; or why they are as they are, rather than otherwise. Thus the absence of the sun in the night, is not the cause of the falling of the dew at that time, in the same manner as its beams are the cause of the ascending of the vapors in the daytime; and its withdrawment in the winter, is not in the same manner the cause of the freezing of the waters, as its approach in the spring is the cause of their thawing. But yet the withdrawment or absence of the sun is an antecedent, with which these effects in the night and winter are connected, and on which they depend; and is one thing that belongs to the ground and reason why they come to pass at that time, rather than at other times; though the absence of the sun is nothing positive, nor has any positive influence.

It may be further observed, that when I speak of connection of causes and effects, I have respect to moral causes, as well as those that are called natural in distinction from them. Moral causes may be causes in as proper a sense as any causes whatsoever; may have as real an influence, and may as truly be the ground and reason of an event's coming to pass.

Therefore I sometimes use the world *cause*, in this inquiry, to signify any antecedent, either natural or moral, positive or negative, on which an event, either a thing, or the manner and circumstance of a thing, so depends, that it is the ground and reason, either in whole, or in part, why it is, rather than not; or why it is as it is, rather than otherwise; or, in other words, any antecedent with which a consequent event is so connected, that it truly belongs to the reason why the proposition which affirms that event, is true; whether it has any positive influence, or not. And in agreement with this, I sometimes use the word *effect* for the consequence of another thing, which is perhaps rather an occasion than a cause, most properly speaking. . . .

Having thus explained what I mean by *cause*, I assert, that nothing ever comes to pass without a cause. What is self-existent must be from eternity, and must be unchangeable: but as to all things that begin to be, they are not self-existent, and therefore must have some foundation of their existence without themselves. That whatsoever begins to be, which before was not, must have a cause why it then begins to exist, seems to be the first dictate of the common and natural sense which God hath implanted in the minds of all mankind, and the main foundation of all our reasonings about the existence of things, past, present, or to come.

And this dictate of common sense equally respects substances and modes, or things and the manner and circumstances of things. Thus, if we see a body which has hitherto been at rest, start out of a state

of rest and begin to move, we do as naturally and necessarily suppose
there is some cause or reason of this new mode of existence, as of
the existence of a body itself which had hitherto not existed. And
so if a body, which had hitherto moved in a certain direction, should
suddenly change the direction of its motion; or if it should put off
its old figure, and take a new one; or change its color: the beginning
of these new modes is a new event, and the mind of mankind necessarily supposes that there is some cause or reason of them.

If this grand principle of common sense be taken away, all arguing
from effects to causes ceases, and so all knowledge of any existence,
besides what we have by the most direct and immediate intuition.
Particularly all our proof of the being of God ceases: we argue his
being from our own being, and the being of other things, which we
are sensible once were not, but have begun to be; and from the being
of the world, with all its constituent parts, and the manner of their
existence; all which we see plainly are not necessary in their own
nature, and so not self-existent, and therefore must have a cause. But
if things, not in themselves necessary, may begin to be without a
cause, all this arguing is vain. . . .

But if once this grand principle of common sense be given up, that
what is not necessary in itself, must have a cause; and we begin to
maintain, that things may come into existence, and begin to be,
which heretofore have not been, of themselves, without any cause;
all our means of ascending in our arguing from the creature to the
Creator, and all our evidence of the being of God, is cut off at one
blow. In this case, we cannot prove that there is a God, either from
the being of the world, and the creatures in it, or from the manner
of their being, their order, beauty and use. . . .

And indeed, according to the hypothesis I am opposing, of the acts
of the will coming to pass without a cause, it is the case in fact, that
millions of millions of events are continually coming into existence
contingently, without any cause or reason why they do so, all over the
world, every day and hour, through all ages. So it is in a constant
succession, in every moral agent. This contingency, this efficient
Nothing, this effectual No-Cause, is always ready at hand, to produce
this sort of effect, as long as the agent exists, and as often as he has
occasion. . . .

So that it is indeed as repugnant to reason, to suppose that an act
of the will should come into existence without a cause, as to suppose
the human soul, or an angel, or the globe of the earth, or the whole
universe, should come into existence without a cause. And if once
we allow that such a sort of effect as a volition may come to pass
without a cause, how do we know but that many other sorts of effects
may do so too? It is not the particular kind of effect that makes the

absurdity of supposing it has being without a cause, but something which is common to all things that ever begin to be, viz. that they are not self-existent, or necessary in the nature of things.

§10. *Volition Necessarily Connected with the Influence of Motives; with Particular Observations on the Great Inconsistence of Mr. Chubb's Assertions and Reasonings, About the Freedom of the Will*

That every act of the will has some cause, and consequently (by what has been already proved) has a necessary connection with its cause, and so is necessary by a necessity of connection and consequence, is evident by this: that every act of the will whatsoever is excited by some motive; which is manifest, because, if the will or mind, in willing and choosing after the manner that it does, is excited so to do by no motive or inducement, then it has no end which it proposes to itself, or pursues in so doing; it aims at nothing, and seeks nothing. And if it seeks nothing, then it does not go after anything, or exert any inclination or preference toward anything. Which brings the matter to a contradiction; because for the mind to will something, and for it to go after something by an act of preference and inclination, are the same thing.

But if every act of the will is excited by a motive, then that motive is the cause of the act of the will. If the acts of the will are excited by motives, then motives are the causes of their being excited; or, which is the same thing, the cause of their being put forth into act and existence. And if so, the existence of the acts of the will is properly the effect of their motives. Motives do nothing as motives or inducements, but by their influence; and so much as is done by their influence, is the effect of them. For that is the notion of an effect, something that is brought to pass by the influence of another thing.

And if volitions are properly the effects of their motives, then they are necessarily connected with their motives. Every effect and event being, as we proved before, necessarily connected with that which is the proper ground and reason of its existence. Thus it is manifest, that volition is necessary, and is not from any self-determining power in the will: the volition which is caused by previous motive and inducement, is not caused by the will exercising a sovereign power over itself, to determine, cause and excite volitions in itself. This is not consistent with the will's acting in a state of indifference and equilibrium, to determine itself to a preference; for the way in which motives operate is by biasing the will, and giving it a certain inclination or preponderance one way. . . .

§11. *The Evidence of God's Certain Foreknowledge of the Volitions of Moral Agents*

That the acts of the wills of moral agents are not contingent events, in that sense as to be without all necessity, appears by God's certain foreknowledge of such events.

In handling this argument, I would in the first place prove that God has a certain foreknowledge of the voluntary acts of moral agents; and secondly, show the consequence, or how it follows from hence, that the volitions of moral agents are not contingent, so as to be without necessity of connection and consequence.

First, I am to prove that God has an absolute and certain foreknowledge of the free actions of moral agents.

One would think, it should be wholly needless to enter on such an argument with any that profess themselves Christians: but so it is; God's certain foreknowledge of the free acts of moral agents, is denied by some that pretend to believe the Scriptures to be the Word of God; and especially of late. I therefore shall consider the evidence of such a prescience in the most High, as fully as the designed limits of this essay will admit of; supposing myself herein to have to do with such as own the truth of the Bible.

My first argument shall be taken from God's prediction of such events. Here I would in the first place lay down these two things as axioms.

(1) If God does not foreknow, he cannot foretell such events; that is, he cannot peremptorily and certainly foretell them. If God has no more than an uncertain guess concerning events of this kind, then he can declare no more than an uncertain guess. Positively to foretell, is to profess to foreknow, or to declare positive foreknowledge.

(2) If God does not certainly foreknow the future volitions of moral agents, then neither can he certainly foreknow those events which are consequent and dependent on these volitions. The existence of the one depending on the existence of the other, the knowledge of the existence of the one depends on the knowledge of the existence of the other; and the one cannot be more certain than the other.

Therefore, how many, how great, and how extensive soever the consequences of the volitions of moral agents may be; though they should extend to an alteration of the state of things through the universe, and should be continued in a series of successive events to all eternity, and should in the progress of things branch forth into an infinite number of series, each of them going on in an endless line or chain of events; God must be as ignorant of all these consequences, as he is of the volition whence they first take their rise: all these events, and the whole state of things depending on them, how important, extensive and vast soever, must be hid from him. . . .

§12. *God's Certain Foreknowledge of the Future Volitions of Moral Agents, Inconsistent with Such a Contingence of Those Volitions, as Is Without All Necessity*

Having proved that God has a certain and infallible prescience of the acts of the will of moral agents, I come now, in the second place, to show the consequence; to show how it follows from hence, that these events are necessary, with a necessity of connection or consequence.

The chief Arminian divines, so far as I have had opportunity to observe, deny this consequence; and affirm, that if such foreknowledge be allowed, it is no evidence of any necessity of the event foreknown. Now I desire, that this matter may be particularly and thoroughly inquired into. I cannot but think, that on particular and full consideration, it may be perfectly determined whether it be indeed so, or not.

In order to give a proper consideration of this matter, I would observe the following things.

(1) It is very evident, with regard to a thing whose existence is infallibly and indissolubly connected with something which already has, or has had existence, the existence of that thing is necessary. . . .

To say, the foreknowledge is certain and infallible, and yet the connection of the event with that foreknowledge is not indissoluble, but dissoluble and fallible, is very absurd. To affirm it would be the same thing as to affirm that there is no necessary connection between a proposition's being infallibly known to be true, and its being true indeed. So that it is perfectly demonstrable, that if there be any infallible knowledge of future volitions, the event is necessary; or, in other words, that it is impossible but the event should come to pass. For if it be not impossible but that it may be otherwise, then it is not impossible but that the proposition which affirms its future coming to pass, may not now be true. But how absurd is that, on the supposition that there is now an infallible knowledge (*i.e.* knowledge which it is impossible should fail) that it is true. There is this absurdity in it, that it is not impossible but that there now should be no truth in that proposition, which is now infallibly known to be true.

(2) That no future event can be certainly foreknown, whose existence is contingent, and without all necessity, may be proved thus; it is impossible for a thing to be certainly known to any intellect without evidence. To suppose otherwise, implies a contradiction: because for a thing to be certainly known to any understanding, is for it to be evident to that understanding: and for a thing to be evident to any understanding, is the same thing as for that understanding to see

evidence of it: but no understanding, created or uncreated, can see evidence where there is none: for that is the same thing as to see that to be which is not. And therefore, if there be any truth which is absolutely without evidence, that truth is absolutely unknowable, insomuch that it implies a contradiction to suppose that it is known.

But if there be any future event, whose existence is contingent, without all necessity, the future existence of that event is absolutely without evidence. . . .

(3) To suppose the future volitions of moral agents not to be necessary events; or, which is the same thing, events which it is not impossible but that they may not come to pass; and yet to suppose that God certainly foreknows them, and knows all things; is to suppose God's knowledge to be inconsistent with itself. . . .

From what has been observed it is evident that the absolute decrees of God are no more inconsistent with human liberty, on account of any necessity of the event which follows from such decrees, than the absolute foreknowledge of God. Because the connection between the event and certain foreknowledge is as infallible and indissoluble as between the event and an absolute decree. That is, it is no more impossible that the event and decree should not agree together, than that the event and absolute knowledge should disagree. The connection between the event and foreknowledge is absolutely perfect, by the supposition: because it is supposed that the certainty and infallibility of the knowledge is absolutely perfect. And it being so, the certainty cannot be increased; and therefore the connection between the knowledge and thing known, cannot be increased; so that if a decree be added to the foreknowledge, it does not at all increase the connection, or make it more infallible and indissoluble. If it were not so, the certainty of knowledge might be increased by the addition of a decree; which is contrary to the supposition, which is, that the knowledge is absolutely perfect, or perfect to the highest possible degree.

PART 4: REASONS FOR SELF-DETERMINISM CONSIDERED. (Wherein the Chief Grounds of the Reasonings of Arminians, in Support and Defense of the Forementioned Notions of Liberty, Moral Agency, etc. and Against the Opposite Doctrine, Are Considered)

§5. *Objections, That This Scheme of Necessity Renders All Means and Endeavors for the Avoiding of Sin, or the Obtaining Virtue and Holiness, Vain, and to No Purpose; and That It Makes Men No More Than Mere Machines in Affairs of Morality and Religion, Answered*

Arminians say, if it be so, that sin and virtue come to pass by a necessity consisting in a sure connection of causes and effects, antecedents and consequents, it can never be worth the while to use any means or endeavors to obtain the one, and avoid the other; seeing no endeavors can alter the futurity of the event, which is become necessary by a connection already established.

But I desire that this matter may be fully considered; and that it may be examined with a thorough strictness, whether it will follow that endeavors and means, in order to avoid or obtain any future thing, must be more in vain, on the supposition of such a connection of antecedents and consequents, than if the contrary be supposed.

For endeavors to be in vain, is for them not to be successful; that is to say, for them not eventually to be the means of the thing aimed at, which cannot be, but in one of these two ways; either, first, that although the means are used, yet the event aimed at does not follow: or, secondly, if the event does follow, it is not because of the means, or from any connection or dependence of the event on the means, the event would have come to pass, as well without the means, as with them. If either of these two things are the case, then the means are not properly successful, and are truly in vain. The successfulness or unsuccessfulness of means, in order to an effect, or their being in vain or not in vain, consists in those means being connected, or not connected, with the effect, in such a manner as this, viz. that the effect is *with* the means, and not *without* them; or, that the being of the effect is, on the one hand, connected with the means, and the want of the effect, on the other hand, is connected with the want of the means. If there be such a connection as this between means and end, the means are not in vain: the more there is of such a connection, the further they are from being in vain; and the less of such a connection, the more are they in vain.

Now therefore the question to be answered (in order to determine, whether it follows from this doctrine of the necessary connection between foregoing things and consequent ones, that means used in order to any effect, are more in vain than they would be otherwise) is, whether it follows from it, that there is less of the forementioned connection between means and effect; that is, whether on the supposition of there being a real and true connection between antecedent things and consequent ones, there must be less of a connection between means and effect, than on the supposition of there being no fixed connection between antecedent things and consequent ones: and the very stating of this question is sufficient to answer it. It must appear to everyone that will open his eyes, that this question cannot be affirmed, without the grossest absurdity and inconsistence. Means are foregoing things, and effects are following things: and if there were no connection between foregoing things and following ones, there could be no connection between means and end; and so all means would be wholly vain and fruitless. For it is by virtue of some connection only, that they become successful: it is some connection observed, or revealed, or otherwise known, between antecedent things and following ones, that is what directs in the choice of means. And if there were no such thing as an established connection, there could be no choice as to means; one thing would have no more tendency to an effect than another; there would be no such thing as tendency in the case. All those things which are successful means of other things, do therein prove connected antecedents of them: and therefore to assert that a fixed connection between antecedents and consequents makes means vain and useless, or stands in the way to hinder the connection between means and end, is just so ridiculous as to say that a connection between antecedents and consequents stands in the way to hinder a connection between antecedents and consequents.

. . . I say no such necessary connection of a series of antecedents and consequents can in the least tend to hinder, but that the means we use may belong to the series; and so may be some of those antecedents which are connected with the consequents we aim at, in the established course of things. Endeavors which we use, are things that exist; and therefore they belong to the general chain of events; all the parts of which chain are supposed to be connected: and so endeavors are supposed to be connected with some effects, or some consequent things, or other. And certainly this does not hinder but that the events they are connected with, may be those which we aim at, and which we choose, because we judge them most likely to have a connection with those events, from the established order and course of things which we observe, or from something in divine revelation. . . .

So that the objection we are upon, does not lie against the doctrine of the necessity of events by a certainty of connection and consequence: on the contrary, it is truly forcible against the Arminian doctrine of contingence and self-determination; which is inconsistent with such a connection. If there be no connection between those events wherein virtue and vice consist, and anything antecedent; then there is no connection between these events and any means or endeavors used in order to them: and if so, then those means must be in vain. The less there is of connection between foregoing things and following ones, so much the less there is between means and end, endeavors and success; and in the same proportion are means and endeavors ineffectual and in vain. . . .

Hence it follows, that there cannot, in any consistence with the Arminian scheme, be any reasonable ground of so much as a conjecture concerning the consequence of any means and endeavors, in order to escape vice or obtain virtue, or any choice or preference of means, as having a greater probability of success by some than others;

either from any natural connection or dependence of the end on the means, or through any divine constitution, or revealed way of God's bestowing or bringing to pass these things, in consequence of any means, endeavors, prayers or deeds. Conjecture in this latter case depends on a supposition that God himself is the giver, or determining cause of the events sought: but if they depend on self-determination, then God is not the determining or disposing author of them: and if these things are not of his disposal, then no conjecture can be made from any revelation he has given concerning any way or method of his disposal of them. . . .

§10. *Concerning Sin's First Entrance into the World*

The things which have already been offered, may serve to obviate or clear many of the objections which might be raised concerning sin's first coming into the world; as though it would follow from the doctrine maintained, that God must be the author of the first sin, through his so disposing things, that it should necessarily follow from his permission, that the sinful act should be committed, etc. I need not therefore stand to repeat what has been said already, about such a necessity's not proving God to be the author of sin, in any ill sense, or in any such sense as to infringe any liberty of man, concerned in his moral agency, or capacity of blame, guilt and punishment.

But if it should nevertheless be said, supposing the case so, that God, when he had made man, might so order his circumstances, that from these circumstances, together with his withholding further assistance and divine influence, his sin would infallibly follow, why might not God as well have first made man with a fixed prevailing principle of sin in his heart?

I answer: (1) It was meet, if sin did come into existence, and appear in the world, it should arise from the imperfection which properly belongs to a creature, as such, and should appear so to do, that it might appear not to be from God as the efficient or fountain. But this could not have been, if man had been made at first with sin in his heart; nor unless the abiding principle and habit of sin were first introduced by an evil act of the creature. If sin had not arose from the imperfection of the creature, it would not have been so visible that it did not arise from God, as the positive cause, and real source of it.—But it would require room that cannot be here allowed, fully to consider all the difficulties which have been started, concerning the first entrance of sin into the world.

And therefore, (2) I would observe that objections against the doctrine that has been laid down, in opposition to the Arminian notion of liberty, from these difficulties, are altogether impertinent; because no additional difficulty is incurred, by adhering to a scheme in this manner differing from theirs, and none would be removed or avoided, by agreeing with, and maintaining theirs. Nothing that the Arminians say, about the contingence, or self-determining power of man's will, can serve to explain with less difficulty, how the first sinful volition of mankind could take place, and man be justly charged with the blame of it. To say the will was self-determined, or determined by free choice, in that sinful volition; which is to say that the first sinful volition was determined by a foregoing sinful volition; is no solution of the difficulty. It is an odd way of solving difficulties, to advance greater, in order to it. To say two and two makes nine; or that a child begat his father, solves no difficulty: no more does it to say, the first sinful act of choice was before the first sinful act of choice, and chose and determined it, and brought it to pass. Nor is it any better solution to say, the first sinful volition chose, determined and produced itself; which is to say, it was before it was. Nor will it go any further toward helping us over the difficulty to say, the first sinful volition arose accidentally, without any cause at all. . . .

THE CONCLUSION

Whether the things which have been alleged, are liable to any tolerable answer in the ways of calm, intelligible and strict reasoning, I must leave others to judge. . . .

It is easy to see how the decision of most of the points in controversy, between Calvinists and Arminians, depends on the determination of this grand article concerning the freedom of the will requisite to moral agency; and that by clearing and establishing the Calvinistic doctrine in this point, the chief arguments are obviated, by which Arminian doctrines in general are supported, and the contrary doctrines demonstratively confirmed. Hereby it becomes manifest, that God's moral government over mankind, his treating them as moral agents, making them the objects of his commands, counsels, calls, warnings, expostulations, promises, threatenings, rewards and punishments, is not inconsistent with a determining disposal of all events, of every kind, throughout the universe, in his providence; either by positive efficiency, or permission. Indeed such a universal, determining providence, infers some kind of necessity of all events; such a necessity as implies an infallible previous fixedness of the futurity of the event: but no other necessity of moral events, or volitions of intelligent agents, is needful in order to this, than moral necessity; which does as much ascertain the futurity of the event as any other necessity. But, as has been demonstrated, such a necessity is not at all repugnant to moral agency, and the reasonable use of commands, calls, rewards, punishments, etc. . . .

The things which have been said, obviate some of the chief objections of Arminians against the Calvinistic doctrine of the total depravity and corruption of man's nature, whereby his heart is wholly under the power of sin, and he is utterly unable, without the interposition of sovereign grace, savingly to love God, believe in Christ, or do anything that is truly good and acceptable in God's sight. For the main objection against this doctrine is that it is inconsistent with the freedom of man's will, consisting in indifference and self-determining power; because it supposes man to be under a necessity of sinning, and that God requires things of him, in order to his avoiding eternal damnation, which he is unable to do; and that this doctrine is wholly inconsistent with the sincerity of counsels, invitations, etc. Now this doctrine supposes no other necessity of sinning than a moral necessity; which, as has been shown, does not at all excuse sin; and supposes no other inability to obey any command, or perform any duty, even the most spiritual and exalted, but a moral inability, which, as has been proved, does not excuse persons in the nonperformance of any good thing, or make them not to be the proper objects of commands, counsels and invitations. And moreover, it has been shown, that there is not, and never can be, either in existence, or so much as in idea, any such freedom of will, consisting in indifference and self-determination, for the sake of which this doctrine of original sin is cast out; and that no such freedom is necessary, in order to the nature of sin, and a just desert of punishment.

The things which have been observed, do also take off the main objections of Arminians against the doctrine of efficacious grace; and at the same time, prove the grace of God in a sinner's conversion (if there be any grace or divine influence in the affair) to be efficacious, yes, and irresistible too, if by irresistible is meant that which is attended with a moral necessity, which it is impossible should ever be violated by any resistance. The main objection of Arminians against this doctrine is that it is inconsistent with their self-determining freedom of will; and that it is repugnant to the nature of virtue that it should be wrought in the heart by the determining efficacy and power of another, instead of its being owing to a self-moving power; that in that case, the good which is wrought would not be our virtue, but rather God's virtue; because it is not the person in whom it is wrought that is the determining author of it, but God that wrought it in him. But the things which are the foundation of these objections have been considered; and it has been demonstrated that the liberty of moral agents does not consist in self-determining power; and that there is no need of any such liberty, in order to the nature of virtue; nor does it at all hinder, but that the state or act of the will may be the virtue of the subject, though it be not from self-determination, but the determination of an extrinsic cause; even so as to cause the event to be morally necessary to the subject of it. And as it has been proved, that nothing in the state or acts of the will of man is contingent; but that on the contrary, every event of this kind is necessary, by a moral necessity; and has also been now demonstrated, that the doctrine of a universal determining providence follows from that doctrine of necessity, which was proved before: and so, that God does decisively, in his providence, order all the volitions of moral agents, either by positive influence or permission: and it being allowed on all hands, that what God does in the affair of man's virtuous volitions, whether it be more or less, is by some positive influence, and not by mere permission, as in the affair of a sinful volition: if we put these things together, it will follow that God's assistance or influence, must be determining and decisive, or must be attended with a moral necessity of the event; and so, that God gives virtue, holiness and conversion to sinners, by an influence which determines the effect, in such a manner that the effect will infallibly follow by a moral necessity; which is what Calvinists mean by efficacious and irresistible grace.

The things which have been said, do likewise answer the chief objections against the doctrine of God's universal and absolute decree, and afford infallible proof of that doctrine; and of the doctrine of absolute, eternal, personal election in particular. The main objections against these doctrines are that they infer a necessity of the volitions of moral agents, and of the future moral state and acts of men; and so are not consistent with those eternal rewards and punishments, which are connected with conversion and impenitence; nor can be made to agree with the reasonableness and sincerity of the precepts, calls, counsels, warnings and expostulations of the Word of God; or with the various methods and means of grace which God uses with sinners, to bring them to repentance; and the whole of that moral government, which God exercises toward mankind: and that they infer an inconsistence between the secret and revealed will of God; and make God the author of sin. But all these things have been obviated in the preceding discourse. And the certain truth of these doctrines, concerning God's eternal purposes, will follow from what was just now observed concerning God's universal providence; how it infallibly follows from what has been proved, that God orders all events, and the volitions of moral agents amongst others, by such a decisive disposal, that the events are infallibly connected with his disposal. For if God disposes all events, so that the infallible existence of the events is decided by his providence, then he doubtless thus orders and decides things knowingly, and on design. God does not do what he does, nor order what he orders, accidentally and unawares; either without, or beside his intention. And if there be a foregoing design of doing and ordering as he does, this is the same with a purpose or decree. And as it has been shown, that nothing is new to God, in any respect, but all things are perfectly and equally in his view from eternity; hence it will follow, that his designs or purposes are not things formed anew, founded on any new views or appearances, but are all eternal purposes. And as it has been now shown how the doctrine of determining efficacious grace certainly follows from things proved in the foregoing discourse; hence will necessarily follow the doctrine of particular, eternal, absolute election. For if men are made true saints, no otherwise than as God makes them so, and distinguishes them from others, by an efficacious power and influence of his, that decides and fixes the event; and God thus makes some saints, and not others, on design or purpose, and (as has been now observed) no designs of God are new; it follows that God thus distinguished from others, all that ever become true saints, by his eternal design or decree. I might also show how God's certain foreknowledge must suppose an absolute decree, and how such a decree can be proved to a demonstration from it: but that this discourse may not be lengthened out too much, that must be omitted for the present. . . .

By the things which have been proved, are obviated some of the main objections against the doctrine of the infallible and necessary perseverance of saints, and some of the main foundations of this doctrine are established. The main prejudices of Arminians against this doctrine seem to be these; they suppose such a necessary, infallible perseverance to be repugnant to the freedom of the will; that it must be owing to man's own self-determining power, that he first becomes virtuous and holy; and so in like manner, it must be left a thing contingent, to be determined by the same freedom of will, whether he will persevere in virtue and holiness; and that otherwise his continuing steadfast in faith and obedience would not be his virtue, or at all praiseworthy and rewardable; nor could his perseverance be properly the matter of divine commands, counsels and promises, nor his apostasy be properly threatened, and men warned against it. Whereas we find all these things in Scripture: there we find steadfastness and perseverance in true Christianity, represented as the virtue of the saints, spoken of as praiseworthy in them, and glorious rewards promised to it; and also find that God makes it the subject of his commands, counsels and promises; and the contrary, of threatenings and warnings. But the foundation of these objections has been removed, in its being shown that moral necessity and infallible certainty of events is not inconsistent with these things; and that, as to freedom of will lying in the power of the will to determine itself, there neither is any such thing, nor any need of it, in order to virtue, reward, commands, counsels, etc.

And as the doctrines of efficacious grace and absolute election do certainly follow from things which have been provided in the preceding discourse; so some of the main foundations of the doctrine of perseverance are thereby established. If the beginning of true faith and holiness, and a man's becoming a true saint at first, does not depend on the self-determining power of the will, but on the determining efficacious grace of God; it may well be argued that it is so also with respect to men's being continued saints, or persevering in faith and holiness. The conversion of a sinner being not owing to a man's self-determination, but to God's determination and eternal election, which is absolute, and depending on the sovereign will of God, and not on the free will of man; as is evident from what has been said: and it being very evident from the Scriptures, that the eternal election which there is of saints to faith and holiness, is also an election of them to eternal salvation; hence their appointment to salvation must also be absolute, and not depending on their contingent, self-determining will. From all of which it follows, that it is absolutely fixed in God's decree, that all true saints shall persevere to actual eternal salvation. . . .

THE NATURE OF TRUE VIRTUE [5]

Chapter 1

Whatever controversies and variety of opinions there are about the nature of virtue, yet all excepting some skeptics, who deny any real difference between virtue and vice, mean by it something beautiful, or rather some kind of beauty or excellency. It is not all beauty that is called virtue; for instance, not the beauty of a building, of a flower, or of the rainbow; but some beauty belonging to beings that have perception and will. It is not all beauty of mankind that is called virtue; for instance, not the external beauty of the countenance or shape, gracefulness of motion, or harmony of voice: but it is a beauty that has its original seat in the mind. But yet perhaps not everything that may be called a beauty of mind, is properly called virtue. There is a beauty of understanding and speculation; there is something in the ideas and conceptions of great philosophers and statesmen that may be called beautiful: which is a different thing from what is most commonly meant by virtue.

[5] From *The Works of Jonathan Edwards*, ed. by E. Hickman, London, 1834, Vol. I, corrected and edited.

But virtue is the beauty of those qualities and acts of the mind that are of a moral nature, *i.e.* such as are attended with desert or worthiness of praise or blame. Things of this sort it is generally agreed, so far as I know, do not belong merely to speculation; but to the disposition and will, or (to use a general word I suppose commonly well understood) to the heart. Therefore I suppose I shall not depart from the common opinion when I say, that virtue is the beauty of the qualities and exercises of the heart, or those actions which proceed from them. So that when it is inquired, what is the nature of true virtue? this is the same as to inquire what that is, which renders any habit, disposition, or exercise of the heart truly beautiful.

I use the phrase true virtue, and speak of things truly beautiful, because I suppose it will generally be allowed that there is a distinction to be made between some things which are truly virtuous, and others which only seem to be so, through a partial and imperfect view of things: that some actions and dispositions appear beautiful, if considered partially and superficially, or with regard to some things belonging to them, and in some of their circumstances and tendencies, which would appear otherwise in a more extensive and comprehensive view, wherein they are seen clearly in their whole nature, and the extent of their connections in the universality of things.

There is a general and particular beauty. By a particular beauty, I mean that by which a thing appears beautiful when considered only with regard to its connection with, and tendency to, some particular things within a limited, and as it were a private sphere. And a general beauty is that by which a thing appears beautiful when viewed most perfectly, comprehensively and universally, with regard to all its tendencies, and its connections with everything to which it stands related. The former may be without and against the latter. As a few notes in a tune, taken only by themselves and in their relation to one another, may be harmonious, which, when considered with respect to all the notes in the tune, or the entire series of sounds they are connected with, may be very discordant, and disagreeable. That only, therefore, is what I mean by true virtue, which, belonging to the heart of an intelligent being, is beautiful by a general beauty, or beautiful in a comprehensive view, as it is in itself, and as related to everything with which it stands connected. And therefore, when we are inquiring concerning the nature of true virtue—wherein this true and general beauty of the heart does most essentially consist—this is my answer to the inquiry:

True virtue most essentially consists in *benevolence to being in general.* Or perhaps, to speak more accurately, it is that consent, propensity and union of heart to being in general, which is immediately exercised in a general good will.

The things before observed respecting the nature of true virtue, naturally lead us to such a notion of it. If it has its seat in the heart, and is the general goodness and beauty of the disposition and its exercise, in the most comprehensive view, considered with regard to its universal tendency, and as related to everything with which it stands connected; what can it consist in, but a consent and good will to being in general? Beauty does not consist in discord and dissent, but in consent and agreement. And if every intelligent being is some way related to being in general, and is a part of the universal system of existence; and so stands in connection with the whole; what can its general and true beauty be, but its union and consent with the great whole?

If any such thing can be supposed as a union of heart to some particular being, or number of beings, disposing it to benevolence to a private circle or system of beings, which are but a small part of the whole; not implying a tendency to a union with the great system, and not at all inconsistent with enmity toward being in general, this I suppose not to be of the nature of true virtue; although it may in some respects be good, and may appear beautiful in a confined and contracted view of things. But of this more afterward.

It is abundantly plain by the Holy Scriptures, and generally allowed, not only by Christian divines, but by the more considerable deists, that virtue most essentially consists in love. And I suppose it is owned by the most considerable writers, to consist in general love of benevolence, or kind affection: though it seems to me the meaning of some in this affair is not sufficiently explained; which perhaps occasions some error or confusion in discourses on this subject.

When I say true virtue consists in love to being in general, I shall not be likely to be understood, that no one act of the mind or exercise of love is of the nature of true virtue, but what has being in general, or the great system of universal existence, for its direct and immediate object: so that no exercise of love, or kind affection to any one particular being that is but a small part of this whole, has anything of the nature of true virtue. But that the nature of true virtue consists in a disposition to benevolence toward being in general; though from such a disposition may arise exercises of love to particular beings, as objects are presented and occasions arise. No wonder that he who is of a generally benevolent disposition, should be more disposed than another to have his heart moved with benevolent affection to particular persons with whom he is acquainted and conversant, and from whom arise the greatest and most frequent occasions for exciting his benevolent temper. But my meaning is, that no affections toward particular persons or beings are of the nature of true virtue, but such as arise from a generally benevolent temper, or from that habit or frame of mind, wherein consists a disposition to love being in general.

And perhaps it is needless for me to give notice to my readers that when I speak of an intelligent being having a heart united and benevolently disposed to being in general, I thereby mean intelligent being in general: not inanimate things, or beings that have no perception or will; which are not properly capable objects of benevolence.

Love is commonly distinguished into love of benevolence, and love of complacence. Love of benevolence is that affection or propensity of the heart to any being, which causes it to incline to its well-being, or disposes it to desire and take pleasure in its happiness. And if I mistake not, it is agreeable to the common opinion, that beauty in the object is not always the ground of this propensity; but that there may be a disposition to the welfare of those that are not considered as beautiful, unless mere existence be accounted a beauty. And benevolence or goodness in the divine Being is generally supposed, not only to be prior to the beauty of many of its objects, but to their existence; so as to be the ground both of their existence and their beauty, rather than the foundation of God's benevolence; as it is supposed that it is God's goodness which moved him to give them both being and beauty. So that if all virtue primarily consists in that affection of heart to being, which is exercised in benevolence, or an inclination to its good, then God's virtue is so extended as to include a propensity not only to being actually existing and actually beautiful, but to possible being, so as to incline him to give a being beauty and happiness.

What is commonly called love of complacence, presupposes beauty. For it is no other than delight in beauty; or complacence in the person or being beloved for his beauty. If virtue be the beauty of an intelligent being, and virtue consists in love, then it is a plain inconsistence to suppose that virtue primarily consists in any love to its object for its beauty; either in a love of complacence, which is delight in a being for his beauty, or in a love of benevolence, that has the beauty of its object for its foundation. For that would be to suppose that the beauty of intelligent beings primarily consists in love to beauty; or that their virtue first of all consists in their love to virtue. Which is an inconsistence, and going in a circle. Because it makes virtue, or beauty of mind, the foundation or first motive of that love wherein virtue originally consists, or wherein the very first virtue consists; or, it supposes the first virtue to be the consequence and effect of virtue. Which makes the first virtue both the ground and the consequence, both cause and effect of itself. Doubtless virtue primarily consists in something else besides any effect or consequence of virtue. If virtue consists primarily in love to virtue, then virtue, the thing loved, is the love of virtue: so that virtue must consist in the love of the love of virtue—and so on ad infinitum. For there is no end of going back in a circle. We never come to any beginning or foundation; it is without beginning, and hangs on nothing. Therefore, if the essence of virtue, or beauty of mind, lies in love, or a disposition to love, it must primarily consist in something different both from complacence, which is a delight in beauty, and also from any benevolence that has the beauty of its object for its foundation. Because it is absurd to say that virtue is primarily and first of all the consequence of itself; which makes virtue primarily prior to itself.

Nor can virtue primarily consist in gratitude; or one being's benevolence to another for his benevolence to him. Because this implies the same inconsistence. For it supposes a benevolence prior to gratitude, which is the cause of gratitude. The first benevolence cannot be gratitude. Therefore there is room left for no other conclusion, than that the primary object of virtuous love is being, simply considered; or that true virtue primarily consists, not in love to any particular beings, because of their virtue or beauty, nor in gratitude, because they love us; but in a propensity and union of heart to being simply considered; exciting absolute benevolence, if I may so call it, to being in general. I say true virtue primarily consists in this. For I am far from asserting that there is no true virtue in any other love than this absolute benevolence. But I would express what appears to me to be the truth on this subject, in the following particulars.

The first object of a virtuous benevolence is being, simply considered; and if being, simply considered, be its object, then being in general is its object; and what it has an ultimate propensity to is the highest good of being in general. And it will seek the good of every individual being unless it be conceived as not consistent with the highest good of being in general. In which case the good of a particular being, or some beings, may be given up for the sake of the highest good of being in general. And particularly, if there be any being statedly and irreclaimably opposite, and an enemy to being in general, then consent and adherence to being in general will induce the truly virtuous heart to forsake that enemy, and to oppose it.

Further, if being, simply considered, be the first object of a truly virtuous benevolence, then that object who has most of being, or has the greatest share of existence, other things being equal, so far as such a being is exhibited to our faculties, will have the greatest share of the propensity and benevolent affections of the heart. I say, "other things being equal," especially because there is a secondary object of virtuous benevolence, that I shall take notice of presently, which must be considered as the ground or motive to a purely virtuous benevolence. Pure benevolence in its first exercise is nothing else but being's uniting consent, or propensity to being; and inclining to the general highest good, and to each being, whose welfare is consistent with the highest general good, in proportion to the degree of existence,[6] understand, "other things being equal."

The second object of a virtuous propensity of heart is benevolent being. A secondary ground of pure benevolence is virtuous benevolence itself in its object. When anyone under the influence of general benevolence, sees another being possessed of the like general benevolence, this attaches his heart to him, and draws forth greater love to him, than merely his having existence: because so far as the being beloved has love to being in general, so far his own being is, as it were, enlarged; extends to, and in some sort comprehends being in general: and therefore, he that is governed by love to being in general, must of necessity have complacence in him, and the greater degree of benevolence to him, as it were out of gratitude to him for his love to general existence, that his own heart is extended and united to, and so looks on its interest as its own. It is because his heart is thus united to being in general, that he looks on a benevolent propensity to being in general, wherever he sees it, as the beauty of the being in whom it is; an excellency that renders him worthy of esteem, complacence, and the greater good will. But several things may be noted more particularly concerning this secondary ground of a truly virtuous love.

1. That loving a being on this ground necessarily arises from pure benevolence to being in general, and comes to the same thing. For he that has a simple and pure good will to general existence, must love that temper in others, that agrees and conspires with itself. A spirit of consent to being must agree with consent to being. That which truly and sincerely seeks the good of others, must approve of, and love that which joins with him in seeking the good of others.

2. This secondary ground of virtuous love is the thing wherein true moral or spiritual beauty primarily consists. Yes, spiritual beauty consists wholly in this, and in the various qualities and exercises of mind which proceed from it, and the external actions which proceed from these internal qualities and exercises. And in these things consists all true virtue, viz. in this love of being, and the qualities and acts which arise from it.

3. As all spiritual beauty lies in these virtuous principles and acts, so it is primarily on this account they are beautiful, viz. that they imply consent and union with being in general. This is the primary

---

[6] I say, "in proportion to the degree of existence," because one being may have more existence than another, as he may be greater than another. That which is great has more existence, and is further from nothing, than that which is little. One being may have everything positive belonging to it, or everything which goes to its positive existence (in opposition to defect) in a higher degree than another; or a greater capacity and power, greater understanding, every faculty and every positive quality in a higher degree. An archangel must be supposed to have more existence, and to be every way further removed from nonentity, than a worm.—E.

and most essential beauty of everything that can justly be called by the name of virtue, or is any moral excellency in the eye of one who has a perfect view of things. I say, "the primary and most essential beauty," because there is a secondary and inferior sort of beauty; which I shall take notice of afterward.

4. This spiritual beauty, which is but a secondary ground of virtuous benevolence, is the ground not only of benevolence, but complacence, and is the primary ground of the latter; that is, when the complacence is truly virtuous. Love to us in particular, and kindness received may be a secondary ground: but this is the primary objective foundation of it.

5. It must be noted, that the degree of the amiableness of true virtue primarily consisting in consent, and a benevolent propensity of heart to being in general, is not in the simple proportion of the degree of benevolent affection seen, but in a proportion compounded of the greatness of the benevolent being, or the degree of being and the degree of benevolence. One who loves being in general, will necessarily value good will to being in general, wherever he sees it. But if he sees the same benevolence in two beings, he will value it more in two than in one only. Because it is a greater thing, more favorable to being in general, to have two beings to favor it, than only one of them. For there is more being that favors being: both together having more being than one alone. So if one being be as great as two, has as much existence as both together, and has the same degree of general benevolence, it is more favorable to being in general, than if there were general benevolence in a being that had but half that share of existence. As a large quantity of gold, with the same quality, is more valuable than a small quantity of the same metal.

6. It is impossible that anyone should truly relish this beauty, consisting in general benevolence, who has not that temper himself. I have observed that if any being is possessed of such a temper, he will unavoidably be pleased with the same temper in another. And it may in like manner be demonstrated, that it is such a spirit, and nothing else, which will relish such a spirit. For if a being destitute of benevolence, should love benevolence to being in general, it would prize and seek that for which it had no value. For how should one love and value a disposition to a thing, or a tendency to promote it, and for that very reason, when the thing itself is what he is regardless of, and has no value for, nor desires to have promoted.

Chapter 2

From what has been said, it is evident that true virtue must chiefly consist in *love to God*; the Being of beings, infinitely the greatest and best. . . .

Chapter 8

. . . The use of language is to express our sentiments, or ideas, to each other; so that those terms by which things of a moral nature are signified, express those moral sentiments which are common to mankind. Therefore, that moral sense which in its natural conscience, chiefly governs the use of language, and is the mind's rule of language in these matters. It is indeed the general natural rule which God has given to all men, whereby to judge of moral good and evil. By such words, right and wrong, good and evil, when used in a moral sense, is meant in common speech, that which deserves praise or blame, respect or resentment; and mankind in general have a sense of desert, by this natural moral sense.

Therefore here is a question which may deserve to be considered: Seeing sentiment is the rule of language, as to what is called good and evil, worthy and unworthy; and it is apparent that sentiment, at least as to many particulars, is different in different persons, especially in different nations—that being thought to deserve praise by one, which by others is thought to be worthy of blame—how therefore can virtue and vice be any other than arbitrary? not at all determined by the nature of things, but by the sentiments of men with relation to the nature of things.

In order to the answering of this question with clearness, it may be divided into two: viz. Whether men's sentiments of moral good and evil are casual and accidental? And, whether their way of using words in what they call good and evil, is not arbitrary, without respect to any common sentiment conformed to the nature of things?

As to the first I would observe that the general disposition or sense of mind, exercised in a sense of desert of esteem or resentment, may be the same in all: though as to particular objects and occasions with regard to which it is exercised, it may be very various in different men or bodies of men, through the partiality or error that may attend the view or attention of the mind. In all a notion of desert of love or resentment, may consist in the same thing in general—a suitableness, or natural uniformity and agreement between the affections and acts of the agent, and the affection and treatment of others some way concerned—and yet occasions and objects through a variety of apprehensions about them, and the various manner in which they are viewed, by reason of the partial attention of the mind, may be extremely various. Besides, example, custom, education, and association, may contribute to this, in ways innumerable. But it is needless to enlarge here, since what has been said by others, Mr. Hutchison in particular, may abundantly show that the differences which are to be found among different persons and nations concerning moral good and evil, are not inconsistent with a general moral sense, common to all mankind.

Nor, secondly, is the use of the words, good and evil, right and wrong, when used in a moral sense, altogether unfixed and arbitrary, according to the variety of notions, opinions and views, that occasion the forementioned variety of sentiment. For though the signification of words is determined by particular use, yet that which governs in the use of terms, is general or common use. And mankind, in what they would signify by terms, are obliged to aim at a consistent use; because it is easily found that the end of language, which is to be a common medium of manifesting ideas and sentiments, cannot be obtained any other way than by a consistent use of words; both that men should be consistent with themselves, and one with another, in the use of them. But men cannot call anything right or wrong, worthy or ill-deserving, consistently, any other way than by calling things so, which truly deserve praise or blame, *i.e.* things wherein, all things considered, there is most uniformity in connecting with them praise or blame. There is no other way in which they can use these terms consistently with themselves. Thus if thieves or traitors may be angry with informers that bring them to justice, and call their behavior by odious names; yet herein they are inconsistent with themselves; because when they put themselves in the place of those who have injured them, they approve the same things they condemn. And therefore, such are capable of being convinced that they apply these odious terms in an abusive manner. So a nation that prosecutes an ambitious design of universal empire, by subduing other nations with fire and sword, may affix terms that signify the highest degrees of virtue to the conduct of such as show the most engaged, stable, resolute spirit in this affair, and do most of this bloody work. But yet they are incapable of being convinced that they use these terms inconsistently, and abuse language in it, and so having their mouths stopped. And not only will men use such words inconsistently with themselves but also with one another, by using them any otherwise than to signify true merit or ill-deserving, as before explained. For there is no way else wherein men have any notion of good or ill desert, in which mankind in general can agree. Mankind in general seem to suppose some general standard, or foundation in nature, for a universal consistence in the use of the terms whereby they express moral good and evil; which none can depart from but through error and mistake. This is evidently supposed in all their disputes about right and wrong; and in all endeavors used to prove that anything is either good or evil, in a moral sense.

RELIGIOUS AFFECTIONS [7]

PART 1. Concerning the Nature of the Affections, and Their Importance on Religion

. . . The proposition or doctrine that I would raise . . . is this: true religion, in great part, consists in holy affections.

We see that the apostle, in remarking the operations and exercises of religion in these Christians, when it had its greatest trial by persecution, as gold is tried in the fire—and when it not only proved true, but was most pure from dross and mixtures—and when it appeared in them most in its genuine excellency and native beauty, and was found to praise, and honor, and glory—he singles out the religious affections of *love* and *joy*, as those exercises, wherein their religion did thus appear true, pure and glorious.

Here it may be inquired, what the affections of the mind are? I answer, The affections are no other than the more vigorous and sensible exercises of the inclination and will of the soul.

God has endowed the soul with two principal faculties: The one, that by which it is capable of perception and speculation, or by which it discerns, and judges of things; which is called the understanding. The other, that by which the soul is some way inclined with respect to the things it views or considers: or it is the faculty by which the soul beholds things—not as an indifferent unaffected spectator, but—either as liking or disliking, pleased or displeased, approving or rejecting. This faculty is called by various names: it is sometimes called the inclination; and, as it respects the actions determined and governed by it, the will: and the mind, with regard to the exercises of this faculty, is often called the heart.

The exercises of this last faculty are of two sorts; either those by which the soul is carried out toward the things in view in approving them, being pleased with, and inclined to them; or, those in which the soul opposes the things in view, in disapproving them; and in being displeased with, averse from, and rejecting them. And as the exercises of the inclination are various in their kinds, so they are much more various in their degrees. There are some exercises of pleasedness or displeasedness, inclination or disinclination, wherein the soul is carried but a little beyond a state of perfect indifference. And there are other degrees, wherein the approbation or dislike, pleasedness or aversion, are stronger; wherein we may rise higher and higher, till the soul

---

[7] From *A Treatise Concerning Religious Affections*. Reprinted in *The Works of Jonathan Edwards*, ed. by E. Hickman, Vol. I, corrected and edited.

comes to act vigorously and sensibly, and its actings are with that strength, that (through the laws of union which the Creator has fixed between soul and body) the motion of the blood and animal spirits begins to be sensibly altered: whence oftentimes arises some bodily sensation, especially about the heart and vitals, which are the fountain of the fluids of the body. Whence it comes to pass that the mind, with regard to the exercises of this faculty, perhaps in all nations and ages, is called the heart. And it is to be noted that they are these more vigorous and sensible exercises of this faculty, which are called the affections.

The will and the affections of the soul are not two faculties; the affections are not essentially distinct from the will, nor do they differ from the mere actings of the will and inclination, but only in the liveliness and sensibility of exercise. It must be confessed that language is here somewhat imperfect, the meaning of words in a considerable measure loose and unfixed, and not precisely limited by custom which governs the use of language. In some sense, the affection of the soul differs nothing at all from the will and inclination, and the will never is in any exercise further than it is affected; it is not moved out of a state of perfect indifference, any otherwise than as it is affected one way or other. But yet there are many actings of the will and inclination that are not so commonly called affections. In everything we do, wherein we act voluntarily, there is an exercise of the will and inclination. It is our inclination that governs us in our actions; but all the actings of the inclination and will are not ordinarily called affections. Yet, what are commonly called affections are not essentially different from them, but only in the degree and manner of exercise. In every act of the will whatsoever, the soul either likes or dislikes, is either inclined or disinclined to what is in view. These are not essentially different from the affections of love and hatred. A liking or inclination of the soul to a thing, if it be in a high degree vigorous and lively, is the very same thing with the affection of love: and a disliking and disinclining, if in a great degree, is the very same with hatred. In every act of the will for, or toward something not present, the soul is in some degree inclined to that thing; and that inclination, if in a considerable degree, is the very same with the affection of desire. And in every degree of an act of the will, wherein the soul approves of something present, there is a degree of pleasedness, and that pleasedness, if it be in a considerable degree, is the very same with the affection of joy or delight. And if the will disapproves of what is present, the soul is in some degree displeased, and if that displeasedness be great, it is the very same with the affection of grief or sorrow.

Such seems to be our nature, and such the laws of the union of soul and body, that there never is in any case whatsoever, any lively and vigorous exercise of the inclination, without some effect upon the body, in some alteration of the motion of its fluids, and especially of the animal spirits. And, on the other hand, from the same laws of union, over the constitution of the body, and the motion of its fluids, may promote the exercise of the affections. But yet, it is not the body, but the mind only that is the proper seat of the affections. The body of man is no more capable of being really the subject of love or hatred, joy or sorrow, fear or hope, than the body of a tree, or than the same body of man is capable of thinking and understanding. As it is the soul only that has ideas, so it is the soul only that is pleased or displeased with its ideas. As it is the soul only that thinks, so it is the soul only that loves or hates, rejoices or is grieved at what it thinks of. Nor are these motions of the animal spirits, and fluids of the body, anything properly belonging to the nature of the affections; though they always accompany them in the present state; but are only effects or concomitants of the affections, which are entirely distinct from the affections themselves, and no way essential to them; so that an unbodied spirit may be as capable of love and hatred, joy or sorrow, hope or fear, or other affections, as one that is united to a body.

The affections and passions are frequently spoken of as the same; and yet, in the more common use of speech, there is in some respect a difference. Affection is a word, that in its ordinary signification, seems to be something more extensive than passion, being used for all vigorous lively actings of the will or inclination; but passion is used for those that are more sudden, and whose effects on the animal spirits are more violent, the mind being more overpowered, and less in its own command.

As all the exercises of inclination and will are concerned either in approving and liking, or disapproving and rejecting; so the affections are of two sorts; they are those by which the soul is carried out to what is in view, cleaving to it, or seeking it; or those by which it is averse from it, and opposes it. Of the former sort are love, desire, hope, joy, gratitude, complacence. Of the latter kind, are hatred, fear, anger, grief, and suchlike; which it is needless now to stand particularly to define.

And there are some affections wherein there is a composition of each of the aforementioned kinds of actings of the will; as in the affection of pity, there is something of the former kind, toward the person suffering, and something of the latter, toward what he suffers. And so in zeal, there is in it high approbation of some person or thing, together with vigorous opposition to what is conceived to be contrary to it. . . .

From hence it clearly and certainly appears that great part of true religion consists in the affections. For love is not only one of the affections, but it is the first and chief of them, and the fountain of all the others. From love arises hatred of those things which are contrary to what we love, or which oppose and thwart us in those things that we delight in; and from the various exercises of love and hatred, according to the circumstances of the objects of these affections, as present or absent, certain or uncertain, probable or improbable, arise all those other affections of desire, hope, fear, joy, grief, gratitude, anger, etc. From a vigorous, affectionate, and fervent love to God, will necessarily arise other religious affections; hence will arise an intense hatred and a fear of sin; a dread of God's displeasure; gratitude to God for his goodness; complacence and joy in God when he is graciously and sensibly present; grief when he is absent; a joyful hope when a future enjoyment of God is expected; and fervent zeal for the divine glory. In like manner, from a fervent love to men, will arise all other virtuous affections toward them.

Upon the whole, I think it clearly and abundantly evident that true religion lies very much in the affections. Not that I think these arguments prove that religion in the hearts of the truly godly is ever in exact proportion to the degree of affection and present emotion of the mind: for, undoubtedly, there is much affection in the true saints which is not spiritual; their religious affections are often mixed; all is not from grace, but much from nature. And though the affections have not their seat in the body, yet the constitution of the body may very much contribute to the present emotion of the mind. The degree of religion is to be estimated by the fixedness and strength of habit exercised in affection, whereby holy affection is habitual, rather than by the degree of the present exercise: and the strength of that habit is not always in proportion to outward effects and manifestations, or indeed inward ones, in the hurry, vehemence, and sudden changes of the course of the thoughts. But yet it is evident that religion consists so much in the affections, as that without holy affection there is no true religion. No light in the understanding is good which does not produce holy affection in the heart; no habit or principle in the heart is good which has no such exercise; and no external fruit is good which does not proceed from such exercises. . . .

PART 3. Showing What Are Distinguishing Signs of Truly Gracious and Holy Affections

Having premised these things, I now proceed directly to take notice of those things in which true religious affections are distinguished from false.

§1. Affections that are truly spiritual and gracious, arise from those influences and operations on the heart, which are spiritual, supernatural, and divine.

I will explain what I mean by these terms, whence will appear their use to distinguish between those affections which are spiritual, and those which are not so. We find that true saints, or those persons who are sanctified by the Spirit of God, are in the New Testament called spiritual persons. And their being spiritual is spoken of as their peculiar character, and that wherein they are distinguished from those who are not sanctified. This is evident, because those who are spiritual are set in opposition to natural men, and carnal men. Thus the spiritual man and the natural man are set in opposition one to another. . . .

. . . Those gracious influences of the saints, and the effects of God's Spirit which they experience, are entirely above nature, and altogether of a different kind from anything that men find in themselves by the exercise of natural principles. No improvement of those principles that are natural, no advancing or exalting of them to higher degrees, and no kind of composition will ever bring men to them; because they not only differ from what is natural, and from everything that natural men experience, in degree and circumstances, but also in kind; and are of a nature vastly more excellent. And this is what I mean by supernatural when I say, that gracious affections are from those influences that are supernatural. . . .

. . . All spiritual and gracious affections are attended with, and arise from some apprehension, idea, or sensation of mind, which is in its whole nature different, yes, exceeding different from all that is or can be in the mind of a natural man. The natural man discerns nothing of it (1 Cor. ii. 14.) any more than a man without the sense of tasting can conceive of the sweet taste of honey; or a man without the sense of hearing can conceive of the melody of a tune; or a man born blind can have a notion of the beauty of a rainbow. . . .

NOTES ON NATURAL SCIENCE: [8] OF BEING

That there should absolutely be Nothing at all, is utterly impossible. The mind, let it stretch its conceptions ever so far, can never so much as bring itself to conceive of a state of perfect Nothing. It puts the mind into mere convulsion and confusion to think of such a state: and

[8] Reprinted in *The Works of President Edwards*, ed. by S. E. Dwight, New York, 1830, Vol. I. Rearranged.

it contradicts the very nature of the soul to think that such a state should be. It is the greatest of contradictions, and the aggregate of all contradictions, to say that a thing should not be. It is true, we cannot so distinctly show the contradiction in words; because we cannot talk about it, without speaking stark nonsense, and contradicting ourselves at every word: and because Nothing is that, whereby we distinctly show other particular contradictions. But here we are run up to our first principle, and have no other to explain the nothingness, or not-being of Nothing by. Indeed, we can mean nothing else by Nothing, but a state of absolute contradiction; and if any man thinks that he can conceive well enough how there should be Nothing, I will engage, that what he means by Nothing, is as much something, as anything that he ever thought of in his life. And I believe, that if he knew what Nothing was, it would be intuitively evident to him that it could not be.

Thus we see it is necessary that some being should eternally be. And it is a more palpable contradiction still to say, that there must be Being somewhere, and not otherwhere, for the words *Absolute Nothing,* and *Where,* contradict each other. And, besides, it gives as great a shock to the mind to think of pure Nothing being in any one place, as it does to think of it in all places: and it is self-evident, that there can be Nothing in one place, as well as in another; and if there can be in one, there can be all. So that we see that this necessary, Eternal Being must be infinite and omnipresent.

This infinite and omnipresent being cannot be solid. Let us see how contradictory it is, to say that an infinite being is solid; for solidity surely is nothing but resistance to other solidities.

Space is this necessary, eternal, infinite, and omnipresent being. We find that we can, with ease, conceive how all other beings should not be. We can remove them out of our minds, and place some other in the room of them: but space is the very thing that we can never remove, and conceive of its not being. If a man would imagine space anywhere to be divided, so as there should be nothing between the divided parts, there remains space between, notwithstanding, and so the man contradicts himself. And it is self-evident I believe to every man, that space is necessary, eternal, infinite and omnipresent. But I had as good speak plain: I have already said as much as, that space is God. And it is indeed clear to me, that all the space there is, not proper to body, all the space there is without the bonds of creation, all the space there was before the creation, is God himself; and nobody would in the least pick at it, if it were not because of the gross conceptions that we have of space.

A state of absolute nothing is a state of absolute contradiction. Absolute nothing is the aggregate of all the contradictions in the world: a state wherein there is neither body, nor spirit, nor space, neither empty space nor full space, neither little nor great, narrow nor broad, neither infinite space nor finite space, not even a mathematical point, neither up nor down, neither north nor south (I do not mean as it is with respect to the body of the earth, or some other great body), but no contrary points, positions or directions, no such thing as either here or there, this way or that way, or any way. When we go about to form an idea of perfect nothing, we must shut out all these things: we must shut out of our minds both space that has something in it, and space that has nothing in it. We must not allow ourselves to think of the least part of space, be it ever so small. Nor must we suffer our thoughts to take sanctuary in a mathematical point. When we go to expel being out of our thoughts, we must be careful not to leave empty space in the room of it; and when we go to expel emptiness from our thoughts, we must not think to squeeze it out by anything close, hard and solid; but we must think of the same that the sleeping rocks do dream of; and not till then shall we get a complete idea of Nothing.

When we go to inquire, whether or no there can be absolutely Nothing? we utter nonsense in so inquiring. The stating of the question is nonsense; because we make a disjunction where there is none. Either Being, or absolute Nothing, is no disjunction; no more than whether a triangle is a triangle, or not a triangle. There is no other way, but only for there to be existence: there is no such thing as absolute Nothing. There is such a thing as Nothing, with respect to this ink and paper: there is such a thing as Nothing, with respect to you and me: there is such a thing as Nothing, with respect to this globe of earth, and with respect to this universe. There is another way, beside these things, having existence; but there is no such thing as Nothing, with respect to entity, or Being, absolutely considered. We do not know what we say, if we say, that we think it possible in itself, that there should not be entity.

And how it grates upon the mind, to think that something should be from all eternity, and yet Nothing all the while be conscious of it. To illustrate this: Let us suppose that the world had a being from all eternity, and had many great changes, and wonderful revolutions, and all the while Nothing knew it, there was no knowledge in the universe of any such thing. How is it possible to bring the mind to imagine this? Yes, it is really impossible it should be, that anything should exist, and Nothing know it. Then you will say, If it be so, it is because Nothing has any existence but in consciousness: No, certainly, nowhere else, but either in created or uncreated consciousness.

Suppose there were another universe, merely of bodies, created at a great distance from this; created in excellent order, harmonious

motions, and a beautiful variety; and there was no created intelligence
in it, nothing but senseless bodies, and nothing but God knew anything
of it. I demand where else that universe would have a being, but only
in the Divine consciousness? Certainly in no other respect. There
would be figures, and magnitudes, and motions, and proportions; but
where, where else, except in the Almighty's knowledge? How is it
possible there should?

But then you will say, For the same reason, in a room closely shut
up, which nobody sees, there is nothing, except in God's knowledge.

I answer, Created beings are conscious of the effects of what is in
the room; for, perhaps, there is not one leaf of a tree, nor a spire of
grass, but what produces effects all over the universe, and will produce
them to the end of eternity. But any otherwise, there is nothing in a
room to shut up, but only in God's consciousness. How can anything
be there, any other way? This will appear to be truly so, to anyone
who thinks of it with the whole united strength of his mind. Let us
suppose, for illustration, this impossibility: that all the spirits in the
universe were, for a time, deprived of their consciousness, and that
God's consciousness, at the same time, were to be intermitted. I say
the universe, for that time, would cease to be, of itself; and this not
merely, as we speak, because the Almighty could not attend to uphold
it; but because God could know nothing of it. It is our foolish imagination, that will not suffer us to see it. We fancy there may be figures
and magnitudes, relations and properties, without anyone knowing
of it. But it is our imagination hurts us. We do not know what figures
and properties are.

Our imagination makes us fancy, that we see shapes, and colors,
and magnitudes, though nobody is there to behold it. But to help our
imagination, let us thus state the case: Let us suppose the creation
deprived of every ray of light, so that there should not be the least
glimmering of light in the universe. Now all will own, that in such
case, the universe would really be immediately deprived of all its
colors. No one part of the universe is any more red, or blue, or green,
or yellow, or black, or white, or light, or dark, or transparent, or
opaque. There would be no visible distinction between the universe
and the rest of the incomprehensible void: yes, there would be no
difference, in these respects, between the universe and the infinite
void; so that any part of that void would really be as light and as
dark, as white and as black, as red and as green, as blue and as brown,
as transparent and as opaque, as any part of the universe: so that,
in such case, there would be no difference, in these respects, between
the universe and Nothing. So also, there would be no difference, between one part of the universe and another: all, in these respects, is
alike confounded with, and undistinguished from, infinite emptiness.

At the same time, also, let us suppose the universe to be altogether deprived of motion, and all parts of it to be at perfect rest. Then, the universe would not differ from the void, in this respect: there would be no more motion in the one than in the other. Then, also, solidity would cease. All that we mean, or can be meant, by solidity, is resistance; resistance to touch, the resistance of some parts of space. This is all the knowledge we get of solidity, by our senses, and, I am sure, all that we can get, any other way. But solidity shall be shown to be nothing else, more fully, hereafter. But there can be no resistance if there is no motion. One body cannot resist another when there is perfect rest among them. But, you will say, Though there is no actual resistance, yet there is potential resistance: that is, such and such parts of space would resist upon occasion. But this is all that I would have, that there is no solidity now; not but that God could cause there to be, on occasion. And if there is no solidity, there is no extension, for extension is the extendedness of solidity. Then, all figure, and magnitude, and proportion, immediately cease. Put, then, both these suppositions together: that is, deprive the universe of light and motion, and the case would stand thus with the universe: There would be neither white nor black, neither blue nor brown, neither bright nor shaded, pellucid nor opaque, no noise nor sound, neither heat nor cold, neither fluid nor solid, neither wet nor dry, neither hard nor soft, nor solidity, nor extension, nor figure, nor magnitude, nor proportion, nor body, nor spirit. What, then, is to become of the universe? Certainly it exists nowhere but in the Divine mind. This will be abundantly clearer to one, after having read what I have further to say of solidity, etc.: so that we see that a universe without motion, can exist nowhere else, but in the mind—either infinite or finite.

Corollary. It follows from hence, that those beings, which have knowledge and consciousness, are the only proper, and real, and substantial beings; inasmuch as the being of other things is only by these. From hence, we may see the gross mistake of those, who think material things the most substantial beings, and spirits more like a shadow; whereas, spirits only are properly substance. . . .

THE MIND [9]

. . . Since all material existence is only idea, this question may be asked: In what sense may those things be said to exist, which are

---

[9] Reprinted in *The Works of President Edwards*, ed. by S. E. Dwight, New York, 1830, Vol. I. Rearranged.

supposed, and yet are in no actual idea of any created minds? I answer, they exist only in uncreated idea. But how do they exist, otherwise than they did from all eternity, for they always were in uncreated idea and Divine appointment. I answer: They did exist from all eternity in uncreated idea, as did everything else, and as they do at present, but not in created idea. But it may be asked: How do those things exist, which have an actual existence, but of which no created mind is conscious?—for instance, the furniture of this room, when we are absent, and the room is shut up, and no created mind perceives it. How do these things exist? I answer: There has been in times past such a course and succession of existences, that these things must be supposed to make the series complete, according to Divine appointment of the order of things. And there will be innumerable things consequential, which will be out of joint, out of their constituted series, without the supposition of these. For, upon supposition of these things, are infinite numbers of things otherwise than they would be, if these were not by God thus supposed. Yes, the whole universe would be otherwise; such an influence have these things, by their attraction and otherwise. Yes, there must be a universal attraction, in the whole system of things, from the beginning of the world to the end; and, to speak more strictly and metaphysically, we must say, in the whole system and series of ideas in all created minds; so that these things must necessarily be put in, to make complete the system of the ideal world. That is, they must be supposed, if the train of ideas be, in the order and course, settled by the supreme mind. So that we may answer in short: That the existence of these things is in God's supposing of them, in order to render complete the series of things (to speak more strictly, the series of ideas), according to his own settled order, and that harmony of things which he has appointed.

The supposition of God, which we speak of, is nothing else but God's acting, in the course and series of his exciting ideas, as if they—the things supposed—were in actual idea.

But you may object: But there are many things so infinitely small, that their influence is altogether insensible; so that, whether they are supposed or not, there will be no alteration made in the series of ideas. I answer: But though the influence is so small that we do not perceive, yet, who knows how penetrating other spirits may be, to perceive the minutest alterations? And whether the alterations be sensible or not, at present, yet the effect of the least influence will be sensible, in time. For instance, let there be supposed to be a leaden globe, of a mile in diameter, to be moving in a right line, with the swiftness of a cannon ball, in the infinite void, and let it pass by a very small atom, supposed to be at rest. This atom will somewhat retard this leaden globe in its motion, though at first, and perhaps for many ages, the difference is altogether insensible. But let it be never so little, in time it will become very sensible. For if the motion is made so much slower, that in a million years it shall have moved one inch less than it would have done otherwise, in a million million it will have moved a million inches less. So now the least atom, by its existence or motion, causes an alteration, more or less, in every other atom in the universe; so the alteration in time will become very sensible; so the whole universe, in time, will become all over different from what it would otherwise have been. For if every other atom is supposed to be either retarded, or accelerated, or diverted; every atom, however small for the present, will cause great alterations, as we have shown already, of retardation. The case is the same as to acceleration; and so as to diversion, or varying the direction of the motion. For let the course of the body be never so little changed, this course, in time, may carry it to a place immensely distant from what the other would have carried it to, as is evident enough. And the case is the same still, if the motion that was before was never so slow is wholly stopped; the difference, in time, will be immense; for this slow motion would have carried it to an immense distance, if it were continued.

But the objector will say: I acknowledge it would be thus if the bodies, in which these insensible alterations are made, were free, and alone, in an infinite void, but I do not know but the case may be far otherwise when an insensible alteration is made in a body that is among innumerable others, and subject to infinite jumbles among them.

I answer: The case is the same, whether the bodies be alone in a void, or in a system of other bodies; for the influence of this insensible alteration continues as steadily forever, through all its various inter-changes and collisions with other bodies, as it would if it were alone in an infinite void: so that in time, a particle of matter that shall be on this side of the universe, might have been on the other. The existence and motion of every atom, has influence, more or less, on the motion of all other bodies in the universe, great or small, as is most demonstrable from the laws of gravity and motion. An alteration, more or less, as to motion, is made on every fixed star, and on all its planets, primary and secondary. Let the alteration made in the fixed stars, be never so small, yet in time it will make an infinite alteration, from what otherwise would have been. Let the fixed stars be supposed, for instance, before to have been in perfect rest; let them now be all set in motion, and this motion be never so small. Yet, continued for-ever, where will it carry those most immense bodies, with their systems? Let a little alteration be made in the motion of the planets, either retardation or acceleration; this, in time, will make a difference of many millions of revolutions. And how great a difference will that make in the floating bodies of the Universe!

By this we may answer a more difficult question, viz.: If material existence be only mental, then our bodies and organs are ideas only. And then in what sense is it true, that the mind receives ideas by the organs of sense; seeing that the organs of sense, themselves, exist nowhere but in the mind?

I answer: Seeing our organs, themselves, are ideas; the connection that our ideas have with such and such a mode of our organs, is no other than God's constitution, that some of our ideas shall be connected with others, according to such a settled law and order, so that some ideas shall follow from others as their cause. . . .

BIBLIOGRAPHY

EDWARDS, Jonathan, *The Works of President Edwards, with a Memoir of his Life*, ed. by S.E. Dwight. New York: 1830, 10 vols.

——— *The Works of Jonathan Edwards*, ed. by E. Hickman, London: 1834, 2 vols.

——— *The Works of Jonathan Edwards*. Perry Miller, general editor. New Haven: Yale U. Press. Vol. I, *Freedom of the Will*, ed. by Paul Ramsey, 1957. Vol. II, *Religious Affections*, ed. by John E. Smith, 1959.

——— *The Philosophy of Jonathan Edwards from His Private Notebooks*, ed. by H.G. Townsend. Eugene, Oregon: U. of Oregon, 1955.

——— *Images or Shadows of Divine Things*, ed. by Perry Miller. New Haven: Yale U. Press, 1948.

——— *The Nature of True Virtue*, with a Foreword by William K. Frankena. Ann Arbor: U. of Michigan Press, 1960.

ALLEN, Alexander V.G., *Jonathan Edwards*. Boston: Houghton Mifflin, 1889.

CARPENTER, Frederick, "The Radicalism of Jonathan Edwards." *New England Quarterly*, Vol. IV, (1931), pp. 629–44.

ELWOOD, Douglas J., *The Philosophical Theology of Jonathan Edwards*. New York: Columbia U. Press, 1960.

FAUST, C.H., and JOHNSON, T.H., *Jonathan Edwards; Representative Selections*, with Introduction, Bibliography and Notes. New York: American Book Co., 1935.

FERM, Vergilius, *Puritan Sage; Collected Writings of Jonathan Edwards*. New York: Library Publishers, 1953.

GARDINER, H. Norman, "The Early Idealism of Jonathan Edwards." *Philosophical Review*, Vol. IX, (1900), pp. 573–96.

MACCRACKEN, John H., "The Sources of Jonathan Edwards' Idealism." *Philosophical Review*, Vol. XII, (1902), pp. 26–42.

MCGIFFERT, A.C., Jr., Jonathan Edwards. New York: Harper and Bros., 1932.

MILLER, Perry, *Jonathan Edwards*. New York: William Sloane Assoc., 1949.

PARKES, Henry Bamford, *Jonathan Edwards, The Fiery Puritan*. New York: Minton, 1930.

SCHNEIDER, Herbert W., *The Puritan Mind*. New York: Henry Holt, 1930.

SUTER, Rufus, "The Conception of Morality in the Philosophy of Jonathan Edwards." *Journal of Religion*, Vol. XIV, (1934), pp. 265–72.

TUFTS, J. H., "Edwards and Newton." *Philosophical Review*, Vol. IL, (1940), pp. 609–22.

WINSLOW, Ola E., *Jonathan Edwards, 1703–1758*. New York: Macmillan Co., 1940; Collier Books, 1961.

WRIGHT, Conrad, "Edwards and The Arminians on the Freedom of the Will." *Harvard Theological Review*, Vol. XXXV, (1942), pp. 241–61.

Samuel Johnson

[1696–1772]

Samuel Johnson was born in Guilford, Connecticut, and was graduated from Yale College in 1698, where he remained for a year as tutor to Jonathan Edwards and other students. Quite early in his life Johnson broke with Congregationalism, and in 1722 he entered the Anglican Church. Johnson was impressed by the richness of the tradition he found in England and dismayed by the comparative intellectual backwardness of the Colonies. He preferred the quiet conservatism of the Church of England to the evangelical enthusiasm then sweeping through the Puritan churches: "The way of these teachers and exhorters was . . . to say all the most frightful things they could think of about the devil, hell and damnation, so as to scare people almost out of their wits, in order to bring them to what they called conversion."[1]

Johnson was interested in philosophical questions; and he engaged in extensive correspondence with George Berkeley and Cadwallader Colden. *The Correspondence Between Johnson and Berkeley* (1729–30), reprinted below, clearly shows the influence of Berkeley's works, which Johnson accepted as a support of true religion—though in these letters he shows his doubts on certain points, particularly concerning Berkeley's position on the existence of "archetypes." Berkeley was a critic of the materialism of Newton and Locke, which he thought might lead to skepticism, freethinking and atheism, all of which he abhorred. Johnson approved of Berkeley's immaterialism and idealism. Berkeley did not deny Newtonian science, only reinterpreted it: *esse* is *percipi*, spiritual, not material substances, were real, the human mind receiving what the Divine Mind impressed upon it.

The correspondence with Colden, the philosophical materialist and critic of Berkeley, is reprinted in the section on Colden.

When Berkeley visited America to establish a college for Indians in the Bermudas (unsuccessfully), he also visited his friend Johnson. The immaterialism of Berkeley and Johnson, however, had little effect on late eighteenth-century American thought, possibly because of its Anglican association, though in the nineteenth century transcendentalism and idealism were again popular.

Johnson was also the author of the first philosophy text to appear in America, *Elementa Philosophica*, which was printed by Benjamin Franklin in 1752. He also had the distinction of being the founder and first president of King's College (later Columbia University) in New York (1754–63). Johnson's religious

[1] *Samuel Johnson*, ed. by Schneider, Vol. I, "Autobiography," p. 28.

devotion led him to study Hebrew and to publish a Hebrew grammar (1771). Throughout his life Johnson's interests in science and philosophy were subservient to his religion. But neither the Puritanism of the religious dissenters, nor the calls for independence from the mother country beginning to make themselves felt in the Colonies, were receptive to Johnson's thought; and his defense of the Church of England and of the monarchy proved to be out of step with the times.

THE PHILOSOPHICAL CORRESPONDENCE BETWEEN SAMUEL JOHNSON AND BISHOP BERKELEY [2]

JOHNSON TO BERKELEY, Sept. 10, 1729

. . . These books . . . contain speculations the most surprisingly ingenious I have ever met with; and I must confess that the reading of them has almost convinced me that matter as it has been commonly defined for an unknown quiddity is but a mere nonentity. That it is a strong presumption against the existence of it, that there never could be conceived any manner of connection between it and our ideas. That the *esse* of things is only their *percipi*; and that the rescuing us from the absurdities of abstract ideas and the gross notion of matter that have so much obtained, deserves well of the learned world, in that it clears away very many difficulties and perplexities in the sciences.

And I am of opinion that this way of thinking cannot fail of prevailing in the world, because it is likely to prevail very much among us in these parts, several ingenious men having entirely come in to it. But there are many others, on the other hand, that cannot be reconciled to it; though of these there are some who have a very good opinion of it and plainly see many happy consequences attending it, on account of which they are well inclined to embrace it, but think they find some difficulties in their way which they cannot get over, and some objections not sufficiently answered to their satisfaction. And since you have condescended to give me leave to do so, I will make bold to lay before you sundry things, which yet remain in the dark either to myself or to others, and which I cannot account for either to my own, or at least to their satisfaction.

The great prejudice that lies against it with some is its repugnancy to and subversion of Sir I. Newton's philosophy in sundry points; to

2 Johnson's letters are reprinted in *Samuel Johnson, President of King's College: His Career and Writings*, ed. by H. W. and C. Schneider. N. Y.; Columbia U. Press, 1929, Vol. II, pp. 263–69; 275–81. The extracts are here reproduced with the permission of Columbia University Press.

which they have been so much attached that they cannot suffer themselves in the least to call it in question in any instance, but indeed it does not appear to me so inconsistent therewith as at first blush it did, for the laws of nature which he so happily explains are the same whether matter be supposed or not. However, let Sir Isaac Newton, or any other man, be heard only so far as his opinion is supported by reason—but after all I confess I have so great a regard for the philosophy of that great man, that I would gladly see as much of it as may be, to obtain in this ideal scheme.

The objection, that it takes away all subordinate natural causes, and accounts for all appearances merely by the immediate will of the Supreme Spirit, does not seem to many to be answered to their satisfaction. It is readily granted that our ideas are inert, and cannot cause one another, and are truly only signs one of another. For instance, my idea of fire is not the cause of my idea of burning and of ashes. But inasmuch as these ideas are so connected as that they seem necessarily to point out to us the relations of cause and effect, we cannot help thinking that our ideas are pictures of things without our minds at least, though not without the Great Mind, and which are their archetypes, between which these relations do obtain. I kindle a fire and leave it, no created mind beholds it; I return again and find a great alteration in the fuel; has there not been in my absence all the while that gradual alteration making in the archetype of my idea of wood which I should have had the idea of if I had been present? And is there not some archetype of my idea of the fire, which under the agency of the Divine Will has gradually caused this alteration? And so in all other instances, our ideas are so connected, that they seem necessarily to refer our minds to some originals which are properly (though subordinate) causes and effects one of another; insomuch that unless they be so, we cannot help thinking ourselves under a perpetual delusion.

That all the phenomena of nature, must ultimately be referred to the will of the Infinite Spirit, is what must be allowed; but to suppose his immediate energy in the production of every effect, does not seem to impress so lively and great a sense of his power and wisdom upon our minds, as to suppose a subordination of causes and effects among the archetypes of our ideas, as he that should make a watch or clock of ever so beautiful an appearance and that should measure the time ever so exactly yet if he should be obliged to stand by it and influence and direct all its motions, he would seem but very deficient in both his ability and skill in comparison with him who should be able to make one that would regularly keep on its motion and measure the time for a considerable while without the intervention of any immediate force of its author or any one else impressed upon it.

And as this tenet seems thus to abate our sense of the wisdom and power of God, so there are some that cannot be persuaded that it is sufficiently cleared from bearing hard on his holiness; those who suppose that the corrupt affections of our souls and evil practices consequent to them, are occasioned by certain irregular mechanical motions of our bodies, and that these motions come to have an habitual irregular bias and tendency by means of our own voluntary indulgence to them, which we might have governed to better purpose, do in this way of thinking, sufficiently bring the guilt of those ill habits and actions upon ourselves; but if in an habitual sinner, every object and motion be but an idea, and every wicked appetite the effect of such a set of ideas, and these ideas, the immediate effect of the Almighty upon his mind; it seems to follow, that the immediate cause of such ideas must be the cause of those immoral appetites and actions; because he is borne down before them seemingly, even in spite of himself. At first indeed they were only occasions, which might be withstood, and so, proper means of trial, but now they become causes of his immoralities. When therefore a person is under the power of a vicious habit, and it cannot but be foreseen that the suggestion of such and such ideas will unavoidably produce those immoralities, how can it consist with the holiness of God to suggest them?

It is, after all that has been said on that head, still something shocking to many to think that there should be nothing but a mere show in all the art and contrivance appearing in the structure (for instance) of a human body, particularly of the organs of sense. The curious structure of the eye, what can it be more than merely a fine show, if there be no connection more than you admit of, between that and vision? It seems from the make of it to be designed for an instrument or means of conveying the images of external things to the perceptive faculty within; and if it be not so, if it be really of no use in conveying visible objects to our minds, and if our visible ideas are immediately created in them by the will of the Almighty, why should it be made to seem to be an instrument or medium as much as if indeed it really were so? It is evident, from the conveying of images into a dark room through a lens, that the eye is a lens, and that the images of things are painted on the bottom of it. But to what purpose is all this, if there be no connection between this fine apparatus and the act of vision; can it be thought a sufficient argument that there is no connection between them because we cannot discover it, or conceive how it should be?

There are some who say, that if our sensations do not depend on any bodily organs, they do not see how death can be supposed to make any alteration in the manner of our perception, or indeed how there should be (properly speaking) any separate state of the soul at all. For if our bodies are nothing but ideas, and if our having ideas in this present state does not depend upon what are thought to be the organs of sense, and lastly, if we are supposed (as doubtless we must) to have ideas in that state; it should seem that immediately upon our remove from our present situation, we should still be attended with the same ideas of bodies as we have now, and consequently with the same bodies or at least with bodies however different, and if so, what room is there left for any resurrection, properly so-called? So that while this tenet delivers us from the embarrassments that attend the doctrine of a material resurrection, it seems to have no place for any ressurrection at all, at least in the sense that word seems to bear in St. John 5; 28, 29.

Some of us are at a loss to understand your meaning when you speak of archetypes. You say the beings of things consists in their being perceived. And that things are nothing but ideas, that our ideas have no unperceived archetypes, but yet you allow archetypes to our ideas when things are not perceived by our minds; they exist in, *i. e.*, are perceived by, some other mind. Now I understand you, that there is a two-fold existence of things or ideas, one in the divine mind, and the other in created minds; the one archetypal, and the other ectypal; that, therefore, the real original and permanent existence of things is archetypal, being ideas in *mente Divina*, and that our ideas are copies of them, and so far forth real things as they are correspondent to their archetypes and exhibited to us, or begotten in us by the will of the Almighty, in such measure and degrees and by such stated laws and rules as He is pleased to observe; that, therefore, there is no un-perceived substance intervening between the divine ideas and ours as a medium, occasion or instrument by which He begets our ideas in us, but that which was thought to be the material existence of things is in truth only ideal in the divine mind. Do I understand you right? Is it not therefore your meaning, that the existence of our ideas (*i. e.*, the ectypal things) depends upon our perceiving them, yet there are external to any created mind, in the all-comprehending Spirit, real and permanent archetypes (as stable and permanent as ever matter was thought to be), to which these ideas of ours are correspondent, and so that (though our visible and tangible ideas are *toto coelo* different and distinct things, yet) there may be said to be external to my mind, in the divine mind, an archetype (for instance of the candle that is before me) in which the originals of both my visible and tangible ideas, light, heat, whiteness, softness, etc., under such a particular cylindrical figure, are united, so that it may be properly said to be the same thing that I both see and feel?

If this, or something like it might be understood to be your meaning, it would seem less shocking to say that we do not see and feel the same thing, because we cannot dispossess our minds of the notion of an external world, and would be allowed to conceive that, though there were no intelligent creature before Adam to be a spectator of it, yet the world was really six days in *archetypo*, gradually proceeding from an informal chaotic state into that beautiful show wherein it first appeared to his mind, and that the comet that appeared in 1680 (for instance) has now, though no created mind beholds it, a real existence in the all-comprehending spirit, and is making its prodigious tour through the vast fields of ether, and lastly that the whole vast congeries of heaven and earth, the mighty systems of worlds with all their furniture, have a real being in the eternal mind antecedent to and independent on the perception of created spirit, and that when we see and feel, etc., that that almighty mind, by his immediate fiat, begets in our minds (*pro nostro modulo*) ideas correspondent to them, and which may be imagined in some degree resemblances of them.

But if there be archetypes to our ideas, will it not follow that there is external space, extention, figure and motion, as being archetypes of our ideas, to which we give these names. And indeed for my part I cannot disengage my mind from the persuasion that there is external space; when I have been trying ever so much to conceive of space as being nothing but an idea in my mind, it will return upon me even in spite of my utmost efforts, certainly there must be, there cannot but be, external space. The length, breadth, and thickness of any idea, it is true, are but ideas; the distance between two trees in my mind is but an idea, but if there are archetypes to the ideas of the trees, there must be an archetype to the idea of the distance between them. Nor can I see how it follows that there is no external absolute height, bigness, or distance of things, because they appear greater or less to us according as we are nearer or remote from them, or see them with our naked eyes, or with glasses; any more than it follows that a man, for instance, is not really absolutely six foot high measured by a two foot rule applied to his body, because divers pictures of him may be drawn some six, some four, some two foot long according to the same measure. Nobody ever imagined that the idea of distance is without the mind, but does it therefore follow that there is no external distance to which the idea is correspondent, for instance, between Rhode Island and Stratford? Truly I wish it were not so great, that I might be so happy as to have a more easy access to you, and more nearly enjoy the advantages of your instructions.

You allow spirits to have a real existence external to one another. Methinks, if so, there must be distance between them, and space wherein they exist, or else they must all exist in one individual spot or point, and as it were coincide one with another. I cannot see how external space and duration are any more abstract ideas than spirits. As we have (properly speaking) no ideas of spirits, so, in-

deed, neither have we of external space and duration. But it seems
to me that the existence of these must unavoidably follow from
the existence of those, insomuch that I can no more conceive of their
not being, than I can conceive of the nonexistence of the infinite
and eternal mind. They seem as necessarily existent independent
of any created mind as the Deity Himself. Or must we say there
is nothing in Dr. Clarke's argument a priori, in his demonstration
of the being and attributes of God, or in what Sir Isaac Newton says
about the infinity and eternity of God in his *Scholium Generale* to
his *Principia*? I should be glad to know your sense of what those two
authors say upon this subject.

You will forgive the confusedness of my thoughts and not wonder
at my writing like a man something bewildered, since I am, as it
were, got into a new world amazed at everything about me. These
ideas of ours, what are they? Is the substance of the mind the sub-
stratum to its ideas? Is it proper to call them modifications of our
minds? Or impressions upon them? Or what? Truly I cannot tell
what to make of them, any more than of matter itself. What is the
esse of spirits?—you seem to think it impossible to abstract their
existence from their thinking. (*Princ.* p. 143. sec. 98.) Is then the
esse of minds nothing else but *percipere*, as the *esse* of ideas is
percipi? Certainly, methinks there must be an unknown somewhat
that thinks and acts, as difficult to be conceived of as matter, and
the creation of which, as much beyond us as the creation of matter.
Can actions be the *esse* of anything? Can they exist or be exerted
without some being who is the agent? And may not that being be
easily imagined to exist without acting, *e. g.*, without thinking? And
consequently (for you are there speaking of duration) may he not be
said *durare, etsi non cogitet*, to persist in being, though thinking
were intermitted for a while? And is not this sometimes fact? The
duration of the eternal mind must certainly imply something besides
an eternal succession of ideas. May I not then conceive that, though
I get my idea of duration by observing the succession of ideas in
my mind, yet there is a *perseverare in existendo*, a duration of my
being, and of the being of other spirits distinct from, and independent
of, this succession of ideas. . . .

JOHNSON TO BERKELEY, Feb. 5, 1730

. . . For my part I am content to give up the cause of matter, glad
to get rid of the absurdities thereon depending if it be defensible,
I am sure, at least, it is not in my power to defend it. And being
spoiled of that sandy foundation, I only want now to be more
thoroughly taught how and where to set down my foot again and
make out a clear and consistent scheme without it. . . .

As to those difficulties that yet remain with me, I believe all my hesitation about the first of them (and very likely the rest) is owing to my dullness and want of attention so as not rightly to apprehend your meaning. I believe I expressed myself unworthily about archetypes in my seventh and eighth articles, but upon looking back upon your *Dialogues*, and comparing again three or four passages, I cannot think I mean anything different from what you intended.

You allow, in *Dialogues* p. 74, "That things have an existence distinct from being perceived by us" (*i. e.*, any created spirits), "and that they exist in, *i. e.*, are perceived by, the infinite and omnipresent mind who contains and supports this sensible world as being perceived by him." And p. 109, "That things have an existence exterior to our minds, and that during the intervals of their being perceived by us, they exist in another (*i. e.*, the infinite) mind"; from whence you justly and excellently infer the certainty of his existence, "who knows and comprehends all things and exhibits them to our view in such manner and according to such rules as he himself has ordained." And p. 113, "That, *e. g.*, a tree, when we do not perceive it, exists without our minds in the infinite mind of God." And this exterior existence of things (if I understand you right) is what you call the archetypal state of things, p. 150.

From these and the like expressions, I gathered what I said about the archetypes of our ideas, and thence inferred that there is exterior to us, in the divine mind, a system of universal nature, whereof the ideas we have are in such a degree resemblances as the Almighty is pleased to communicate to us. And I cannot yet see but my inference was just; because according to you, the idea we see is not in the divine mind, but in our own. When, therefore, you say sensible things exist in, as understood by, the infinite mind, I humbly conceive you must be understood that the originals or archetypes of our sensible things or ideas exist independent of us in the infinite mind, or that sensible things exist *in archetypo* in the divine mind. The divine idea, therefore, of a tree suppose (or a tree in the divine mind), must be the original or archetype of ours, and ours a copy or image of His (our ideas images of His, in the same sense as our souls are images of Him) of which there may be several, in several created minds, like so many several pictures of the same original to which they are all to be referred.

When therefore, several people are said to see the same tree or star, etc., whether at the same or at so many several distances from it, it is (if I understand you) *unum et idem in Archetypo*, though *multiplex et diversum in Ectypo*, for it is as evident that your idea is not mine nor mine yours when we say we both look on the same tree, as that you are not I nor I you. But in having each our idea being dependent upon and impressed upon by the same almighty mind, wherein you say this tree exists, while we shut our eyes (and doubtless you mean the same also, while they are open), our several trees must, I think be so many pictures (if I may so call them) of the one original, the tree in the infinite mind, and so of all other things. Thus I understand you not indeed, that our ideas are in any measure adequate resemblances of the system in the divine mind, but however that they are just and true resemblances or copies of it, so far as He is pleased to communicate His mind to us.

As to space and duration, I do not pretend to have any other notion of their exterior existence than what is necessarily implied in the notion we have of God; I do not suppose they are anything distinct from, or exterior to, the infinite and external mind; for I conclude with you that there is nothing exterior to my mind but God and other spirits with the attributes or properties belonging to them and ideas contained in them.

External space and duration therefore I take to be those properties or attributes in God, to which our ideas, which we signify by those names, are correspondent, and of which they are the faint shadows. This I take to be Sir Isaac Newton's meaning when he says, *Schol. General. Deus*: "*durat semper et adest ubique et existendo semper et ubique, durationem et spacium, eternitatem et infinitatem constituit.*" And in his *Optics* calls space "as it were God's boundless sensorium," nor can I think you have a different notion of these attributes from that great philosopher, though you may differ in your ways of expressing or explaining yourselves. However it be, when you call the Deity infinite and eternal, and in that most beautiful and charming description, *Dialogues* p. 71. etc., when you speak of the "abyss of space and boundless extent beyond thought and imagination," I do not know how to understand you any otherwise than I understood Sir Isaac, when he uses the like expressions. The truth is we have no proper ideas of God or His attributes, and conceive of them only by analogy from what we find in ourselves; and so, I think we conceive His immensity and eternity to be what in Him are correspondent to our space and duration.

As for the *punctum stans* of the Schools, and the *to nun* of the Platonists, they are notions too fine for my gross thoughts; I cannot tell what to make of those words, they do not seem to convey any ideas or notions to my mind, and whatever the matter is, the longer I think of them, the more they disappear, and seem to dwindle away into nothing. Indeed they seem to me very much like abstract ideas, but I doubt the reason is because I never rightly understood them. I do not see why the term *punctum stans* may not as well, at least, be applied to the immortality as the eternity of God; for the word *punctum* is more commonly used in relation to extension or space than duration; and to say that a being is immense, and yet that it is but a point, and that its duration is perpetual without beginning or end, and yet that it is but a *to nun* looks to me like a contradiction.

I cannot therefore understand the term *to nun* unless it be designed to adumbrate the divine omnisciency or the perfection of the divine knowledge, by the more perfect notion we have of things present than of things past; and in this sense it would imply that all things past, present and to come are always at every point of duration equally perfectly known or present to God's mind (though in a manner infinitely more perfect), as the things that are known to us are present to our minds at any point of our duration which we call *now*. So that with respect to His equally perfect knowledge of things past, present or to come, it is in effect always *now* with Him. To this purpose it seems well applied and intelligible enough, but His duration I take to be a different thing from this, as that point of our duration which we call *now*, is a different thing from our actual knowledge of things, as distinguished from our remembrance. And it may as well be said that God's immensity consists in His knowing at once what is, and is transacted in all places (e. g., China, Jupiter, Saturn, all the systems of fixed stars, etc.) everywhere, however so remote from us (though in a manner infinitely more perfect), as we know what is, and is transacted in us and about us just at hand; as that His eternity consists in this *to nun* as above explained, *i. e.*, in His knowing things present, past and to come, however so remote, all at once or equally perfectly as we know the things that are present to us *now*.

In short our ideas expressed by the terms immensity and eternity are only space and duration considered as boundless or with the negation of any limits, and I cannot help thinking there is something analogous to them without us, being in and belonging to, or attributes of, that glorious mind, whom for that reason we call immense and eternal, in whom we and all other spirits, live, move and have their being, not all in a point, but in so many different points places or *alicubis*, and variously situated with respect one to another, or else as I said before, it seems as if we should all coincide one with another.

I conclude, if I am wrong in my notion of eternal space, and duration, it is owing to the riveted prejudices of abstract ideas; but really, when I have thought it over and over again in my feeble way of thinking, I cannot see any connection between them (as I understand them) and that doctrine. They do not seem to be any more abstract ideas than spirits, for, as I said, I take them to be attributes of the necessarily existing spirit; and consequently the same reasons that convince me of his existence, bring with them the existence of these attributes. So that of the ways of coming to the knowledge of things that you mention, it is that of inference or deduction by which I seem to know that there is external infinite space and duration because there is without me a mind infinite and eternal.

As to the *esse* of spirits, I know Descartes held the soul always thinks, but I thought Mr. Locke had sufficiently confuted this notion, which he seems to have entertained only to serve a hypothesis. The Schoolmen, it is true, call the soul *Actus* and God *Actus purus*; but I confess I could never well understand their meaning, perhaps because I never had opportunity to be much versed in their writings. I should have thought the Schoolmen to be of all sorts of writers the most unlikely to have had recourse to for the understanding of your sentiments, because they of all others, deal the most in abstract ideas; though to place the very being of spirits in the mere act of thinking, seems to me very much like making abstract ideas of them.

There is certainly something passive in our souls, we are purely passive in the reception of our ideas; and reasoning and willing are actions of something that reasons and wills, and therefore must be only modalities of that something. Nor does it seem to me that when I say [something] I mean an abstract idea. It is true I have no idea of it, but I feel it; I feel that it is, because I feel or am conscious of the exertions of it; but the exertions of it are not the thing but the modalities of it distinguished from it as actions from an agent, which seems to me distinguishable without having recourse to abstract ideas.

And, therefore, when I suppose the existence of a spirit while it does not actually think, it does not appear to me that I do it by supposing an abstract idea of existence, and another of absolute time. The existence of John asleep by me, without so much as a dream is not an abstract idea. Nor is the time passing the while an abstract idea, they are only partial considerations of him. *Perseverare in existendo* in general, without reflecting on any particular thing existing, I take to be what is called an abstract idea of time or duration; but the *perseverare in existendo* of John is, if I mistake not, a partial consideration of him. And I think it is as easy to conceive of him as continuing to exist without thinking as without seeing.

Has a child no soul till it actually perceives? And is there not such a thing as sleeping without dreaming, or being in a *deliquium* without a thought? If there be, and yet at the same time the *esse* of a spirit be nothing else but its actual thinking, the soul must be dead during those intervals; and if ceasing or intermitting to think be the ceasing to be, or death of the soul, it is many times and easily put to death. According to this tenet, it seems to me the soul may sleep on to the resurrection, or rather may wake up in the resurrection state, the next moment after death. Nay I do not see upon what we can build any natural argument for the soul's immortality. I think I once heard you allow a principle of perception and spontaneous motion in beasts. Now if their *esse* as well as ours consists in perceiving, upon what is the natural immortality of our souls founded that will not equally conclude in favor of them? I mention this last consideration because I am at a loss to understand how you state the argument for the soul's natural immortality; for the argument from thinking to immaterial and from thence to indivisible, and from thence to immortal does not seem to obtain in your way of thinking.

If *esse* be only *percipere*, upon what is our consciousness founded? I perceived yesterday, and I perceive now, but last night between my yesterday's and today's perception there has been an intermission when I perceived nothing. It seems to me there must be some principle common to these perceptions, whose *esse* does not depend on them, but in which they are, as it were, connected, and on which they depend, whereby I am and continue conscious of them.

Lastly, Mr. Locke's argument (B. 2. Ch. 19. Sec. 4.) from the intention and remission of thought, appears to me very considerable; according to which, upon this supposition the soul must exist more or have a greater degree of being at one time than at another, according as it thinks more intensely or more remissly.

I own I said very wrong when I said I did not know what to make of ideas more than of matter. My meaning was, in effect, the same as I expressed afterward about the substance of the soul's being a somewhat as unknown as matter. And what I intended by those questions was whether our ideas are not the substance of the soul itself, under so many various modifications, according to that saying (if I understand it right) *Intellectus intelligendo fit omnia?* It is true, those expressions (modifications, impressions, etc.) are metaphorical, and it seems to me to be no less so, to say that ideas exist in the mind, and I am under some doubt whether this last way of speaking does not carry us further from the thing, than to say ideas are the mind variously modified; but as you observe, it is scarce possible to speak of the mind without a metaphor. . . .

BERKELEY TO JOHNSON, Mar. 24, 1730 [3]

. . . I have no objection against calling the ideas in the mind of God, archetypes of ours. But I object against those archetypes by

[3] Reprinted in E. Edwards Beardsley, *Life and Correspondence of Samuel Johnson, D.D.* New York: Hurd and Houghton, 1874, pp. 73–75.

philosophers supposed to be real things, and to have an absolute rational existence distinct from their being perceived by any mind whatsoever, it being the opinion of all materialists that an ideal existence in the divine mind is one thing, and the real existence of material things another.

As to space, I have no notion of any but that which is relative. I know some late philosophers have attributed extension to God, particularly mathematicians; one of whom, in a treatise *de Spacio reali*, pretends to find out fifteen of the incommunicable attributes of God in space. But it seems to me, that they being all negative, he might as well have found them in nothing; and that it would have been as justly inferred from space being impassive, uncreated, indivisible, etc., that it was nothing, as that it was God.

Sir Isaac Newton supposes an absolute space different from relative, and consequent thereto, absolute motion different from relative motion; and with all other mathematicians, he supposes the infinite divisibility of the finite parts of this absolute space; he also supposes material bodies to drift therein. Now, though I do acknowledge Sir Isaac to have been an extraordinary man and most profound mathematician, yet I cannot agree with him in these particulars. I make no scruple to use the word space, as well as other words in common use, but I do not mean thereby a distinct absolute being. For my meaning I refer you to what I have published.

By the *to nun* I suppose to be implied that all things past and to come are actually present to the mind of God, and that there is in Him no change, variation, or succession—a succession of ideas I take to constitute time and not to be only the sensible measure thereof, as Mr. Locke and others think. But in these matters every man is to think for himself, and speak as he finds. One of my earliest inquiries was about time, which led me into several paradoxes that I did not think fit or necessary to publish, particularly into the notion that the resurrection follows next moment to death. We are confounded and perplexed about time. (1) Supposing a succession in God. (2) Conceiving that we have an abstract idea of time. (3) Supposing that the time in one mind is to be measured by the succession of ideas in another. (4) Not considering the true use and ends of words, which as often terminate in the will as the understanding, being employed rather to excite influence, and direct action than to produce clear and distinct ideas.

That the soul of man is passive as well as active I make no doubt. Abstract general ideas was a notion that Mr. Locke held in common with the Schoolmen, and I think all other philosophers; it runs through his whole book *Of Human Understanding*. He holds an abstract idea of existence exclusive of perceiving and being perceived. I cannot find I have any such idea, and this is my reason against it. Descartes proceeds upon other principles. One square foot of snow is as white as one thousand yards; one single perception is as truly a perception as one hundred. Now any degree of perception being sufficient to existence, it will not follow that we should say one existed more at one time than another, any more than we should say one thousand yards of snow are whiter than one yard. But after all, this comes to a verbal dispute. I think it might prevent a good deal of obscurity and dispute to examine well what I have said about abstraction, and about the true use of sense and significancy of words, in several parts of these things that I have published, though much remains to be said on that subject.

You say you agree with me that there is nothing within your mind but God and other spirits, with the attributes or properties belonging to them, and the ideas contained in them. This is a principle or main point from which, and from what I had laid down about abstract ideas, much may be deduced. But if in every inference we should not agree, so long as the main points are settled and well understood, I should be less solicitous about conjectures. . . .

BIBLIOGRAPHY

JOHNSON, Samuel, *Samuel Johnson, President of King's College: His Career and Writings*, ed. by Herbert and Carl Schneider. New York: Columbia U. Press, 1929, 4 vols. Esp. Vol. II, *The Philosopher*.

BEARDSLEY, E. Edwards, *Life and Correspondence of Samuel Johnson, D.D.* New York, 1874.

CHANDLER, Thomas Bradbury, *The Life of Samuel Johnson, D.D.: with an Appendix Containing Many Original Letters*. New York, 1805.

HORNBERGER, Theodore, "Samuel Johnson of Yale and King's College: A Note on the Relation of Science and Religion in Provincial America." *New England Quarterly*, Vol. VII, (1935), pp. 378–97.

JONES, Adam Leroy, *Early American Philosophers*. New York: Macmillan Co., 1898, chaps. 2–3, pp. 22–45.

WILD, John, *George Berkeley, A Study of His Life and Philosophy*. Cambridge: Harvard U. Press, 1936, with an analysis of the Berkeley-Johnson Correspondence, pp. 311–19.

Cadwallader Colden
[1688–1776]

Cadwallader Colden was probably the ablest representative of Newtonian philosophy and materialism in the Colonies. He was a learned man of wide interests and indefatigable energies. Colden was born in Ireland of Scottish parents in 1688. He studied at the University of Edinburgh and later prepared in London for the practice of medicine. Emigrating to America in 1710, he eventually gave up medicine for politics. Colden was appointed to the post of Surveyor-General of the Province of New York. Eventually he became Lieutenant-Governor, a position which he held from 1761 until his death at the outbreak of the Revolutionary War in 1776. Had his name not been so closely associated with the Tory cause, his accomplishments might have been more fully appreciated in America.

Colden was alive to many of the intellectual crosscurrents of his day. He corresponded with Halley, Newton, Linnaeus, Euler, Franklin, and others; he also was known for his experimental work in botany, cancer, and the control of epidemic diseases.

Colden carried on an extensive correspondence with Samuel Johnson on the topic of idealism versus materialism, portions of which are reprinted below as *The Philosophical Correspondence Between Cadwallader Colden and Samuel Johnson on Materialism and Immaterialism* (1744–53). In these lively letters

Johnson hoped to persuade Colden to accept Berkeley's immaterialism; but Colden found such a position absurd, and he elaborated his own brand of Newtonian materialism.

Colden wrote much, but published little. His early book, *History of the Five Indian Nations Depending on the Province of New York* (1727), was a detailed study of various tribes in his region. But his most important philosophical inquiries were contained in *An Explication of the First Causes of Action; And of Gravitation* (1745)—which was probably the first scientific work of its kind printed in America—and in a revision of that work, *The Principles of Action in Matter, The Gravitation of Bodies, and the Motion of Planets Explained from These Principles* (1751).

Colden attempted to go beyond Newton by suggesting an explanation for gravitation. For Newton, the mutual attraction of bodies was only apparent, perhaps an effect rather than a cause. For Colden, gravitation was a cause that might be explained by reference to the joint action of the various powers of matter. Material substance, Colden conceded, was itself unknowable. But we could know the *actions* of bodies: (1) resisting, (2) moving, and (3) elastic matter (ether). Colden recapitulated his main position in a private notebook in 1755. Part of this notebook, *A Summary of the Principles of Ac-*

tion, is published below for the first time.

Colden was not a pure materialist. And in this piece he suggests a semi-dualistic theory, which allows for the existence of "intelligent being." Like body, intelligent being is active and known by its effects, but it differs from material being in its essential nature. How these different powers interact is a problem that Colden never quite resolves. Colden was sympathetic to deism: God as First Cause gave direction to the action of matter, but did not intervene in its operations.

Colden wrote many other works, most of them still in unpublished manuscript. *An Introduction to the Doctrine of Fluxions* (1743) contains his mathematical reflections. *First Principles of Morality* (written about 1746) presents a materialistic hedonism: the body is a machine and pleasure is the end cause of the virtues. *The Introduction to the Study of Physics*, later revised as *An Introduction to the Study of Philoso-*

phy Wrote in America for the Use of a Young Gentleman (1760), contains a summary of his main ideas. Another piece, stimulated by the reading of a treatise on the eye by Dr. Porterfield, is the occasion for some forty pages of *Reflections* (c. 1761) on a variety of topics. The *Inquiry into the Main Principles of Vital Motions* (1766) suggests a theory of physiological atomism; and his undated *Treatise on Animal Oeconomy* attempts to explain the properties of animals "according to the laws of matter in motion."

Throughout Colden's writings one finds a modern mind, critical of "mere authority," directing the individual to think for himself, unencumbered by prejudice and received tradition, and basing its inquiries on the methods of science. Although conservative in his political beliefs and opposed to the impending Revolution, he was nonetheless devoted to Reason and sympathetic to the emerging naturalism of the Enlightenment.

THE PHILOSOPHICAL CORRESPONDENCE BETWEEN CADWALLADER COLDEN AND SAMUEL JOHNSON ON MATERIALISM AND IMMATERIALISM [1]

COLDEN TO JOHNSON, Mar. 26, 1744

. . . As to the Bishop's *New Theory of Vision*, I think he has explained some things better than had been done before, but as to the main design he labors at, I cannot say that I comprehend it. I allow that the object which reflects light is not in a proper sense the object of vision, no more than a bell or any other sounding body is the object of the sense of hearing, and yet I think we may without much impropriety say that we see or hear a bell as well as that we feel it,

[1] Reprinted in E. Edwards Beardsley, *Life and Correspondence of Samuel Johnson, D.D.*, New York: Hurd and Houghton, 1874, pp. 129–84.

though it be certain that the bell is not the immediate object of the senses of seeing and hearing, as it is of the sense of feeling, and that it is only from reasoning and experience that we form the conception of the same objects affecting all the senses. If his sentiments do not differ from this conception of the matter, then I must look on a great part of his books to contain a most subtle disputation about the use of words. If his sentiments be different, I can form no conception of them. His mistake in the "Analyst," in my opinion, may be made very apparent, that he does not understand the doctrine of infinites or fluxions, as received by mathematicians, and this I think I can demonstrate. I formerly had illustrated the principles of that doctrine in writing, in order to assist my own imagination in forming a regular and true conception of it. . . .

I assume the liberty always to be allowed in philosophizing to differ from any man without disrespect or disregard to his character, as I now do with respect to Bishop Berkeley, whose merit is very conspicuous, and whom I highly esteem.

JOHNSON TO COLDEN, April 18, 1744

. . . I am much obliged to you for the observations you have made upon Bishop Berkeley's *Principles* that I lent you. I take it that the great design of that gentleman, in what he wrote, was to banish scholasticism and all talk without any meaning out of philosophy, which you very well know, has been the bane of science in all other parts of learning, as well as in religion and morality. Mr. Locke went a great way in this, and did much service, but yet, while he continued the doctrine of abstract ideas, he was led to think and teach that there are some ideas common to several senses, in which the Bishop justly suggested he was mistaken; and indeed, to me it looks as if he had demonstrated against him that tangible and visible extension are things *toto coelo* different though they both go by the same general name, and so of the rest.

If indeed you mean nothing by matter but what is immediately perceived by sense, as you do not at all differ from what he would be at, so you would, in this case, be right in thinking that a great part of his book is only a subtle dissertation about the use of words; but if you conceive matter to be something abstracted and prescinded from all the immediate objects of the senses, according to the old scholastical say of it, and that it is *neque quid, neque quantum, neque quale, neque quod potest digito demonstrari*, you might perhaps think that a mere dispute about words was the very thing, and that only, which he opposed, and that he had a great deal of reason so to do. As to his mathematical series I confess I am not versed enough in the sublime mathematics to be a judge of them, and so can pronounce nothing on this subject. . . .

COLDEN TO JOHNSON, June 2, 1746

. . . One thing I am desirous to be more fully informed of from you, how consciousness and intelligence become essential to all agents that act from a power in themselves. As to my own part, I do not perceive the necessary connection between power or force and intelligence or consciousness. We may certainly in a thousand objects of our senses discover power and force without perceiving any intelligence in them. And though this power or force should be only apparent, and the consequence or effect of some other primary cause, yet I am certainly to be excused in my thinking it real till it appear otherwise to me, as I believe every man is to be excused who does not understand astronomy, and thinks that the sun moves, and this opinion cannot in any proper sense be called an absurdity in him.

In the next place I must beg you will give me a definition of matter, or of any other being merely passive, without any power or force or action. Such a being I cannot conceive, and therefore as to me does not exist.

You will oblige me exceedingly by giving your opinion of the printed "Treatise" or of any part of it without reserve. For my design only is to discover and be assured of the truth. You will find by some parts of that piece that though I have the greatest esteem of Sir Isaac Newton's knowledge and performances, I take the liberty to differ from him in some points. That man never existed who never erred. . . .

JOHNSON TO COLDEN, June 23, 1746

. . . There is one thing that I am much pleased with, which is, that you make the resistance of what you call matter to be an action deriving from a self-exerting principle. This I take to be a point of very great importance and use both in physics and metaphysics as well as religion. All the odds between you and me is that you make matter a self-exerting active principle, whereas I give that denomination only to what is merely passive and inert and give the name of spirit to that which is the principle of activity, pervading and agitating all things, according to Virgil's philosophy, *mens agitat molem*, etc., which though it be the most ancient, I take to be nevertheless the most true and undoubted system; and that elasticity, attraction or pulsion and repulsion as well as resistance, or what Sir Isaac calls *vis inertiae*, and perhaps some other forces are so many exertions of

the one universal intelligent self-exerting active principle who
pervades all things, and in whom we live and move and have our
being. Your attempt to assign the cause of gravitation appears
to me a curious dissertation—but I have hardly furniture and force
of mind enough to comprehend it, having for many years discontinued
those kind of studies, and indeed never turned my thoughts that
way so closely as I find you have done, nor had proper means to
enable me for it; your system seems to me pretty near of kin to Mr.
Hutchinson's, as far as I have had opportunity to be acquainted with
his from my Lord Forbes, but I believe you have much outdone
him in the exactness of your range of thoughts and mathematical
reasoning, but I think his notion of pulsion or protrusion is something like yours; however, I dare not pronounce.

And now in answer to your candid inquiries. You ask: how
consciousness and intelligence become essential to all agents that act
from a power within themselves? Where, by a *power within themselves* I apprehend you mean a *principle of activity* belonging to
their own proper essence, and not either arbitrarily annexed to
them or exerting itself in and by them. To which I answer: A
power [of] action without a principle of self-exertion and activity
in which it resides I can have no notion of; and a blind senseless
power or principle of activity appears to me repugnant and if it
were possible, it would be [so] far from being of any use in nature
that it would be mischievous without a mind to direct and overrule it. In fact we find that all the motions and consequently actions
in nature are conformable to the wisest laws and rules ever aiming
at some useful end which evidently discovers design and contrivance, and must therefore be under the active management of a most
wise and designing principle or cause; so that it seems to me
repugnant to place intelligence and activity in or derive them from
different principles; I can have no notion of action without volition.
For if you suppose a blind principle of action in matter, you must
still suppose it under the overruling force of an intelligent and
designing principle. And, as it is not the part of a philosopher to
multiply beings and causes without necessity, it seems plain to me
that we ought not to imagine any other principle of action than the
principle of intelligence, which we know from our own soul has,
and in nature must have, a power of self-exertion and activity. We
must come to it eventually in our inquiries and I see not how we can
avoid admitting it immediately as soon as ever we begin to inquire
after efficient causes. For my part I can find nothing but what is
merely passive in any immediate object either of sense or imagination, and must therefore conceive of what is called matter to be no
more than a mere passive instrument or medium acted by the one

principle of intelligence and activity. Thus I say things appear to me; nor can I with the utmost force of mind that my capacity will admit of, conceive of things any otherwise. After all I do not see that my way of defining things affects your ingenious performance considered as a physical essay. If there be any difference in our thoughts divested of all words, as perhaps there is none, it is, as I apprehend, not of physical, but rather of metaphysical consideration. . . .

COLDEN TO JOHNSON, Nov. 19, 1746

I shall add something on this occasion, in defense of my system, that from it a certain proof may be given of the evidence of spirits, or immaterial beings. For as in the idea of all immaterial beings, quantity or shape or form is included, and their actions are all divisible into degrees or quantities of action; the being from whence thinking proceeds cannot be material, because no kind of quantity enters our conception thereof, neither can any kind of measure or division be applied to it, so much as in imagination.

All allow that when God created matter, He gave it some essential property; otherwise there can be no essential difference between matter and spirit, and why may not I say, in my way of speaking, that God gave at the creation to different kinds of matter, different and distinct kinds of action. As to my part, I can discover no kind of ill consequence in the one more than in the other.

In answer to your demand of my opinion of Dr. Berkeley's book *De Motu*, I shall give it with the freedom requisite to philosophy. I think that the Doctor has made the greatest collection in this and his other performances, of indistinct and indigested conceptions from the writings of both the ancients and the moderns that I ever met with in any man's performances; that he has the art of puzzling and confounding his readers in an elegant style not common to such kind of writers; and that he is as great an abuser of the use of words as any one of those he blames most for that fault. I hope you will pardon me for writing so freely of your friend, and of so great a man. I do it with the less concern in hopes thereby to provoke you to use the same freedom with me. Compliments without sincerity spoil all philosophy. . . .

COLDEN TO JOHNSON, Jan. 27, 1747

In my last I told you how much I had been involved in the public affairs, that I had not been able to consider your new *System of Morality* with the attention which I designed to give to the reading of it, and which it truly deserves. Nothing has been a greater injury to true religion than the pretenses that some people have set up that religion is not the object of the understanding, but is merely founded on authority, for in such case it could not with any propriety be designed for the use of an intelligent being, and there are no means left to distinguish between true and false religion when we are not allowed to use our understanding in forming our judgment, and the false may set up as strong pretenses to authority as the true, and in fact always does.

You have by your performance clearly evinced the contrary of this, that true religion is founded on the reason or nature of things, and you have shown this in a manner adapted to common capacities and the commonly received conceptions, which makes it more generally useful and the more valuable.

I have considered the same in my own *Principles of Natural Philosophy*, and I have done this for two reasons: viz. thereby to remove some metaphysical objections which you made to my principles, and which I hope by this method to remove more easily than by a direct answer; the other reason is in hopes to give you some hints which may perhaps be of use to you in reconsidering your subject, as you tell me that you intend to publish a second edition of that work. I hope you will give me your sentiments with the same freedom that you see I write to you, and thereby I shall judge that the freedom I take is not disagreeable to you. I have no other view but truth, and for that reason I shall myself be more obliged by having my mistakes shown to me than by any applause.

JOHNSON TO COLDEN, April 15, 1747

. . . Your beautiful little draft of the *First Principles of Morality* is what I have been very much pleased with; I have read it with attention three times, and every time with a fresh increase of pleasure, and now at length return my hearty thanks for it, and for the candor you express toward the piece I had the presumption to publish. You have in this little piece of yours made such an easy, gradual, and natural progress from physics to metaphysics, and from thence to morality, as is very pleasing to the mind; and I think, if I rightly apprehend, you have now so explained yourself that we do not much differ, and what difference yet remains I believe is but merely verbal. My chief objection was against your using the term *action* as expressing anything in matter, which I take to be a mere passive thing, and that action cannot in strict propriety of speaking be attributed to it; for which reason that expression still grated upon my mind till I came to your seventh section, in which, when you come to explain the difference between spirit and body, you say "the actions of the latter are altered by efficient causes *always* external to themselves."

This seems evidently to conclude what I would be at, and that at the bottom we think alike, viz. that when we speak of matter and the action of it we use that word for want of a better, in a sense rather figurative than literal, and understand it in a vulgar sense rather than a sense that is strictly philosophical, [as we] do the rising and setting of the sun. So we may call writing the action of the pen, when it is only in reality merely acted [on], and consequently that by the action of matter you do not mean any exertion of its own, much less a designed conscious self-exertion which always enters into my notion of efficient causes; and that therefore when you say it is *determined* by the (exertion I would say of) *efficient causes always* external *to itself*, those efficient causes must always be self-exerting and intelligent beings *i. e. spirits*, which therefore only are properly agents, and consequently that all the actions in all nature that affect our senses and excite ideas in our minds are really the actions of that great, supreme, almighty being or spirit whom you call (25) *the soul of the universe*.

I do not, with Sir Isaac in section 9, quite like that expression. It may however be admitted, if it means that he animates and governs the world as the soul does the body, which is merely passive to it: it is so far right—he being in this sense the natural governor of the natural world; but this seems not sufficient unless you also conceive him as the moral governor of the intelligent or moral world, rewarding or punishing men according as they behave— which is what I would apprehend you to mean by the real words.

You say very truly, section 9, "we have no idea of matter"; by which it is plain that by matter you mean something that is not the object either of our senses or minds. Of what use then is it in philosophy? Why may we not wholly drop it, and do as well without it, perhaps much better, and suppose what you call the action of it to be the action of that Almighty Spirit in whom we live, move, and have our being, and consider all nature as being the glorious system of His incessant exertions and operations, with which by His own action governed by fixed rules of His most wise establishment called the laws of nature, He perpetually and with endless variety of objects affects our senses and minds. This will sufficiently account for everything, whereas matter whereof we have no idea, can account for nothing.

You use the expression, sections 20 and 21, *during the time of our existence*, which sounds as though it was to have a period with this vain life. This I cannot suppose your meaning (and therefore might perhaps be better left out), because I apprehend you must think it evident from the wisdom, justice, and goodness of God, compared with that excellent nature He has given us, that we must be designed for nobler ends than can be answered by our existence only in this short, uncertain, and troublesome life. . . .

COLDEN TO JOHNSON, May 18, 1747

. . . I did not think of the old opinion of the soul of the world when I wrote that paragraph. My design was only to avoid all expressions which could raise any idea of matter or corporeity, as the word spirit in its natural signification is apt to do, and for that reason only I made use of the words soul or mind. Please then to put in their place *infinitely intelligent being*. It was by the same inadvertency the words, *during the time of our existence*, were made use of, and I am obliged to you for the correction which you have made of them.

But now to come to the matter itself, I cannot have any idea of anything merely passive or without any kind of action. I can have no idea of a mere negative, and since, as I observed, all our ideas of everything external to us must arise from the actions of those things on our minds, everything of which we have any idea must be active. This is my fundamental argument, to which I suspect you have not given sufficient attention; and from whence I conclude that all matter is active. You seem likewise not to have alluded to the distinction which I make between the substance and the action of that substance. We have no idea of the substance of intelligent beings, as little as of material. We have only ideas of their actions. Or, the ideas are the effects of their actions on our minds. But, Sir, if you attribute all action immediately to that "Almighty Spirit in whom we live, move, and have our being, all nature" (as you say) "being a system of His incessant exertions, etc.," I do not see how any thing or action can be morally evil in a proper sense, and the foundation of morality seems merely to be sapped. It seems to be a kind of Spinozism in other words. But as this is inconsistent with the whole tenor and end of your treatise, I can only conclude that I have not been able to form any conception of the first principles of your and Dr. Berkeley's system of philosophy. I am afraid you will find me of a much duller apprehension than you at first imagined, and that if you are willing to make me understand your system, it will give you more trouble than perhaps anything that can be expected from me on the subject, can deserve. . . .

JOHNSON TO COLDEN, June 7, 1747

. . . I am entirely satisfied and well-pleased with the amendments you allow me to make in the ingenious draft you were so good as to send me of your notion of the first principles of morality; with which it now runs clearly to my mind and is equally pleasing to my friends here, to whom I have communicated it. As for the incidental turn I made upon an expression of yours in favor of Bishop Berkeley's system, I was little more than jocular on that occasion, being not dogmatically tenacious of his peculiar sentiments, much less zealous of making you a proselyte to them. I would however observe that you have made a considerable approach toward them, at least as far as I am concerned to wish you to do, particularly in your allowing that all our ideas of sensible things are the effects of the actions of something external to our minds, and that even resistance is an action. Your supposing an active medium which you call matter intervening between the action of the Deity and our minds perceiving, to which they are immediately passive, though I am not clear in it, does not affect me so long as you allow all action throughout all sensible nature to derive originally from Him.

I doubt I expressed myself sometimes uncouthly, at least very incorrectly, otherwise you would not have inferred from what I wrote that I attributed all action immediately to the Almighty Spirit. I meant only all the actions in sensible nature only, or which produce in our minds the ideas of sense and imagination; but I was far from meaning that there are no other actions besides those of the Deity. For this would be in effect to deny or doubt whether there be any other beings besides Him and our ideas. This would sap the foundation of morality sure enough, and would be at least as bad as Spinozism. Bishop Berkeley, any more than I, never doubted of the existence or actions of other inferior created spirits, free agents and subject to moral government. All he contends for is that there are no other than two sorts of beings, the one active and the other passive—that spirit, the Deity, and created intelligence alone are the active beings, and the objects of sense alone are merely passive; and that there is no active medium intervening between the actions of the Deity and our minds whom He has made to be perceptive and self-active beings. These I take to be the first principles of his system. . . .

COLDEN TO JOHNSON, Dec. 20, 1752

. . . In the sixth page of your *Noetica*, you say our perceptions cannot be produced in our minds without a cause (so far we agree); or, which is the same thing, by any imagined, unintelligent, inert, or unactive cause. I likewise agree than an unactive cause and no cause are synonymous; but I am not convinced that intelligence is an essential concomitant to all action, for then I could not conceive the action of a mill without supposing it endowed with intelligence. You seem likewise to think that the words *inert* and *unactive* are synonymous. Sir Isaac Newton was certainly of a different opinion, as appears by the third definition in the beginning of his *Principia*, viz., *Materiae vis inerta est Potentia resistendi*, etc. We certainly can have no conception of force or power devoid of all kind of action. Now, Sir, these are fundamental differences. One of us must be under a very great mistake, and if you incline to write with the same freedom that I incline to think on these subjects, I hope we shall not continue long of a different opinion. Inert, in common discourse, is often synonymous with unactive, but I take it in the sense that philosophers of late use the word inertia when they say *vis inertiae*, which certainly cannot mean mere inaction. . . .

JOHNSON TO COLDEN, Feb. 19, 1753

. . . I do not differ with you at all, considered as a natural philosopher, which is the light in which you are principally to be considered in that treatise. For it is evident there are those three distinct principles of action in nature you go upon—media or endings of action I should call them as a metaphysician, referring the same origin of them to the one great principle of natural discovery and action; but which you as a natural philosopher—as such going no higher—do very well to consider as distinct principles. The principle of resistance of motion and of elasticity—and the contemporative (if I may so speak) of those principles in their various exertions and operations you seem to have happily demonstrated—will well account for the phenomena, and as to what is metaphysical in your treatise, I think you have explained yourself to my satisfaction in your chapter of the Intelligent Being, section 10—where you allow the Intelligent Being to be the real author of all material (I should call them sensible) beings, and to govern or direct their actions in such a manner as is most conducive to the advantage of the whole, which you rightly deduce from the power of our minds over the ether in the nerves which we observe to quiesce till put in action by our hands. The reasons indeed we know not, but it is the fact.

So that I believe what we seem to differ in, if at all, will amount to little more than words. I agree with you in saying, "we can certainly have no conception of force or power devoid of all kind of action," and when I do so, it seems to me that you must with me allow that Sir Isaac's *vis inertiae* is a contradiction in terms, and that that great man, in that definition and the explication of it, has some expressions that have no meaning; for I must think it is plain that by inertia (as in Ovid, *pondus iners*) the old Romans meant an utter destitution of any principle of activity *in se*, or power of self-exertion or action, terminating on anything without, and I do not see what right he had to use or define it in a quite contrary sense; at best his expressions are figurative.

As to that question whether the same being that is the principle of action must as such be also a principle of intelligence, I have nothing to say for it more than I said in a former letter, that it seems to follow from that principle *"Non est philosophia exerta multiplicare sine necessitate,"* and that a blind principle or power of action without intelligence seems repugnant and useless. However it seems a question of little real consequence, or indeed of scarce any meaning after what you allow in the chapter of the Intelligent Being, the action of what you call matter being according to you derived originally from and directed by the Intelligent Being. And so matter is no more than merely His instrument, so that what you call the action of a mill or watch is really only a successive series of passions till you come to the principle of intelligence, which will ultimately prove to be also the principle of the action.

That expression of yours, page 164, "that perfect intelligence will not act in contradiction to the action of matter," I should have chosen to express thus: will not in the settled course of things act in contradiction to the laws He hath established according to which He wills matter to act. For I cannot conceive you to imagine the action of matter to be independent of the divine will. I rather imagine from other passages that you do with me conceive it to be entirely dependent, as well as matter itself, on the constant free exertion of the divine will and power.

I do not deny, Sir, but that I am yet a little in the dark about the operations of that elastic fluid by which you account for gravitation. I should scarce ever say that there should be a perpetual return of the ethereal fluid to the sun as well as a perpetual flow from it, agreeable to Mr. Hutchinson's notion, who imagines a perpetual circulation of it from the sun, and after a kind of condensation of it at the utmost bounds of the system, a reverberation and return of it to the sun again; so that according to that great man the effects of gravitation, circular motion, and rotation, will be the result of the struggle between those contrary tendencies. This being supposed, you and he seem well to coincide. I wish you had opportunity, if you have not had, to read his system with some attention and exactness, if not in his works, which are something tedious, at least in that beautiful short sketch of them set forth by your excellently great and good countryman, Lord President Forbes, in his "Letter to a Bishop and Thoughts on Religion." But what you call the different principles of light and ether, he supposes to be the one ethereal fluid or fire of the sun in the different conditions of light and spirit as it flies from or returns to its fountain. Perhaps your notion and his may come nearly to the same thing. The Abbé Pluche of France, as well as he and Bishop Berkeley, agree that this ethereal fire is the light and life of the whole sensible world, and grand agent in all nature, or the immediate engine from whence all the phenomena mechanically derive: and that this was the original philosophy of Moses and in all the Hebrew Scriptures, and taught mankind from the beginning. And I am pleased in thinking that your demonstrations and Mr. Franklin's experiments illustrate and confirm it to be the only true and genuine philosophy. . . .

A SUMMARY OF THE PRINCIPLES OF ACTION [2]

A recapitulation of the general remarks on the several powers by which as Principles of Action the phenomena are produced and are necessary consequences or effects of their action.

All the knowledge we have of things external to us is derived from the impressions they make on our senses, that is from the phenomena, or from the effects of the action of those things. Then we can have no conception of the difference of things but from the effects of their different actions, which when they are so very different or opposite that we clearly perceive that they must arise from different powers, they constitute so far as our conceptions reach the different essences of these different things. We can have no idea of power or virtue, without conceiving something which has that power, which thing is commonly called *substance. Virtus sine substantia subsistive non potest* is a universally received maxim. But we have no idea of substances, other than what is derived from their power of acting. Since then virtue or power constitutes the essences of things, at least so far as we can know them, the power of acting cannot pass from one thing or substance to another. For if it did, the essence of things would be changed, nothing could remain fixed and stable, and we could have no certain knowledge of anything, and it appears likewise from the constant observations of the phenomena that things never change or lose their powers of acting.

Simple or uncompounded beings can only have one power, essential to them: for otherwise there can be no distinction between simple

[2] From Colden's unpublished scientific papers, on file at the New York Historical Society Library, New York City. Published with the kind permission of the Society.

and compound, since all the difference of things arises from the difference of their powers and actions.

That there are three different powers is evidently deduced from the phenomena, or from the effects of the action of those powers.

One is denominated from the perpetual and manifest effect of its action, whereby it *resists* any change of its present state. From this resisting power arises, that property of matter called *impenetrability* or *solidity*, and which is allowed to be its essential property by all writers. We have no conception of this property, but what arises from its resisting all change of its present state.

Motion in resisting matter is only the effect of the action of the moving power on a resisting body. The power of moving is not thereby communicated: for, if the action communicated be by any means stopped, resisting matter cannot of itself recover motion. For this reason, motion in a resisting body is not a simple, but compound action of two different powers, viz. of the moving and resisting powers in a compound ratio of the quantity of resisting matter and degree of motion or velocity. It is called by Sir Isaac Newton *momentum* to distinguish it from simple motion.

It is evident, that the power of moving cannot be in resisting matter. For the resisting all change of its present state and a perpetual change by motion are inconsistent, or opposite, or negative powers to each other. Innumerable appearances lead us to *light*, as the substance to which the power of moving is essential. Take away motion from light and we have no idea of what remains. All the phenomena or effects of light cease on supposition of its having no motion. Besides, we everywhere, and at all times discover that the rays or parts of light are mutually penetrable. No ray of light can be given to which another ray is not directly opposite in the direction of its motion, and yet neither of these rays obstruct the other's motion. Every ray is intersected in every part by other rays, and yet the direction of no ray is thereby changed or altered. Therefore light and resisting matter are essentially different substances.

Gravitation and the mutual apparent attraction of bodies, at a distance from each other, are phenomena which discover the necessity of the existence of some medium, by which the action of the one can be communicated to the other: for nothing can act where it is not. It is only from the phenomena or from the effects that we can deduce their causes, or discover the powers, which produce the effects. It is from the phenomena or from the effects that we have any evidence of the existence of anything. From the phenomena therefore I conclude, that some medium universally diffused exists, which I call *other*: that the peculiar power of this medium is to *react* every action, which it receives from the contiguous powers, either of moving or resisting. Supposing the two powers of resisting and moving were annihilated, or ceased to act, the other, so far as can be discovered from the phenomena, must be inactive; but as the other powers are always acting, it must be continually reacting the action which it receives from them. It is in continual fits or turns of receiving and reacting their action. Reaction is observed everywhere, and universally allowed; but reaction can neither be the effect of the resisting power nor of the moving: not of the resisting, because the effect of resisting is to oppose the action of the other powers, and therefore cannot continue them by reaction; nor of the moving, because in the reaction of motion something distinct is conceived which reacts that motion and which in some sort opposes the motion which it reacts.

The resisting substance is collected into large quantities or bodies, such as the planets. These again consist of smaller bodies, and the smallest bodies may be divided and subdivided into smaller parts. Not only the great bodies are observed to be at a great distance from each other, but likewise the smallest compounding parts of bodies are separated from each other at a great distance, in proportion to their bulk, so that the quantity of space occupied by resisting matter bears but a small proportion to space void of resisting matter.

Every part of space, not occupied by the resisting substance, is filled with other, not only between the great bodies, but likewise between the smallest divisions or compounding parts of bodies. The mutual apparent attraction between the great bodies shows the necessity of such a medium between them, and the gravitation of the smaller bodies, being in proportion to the quantity of matter in them, shows that this medium acts on every part of these bodies. It likewise appears from the resistance of bodies, being in proportion to their bulk or quantity of matter in them. For since there is nothing of motion in resistance, the resisting action of the compounding parts of bodies could not be communicated from one to another, so as to form a united force of resistance, if this medium were not between the compounding and distant parts of bodies to communicate the action of the one to the other. And as the action of every part on this medium lessens as the squares of the distances, the power of resisting in great bodies, in proportion to their bulks, is less than in small bodies. Since light has no power of resisting, and is therefore penetrable, it does not exclude the other from the same place in which it is.

The parts of the other are everywhere contiguous to each other, except where they are separated by resisting matter, otherwise there is no separation of its parts. This is evident from the action of resistance which has nothing of motion, its being communicated to so vast a distance, as from the phenomena it appears to be: nor could otherwise the action and reaction be continued to the greatest distance severally in one instant. At the same time that there are evidently no separation of parts, it must be conceived as consisting of points, from each of which the reaction is expanded in all directions.

Though the other be thus in general diffused through the whole extent of space, and cannot be conceived otherwise, than as one uniform diffused substance, without any distinction of different parts; yet its action may be properly considered as distinguished into parts of all magnitudes and dimensions. For example, the direction of the reaction of the other toward the sun makes an immense sphere, within which the planets and comets perform their periodic motions. Again, the other may be supposed to be divided into much less, but very large spheres round each of the planets. Lastly, the elementary parts of bodies have their respective spheres of other round them: and that, in respect to the bulk of these elementary parts, the sphere of reaction extends to a much greater distance, than the sphere of reaction round the sun. Though these several spheres of reaction be continually changing place, by the motion of the bodies round which they are formed, it does not from thence follow, that there is any change of place in any part of the other. These remarks on the other perhaps may likewise be of use in considering some other things, which have generally perplexed philosophers in their inquiries.

The phenomena likewise show, by a proper deduction from them, that several propositions hitherto received as general maxims are not absolutely true. It is demonstrated from the phenomena of light that the parts of it are mutually penetrable, and that therefore any quantity of light may be contained in any space. It appears from the phenomena, that however light be expanded, by the diverging of its rays, it entirely fills the space in which it is contained, without any separation of the parts of light, and therefore that this diverging only is the cause that light grows less and less dense, as the distance from the luminous body increases.

From a consideration of the different phenomena it appears evident that no part of space is without light, except where space is occupied by the elementary parts of bodies, and how small the space is which is occupied by them, in respect to the remaining part of space, is scarce conceivable. The velocity of light is so very great, that no progressive motion, which is perceived by our senses, can be compared with it: neither does it of itself lose any degree of its velocity. The light of the fixed stars after it has moved the inconceivable distance between them and the earth, moves with no less velocity than that of any other light. Light of the least density moves with the same velocity with that of the greatest density. Therefore the different force of light is everywhere as its superficial density, at different distances, reciprocal to the squares of the distances from the luminous body, emitting the light. For the rays diverge from the emitting point in all directions, and it is only the extremity of these rays which in one instant act on any resisting body, and these extremities at equal distances from the luminous point form spherical surfaces.

The action of light cannot be stopped or retarded otherwise than by resistance, that is by the resisting substance, or by the action of resistance communicated to the other. Since the resistance communicated to the other decreases as the squares of the distances from the resisting body, accurate observations show, that light is only stopped by the other at or very near the surfaces of bodies. And if it be considered, to how great a distance from resisting bodies, the effect of the resistance communicated to the other is observed, and how much greater, in proportion to their bulk, the force of resistance is greater in small bodies than in large, the force of resistance in the elementary parts of bodies must be immensely great. Indeed considering that the essence of resisting bodies consists in their power of resisting, in the elementary or uncompounded parts it must be infinitely great, or they must be perfectly impenetrable. Otherwise their essence may be destroyed or they may be annihilated.

From a like reasoning it follows, that the velocity of light, where there is nothing to oppose or retard it, must be infinitely great. Yet notwithstanding of this, supposing that the resistance of the elementary parts of bodies is infinitely great, and the velocity of the rays or parts of light is likewise infinitely great, there may be an infinite diversity in the different degrees of force of resisting in the elementary parts of bodies, and an infinite variety of degrees of velocity, in the elementary parts of rays or parts of light essential to them severally as is evident from the doctrine of infinites.

But there is nothing in the phenomena to show any diversity in the parts of the other, on the contrary they show an entire uniformity or sameness throughout the whole. Notwithstanding of this, when the time is considered, in which the returns of receiving and reacting are performed, we are brought to an infinitely small division of time, in which these returns are made. Light is supposed to move in about eight minutes of time from the sun to the earth, and Sir Isaac Newton has observed, that light passes only the one hundred and eighty seven thousandth part of an inch in the interval of these returns. If then the distance between the earth and the sun be divided by this exceedingly small part of an inch, the quotient must become an immensely great sum, and if again eight minutes of time be divided by this immense sum, the time between the intervals of the reaction of the other must be an inconceivably small part of time. So that everywhere we discover, that infinite ratios are really founded in nature.

The elementary parts of bodies are absolutely impenetrable, as before shown, and the parts of the other contiguous to the surface of these bodies must likewise be impenetrable, in the time of reaction: for the reaction is always equal to the action received. Then, by this reaction of the other on the surfaces of bodies, light must be retained or entirely obstructed in the time of this reaction: and since these returns are in such inconceivably small portions of time, only so much light can pass as moves in that small time, or only surfaces of light are emitted from luminous bodies, by a kind of repeated vibrations, which surfaces expand themselves in straight lines in all directions, in which they are not obstructed by resisting matter.

Light communicates its action of motion to resisting bodies, if nothing hinders, in the direction of its rays; but if the action of light be obstructed in that direction, it communicates its action in any other direction, in which it meets with the least resistance. This is everywhere evident in fire and more particularly in gunpowder. Both fire and gunpowder in the open air, where the resistance is nearly equal, communicates its action nearly equally in all directions; but if its action be obstructed in every division except one, the fire or more properly the light contained in it, exerts its united force in that one direction; for every action must produce its effect in whatever way it can be produced.

Resistance, motion and reaction are observed everywhere, and allowed by all naturalists. These can in no sense be called occult qualities. If then from these, as principles of action, all the phenomena can be deduced, as I think they can, wherever we have sufficiently accurate observations of the phenomena, and of the circumstances attending them, no doubt can remain of their being really the principles of action, so far as it is the object of our senses. I have given in the proceeding chapters some instances of this, by explaining from them the general phenomena of gravitation, in the phenomena of light and colors, in the phenomena arising from the motion of the planets, and more particularly of the earth, where our observations are most accurate, and from the phenomena in the cohesion of the parts of bodies. I may be allowed to hope therefore, that the like may be done as to the other phenomena, when attempted with sufficient capacity, and accurate knowledge of the phenomena. Though I may have erred on some of the deductions, this may happen without any prejudice to the truth and reality of the principles themselves, and after repeated reflections, for some years, on these principles and the effects that many be deduced from them, I am fully persuaded they will stand the test of the most accurate of judicious examination, notwithstanding of any errors I may have fallen into by want of sufficient capacity.

It is unquestionably true, that all the knowledge we have is from our consciousness of our own actions, and from the phenomena, or from the effects of the actions of things external to us on our senses: and therefore from the effects of intelligence, which everywhere appears, it necessarily follows that some intellectual principle exists. From what we are conscious of in our own actions, and from an evident design, view and purpose, which appears in the formation of the innumerable systems, which come within our knowledge, all of them formed to serve some particular end or purpose, we receive the idea of an intelligent being necessarily existing. Force or power, however great, gives no idea of intelligence; but when actions are all directed to certain purposes or ends, we cannot doubt of their being directed by intelligence: and where we discover no view, design or purpose in any action, we cannot conceive that such action is directed by intelligence. Design, view and purpose, which is generally called the *final cause* or the motive of intelligent actions, distinguishes them from the actions of the material powers.

It is true that we cannot conceive design, view or purpose as an active principle. But if it be considered that we have no idea of any power, or of its manner of acting, and that all the powers are really denominated from the constant effect of their action, the intellectual power may be truly and well denominated from the perpetual effect of intelligence, viz. design, view or purpose. Resistance is only the effect of the resisting power, it gives no idea of the power itself or of its manner of acting. Motion or change of place is the effect of the moving power, it gives no idea of the power itself, or of its manner of acting. Then the intellectual power may be as properly denominated from the perpetual effect, which accompanies all its actions, and without which we have no conception of it.

The intelligent being never acts in opposition to the material powers, but directs their actions to some particular purpose, by some particular and regular disposition and composition of their several powers. This disposition of the several powers is called mechanism, and the several mechanical forms are called systems, or machines, and are as various as the various purposes of the intelligent being. Mere mechanism, without power or force, can produce no effect; and mere force or power gives no idea of intelligence. If a man by mere force should turn wheat into flour, we must receive an idea of his great strength, but no conception of his intelligence; but if he contrives a machine, by which with the help of the natural powers, which form the parts of the machine, he perform this, then we have a conception of his wisdom or knowledge, and the greater opinion of his wisdom or it appears the more clearly, the less bodily strength he is supposed to have.

There is nothing in the conception of intelligence opposite or negative to the material power, and though in the resisting power there be a negation or want of intelligence, there is nothing in the conception of it negative or opposite to intelligence. Therefore, there is nothing in the material powers to exclude the intelligent being from the same place, in which they are, neither is there anything in intelligence to exclude the material powers, from the same place in which it is. Therefore, though the intelligent being occupies no place exclusively of matter, yet certainly it includes a contradiction to say, it is in no place or no where. The phenomena discover intelligence everywhere.

There is this remarkable or essential distinction between the material and intelligent powers, that in the material the one communicates its action to the other, or opposes or resists the action of the other. But the material does not communicate the action of moving or resisting to the intelligent, nor does the intelligent communicate view, design or purpose to the material powers; but where the material powers and their actions are necessary for the views and purposes of the intelligent, it so disposes these powers into mechanical systems, that they by their united actions produce the effects which the intelligent has in view, or designs to produce. This plainly appears everywhere from the phenomena. If it were otherwise, all our knowledge and distinction of different beings must be confounded.

From what we are conscious of within ourselves, we may with certainty conclude, that the several material powers excite different ideas in our minds, that every degree of force in the resisting power and of velocity in the moving power excite distinct ideas, that their complicated actions excite complicated ideas, and that the same degree of action in either power excites always the same idea. We are conscious likewise, that in the machine which constitutes our body, certain material actions, as motion or resisting motion, always accompany certain volitions or actions of the mind, and that a certain frame or composition of the material substances, so as to produce a communication and union of every part with the whole, the distinguishing constitution of every machine, is necessary for the production of the material actions, by the will or action of the mind. But in what manner the material beings act on the intelligent, or the intelligent on the material, we in no wise know. It is highly probable that this knowledge cannot be acquired. Since we have no conception of any power, or of its manner of acting, but only of the effects of its action, the manner by which the material and intelligent powers act on each other, is without the reach of human understanding. This is carefully to be observed, for nothing has occasioned more perplexity, and fruitless vain labor, than the attempting to explain what is in itself inexplicable, and beyond the limits of human conception.

Many more corollaries readily offered themselves to my conception than I have put in writing. Where they are obvious some readers will have more pleasure in discovering them of themselves, than by learning them from another. In some cases theorems evident from these principles contradict firmly received opinions. These prejudices, I think, will be more early got over by one who of himself discovers their falsity than by another's directly contradicting a favorite opinion. . . .

BIBLIOGRAPHY

COLDEN, Cadwallader, *An Explication of the First Causes of Action in Matter; And of the Cause of Gravitation.* New York, 1745, London, 1746.

———— *The Principles of Action in Matter, the Gravitation of Bodies, and the Motion of the Planets, Explained from those Principles.* London, 1751.

———— *An Introduction to the Study of Philosophy Wrote in America for the Use of a Young Gentleman.* (1760) Printed in Joseph L. Blau's *American Philosophic Addresses, 1700–1900.* New York: Columbia U. Press, 1946, pp. 289–311.

———— *The Colden Letter Books.* New York: Collections of the New York Historical Society, 1876–77, 2 vols.

———— *The Letters and Papers of Cadwallader Colden.* New York, 1917–23, 1934–35, 9 vols. Vol. VII, pp. 359–76 contains a list of Colden's unpublished manuscripts and papers.

———— "The Philosophical Correspondence Between Samuel Johnson and Cadwallader Colden." Reprinted in *The Letters and Papers of Cadwallader Colden,* Vol. III; H.W. and C. Schneider, *Samuel Johnson,* Vol. II; E.E. Beardsley, *Life and Correspondence of Rev. Samuel Johnson, D.D.*

INGRAHAM, Charles A., "A Great Colonial Executive and Scholar—Cadwallader Colden." *Americana,* Vol. XIX, (1925), pp. 295–314.

KEYS, Alice M., *Cadwallader Colden: A Representative Eighteenth Century Official.* New York: Columbia U. Press, 1906.

RILEY, I. Woodbridge, *American Philosophy: the Early Schools.* New York: Dodd, Mead and Co., 1907, pp. 329–72.

Benjamin Franklin

[1706–1790]

In a letter to Benjamin Franklin, David Hume wrote: "America has sent us many good things . . . but you are the first philosopher, and indeed the first great man of letters, for whom we are beholden to her."[1] It is significant that this view was widely shared abroad. Yet Franklin never published what we might today consider a substantial philosophical work; nor did he engage in any protracted philosophical inquiry. Franklin's reputation was based on the famous experiments which he conducted in electricity (his scientific inquiries here were more experimental than theoretical in nature) and on his practical inventions—the lightning rod, the Franklin stove, etc. In his scientific work, however, Franklin both applied Newton's physical principles and illustrated Newtonian natural philosophy and the possibility of a completely mechanical explanation of the universe. Franklin corresponded with Peter Collinson and the Royal Society of London. His paper, *Opinions and Conjectures Concerning the Properties and Effects of Electrical Matter, etc.*, which is partly reproduced below, was sent to Collinson and read at the Royal Society in 1750. It offers Franklin's most complete statement of his work in electricity until that time; and it shows the influence of materialism on his thought. In speaking of the correspondence between Franklin and Collinson, Joseph Priestley in his *History of Electricity* (1767) asserted that "Nothing was ever written upon the subject of electricity . . . which was more generally read and admired in all parts of Europe, than these letters." Franklin's interest in science was not confined to his electrical experiments, he carefully followed the scientific developments of his day. Thus he was considered by his contemporaries—because of his work in physical science—a "natural philosopher."

Franklin also owed his philosophical reputation to the fact that he was broadly educated and interested in many fields of human endeavor. Moreover, he displayed a wisdom for life, both intellectual and practical. His *Autobiography* (written 1771–89 and published after his death) is his most famous published work and reveals a man of extraordinary talents for conducting life with prudence.

Franklin was born in Boston in 1706. He became apprenticed to his brother James, a printer. Later he moved to Philadelphia (1723) and continued in the trade of printer. There he bought the *Pennsylvania Gazette* (1729) and began his *Poor Richard's Almanack* (1732), which

[1] May 10, 1762. *The Works of Benjamin Franklin*, ed. by J. Bigelow, New York: G. P. Putnam's Sons, 1904, Vol. III, p. 403.

enjoyed great popularity in the Colonies. Franklin was a signer of the Declaration of Independence and was the first Postmaster-General under the Confederation. He helped found the American Philosophical Society, and helped establish the first fire-fighting company and the first library in Philadelphia. Franklin's international reputation was due in no small part to the fact that he was appointed Ambassador to France and was feted by Parisian literary and philosophical circles.

Franklin was actually a transitional figure. Bred a New England Calvinist, he also bore the imprint of the Enlightenment. Franklin was a deist. His early piece, *Articles of Belief and Acts of Religion* (1730), and a number of his letters show, however, that he was somewhat more conservative than many other deists of his time. Thus he was critical of the religious extremes of which he thought Thomas Paine guilty, and he urged Paine not to publish a manuscript which he thought too irreligious. In a letter to Benjamin Stiles (1790), he said that while he believed in God and accepted the morality of Christianity, he was somewhat dubious about the divinity of Jesus. In ethics, Franklin secularized the typical Puritan virtues of thrift, temperance, punctuality, and industry. The combination of virtue and reason was defended as the true source of happiness. In the two *Dialogues Between Philocles and Horatio Concerning Virtue and Pleasure* (1730), the second of which is reprinted here, Franklin justified the "rational" or "moral good" over the "natural" or "sensual good." In politics, Franklin was a stanch defender of the ideals of republicanism and revolution. Franklin was a highly civilized man—fair-minded, humane, charitable, and a source of worldly wisdom—qualities which were rather unique in the American Colonies.

OPINIONS AND CONJECTURES CONCERNING THE PROPERTIES AND EFFECTS OF ELECTRICAL MATTER [2]

The electrical matter consists of particles extremely subtile, since it can permeate common matter, even the densest metals, with such ease and freedom as not to receive any perceptible resistance.

If anyone should doubt whether the electrical matter passes through the substance of bodies, or only over and along their surfaces, a shock from an electrified large glass jar, taken through his own body, will probably convince him.

Electrical matter differs from common matter in this, that the parts of the latter mutually attract, those of the former mutually repel, each

[2] The complete title continues: *and the Means of Preserving Buildings, Ships, etc., from Lightening, Arising from Experiments and Observations Made at Philadelphia,* 1749. The paper was sent to Peter Collinson, July 29, 1750. Reprinted in *The Works of Benjamin Franklin,* ed. by J. Bigelow, Vol. II, pp. 287-98.

other. Hence the appearing divergency in a stream of electrified effluvia.

But, though the particles of electrical matter do repel each other, they are strongly attracted by all other matter.[3]

From these three things, the extreme subtility of the electrical matter, the mutual repulsion of its parts, and the strong attraction between them and other matter, arises this effect, that, when a quantity of electrical matter is applied to a mass of common matter, of any bigness or length, within our observation (which has not already got its quantity), it is immediately and equally diffused through the whole.

Thus, common matter is a kind of sponge to the electrical fluid. And as a sponge would receive no water, if the parts of water were not smaller than the pores of the sponge; and even then but slowly, if there were not a mutual attraction between those parts and the parts of the sponge; and would still imbibe it faster, if the mutual attraction among the parts of the water did not impede, some force being required to separate them; and fastest, if, instead of attraction, there were a mutual repulsion among those parts, which would act in conjunction with the attraction of the sponge; so is the case between the electrical and common matter.

But in common matter there is (generally) as much of the electrical as it will contain within its substance. If more is added, it lies without upon the surface, and forms what we call an electrical atmosphere; and then the body is said to be electrified.

It is supposed that all kinds of common matter do not attract and retain the electrical with equal strength and force, for reasons to be given hereafter. And that those called electrics per se, as glass, etc., attract and retain it strongest, and contain the greatest quantity.

We know that the electrical fluid is *in* common matter, because we can pump it *out* by the globe or tube. We know that common matter has near as much as it can contain, because, when we add a little more to any portion of it, the additional quantity does not enter, but forms an electrical atmosphere. And we know that common matter has not (generally) more than it can contain, otherwise all loose portions of it would repel each other, as they constantly do when they have electric atmospheres.

The beneficial uses of this electric fluid in the creation we are not yet well acquainted with, though doubtless such there are, and those very considerable; but we may see some pernicious consequences that would attend a much greater proportion of it. For, had this globe we live on as much of it in proportion as we can give to a globe of iron, wood, or the like, the particles of dust and other light matters that

[3] See the ingenious essays on Electricity, in the *Transactions*, by Mr. Ellicot.—F.

get loose from it would, by virtue of their separate electrical atmospheres, not only repel each other, but be repelled from the earth, and not easily be brought to unite with it again; whence our air would continually be more and more clogged with foreign matter and grow unfit for respiration. This affords another occasion of adoring that wisdom which has made all things by weight and measure!

If a piece of common matter be supposed entirely free from electrical matter, and a single particle of the latter be brought nigh, it will be attracted and enter the body, and take place in the center, or where the attraction is every way equal. If more particles enter, they take their places where the balance is equal between the attraction of the common matter and their own mutual repulsion. It is supposed they form triangles, whose sides shorten as their number increases, till the common matter has drawn in so many that its whole power of compressing those triangles by attraction is equal to their whole power of expanding themselves by repulsion; and then will such a piece of matter receive no more.

When part of this natural proportion of electrical fluid is taken out of a piece of common matter, the triangles formed by the remainder are supposed to widen, by the mutual repulsion of the parts, until they occupy the whole piece.

When the quantity of electrical fluid taken from a piece of common matter is restored again, it enters the expanded triangles, being again compressed till there is room for the whole.

To explain this: take two apples, or two balls of wood or other matter, each having its own natural quantity of the electrical fluid. Suspend them by silk lines from the ceiling. Apply the wire of a well-charged phial, held in your hand, to one of them (A) and it will receive from the wire a quantity of the electrical fluid, but will not imbibe it, being already full. The fluid, therefore, will flow round its surface and form an electrical atmosphere. Bring A into contact with B, and half the electrical fluid is communicated, so that each has now an electrical atmosphere, and therefore they repel each other. Take away these atmospheres, by touching the balls, and leave them in their natural state; then, having fixed a stick of sealing wax to the middle of the phial to hold it by, apply the wire to A, at the same time the coating touches B. Thus will a quantity of the electrical fluid be drawn out of B, and thrown on A. So that A will have a redundance of this fluid, which forms an atmosphere round, and B an exactly equal deficiency. Now, bring these balls again into contact, and the electrical atmosphere will not be divided between A and B, into two smaller atmospheres as before; for B will drink up the whole atmosphere of A, and both will be found again in their natural state.

The form of the electrical atmosphere is that of the body it surrounds. This shape may be rendered visible in a still air, by raising a smoke from dry rosin dropped into a hot teaspoon under the electrified body, which will be attracted, and spread itself equally on all sides, covering and concealing the body. And this form it takes, because it is attracted by all parts of the surface of the body, though it cannot enter the substance already replete. Without this attraction, it would not remain round the body, but dissipate in the air.

The atmosphere of electrical particles surrounding an electrified sphere is not more disposed to leave it, or more easily drawn off from any one part of the sphere than another, because it is equally attracted by every part. But that is not the case with bodies of any other figure. From a cube it is more easily drawn at the corners than at the plane sides, and so from the angles of a body of any other form, and still more easily from the angle that is most acute. . . . We suppose electrified bodies discharge their atmospheres upon unelectrified bodies more easily, and at a greater distance from their angles and points than from their smooth sides. Those points will also discharge into the air, when the body has too great an electrical atmosphere, without bringing any non-electric near to receive what is thrown off. For the air, though an electric per se, yet has always more or less water and other non-electric matters mixed with it; and these attract and receive what is so discharged.

But points have a property, by which they *draw on* as well as *throw off* the electrical fluid, at greater distances than blunt bodies can. That is, as the pointed part of an electrified body will discharge the atmosphere of that body, or communicate it farthest to another body, so the point of an unelectrified body will draw off the electrical atmosphere from an electrified body, farther than a blunter part of the same unelectrified body will do. Thus, a pin held by the head, and the point presented to an electrified body, will draw off its atmosphere at a foot distance; where, if the head were presented instead of the point, no such effect would follow. To understand this, we may consider that, if a person standing on the floor would draw off the electrical atmosphere from an electrified body, an iron crow and a blunt knitting needle held alternately in his hand, and presented for that purpose, do not draw with different forces in proportion to their different masses. For the man, and what he holds in his hand, be it large or small, are connected with the common mass of unelectrified matter; and the force with which he draws is the same in both cases, it consisting in the different proportion of electricity in the electrified body and that common mass. But the force with which the electrified body retains its atmosphere by attracting it, is proportioned to the surface over which the particles are placed; that is, four square inches of that surface retain their atmosphere with four times the force that one square inch retains its atmosphere. And as in plucking the hairs from a horse's tail a degree of strength not sufficient to pull away a handful at once could yet easily strip it hair by hair, so a blunt body presented cannot draw off a number of particles at once, but a pointed one, with no greater force, takes them away easily, particle by particle.

These explanations of the power and operation of points when they first occurred to me, and while they first floated in my mind, appeared perfectly satisfactory; but now I have written them, and considered them more closely, I must own I have some doubts about them; yet, as I have at present nothing better to offer in their stead, I do not cross them out; for, even a bad solution read, and its faults discovered, has often given rise to a good one, in the mind of an ingenious reader.

Nor is it of much importance to us to know the manner in which nature executes her laws; it is enough if we know the laws themselves. It is of real use to know that china left in the air unsupported will fall and break; but *how* it comes to fall, and *why* it breaks, are matters of speculation. It is a pleasure indeed to know them, but we can preserve our china without it.

Thus, in the present case, to know this power of points may possibly be of some use to mankind, though we should never be able to explain it. The . . . experiments . . . show this power. . . .

AUTOBIOGRAPHY [4]

. . . I conceived the bold and arduous project of arriving at moral perfection. I wished to live without committing any fault at any time; I would conquer all that either natural inclination, custom, or company might lead me into. As I knew, or thought I knew, what was right and wrong, I did not see why I might not always do the one and avoid the other. But I soon found I had undertaken a task of more difficulty than I had imagined. While my care was employed in guarding against one fault, I was often surprised by another; habit took the advantage of inattention; inclination was sometimes too strong for reason. I concluded, at length, that the mere speculative conviction that it was our interest to be completely virtuous, was not sufficient to prevent our slipping; and that the contrary habits must be broken, and good ones acquired and established, before we can have any dependence on a steady, uniform rectitude of conduct. For this purpose I therefore contrived the following method.

[4] *The Works of Benjamin Franklin,* ed. by J. Bigelow, Vol. I, pp. 88–203.

In the various enumerations of the moral virtues I had met with in my reading, I found the catalogue more or less numerous, as different writers included more or fewer ideas under the same name. Temperance, for example, was by some confined to eating and drinking, while by others it was extended to mean the moderating every other pleasure, appetite, inclination, or passion, bodily or mental, even to our avarice and ambition. I proposed to myself, for the sake of clearness, to use rather more names, with fewer ideas annexed to each, than a few names with more ideas; and I included under thirteen names of virtues all that at that time occurred to me as necessary or desirable, and annexed to each a short precept, which fully expressed the extent I gave to its meaning.

These names of virtues, with their precepts, were:

1. TEMPERANCE

Eat not to dullness; drink not to elevation.

2. SILENCE

Speak not but what may benefit others or yourself; avoid trifling conversation.

3. ORDER

Let all your things have their places; let each part of your business have its time.

4. RESOLUTION

Resolve to perform what you ought; perform without fail what you resolve.

5. FRUGALITY

Make no expense but to do good to others or yourself; *i.e.*, waste nothing.

6. INDUSTRY

Lose no time; be always employed in something useful; cut off all unnecessary actions.

7. SINCERITY

Use no hurtful deceit; think innocently and justly; and, if you speak, speak accordingly.

8. JUSTICE

Wrong none by doing injuries, or omitting the benefits that are your duty.

9. MODERATION

Avoid extremes; forbear resenting injuries so much as you think they deserve.

10. CLEANLINESS

Tolerate no uncleanliness in body, clothes, or habitation.

11. TRANQUILLITY

Be not disturbed at trifles, or at accidents common or unavoidable.

12. CHASTITY

Rarely use venery but for health or offspring, never to dullness, weakness, or the injury of your own or another's peace or reputation.

13. HUMILITY

Imitate Jesus and Socrates.

My intention being to acquire the habitude of all these virtues, I judged it would be well not to distract my attention by attempting the whole at once, but to fix it on one of them at a time; and, when I should be master of that, then proceed to another, and so on till I had gone through the thirteen; and, as the previous acquisition of some might facilitate the acquisition of certain others, I arranged them with that view, as they stand above. Temperance first, as it tends to procure that coolness and clearness of head, which is so necessary where constant vigilance was to be kept up, and guard maintained against the unremitting attraction of ancient habits, and the force of perpetual temptations. This being acquired and established, Silence would be more easy; and my desire being to gain knowledge at the same time that I improved in virtue, and considering that in conversation it was obtained rather by the use of the ears than of the tongue, and therefore wishing to break a habit I was getting into of prattling, punning, and joking, which only made me acceptable to trifling company, I gave Silence the second place. This and the next, Order, I expected would allow me more time for attending to my project and my studies. Resolution, once become habitual, would keep me firm in my endeavors to obtain all the subsequent virtues; Frugality and Industry freeing me from my remaining debt, and producing affluence and independence, would make more easy the practice of Sincerity and Justice, etc. Conceiving, then, that, agreeably to the advice of Pythagoras in his *Golden Verses*, daily examination would be necessary, I contrived the following method for conducting that examination.

I made a little book in which I allotted a page for each of the virtues. I ruled each page with red ink, so as to have seven columns, one for each day of the week, marking each column with a letter for the day. I crossed these columns with thirteen red lines, marking the beginning of each line with the first letter of one of the virtues; on which line, and in its proper column, I might mark, by a little black spot, every fault I found upon examination to have been committed respecting that virtue upon that day.

TEMPERANCE						
Eat Not to Dullness Drink Not to Elevation						
	S.	M.	T.	W.	T.	F.	S.
T.							
S.	*	*		*		*	
O.	* *	*	*		*	*	*
R.			*			*	
F.		*			*		
I.			*				
S.							
J.							
M.							
C.							
T.							
C.							
H.							

I determined to give a week's strict attention to each of the virtues successively. Thus, in the first week, my great guard was to avoid every the least offense against Temperance, leaving the other virtues to their ordinary chance, only marking every evening the faults of the day. Thus, if in the first week I could keep my first line, marked T, clear of spots, I supposed the habit of that virtue so much strengthened, and its opposite weakened, that I might venture extending my attention to include the next, and for the following week keep both lines clear of spots. Proceeding thus to the last, I could go through a course complete in thirteen weeks, and four courses in a year. And like him who, having a garden to weed, does not attempt to eradicate all the bad herbs at once, which would exceed his reach and his strength, but works on one of the beds at a time, and, having accomplished the first, proceeds to a second, so I should have, I hoped, the encouraging pleasure of seeing on my pages the progress I made in virtue, by clearing successively my lines of their spots, till in the end, by a number of courses, I should be happy in viewing a clean book, after a thirteen weeks' daily examination.

This my little book had for its motto these lines from Addison's *Cato:*

> Here will I hold. If there's a power above us
> (And that there is, all nature cries aloud
> Thro' all her works), He must delight in virtue;
> And that which He delights in must be happy.

Another from Cicero:

> O vitæ Philosophia dux! O virtutum indagatrix expultrixque vitiorum! Unus dies, bene et ex præceptis tuis actus, peccanti immortalitati est anteponendus.

Another from the Proverbs of Solomon, speaking of wisdom or virtue:

> Length of days is in her right hand, and in her left hand riches and honor. Her ways are ways of pleasantness, and all her paths are peace.—iii. 16, 17.

And conceiving God to be the fountain of wisdom, I thought it right and necessary to solicit his assistance for obtaining it; to this end I formed the following little prayer, which was prefixed to my tables of examination, for daily use.

> O powerful Goodness! bountiful Father! merciful Guide! Increase in me that wisdom which discovers my truest interest. Strengthen my resolutions to perform what that wisdom dictates. Accept my kind offices to thy other children as the only return in my power for thy continual favors to me.

I used also sometimes a little prayer which I took from Thomson's *Poems*, viz.:

> Father of light and life, thou Good Supreme!
> O teach me what is good; teach me Thyself!
> Save me from folly, vanity, and vice,
> From every low pursuit; and fill my soul
> With knowledge, conscious peace, and virtue pure;
> Sacred, substantial, never-fading bliss!

The precept of Order requiring that every part of my business should have its allotted time, one page in my little book contained the following scheme of employment for the twenty-four hours of a natural day.

THE MORNING. *Question.* What good shall I do this day?	5 6 7 8	Rise, wash, and address *Powerful Goodness!* Contrive day's business, and take the resolution of the day; prosecute the present study, and breakfast.
	9 10 11	Work.
NOON.	12 1	Read, or overlook my accounts, and dine.
	2 3 4 5	Work.
EVENING. *Question.* What good have I done today?	6 7 8 9	Put things in their places. Supper. Music or diversion, or conversation. Examination of the day.
NIGHT.	10 11 12 1 2 3 4	Sleep.

I entered upon the execution of this plan for self-examination, and continued it with occasional intermissions for some time. I was surprised to find myself so much fuller of faults than I had imagined; but I had the satisfaction of seeing them diminish. To avoid the trouble of renewing now and then my little book, which, by scraping out the marks on the paper of old faults to make room for new ones in a new course, became full of holes, I transferred my tables and precepts to the ivory leaves of a memorandum book, on which the lines were drawn with red ink, that made a durable stain, and on those lines I marked my faults with a black-lead pencil, which marks I could easily wipe out with a wet sponge. After a while I went through one course only in a year, and afterward only one in several years, till at length I omitted them entirely, being employed in voyages and business abroad, with a multiplicity of affairs that interfered; but I always carried my little book with me.

My scheme of Order gave me the most trouble; and I found that, though it might be practicable where a man's business was such as to leave him the disposition of his time, that of a journeyman printer, for instance, it was not possible to be exactly observed by a master who must mix with the world and often receive people of business at their own hours. Order, too, with regard to places for things, papers, etc., I found extremely difficult to acquire. I had not been early accustomed to it, and, having an exceeding good memory, I was not so sensible of the inconvenience attending want of method. This article, therefore cost me so much painful attention and my faults in it vexed me so much, and I made so little progress in amendment, and had such frequent relapses that I was almost ready to give up the attempt, and content myself with a faulty character in that respect, like the man who, in buying an ax of a smith, my neighbor, desired to have the whole of its surface as bright as the edge. The smith consented to grind it bright for him if he would turn the wheel; he turned while the smith pressed the broad face of the ax hard and heavily on the stone which made the turning of it very fatiguing. The man came every now and then from the wheel to see how the work went on and at length would take his ax as it was, without farther grinding. "No," said the smith, "turn on, turn on; we shall have it bright by and by; as yet, it is only speckled." "Yes," says the man, "*but I think I like a speckled ax best.*" And I believe this may have been the case with many who, having, for want of some such means as I employed, found the difficulty of obtaining good and breaking bad habits in other points of vice and virtue, have given up the struggle, and concluded that "a speckled ax was best"; for something, that pretended to be reason, was every now and then suggesting to me that such extreme nicety as I exacted of myself might be a kind of foppery in morals, which, if it were known, would make me ridiculous; that a perfect character might be attended with the inconvenience of being envied and hated; and that a benevolent man should allow a few faults in himself, to keep his friends in countenance.

In truth, I found myself incorrigible with respect to Order; and now I am grown old and my memory bad, I feel very sensibly the want of it. But, on the whole, though I never arrived at the perfection I had been so ambitious of obtaining, but fell far short of it, yet I was, by the endeavor, a better and a happier man than I otherwise should have been if I had not attempted it; as those who aim at perfect writing by imitating the engraved copies, though they never reach the wished-for excellence of those copies, their hand is mended by the endeavor, and is tolerable while it continues fair and legible.

It may be well my posterity should be informed that to this little artifice, with the blessing of God, their ancestor owed the constant felicity of his life, down to his seventy-ninth year, in which this is written. What reverses may attend the remainder is in the hand of

Providence; but, if they arrive, the reflection on past happiness enjoyed ought to help his bearing them with more resignation. To Temperance he ascribes his long-continued health, and what is still left to him of a good constitution; to Industry and Frugality, the early easiness of his circumstances and acquisition of his fortune, with all that knowledge that enabled him to be a useful citizen, and obtained for him some degree of reputation among the learned; to Sincerity and Justice, the confidence of his country, and the honorable employs it conferred upon him; and to the joint influence of the whole mass of virtues, even in the imperfect state he was able to acquire them, all that evenness of temper, and that cheerfulness in conversation, which makes his company still sought for and agreeable even to his younger acquaintances. I hope, therefore, that some of my descendants may follow the example and reap the benefit.

It will be remarked that, though my scheme was not wholly without religion, there was in it no mark of any of the distinguishing tenets of any particular sect. I had purposely avoided them; for, being fully persuaded of the utility and excellence of my method, and that it might be serviceable to people in all religions, and intending sometime or other to publish it, I would not have anything in it that should prejudice anyone, of any sect, against it. I purposed writing a little comment on each virtue, in which I would have shown the advantages of possessing it, and the mischiefs attending its opposite vice; and I should have called my book *The Act of Virtue*,[5] because it would have shown the means and manner of obtaining virtue, which would have distinguished it from the mere exhortation to be good, that does not instruct and indicate the means, but is like the apostle's man of verbal charity, who only, without showing to the naked and hungry how or where they might get clothes or victuals, exhorted them to be fed and clothed. —James ii. 15, 16.

But it so happened that my intention of writing and publishing this comment was never fulfilled. I did, indeed, from time to time, put down short hints of the sentiments, reasonings, etc., to be made use of in it, some of which I have still by me; but the necessary close attention to private business in the earlier part of my life, and public business since, have occasioned my postponing it; for, it being connected in my mind with a great and extensive project that required the whole man to execute, and which an unforeseen succession of employs prevented my attending to, it has hitherto remained unfinished.

In this piece, it was my design to explain and enforce this doctrine, that vicious actions are not hurtful because they are forbidden, but

---

[5] Nothing so likely to make a man's fortune as virtue.—Marginal note by F.

forbidden because they are hurtful, the nature of man alone considered; that it was, therefore, everyone's interest to be virtuous who wished to be happy even in this world; and I should, from this circumstance (there being always in the world a number of rich merchants, nobility, states, and princes, who have need of honest instruments for the management of their affairs, and such being rare), have endeavored to convince young persons that no qualities were so likely to make a poor man's fortune as those of probity and integrity.

My list of virtues contained at first but twelve; but a Quaker friend having kindly informed me that I was generally thought proud; that my pride showed itself frequently in conversation; that I was not content with being in the right when discussing any point, but was overbearing, and rather insolent, of which he convinced me by mentioning several instances; I determined endeavoring to cure myself, if I could, of this vice or folly among the rest, and I added Humility to my list, giving an extensive meaning to the word.

I cannot boast of much success in acquiring the reality of this virtue, but I had a good deal with regard to the appearance of it. I made it a rule to forbear all direct contradiction to the sentiments of others, and all positive assertion of my own. I even forbid myself, agreeably to the old laws of our Junto, the use of every word or expression in the language that imported a fixed opinion, such as *certainly, undoubtedly,* etc., and I adopted, instead of them, *I conceive, I apprehend,* or *I imagine* a thing to be so or so; or it *so appears to me at present.* When another asserted something that I thought an error, I denied myself the pleasure of contradicting him abruptly, and of showing immediately some absurdity in his proposition; and in answering I began by observing that in certain cases or circumstances his opinion would be right, but in the present case there *appeared* or *seemed* to me some difference, etc. I soon found the advantage of this change in my manner; the conversations I engaged in went on more pleasantly. The modest way in which I proposed my opinions procured them a readier reception and less contradiction; I had less mortification when I was found to be in the wrong, and I more easily prevailed with others to give up their mistakes and join with me when I happened to be in the right.

And this mode, which I at first put on with some violence to natural inclination, became at length so easy, and so habitual to me, that perhaps for these fifty years past no one has ever heard a dogmatical expression escape me. And to this habit (after my character of integrity) I think it principally owing that I had early so much weight with my fellow citizens when I proposed new institutions, or alterations in the old, and so much influence in public councils when I became a member; for I was but a bad speaker, never eloquent, subject to much hesitation in my choice of words, hardly correct in language, and yet I generally carried my points.

In reality, there is, perhaps, no one of our natural passions so hard to subdue as pride. Disguise it, struggle with it, beat it down, stifle it, mortify it as much as one pleases, it is still alive, and will every now and then peep out and show itself; you will see it, perhaps, often in this history; for, even if I could conceive that I had completely overcome it, I should probably be proud of my humility. . . .

DIALOGUE BETWEEN PHILOCLES AND HORATIO CONCERNING VIRTUE AND PLEASURE [6]

Philocles—Dear Horatio, where hast thou been these three or four months? What new adventures have you fallen upon since I met you in these delightful, all-inspiring fields, and wondered how such a pleasure hunter as you could bear being alone?

Horatio—O Philocles, thou best of friends, because a friend to reason and virtue, I am very glad to see you. Do not you remember, I told you then that some misfortunes in my pleasures had sent me to philosophy for relief? But now I do assure you I can, without a sigh, leave other pleasures for those of philosophy; I can hear the word *reason* mentioned, and *virtue* praised, without laughing. Do not I bid fair for conversion, think you?

Phil.—Very fair, Horatio; for I remember the time when reason, virtue, and pleasure were the same thing with you; when you counted nothing good but what pleased, nor anything reasonable but what you gained by; when you made a jest of mind and the pleasures of reflection, and elegantly placed your sole happiness, like the rest of the animal creation, in the gratification of sense.

Hor.—I did so; but in our last conversation, when walking upon the brow of this hill, and looking down on that broad, rapid river, and yon widely-extended beautifully-varied plain, you taught me another doctrine; you showed me that self-denial, which above all things I abhorred, was really the greatest good and the highest self-gratification and absolutely necessary to produce even my own darling sole good, pleasure.

Phil.—True; I told you that self-denial was never a duty but when it was a natural means of procuring more pleasure than we could taste without it; that as we all strongly desire to live, and to live only to enjoy, we should take as much care about our future as our present

[6] A Second Dialogue, from the *Pennsylvania Gazette*, July 9, 1739. *The Works of Benjamin Franklin*, ed. by J. Bigelow, Vol. I, pp. 401–08.

happiness, and not build one upon the ruins of the other; that we should look to the end and regard consequences, and if through want of attention we had erred and exceeded the bounds which nature had set us, we were then obliged, for our own sakes, to refrain or deny ourselves a present momentary pleasure for a future constant and durable good.

Hor.—You have shown, Philocles, that self-denial, which weak or interested men have rendered the most forbidding, is really the most delightful and amiable, the most reasonable and pleasant thing in the world. In a word, if I understand you aright, self-denial is in truth self-recognizing, self-acknowledging, or self-owning. But now, my friend, you are to perform another promise, and show me the path that leads up to that constant, durable, and invariable good, which I have heard you so beautifully describe and which you seem so fully to possess. Is not this good of yours a mere chimera? Can anything be constant in a world which is eternally changing, and which appears to exist by an everlasting revolution of one thing into another, and where everything without us and everything within us is in perpetual motion? What is this constant, durable good, then, of yours? Prithee, satisfy my soul, for I am all on fire and impatient to enjoy her. Produce this eternal blooming goddess with never-fading charms, and see whether I will not embrace her with as much eagerness and rapture as you.

Phil.—You seem enthusiastically warm, Horatio; I will wait till you are cool enough to attend to the sober, dispassionate voice of reason.

Hor.—You mistake me, my dear Philocles; my warmth is not so great as to run away with my reason; it is only just raised enough to open my faculties, and fit them to receive those eternal truths and that durable good which you so triumphantly boasted of. Begin, then; I am prepared.

Phil.—I will. I believe, Horatio, with all your skepticism about you, you will allow that good to be constant which is never absent from you, and that to be durable which never ends but with your being.

Hor.—Yes, go on.

Phil.—That can never be the good of a creature which when present the creature may be miserable, and when absent is certainly so.

Hor.—I think not; but pray explain what you mean, for I am not much used to this abstract way of reasoning.

Phil.—I mean all the pleasures of sense. The good of man cannot consist in the mere pleasures of sense, because when any one of those objects which you love is absent or cannot be come at, you are certainly miserable; and if the faculty be impaired, though the object be present, you cannot enjoy it. So that this sensual good depends upon a thousand things without and within you and all out of your power. Can this then be the good of man? Say, Horatio, what think you, is not this a checkered, fleeting, fantastical good? Can that, in any propriety of speech, be called the good of man which even while he is tasting he may be miserable, and which when he cannot taste he is necessarily so? Can that be our good which costs us a great deal of pains to obtain, which cloys in possessing, for which we must wait the return of appetite before we can enjoy again? Or is that our good which we can come at without difficulty, which is heightened by possession, which never ends in weariness and disappointment, and which the more we enjoy the better qualified we are to enjoy on?

Hor.—The latter, I think; but why do you torment me thus? Philocles, show me this good immediately.

Phil.—I have showed you what it is not: it is not sensual, but it is rational and moral good. It is doing all the good we can to others, by acts of humanity, friendship, generosity, and benevolence; this is that constant and durable good which will afford contentment and satisfaction always alike, without variation or diminution. I speak to your experience now, Horatio. Did you ever find yourself weary of relieving the miserable, or of raising the distressed into life or happiness? Or rather, do not you find the pleasure grow upon you by repetition, and that it is greater in the reflection than in the act itself? Is there a pleasure upon earth to be compared with that which arises from the sense of making others happy? Can this pleasure ever be absent, or ever end but with your being? Does it not always accompany you? Doth not it lie down and rise with you, live as long as you live, give you consolation in the hour of death, and remain with you when all other things are going to forsake you, or you them?

Hor.—How glowingly you paint, Philocles. Methinks Horatio is amongst the enthusiasts. I feel the passion; I am enchantingly convinced, but I do not know why; overborne by something stronger than reason. Sure some divinity speaks within me. But prithee, Philocles, give me the cause why this rational and moral good so infinitely excels the mere natural or sensual.

Phil.—I think, Horatio, that I have clearly shown you the difference between merely natural or sensual good and rational or moral good. Natural or sensual pleasure continues no longer than the action itself; but this divine or moral pleasure continues when the action is over, and swells and grows upon your hand by reflection. The one is inconstant, unsatisfying, of short duration, and attended with numberless ills; the other is constant, yields full satisfaction, is durable, and no evils preceding, accompanying, or following it. But if you inquire farther into the cause of this difference, and would know why the moral pleasures are greater than the sensual, perhaps the reason is the same as in all other creatures, that their happiness or chief good consists in acting up to their chief faculty, or that faculty which distinguishes them from all creatures of a different species. The chief faculty in man is his reason, and consequently his chief good, or that which may be justly called his good, consists not merely in action, but in reasonable action. By reasonable actions we understand those actions which are preservative of the human kind and naturally tend to produce real and unmixed happiness; and these actions, by way of distinction, we call actions morally good.

Hor.—You speak very clearly, Philocles; but, that no difficulty may remain on my mind, pray tell me what is the real difference between natural good and evil, and moral good and evil, for I know several people who use the terms without ideas.

Phil.—That may be. The difference lies only in this: that natural good and evil are pleasure and pain; moral good and evil are pleasure or pain produced with intention and design; for it is the intention only that makes the agent morally good or bad.

Hor.—But may not a man with a very good intention do an evil action?

Phil.—Yes; but then he errs in his judgment, though his design be good. If his error is inevitable, or such as, all things considered, he could not help, he is inculpable; but if it arose through want of diligence in forming his judgment about the nature of human actions, he is immoral and culpable.

Hor.—I find, then, that in order to please ourselves rightly, or to do good to others morally, we should take great care of our opinions.

Phil.—Nothing concerns you more; for as the happiness or real good of men consists in right action, and right action cannot be produced without right opinion, it behooves us, above all things in this world, to take care that our own opinions of things be according to the nature of things. The foundation of all virtue and happiness is thinking rightly. He who sees an action is right—that is, naturally tending to good— and does it because of that tendency, he only is a moral man; and he alone is capable of that constant, durable, and invariable good which has been the subject of this conversation.

Hor.—How, my dear philosophical guide, shall I be able to know, and determine certainly, what is right and wrong in life?

Phil.—As easily as you distinguish a circle from a square, or light from darkness. Look, Horatio, into the sacred book of nature; read your own nature, and view the relation which other men stand in to you, and you to them, and you will immediately see what constitutes human happiness, and consequently what is right.

Hor.—We are just coming into town, and can say no more at present. You are my good genius, Philocles. You have showed me what is good. You have redeemed me from the slavery and misery of folly and vice, and made me a free and happy being.

Phil.—Then I am the happiest man in the world. Be you steady, Horatio. Never depart from reason and virtue.

Hor.—Sooner will I lose my existence. Good night, Philocles.

Phil.—Adieu, dear Horatio!

BIBLIOGRAPHY

FRANKLIN, Benjamin, *The Works of Benjamin Franklin*, ed. by Jared Sparks. Boston: Hilliard, Gray and Co., 1840, 10 vols.

———— *The Writings of Benjamin Franklin*, ed. by A. H. Smyth. New York: Macmillan Co., 1905–07, 10 vols.

———— *The Works of Benjamin Franklin*, ed. by John Bigelow. New York: G. P. Putnam's Sons, 1904, 12 vols.

———— *Benjamin Franklin's Autobiographical Writings*, ed. by Carl Van Doren. New York: Viking Press, 1945.

———— *The Papers of Benjamin Franklin*, ed. by Leonard W. Labaree and Whitfield J. Bell, Jr. Vols. I, II, III. New Haven: Yale University Press, 1959–   , 40 vols. continuing.

BECKER, Carl L., *Benjamin Franklin*. Ithaca: Cornell U. Press, 1946.

COHEN, I. Bernard, *Benjamin Franklin. His Contributions to the American Tradition.* Indianapolis: Bobbs Merrill Co., 1953.

———— *Franklin and Newton. An Inquiry into Speculative Newtonian Experimental Science and Franklin's Work in Electricity as an Example Thereof.* Philadelphia: American Philosophical Society, 1956.

CRANE, V. W., *Benjamin Franklin, Englishman and American.* Baltimore: Williams & Wilkins Co., 1936.

FAY, Bernard, *Franklin, the Apostle of Modern Times.* Boston: Little, Brown & Co., 1929.

LUCAS, F. L., *The Art of Living; Four Eighteenth-Century Minds: Hume, Horace Walpole, Burke, Benjamin Franklin.* London: Cassell, 1959.

MOTT, F. L., JORGENSON, C. E., *Benjamin Franklin: Representative Selections with Introduction, Bibliography, and Notes.* New York: American Book Co., 1936.

RUSSELL, Phillips, *Benjamin Franklin, the First Civilized American,* New York: Brentano's, 1926.

SCHNEIDER, H. W., "The Significance of Benjamin Franklin's Moral Philosophy." *Studies in the History of Ideas,* New York: Columbia U. Press, 1925. Vol. II, pp. 293–312.

VAN DOREN, Carl, *Benjamin Franklin.* New York: Viking Press, 1938.

———— *Benjamin Franklin and Jonathan Edwards: Selections from Their Writings.* New York: Charles Scribner's Sons, 1920.

PART TWO

Reason and Revolution (1776-1800)

Thomas Jefferson

[1743–1826]

Thomas Jefferson, perhaps better than anyone else, expressed the "American mind," and enunciated and defended in his life its democratic and republican principles. Jefferson was hardly a systematic thinker, nor were his basic ideas original. Jefferson was born of an aristocratic family in Virginia. He played a leading role in the great events of his day: author of the Declaration of Independence (1776), member of the Continental Congress, Governor of Virginia, Ambassador to France after Franklin, Secretary of State under Washington, Vice-President of the United States (1796–1800), and subsequently President (1800–08). A man of insatiable curiosity, widely read and interested in science, the arts, architecture, and philosophy, he is often cited as an example of the universal man.

Jefferson's reflections are scattered throughout many volumes of letters and notes. It is necessary, therefore, to piece these fragments together into a coherent picture. They are here listed under three headings (with some overlappings): Political Philosophy, Religious Philosophy, Moral Philosophy. The fundamental postulate of his political philosophy was his belief in the latent capacities of the people and in the efficacy of majority rule: "Governments derive their just powers from the consent of the governed." Jefferson, like Locke, believed in the doctrine of "natural rights" (based on self-

evidence) and in the right of revolution to secure these rights (he was sympathetic to the ideals of the French Revolution). While he had faith in the common man, he hoped that the best, a natural aristocracy, would be elected to office; and he thought that universal education was central to democracy. His ideal was an agrarian, decentralized society, rather than an industrial one, which, he feared, was more prone to corruption. He was a critic of slavery, though himself a slaveholder. In religion, Jefferson defended toleration and the principle of separation of church and state. A deist and a freethinker, he was bitterly attacked in his own day for atheism; he was a constant critic of Calvinism, of clerical authority, and he did not accept the divinity of Jesus. In moral philosophy, Jefferson took happiness (*eudaemonia*) as the chief good of man, sympathizing with Epicurus rather than Plato; but he also argues for the existence of a "moral sense." Jefferson, like others of the Enlightenment, had faith in reason, science and progress. In his epitaph, written by himself, he wished to be known as "the author of the Declaration of Independence, the statute of Virginia for religious liberty, and the father of the University of Virginia." Perhaps the best single expression of Jeffersonianism is his statement: "I have sworn upon the altar of God, eternal hostility against every form of tyranny over the mind of man."

POLITICAL PHILOSOPHY

THE DECLARATION OF INDEPENDENCE[1]

When in the course of human events it becomes necessary for one people to dissolve the political bands which have connected them with another, and to assume among the powers of the earth, the separate and equal station to which the laws of Nature and of Nature's God entitle them, a decent respect to the opinions of mankind requires that they should declare the causes which impel them to the separation. We hold these truths to be self-evident, that all men are created equal, that they are endowed by their Creator with certain inalienable Rights, that among these are life, liberty and the pursuit of happiness. That to secure these rights, governments are instituted among men, deriving their just powers from the consent of the governed, that whenever any form of government becomes destructive of these ends, it is the right of the people to alter or to abolish it, and to institute new government, laying its foundation on such principles and organizing its powers in such form, as to them shall seem most likely to effect their safety and happiness. Prudence, indeed, will dictate that governments long established should not be changed for light and transient causes; and accordingly all experience hath shown that mankind are more disposed to suffer, while evils are sufferable, than to right themselves by abolishing the forms to which they are accustomed. But when a long train of abuses and usurpations, pursuing invariably the same object evinces a design to reduce them under absolute despotism, it is their right, it is their duty, to throw off such government, and to provide new guards for their future security. . . .

ON THE DISTINCTION BETWEEN
NATURAL AND CIVIL RIGHTS [2]

Suppose twenty persons, strangers to each other, to meet in a country not before inhabited. Each would be a sovereign in his own natural right. His will would be his law, but his power, in many cases, inadequate to his right, and the consequence would be that each might be exposed, not only to each other but to the other nineteen.

[1] In Congress, July 4, 1776.
[2] "Reflections on the Articles of Confederation." Reprinted in G. Chinard, *Thomas Jefferson*, Boston: Little, Brown, 1929, pp. 80–81, from a manuscript in the Library of Congress.

It would then occur to them that their condition would be much improved, if a way could be devised to exchange that quantity of danger into so much protection, so that each individual should possess the strength of the whole number. As all their rights, in the first case are natural rights, and the exercise of those rights supported only by their own natural individual power, they would begin by distinguishing between those rights they could individually exercise fully and perfectly and those they could not.

Of the first kind are the rights of thinking, speaking, forming and giving opinions, and perhaps all those which can be fully exercised by the individual without the aid of exterior assistance—or in other words, rights of personal competency. Of the second kind are those of personal protection, of acquiring and possessing property, in the exercise of which the individual natural power is less than the natural right.

Having drawn this line they agree to retain individually the first class of rights or those of personal competency; and to detach from their personal possession the second class, or those of defective power and to accept in lieu thereof a right to the whole power produced by a condensation of all the parts. These I conceive to be civil rights or rights of compact, and are distinguishable from natural rights, because in the one we act wholly in our own person, in the other we agree not to do so, but act under the guarantee of society.

ON REBELLION[3]

Yet where does this anarchy exist? Where did it ever exist, except in the single instance of Massachusetts?[4] And can history produce an instance of rebellion so honorably conducted? I say nothing of its motives. They were founded in ignorance, not wickedness. God forbid we should ever be twenty years without such a rebellion. The people cannot be all, and always, well-informed. The part which is wrong will be discontented in proportion to the importance of the facts they misconceive. If they remain quiet under such misconceptions it is a lethargy, the forerunner of death to the public liberty. We have had 13 states independent 11 years. There has been one rebellion. That comes to one rebellion in a century and a half for each state. What country before ever existed a century and a half without a rebellion? and what country can preserve its liberties if their rulers are not warned from time to time that their people preserve the spirit of resistance? Let them take arms. The remedy is to set them right

---

[3] Letter to William S. Smith (November 13, 1787). *The Writings of Thomas Jefferson*, ed. by Paul L. Ford, N. Y., G. P. Putnam's Sons, 1892–99, Vol. IV, p. 467.
[4] This refers to Shays's Rebellion.

as to facts, pardon and pacify them. What signify a few lives lost in a century or two? The tree of liberty must be refreshed from time to time with the blood of patriots and tyrants. It is its natural manure.

ON NATURAL ARISTOCRACY[5]

I agree with you that there is a natural aristocracy among men. The grounds of this are virtue and talents. Formerly, bodily powers gave place among the *aristoi*. But since the invention of gunpowder has armed the weak as well as the strong with missile death, bodily strength, like beauty, good humor, politeness and other accomplishments, has become but an auxiliary ground for distinction. There is also an artificial aristocracy, founded on wealth and birth, without either virtue or talents; for with these it would belong to the first class. The natural aristocracy I consider as the most precious gift of nature, for the instruction, the trusts, and government of society. And indeed, it would have been inconsistent in creation to have formed man for the social state, and not to have provided virtue and wisdom enough to manage the concerns of the society. May we not even say, that that form of government is the best, which provides the most effectually for a pure selection of these natural *aristoi* into the offices of government? The artificial aristocracy is a mischievous ingredient in government, and provision should be made to prevent its ascendancy. On the question, what is the best provision, you and I differ; but we differ as rational friends, using the free exercise of our own reason, and mutually indulging its errors. You think it best to put the pseudo-*aristoi* into a separate chamber of legislation, where they may be hindered from doing mischief by their co-ordinate branches, and where, also, they may be a protection to wealth against the agrarian and plundering enterprises of the majority of the people. I think that to give them power in order to prevent them from doing mischief, is arming them for it, and increasing instead of remedying the evil. For if the co-ordinate branches can arrest their action, so may they that of the co-ordinates. Mischief can be done negatively as well as positively. Of this, a cabal in the Senate of the United States has furnished many proofs. Nor do I believe them necessary to protect the wealthy; because enough of these will find their way into every branch of the legislation, to protect themselves. From fifteen to twenty legislatures of our own, in action for thirty years past, have proved that no fears of an equalization of property are to be apprehended from them. I think the best remedy is exactly that provided by all our constitutions,

---

[5] Letter to John Adams (Oct. 28, 1813) in *The Writings of Thomas Jefferson*, ed. by P. L. Ford, Vol. IX, pp. 425–28; *Autobiography*, Vol. I, p. 49.

to leave to the citizens the free election and separation of the *aristoi* from the pseudo-*aristoi*, of the wheat from the chaff. In general they will elect the really good and wise. In some instances, wealth may corrupt, and birth blind them; but not in sufficient degree to endanger the society. . . .

With respect to aristocracy, we should further consider, that before the establishment of the American States, nothing was known to history but the man of the old world, crowded within limits either small or overcharged, and steeped in the vices which that situation generates. A government adapted to such men would be one thing; but a very different one, that for the man of these States. Here everyone may have land to labor for himself, if he chooses; or, preferring the exercise of any other industry, may exact from it such compensation as not only to afford a comfortable subsistence, but wherewith to provide for a cessation from labor in old age. Everyone, by his property, or by his satisfactory situation, is interested in the support of law and order. And such men may safely and advantageously reserve to themselves a wholesome control over their public affairs, and a degree of freedom, which, in the hands of the canaille of the cities of Europe, would be instantly perverted to the demolition and destruction of everything public and private.

In the earlier times of the colony, when lands were to be obtained for little or nothing, some provident individuals procured large grants, and, desirous of founding great families for themselves, settled them on their descendants in fee tail. The transmission of this property from generation to generation in the same name raised up a distinct set of families who, being privileged by law in the perpetuation of their wealth were thus formed into a Patrician order, distinguished by the splendor and luxury of their establishments. . . . To annul this privilege, and instead of an aristocracy of wealth, of more harm and danger, than benefit to society, to make an opening for the aristocracy of virtue and talent, which nature has wisely provided for the direction of the interests of society, and scattered with equal hand through all its conditions, was deemed essential to a well-ordered republic.

ON MAJORITY RULE[6]

It is my principle that the will of the majority should always prevail. If they approve the proposed Convention in all its parts, I shall concur in it cheerfully, in hopes that they will amend it when-

[6] Letter to James Madison (Dec. 20, 1787). *The Writings of Thomas Jefferson*, ed. by P. L. Ford, Vol. IV, pp. 479–80.

ever they shall find it work wrong. I think our governments will remain virtuous for many centuries; as long as they are chiefly agricultural; and this will be as long as there shall be vacant lands in any part of America. When they get piled upon one another in large cities, as in Europe, they will become corrupt as in Europe. Above all things I hope the education of the common people will be attended to; convinced that on their good sense we may rely with the most security for the preservation of a due degree of liberty.

ON THE WILL OF THE NATION[7]

We surely cannot deny to any nation that right whereon our own government is founded, that every one may govern itself under whatever forms it pleases, and change these forms at its own will, and that it may transact its business with foreign nations through whatever organ it thinks proper, whether King, convention, assembly, committee, President, or whatever else it may choose. The will of the nation is the only thing essential to be regarded.

ON THE FREEDOM OF THE PRESS[8]

No government ought to be without censors: and where the press is free, no one ever will. If virtuous, it need not fear the fair operations of attack and defense. Nature has given to man no other means of sifting out the truth either in religion, law, or politics. I think it as honorable to the government neither to know, nor notice, its sycophants or censors, as it would be undignified and criminal to pamper the former and persecute the latter.

ON SLAVERY[9]

I had always hoped that the younger generation receiving their early impressions after the flame of liberty had been kindled in every breast, and had become as it were the vital spirit of every American, that the generous temperament of youth, analogous to the motion of their blood, and above the suggestions of avarice, would have sympathized with oppression, and found their love of liberty beyond their own share in it. But my intercourse with them, since my return has not been sufficient to ascertain that they had made toward this

[7] Letter to the U. S. Minister to France (Dec. 30, 1792). *The Writings of Thomas Jefferson*, ed. by P. L. Ford, Vol. VI, p. 149.

[8] Letter to President Washington (Sept. 9, 1792). *The Writings of Thomas Jefferson*, ed. by P. L. Ford, Vol. VI, p. 108.

[9] Letter to Edward Coles (August 25, 1814). *The Writings of Thomas Jefferson*, ed. by P. L. Ford, Vol. IX, pp. 478–79.

point the progress I had hoped. Your solitary but welcome voice is the first which had brought this sound to my ear; and I have considered the general silence which prevails on this subject as indicating an apathy unfavorable to every hope. Yet the hour of emancipation is advancing, in the march of time. It will come; and whether brought on by the generous energy of our own minds; or by the bloody process of Santo Domingo, excited and conducted by the power of our present enemy, if once stationed permanently within our country, and offering asylum and arms to the oppressed, is a leaf of our history not yet turned over. As to the method by which this difficult work is to be effected, if permitted to be done by ourselves, I have seen no proposition so expedient on the whole, as that of emancipation of those born after a given day, and of their education and expatriation after a given age. This would give time for a gradual extinction of that species of labor and substitution of another, and lessen the severity of the shock which an operation so fundamental cannot fail to produce. For men probably of any color, but of this color we know, brought from their infancy without necessity for thought or forecast, are by their habits rendered as incapable as children of taking care of themselves, and are extinguished promptly wherever industry is necessary for raising young. In the meantime they are pests in society by their idleness, and the depredations to which this leads them. Their amalgamation with the other color produces a degradation to which no lover of his country, no lover of excellence in the human character can innocently consent. . . . My opinion has ever been that, until more can be done for them, we should endeavor, with those whom fortune has thrown on our hands, to feed and clothe them well, protect them from all ill-usage, require such reasonable labor only as is performed voluntarily by freemen, and be led by no repugnancies to abdicate them, and our duties to them. The laws do not permit us to turn them loose, if that were for their good: and to commute them for other property is to commit them to those whose usage of them we cannot control.

ON EDUCATION [10]

By that part of our plan which prescribes the selection of the youths of genius from among the classes of the poor, we hope to avail the State of those talents which nature has sown as liberally among the poor as the rich, but which perish without use, if not sought for and cultivated. But of all the views of this law none is more important,

[10] "Notes on Virginia (1781–82)," *The Writings of Thomas Jefferson*, ed. by A. Bergh, Wash., D. C., 1903, Vol. II, pp. 203–08, 225–8, 300–3.

none more legitimate, than that of rendering the people the safe, as they are the ultimate, guardians of their own liberty. For this purpose the reading in the first stage, where they will receive their whole education, is proposed, as has been said, to be chiefly historical. History, by apprising them of the past, will enable them to judge of the future; it will avail them of the experience of other times and other nations; it will qualify them as judges of the actions and designs of men; it will enable them to know ambition under every disguise it may assume; and knowing it, to defeat its views. In every government on earth is some trace of human weakness, some germ of corruption and degeneracy, which cunning will discover, and wickedness insensibly open, cultivate, and improve. Every government degenerates when trusted to the rulers of the people alone. The people themselves, therefore, are its only safe depositories. And to render even them safe, their minds must be improved to a certain degree. This indeed is not all that is necessary, though it be essentially necessary. An amendment of our constitution must here come in aid of the public education. The influence over government must be shared among all people. If every individual which composes their mass participates of the ultimate authority, the government will be safe; because the corrupting the whole mass will exceed any private resources of wealth; and public ones cannot be provided but by levies on the people. In this case every man would have to pay his own price. The government of Great Britain has been corrupted, because but one man in ten has a right to vote for members of parliament. The sellers of the government, therefore, get nine-tenths of their price clear. It has been thought that corruption is restrained by confining the right of suffrage to a few of the wealthier of the people; but it would be more effectually restrained by an extension of that right to such members as would bid defiance to the means of corruption.

RELIGIOUS PHILOSOPHY

ON THE SEPARATION BETWEEN CHURCH AND STATE [11]

Believing with you that religion is a matter which lies solely between man and his God, that he owes account to none other for his faith or his worship, that the legislative powers of government reach actions only, and not opinions, I contemplate with sovereign reverence

[11] Letter to the Danbury Baptist Association, Conn. (Jan. 1, 1802). *The Writings of Thomas Jefferson*, ed. by H. A. Washington, N. Y., 1854, Vol. VIII, p. 113.

that act of the whole American people which declared that their legislature should "make no law respecting an establishment of religion, or prohibiting the free exercise thereof," thus building a wall of separation between church and state. Adhering to this expression of the supreme will of the nation in behalf of the rights of conscience, I shall see with sincere satisfaction the progress of those sentiments which tend to restore to man all his natural rights, convinced he has no natural right in opposition to his social duties.

ON RELIGIOUS LIBERTY[12]

Well aware that Almighty God hath created the mind free; that all attempts to influence it by temporal punishments or burdens, or by civil incapacitations, tend only to beget habits of hypocrisy and meanness, and are a departure from the plan of the Holy Author of our religion, who being Lord both of body and mind, yet chose not to propagate it by coercions on either, as was in his Almighty power to do; that the impious presumption of legislators and rulers, civil as well as ecclesiastical, who, being themselves but fallible and uninspired men, have assumed dominion over the faith of others, setting up their own opinions and modes of thinking as the only true and infallible, and as such endeavoring to impose them on others, hath established and maintained false religions over the greatest part of the world, and through all time; that to compel a man to furnish contributions of money for the propagation of opinions which he disbelieves, is sinful and tyrannical; that even the forcing him to support this or that teacher of his own religious persuasion, is depriving him of the comfortable liberty of giving his contributions to the particular pastor whose morals he would make his pattern, and whose powers he feels most persuasive to righteousness, and is withdrawing from the ministry those temporal rewards, which, proceeding from an approbation of their personal conduct, are an additional incitement to earnest and unremitting labors for the instruction of mankind; that our civil rights have no dependence on our religious opinions, more than our opinions in physics or geometry; that, therefore, the proscribing any citizen as unworthy the public confidence by laying upon him an incapacity of being called to the offices of trust and emolument, unless he profess or renounce this or that religious opinion, is depriving him injuriously of those privileges and advantages to which in common with his fellow citizens he has a natural right; that it tends also to corrupt the principles of that very religion it is meant to encourage,

---

[12] *An Act for Establishing Religious Freedom Passed in the Assembly of Virginia in the Beginning of the Year 1786* (Jefferson regarded this Act as one of his most important contributions to humanity).

by bribing, with a monopoly of worldly honors and emoluments, those who will externally profess and conform to it; that though indeed these are criminal who do not withstand such temptation, yet neither are those innocent who lay the bait in their way; that to suffer the civil magistrate to intrude his powers into the field of opinion and to restrain the profession or propagation of principles, on the supposition of their ill tendency, is a dangerous fallacy, which at once destroys all religious liberty, because he being of course judge of that tendency, will make his opinions the rule of judgment, and approve or condemn the sentiments of others only as they shall square with or differ from his own; that it is time enough for the rightful purposes of civil government, for its officers to interfere when principles break out into overt acts against peace and good order; and finally, that truth is great and will prevail if left to herself, that she is the proper and sufficient antagonist to error, and has nothing to fear from the conflict, unless by human interposition disarmed of her natural weapons, free argument and debate, errors ceasing to be dangerous when it is permitted freely to contradict them.

Be it therefore enacted by the General Assembly, That no man shall be compelled to frequent or support any religious worship, place, or ministry whatsoever, nor shall be enforced, restrained, molested, or burdened in his body or goods, nor shall otherwise suffer on account of his religious opinions or belief; but that all men shall be free to profess, and by argument to maintain, their opinions in matters of religion, and that the same shall in nowise diminish, enlarge, or affect their civil capacities.

And though we well know this Assembly, elected by the people for the ordinary purposes of legislation only, have no power to restrain the acts of succeeding assemblies, constituted with the powers equal to our own, and that therefore to declare this act irrevocable would be of no effect in law, yet we are free to declare, and do declare, that the rights hereby asserted are of the natural rights of mankind, and that if any act shall be hereafter passed to repeal the present or to narrow its operation, such act will be an infringement of natural right.

ON REASON IN RELIGION[13]

Your reason is now mature enough to examine this object. In the first place divest yourself of all bias in favor of novelty and singularity of opinion. Indulge them in any other subject rather than that of religion. It is too important, and the consequences of error may be too serious. On the other hand shake off all the fears and servile prejudices

[13] Letter to Peter Carr (August 10, 1787). *The Writings of Thomas Jefferson,* ed. by P. L. Ford, Vol. IV, pp. 430–32.

under which weak minds are servilely crouched. Fix reason firmly in her seat, and call to her tribunal every fact, every opinion. Question with boldness even the existence of a god; because, if there be one, he must more approve of the homage of reason, than that of blind-fold fear. You will naturally examine first the religion of your own country. Read the Bible then, as you would read Livy or Tacitus. The facts which are within the ordinary course of nature you will believe on the authority of the writer, as you do those of the same kind in Livy and Tacitus. The testimony of the writer weighs in their favor in one scale, and their not being against the laws of nature does not weigh against them. But those facts in the Bible which contradict the laws of nature, must be examined with more care, and under a variety of faces. Here you must recur to the pretensions of the writer to inspiration from God. Examine upon what evidence his pretensions are founded, and whether that evidence is so strong as that its falsehood would be more improbable than a change in the laws of nature in the case he relates. . . . You will next read the New Testament. It is the history of a personage called Jesus. Keep in your eye the opposite pretensions: (1) of those who say he was begotten by God, born of a virgin, suspended and reversed the laws of nature at will, and ascended bodily into heaven; and (2) of those who say he was a man of illegitimate birth, of a benevolent heart, enthusiastic mind, who set out without pretensions to divinity, ended in believing them, and was punished capitally for sedition by being gibbetted according to the Roman law which punished the first commission of that offense by whipping, and the second by exile or death *in furca*. (See this law in the Digest Lib. 48. tit. 19 #28. 3. & Lipsius Lib. 2. de cruce. cap. 2.) These questions are examined in the books I have mentioned under the head of religion, and several others. They will assist you in your inquiries, but keep your reason firmly on the watch in reading them all. Do not be frightened from this inquiry by any fear of its consequences. If it ends in a belief that there is no God, you will find incitements to virtue in the comfort and pleasantness you feel in its exercise, and the love of others which it will procure you. If you find reason to believe there is a god, a consciousness that you are acting under his eye, and that he approves you, will be a vast addi-tional incitement; if that there be a future state, the hope of a happy existence in that increases the appetite to deserve it; if that Jesus was also a god, you will be comforted by a belief in his aid and love. In fine, I repeat that you must lay aside all prejudice on both sides, and neither believe nor reject anything because any other persons, or description of persons have rejected or believed it. Your own reason is the only oracle given you by heaven, and you are answerable not only for the rightness but uprightness of the decision.

I forgot to observe when speaking of the New Testament that you should read all the histories of Christ, as well of those whom a council of ecclesiastics have decided for us to be pseudo-evangelists, as those they named evangelists. Because these pseudo-evangelists pretended to inspiration as much as the others, and you are to judge their pretensions by your own reason, and not by the reason of those ecclesiastics.

ON DEISM[14]

. . . I can never join Calvin in addressing *his* God. He was indeed an atheist, which I can never be; or rather his religion was daemonism. If ever man worshiped a false God, he did. The being described in his five points, is not the God whom you and I acknowledge and adore, the creator and benevolent governor of the world; but a daemon of malignant spirit. It would be more pardonable to believe in no God at all, than to blaspheme him by the atrocious attributes of Calvin. Indeed, I think that every Christian sect gives a great handle to atheism by their general dogma, that, without a revelation, there would not be sufficient proof of the being of a God. Now one-sixth of mankind only are supposed to be Christians: the other five-sixths then, who do not believe in the Jewish and Christian revelation, are without a knowledge of the existence of a God! This gives completely a *gain de cause* to the disciples of Ocellus, Timaeus, Spinoza, Diderot, and D'Holbach. The argument which they rest on as triumphant and unanswerable is, that in every hypothesis of cosmogony, you must admit an eternal pre-existence of something; and according to the rule of sound philosophy you are never to employ two principles to solve a difficulty when one will suffice. They say then, that it is more simple to believe at once in the eternal pre-existence of the world, as it is now going on, and may forever go on by the principle of reproduction which we see and witness, than to believe in the eternal pre-existence of an ulterior cause, or creator of the world, a being whom we see not and know not, of whose form, substance and mode, or place of existence, or of action, no sense informs us, no power of the mind enables us to delineate or comprehend. On the contrary, I hold (without appeal to revelation) that when we take a view of the universe, in its parts, general or particular, it is impossible for the human mind not to perceive and feel a conviction of design, consummate skill, and indefinite power in every atom of its composition. The movements of the heavenly bodies, so exactly held in their course by the balance

---

[14] Letter to John Adams (April 11, 1823). *The Writings of Thomas Jefferson,* ed. by A. Bergh, Vol. IV, pp. 363-64.

of centrifugal and centripetal forces; the structure of our earth itself, with its distribution of lands, waters and atmosphere; animal and vegetable bodies, examined in all their minutest particles; insects, mere atoms of life, yet as perfectly organized as man or mammoth; the mineral substances, their generation and uses; it is impossible, I say, for the human mind not to believe, that there is in all this, design, cause and effect, up to an ultimate cause, a fabricator of all things from matter and motion, their preserver and regulator while permitted to exist in their present forms, and their regenerator into new and other forms. We see, too, evident proofs of the necessity of a super-intending power, to maintain the universe in its course and order. Stars, well known, have disappeared, new ones have come into view; comets, in their incalculable courses, may run foul of suns and planets, and require renovation under other laws, certain races of animals are become extinct; and were there no restoring power, all existences might extinguish successively, one by one, until all should be reduced to a shapeless chaos. So irresistible are these evidences of an intelligent and powerful agent, that, of the infinite numbers of men who have existed through all time, they have believed, in the proportion of a million at least to unit, in the hypothesis of an external pre-existence of a creator, rather than in that of a self-existent universe. Surely this unanimous sentiment renders this more probable, than that of the few in the other hypothesis. Some early Christians, indeed, have believed in the co-eternal pre-existence of both the creator and the world, without changing their relation of cause and effect. That this was the opinion of Saint Thomas, we are informed by Cardinal Toleta. . . .

ON PLATONISM AND CHRISTIANITY[15]

. . . I am just returned from one of my long absences, having been at my other home for five weeks past. Having more leisure there than here for reading, I amused myself with reading seriously Plato's *Republic*. I am wrong, however, in calling it amusement, for it was the heaviest task-work I ever went through. I had occasionally before taken up some of his other works, but scarcely ever had patience to go through a whole dialogue. While wading through the whimsies, the puerilities, and unintelligible jargon of this work, I laid it down often to ask myself, how it could have been, that the world should have so long consented to give reputation to such nonsense as this? How the *soi-disant* Christian world, indeed, should have done it, is a piece of historical curiosity. But how could the Roman good sense do it? And

[15] From letter to John Adams (July 5, 1814). *The Writings of Thomas Jefferson*, ed. by P. L. Ford, Vol. IX, p. 460.

particularly, how could Cicero bestow such eulogies on Plato? Although Cicero did not wield the dense logic of Demosthenes, yet he was able, learned, laborious, practiced in the business of the world, and honest. He could not be the dupe of mere style, of which he was himself the first master in the world. With the moderns, I think, it is rather a matter of fashion and authority. Education is chiefly in the hands of persons who, from their profession, have an interest in the reputation and the dreams of Plato. They give the tone while at school, and few in their after years have occasion to revise their college opinions. But fashion and authority apart, and bringing Plato to the test of reason, take from him his sophisms, futilities and incomprehensibilities, and what remains? In truth, he is one of the race of genuine sophists, who has escaped the oblivion of his brethren, first, by the elegance of his diction, but chiefly, by the adoption and incorporation of his whimsies into the body of artificial Christianity. His foggy mind is forever presenting the semblances of objects which, half-seen through a mist, can be defined neither in form nor dimension. Yet this, which should have consigned him to early oblivion, really procured him immortality of fame and reverence. The Christian priesthood, finding the doctrines of Christ leveled to every understanding and too plain to need explanation, saw in the mysticisms of Plato materials with which they might build up an artificial system, which might, from its indistinctness, admit everlasting controversy; give employment for their order, and introduce it to profit, power and preeminence. The doctrines which flowed from the lips of Jesus himself are within the comprehension of a child; but thousands of volumes have not yet explained the Platonisms engrafted on them: and for this obvious reason, that nonsense can never be explained. Their purposes, however, are answered. Plato is canonized: and it is now deemed as impious to question his merits as those of an Apostle of Jesus. He is peculiarly appealed to as an advocate of the immortality of the soul; and yet I will venture to say, that were there no better arguments than his in proof of it, not a man in the world would believe it. It is fortunate for us, that Platonic republicanism has not obtained the same favor as Platonic Christianity; or we should now have been all living, men, women and children, pell mell together, like the beasts of the field or forest. Yet "Plato is a great philosopher," said La Fontaine. But, says Fontenelle, "do you find his ideas very clear?" "Oh no! he is of an obscurity impenetrable." "Do you not find him full of contradictions?" "Certainly," replied La Fontaine, "he is but a sophist." Yet immediately after, he exclaims again, "Oh, Plato was a great philosopher." Socrates had reason, indeed, to complain of the misrepresentations of Plato; for in truth, his dialogues are libels on Socrates. . . .

SYLLABUS OF AN ESTIMATE OF THE MERIT OF THE DOCTRINES OF JESUS, COMPARED WITH THOSE OF OTHERS[16]

In a comparative view of the ethics of the enlightened nations of antiquity, of the Jews, and of Jesus, no notice should be taken of the corruptions of reason among the ancients, to wit, the idolatry and superstition of the vulgar, nor of the corruptions of Christianity by the learned among its professors.

Let a just view be taken of the moral principles inculcated by the most esteemed of the sects of ancient philosophy, or of their individuals; particularly Pythagoras, Socrates, Epicurus, Cicero, Epictetus, Seneca, Antoninus.

I. Philosophers. 1. Their precepts related chiefly to ourselves, and the government of those passions which, unrestrained, would disturb our tranquillity of mind.[17] In this branch of philosophy they were really great.

2. In developing our duties to others, they were short and defective. They embraced, indeed, the circles of kindred and friends, and inculcated patriotism, or the love of our country in the aggregate, as a primary obligation: toward our neighbors and countrymen they taught justice, but scarcely view them as within the circle of benevolence. Still less have they inculcated peace, charity and love to our fellow men, or embraced with benevolence the whole family of mankind.

II. Jews. 1. Their system was Deism; that is, the belief in one only God. But their ideas of him and of his attributes were degrading and injurious.

2. Their Ethics were not only imperfect, but often irreconcilable with the sound dictates of reason and morality, as they respect intercourse with those around us; and repulsive and antisocial, as respecting other nations. They needed reformation, therefore, in an eminent degree.

III. Jesus. In this state of things among the Jews, Jesus appeared. His parentage was obscure; his condition poor; his education null; his

---

[16] Letter to Benjamin Rush (April 21, 1803). *The Writings of Thomas Jefferson,* ed. by P. L. Ford, Vol. VIII, p. 223.

[17] To explain, I will exhibit the heads of Seneca's and Cicero's philosophical works, the most extensive of any we have received from the ancients. Of ten heads in Seneca, seven relate to ourselves, viz. *de ira, consolatio, de tranquilitate, de constantia sapientis, de otio sapientis, de vita beata, de brevitate vitae;* two relate to others, *de clementia, de beneficitis;* and one relates to the government of the world, *de providentia.* Of eleven tracts of Cicero, five respect ourselves, viz. *de finibus, Tusculana, academica, paradoxa, de Senectute;* one, *de officiis,* relates partly to ourselves, partly to others; one, *de amicitia,* relates to others; and four are on different subjects, to wit, *de natura deorum, de divinatione, de fato,* and *somnium Scipionis.*—J.

natural endowments great; his life correct and innocent; he was meek, benevolent, patient, firm, disinterested, and of the sublimest eloquence.

The disadvantages under which his doctrines appear are remarkable.

1. Like Socrates and Epictetus, he wrote nothing himself.

2. But he had not, like them, a Xenophon or an Arrian to write for him. I name not Plato, who only used the name of Socrates to cover the whimsies of his own brain. On the contrary, all the learned of his country, entrenched in its power and riches, were opposed to him, lest his labors should undermine their advantages; and the committing to writing his life and doctrines fell on unlettered and ignorant men; who wrote, too, from memory, and not till long after the transactions had passed.

3. According to the ordinary fate of those who attempt to enlighten and reform mankind, he fell an early victim to the jealousy and combination of the altar and the throne, at about thirty-three years of age, his reason having not yet attained the *maximum* of its energy, nor the course of his preaching, which was but of three years at most, presented occasions for developing a complete system of morals.

4. Hence the doctrines which he really delivered were defective as a whole, and fragments only of what he did deliver have come to us, mutilated, misstated, and often unintelligible.

5. They have been still more disfigured by the corruptions of schismatizing followers, who have found an interest in sophisticating and perverting the simple doctrines he taught, by engrafting on them the mysticisms of a Grecian sophist, frittering them into subtleties, and obscuring them with jargon, until they have caused good men to reject the whole in disgust, and to view Jesus himself as an impostor.

Nothwithstanding these disadvantages, a system of morals is presented to us, which, if filled up in the style and spirit of the rich fragments he left us, would be the most perfect and sublime that has ever been taught by man.

The question of his being a member of the Godhead, or in direct communication with it, claimed for him by some of his followers, and denied by others, is foreign to the present view, which is merely an estimate of the intrinsic merit of his doctrines.

1. He corrected the Deism of the Jews, confirming them in their belief of one only God, and giving them juster notions of his attributes and government.

2. His moral doctrines, relating to kindred and friends, were more pure and perfect than those of the most correct of the philosophers, and greatly more so than those of the Jews; and they went far beyond both in inculcating universal philanthropy, not only to kindred and friends, to neighbors and countrymen, but to all mankind, gathering all into one family, under the bonds of love, charity, peace,

common wants and common aids. A development of this head will evince the peculiar superiority of the system of Jesus over all others.

3. The precepts of philosophy, and of Hebrew code, laid hold of actions only. He pushed his scrutinies into the heart of man; erected his tribunal in the region of his thoughts, and purified the waters at the fountainhead.

4. He taught, emphatically, the doctrines of a future state, which was either doubted, or disbelieved by the Jews; and wielded it with efficacy, as an important incentive, supplementary to the other motives to moral conduct.

MORAL PHILOSOPHY

ON MORAL SENSE[18]

The copy of your *Second Thoughts on Instinctive Impulses*, with the letter accompanying it, was received just as I was setting out on a journey to this place, two or three days distant from Monticello. I brought it with me and read it with great satisfaction, and with the more as it contained exactly my own creed on the foundation of morality in man. It is really curious that on a question so fundamental, such a variety of opinions should have prevailed among men, and those, too, of the most exemplary virtue and first order of understanding. It shows how necessary was the care of the Creator in making the moral principle so much a part of our constitution as that no errors of reasoning or of speculation might lead us astray from its observance in practice. Of all the theories on this question, the most whimsical seems to have been that of Wollaston, who considers truth as the foundation of morality. The thief who steals your guinea does wrong only inasmuch as he acts a lie in using your guinea as if it were his own. Truth is certainly a branch of morality, and a very important one to society. But presented as its foundation, it is as if a tree taken up by the roots, had its stem reversed in the air, and one of its branches planted in the ground. Some have made the *love of God* the foundation of morality. This, too, is but a branch of our moral duties, which are generally divided into duties to God and duties to man. If we did a good act merely from the love of God and a belief that it is pleasing to Him, whence arises the morality of the atheist? It is idle to say, as some do, that no such being exists. We have the same evidence of

[18] Letter to Thomas Law (June 13, 1814). *The Writings of Thomas Jefferson,* ed. by A. Bergh, Vol. XIV, pp. 138–44.

the fact as of most of those we act on, to wit: their own affirmations, and their reasonings in support of them. I have observed, indeed, generally, that while in Protestant countries the defections from the Platonic Christianity of the priests is to Deism, in Catholic countries they are to atheism. Diderot, D'Alembert, D'Holbach, Condorcet, are known to have been among the most virtuous of men. Their virtue, then, must have had some other foundation than the love of God.

The τὸ καλόν of others is founded in a different faculty, that of taste, which is not even a branch of morality. We have indeed an innate sense of what we call beautiful, but that is exercised chiefly on subjects addressed to the fancy, whether through the eye in visible forms, as landscape, animal figure, dress, drapery, architecture, the composition of colors, etc., or to the imagination directly, as imagery, style, or measure in prose or poetry, or whatever else constitutes the domain of criticism or taste, a faculty entirely distinct from the moral one. Self-interest, or rather self-love, or egoism, have been more plausibly substituted as the basis of morality. But I consider our relations with others as constituting the boundaries of morality. With ourselves we stand on the ground of identity, not of relation, which last, requiring two subjects, excludes self-love confined to a single one. To ourselves, in strict language, we can owe no duties, obligation requiring also two parties. Self-love, therefore, is no part of morality. Indeed it is exactly its counterpart. It is the sole antagonist of virtue, leading us constantly by our propensities to self-gratification in violation of our moral duties to others. Accordingly, it is against this enemy that are erected the batteries of moralists and religionists, as the only obstacle to the practice of morality. Take from man his selfish propensities, and he can have nothing to seduce him from the practice of virtue. Or subdue those propensities by education, instruction or restraint, and virtue remains without a competitor. Egoism, in a broader sense, has been thus presented as the source of moral action. It has been said that we feed the hungry, clothe the naked, bind up the wounds of the man beaten by thieves, pour oil and wine into them, set him on our own beast and bring him to the inn, because we receive ourselves pleasure from these acts. So Helvetius, one of the best men on earth, and the most ingenious advocate of this principle, after defining "interest" to mean not merely that which is pecuniary, but whatever may procure us pleasure or withdraw us from pain (*De l'esprit*, 1758; 2, 1), says (*ibid.* 2, 2), "The humane man is he to whom the sight of misfortune is insupportable, and who to rescue himself from this spectacle is forced to succor the unfortunate object." This indeed is true. But it is one step short of the ultimate question. These good acts give us pleasure, but how happens it that they give us pleasure? Because nature hath implanted in our breasts a love of others, a sense of duty to them, a moral instinct, in short, which prompts us irresistibly to feel and to succor their distresses, and protest against the language of Helvetius (*ibid.* 2, 5), "what other motive than self-interest could determine a man to generous actions? It is as impossible for him to love what is good for the sake of good, as to love evil for the sake of evil." The Creator would indeed have been a bungling artist, had he intended man for a social animal, without planting in him social dispositions. It is true they are not planted in every man, because there is no rule without exceptions; but it is false reasoning which converts exceptions into the general rule. Some men are born without the organs of sight, or of hearing, or without hands. Yet it would be wrong to say that man is born without these faculties, and sight, hearing and hands may with truth enter into the general definition of man.

The want or imperfection of the moral sense in some men, like the want or imperfection of the senses of sight and hearing in others, is no proof that it is a general characteristic of the species. When it is wanting, we endeavor to supply the defect by education, by appeals to reason and calculation, by presenting to the being so unhappily conformed, other motives to do good and to eschew evil, such as the love, or the hatred, or rejection of those among whom he lives, and whose society is necessary to his happiness and even existence; demonstrations by sound calculation that honesty promotes interest in the long run; the rewards and penalties established by the laws; and ultimately the prospects of a future state of retribution for the evil as well as the good done while here. These are the correctives which are supplied by education, and which exercise the functions of the moralist, the preacher, and legislator; and they lead into a course of correct action all those whose disparity is not too profound to be eradicated. Some have argued against the existence of a moral sense, by saying that if nature had given us such a sense, impelling us to virtuous actions, and warning us against those which are vicious, then nature would also have designated, by some particular earmarks, the two sets of actions which are, in themselves, the one virtuous and the other vicious. Whereas, we find, in fact, that the same actions are deemed virtuous in one country and vicious in another. The answer is, that nature has constituted *utility* to man, the standard and test of virtue. Men living in different countries under different circumstances, different habits and regimens, may have different utilities; the same act, therefore, may be useful, and consequently virtuous in one country which is injurious and vicious in another differently circumstanced. I sincerely, then, believe with you in the general existence of a moral instinct. I think it the brightest gem with which the human character is studded, and the want of it as more degrading than the most hideous of the bodily deformities. I am happy in reviewing the roll of associates in this principle which you present in your second letter, some of which I had not before met with. To these might be added Lord Kaims, one of the ablest of our advocates, who goes so far as to say, in his *Principles of Natural Religion*, that a man owes no duty to which he is not urged by some impulsive feeling. This is correct, if referred to the standard of general feeling in the given case, and not to the feeling of a single individual. Perhaps I may misquote him, it being fifty years since I read his book.

ON HAPPINESS[19]

. . . As you say of yourself, I too am an Epicurian. I consider the genuine (not the imputed) doctrines of Epicurus as containing everything rational in moral philosophy which Greece and Rome have left us. Epictetus indeed, has given us what was good of the Stoics; all beyond, of their dogmas, being hypocrisy and grimace. Their great crime was in their calumnies of Epicurus and misrepresentations of his doctrines; in which we lament to see the candid character of Cicero engaging as an accomplice. Diffuse, vapid, rhetorical, but enchanting. His prototype Plato, eloquent as himself, dealing out mysticisms incomprehensible to the human mind, has been deified by certain sects usurping the name of Christians; because, in his foggy conceptions, they found a basis of impenetrable darkness whereon to rear fabrications as delirious, of their own invention. These they fathered blasphemously on Him whom they claimed as their Founder, but who would disclaim them with the indignation which their caricatures of His religion so justly excite. Of Socrates we have nothing genuine but in the *Memorabilia* of Xenophon; for Plato makes him one of his Collocutors merely to cover his own whimsies under the mantle of his name; a liberty of which we are told Socrates himself complained. Seneca is indeed a fine moralist, disfiguring his work at times with some Stoicisms, and affecting too much of antithesis and point, yet giving us on the whole a great deal of sound and practical morality. But the greatest of all the reformers of the depraved religion of His own country, was Jesus of Nazareth. Abstracting what is really His from the rubbish in which it is buried, easily distinguished by its luster from the dross of His biographers, and as separable from that as the diamond from the dunghill, we have the outlines of a system of the most sublime morality which has ever fallen from the lips of man; outlines which it is lamentable He did not live to fill up. Epictetus and Epicurus give laws for governing ourselves, Jesus a supple-

[19] Letter to William Short (Oct. 31, 1819). *The Writings of Thomas Jefferson*, ed. by P. L. Ford, Vol. X, pp. 143–46.

ment of the duties and charities we owe to others. The establishment of the innocent and genuine character of this benevolent Moralist, and the rescuing it from the imputation of imposture, which has resulted from artificial systems,[20] invented by ultra-Christian sects, unauthorized by a single word ever uttered by Him, is a most desirable object, and one to which Priestley has successfully devoted his labors and learning. It would in time, it is to be hoped, effect a quiet euthanasia of the heresies of bigotry and fanaticism which have so long triumphed over human reason, and so generally and deeply afflicted mankind; but this work is to be begun by winnowing the grain from the chaff of the historians of His life. I have sometimes thought of translating Epictetus (for he has never been tolerably translated into English) by adding the genuine doctrines of Epicurus from the *Syntagma* of Gassendi, and an abstract from the Evangelists of whatever has the stamp of the eloquence and fine imagination of Jesus. The last I attempted too hastily some twelve or fifteen years ago. It was the work of two or three nights only, at Washington, after getting through the evening task of reading the letters and papers of the day. But with one foot in the grave, these are now idle projects for me. My business is to beguile the wearisomeness of declining life, as I endeavor to do, by the delights of classical reading and of mathematical truths, and by the consolations of a sound philosophy, equally indifferent to hope and fear.

I take the liberty of observing that you are not a true disciple of our master Epicurus, in indulging the indolence to which you say you are yielding. One of his canons, you know, was that "That indulgence which presents a greater pleasure, or produces a greater pain, is to be avoided." Your love of repose will lead, in its progress, to a suspension of healthy exercise, a relaxation of mind, an indifference to everything around you, and finally to a debility of body, and hebetude of mind, the farthest of all things from the happiness which the well-regulated indulgences of Epicurus ensure; fortitude, you know, is one of his four cardinal virtues. That teaches us to meet and surmount difficulties; not to fly from them like cowards; and to fly, too, in vain, for they will meet and arrest us at every turn of our road. Weigh this matter well; brace yourself up; take a seat with Correa, and come and see the finest portion of your country, which, if you have not forgotten, you still do not know, because it is no longer the same as when you knew it. It will add much to the happiness of my recovery to be able to receive Correa and yourself, and prove the estimation in which I hold

[20] *E.g.* The immaculate conception of Jesus, His deification, the creation of the world by Him, His miraculous powers, His resurrection and visible ascension, His corporeal presence in the Eucharist, the Trinity, original sin, atonement, regeneration, election, orders of Hierarchy, etc.—J.

you both. Come, too, and see our incipient University, which has advanced with great activity this year. By the end of the next, we shall have elegant accommodations for seven professors, and the year following the professors themselves. No secondary character will be received among them. Either the ablest which America or Europe can furnish, or none at all. They will give us the selected society of a great city separated from the dissipations and levities of its ephemeral insects.

I am glad the bust of Condorcet has been saved and so well-placed. His genius should be before us; while the lamentable, but singular act of ingratitude which tarnished his latter days, may be thrown behind us.

I will place under this a syllabus of the doctrines of Epicurus,[21] somewhat in the lapidary style, which I wrote some twenty years ago; a like one of the philosophy of Jesus, of nearly the same age, it is too long to be copied. *Vale, et tibi persuade carissimum te esse mihi.*

BIBLIOGRAPHY

JEFFERSON, Thomas, *The Writings of Thomas Jefferson*, ed. by Paul L. Ford. New York: G.P. Putnam, 1892–99, 10 vols.

———— *The Writings of Thomas Jefferson*, ed. by A. Bergh. Washington, D.C.: Thomas Jefferson Memorial Assn., 1903, 20 vols.

[21] *Syllabus of the doctrines of Epicurus.*

Physical.—The Universe eternal.

Its parts, great and small, interchangeable.

Matter and Void alone.

Motion inherent in matter which is weighty and declining.

Eternal circulation of the elements of bodies.

Gods, an order of beings next superior to man, enjoying in their sphere, their own felicities; but not meddling with the concerns of the scale of beings below them.

Moral.—Happiness the aim of life.

Virtue the foundation of happiness.

Utility the test of virtue.

Pleasure active and In-do-lent.

In-do-lence is the absence of pain, the true felicity.

Active, consists in agreeable motion; it is not happiness, but the means to produce it.

Thus the absence of hunger is an article of felicity; eating the means to obtain it.

The *summum bonum* is to be not pained in body, nor troubled in mind.

i.e. In-do-lence of body, tranquillity of mind.

To procure tranquillity of mind we must avoid desire and fear, the two principal diseases of the mind.

Man is a free agent.

Virtue consists in: 1. Prudence. 2. Temperance. 3. Fortitude. 4. Justice.

To which are opposed: 1. Folly. 2. Desire. 3. Fear. 4. Deceit.—J.

_____ *The Writings of Thomas Jefferson*, ed. by H.A. Washington. New York: Riker, Thorne, 1854, 9 vols.

_____ *The Complete Jefferson*, ed. by Saul K. Padover. New York: Duell, Sloan & Pearce, 1943.

_____ *Thomas Jefferson on Democracy*. New York: Penguin Books, 1946.

_____ *The Papers of Thomas Jefferson*, ed. by Julian P. Boyd. Princeton: Princeton U. Press, 1950–61, vols. I–XVI available.

_____ *The Life and Morals of Jesus Christ of Nazareth Extracted Textually from the Gospels of Matthew, Mark, Luke, and John*. Philadelphia: David McKay, 1946; Boston: Beacon Press, 1951.

ADAMS, James T., *The Living Jefferson*. New York: Charles Scribner's, 1936.

BECKER, Carl L., *The Declaration of Independence*. New York: Harcourt, Brace, 1922.

BOORSTIN, Daniel J., *The Lost World of Thomas Jefferson*. New York: Henry Holt, 1948.

BOWERS, Claude G., *Jefferson and Hamilton*. Boston: Houghton Mifflin, 1925.

_____ *The Young Jefferson*. Boston: Houghton Mifflin, 1945.

CHINARD, Gilbert, *Thomas Jefferson*. Boston: Little, Brown, 1929.

ETHICS, Vol. LIII, No. 4, (July, 1943), "A Symposium on Jefferson." Papers by Claude G. Bowers, Herbert W. Schneider, Gilbert Chinard, Horace M. Kallen, T.V. Smith, Charles E. Merriam, and Frank P. Bourgin.

KOCH, Adrienne, *The Philosophy of Thomas Jefferson*. New York: Columbia U. Press, 1943.

LEHMANN-HARTLEBEN, Karl, *Thomas Jefferson, American Humanist*. New York: Macmillan Co., 1947.

MALONE, Dumas, *Jefferson and His Time*. Boston: Little, Brown, 1948–62, 3 vols.

MARTIN, Edwin T., *Thomas Jefferson: Scientist*. New York: Henry Schuman, 1952.

PRESCOTT, F.C., *Alexander Hamilton and Thomas Jefferson*. Representative Selections, with Introduction. Cincinnati: American Book Co., 1934.

RANDALL, H.S., *Life of Thomas Jefferson*. New York: Derby & Jackson, 1858, 3 vols.

SCHACHNER, Nathan, *Thomas Jefferson*. New York: Appleton-Century-Crofts, 1951, 2 vols.

WILTSE, C.M., *The Jeffersonian Tradition in American Democracy*. Chapel Hill, N.C.: U. of N.C. Press, 1935.

Thomas Paine

[1737–1809]

Thomas Paine was a spokesman for the Age of Reason and the Spirit of the Revolution, which captured America and France in the latter part of the eighteenth century. Born in England, the son of a Quaker, he migrated to America in 1774. Paine's pamphlet *Common Sense*, published in January of 1776, sold one hundred thousand copies, an enormous number at that time, and literally swept the Colonies. Paine himself believed that it was *Common Sense* which had aroused the Colonies against England and precipitated the Declaration of Independence—an overstatement, perhaps, although *Common Sense* was undeniably a factor in the development of the movement for independence. Paine was the intimate of Jefferson, Washington, Lafayette and the patriots of the Revolution; and during the War he published *The Crisis*, a series of sixteen pamphlets, which continued to have an influence on the course of events.

The Revolution having succeeded in America, Paine was inspired anew by the thought that a similar revolution might change the old order in Europe. After an eventful stay in England, where he became one of the spokesmen of the common people and feared by the government and the defenders of privilege, he fled to France in 1792.

At first he was feted by the French savants and philosophers and the leaders of the Revolution. Indeed he had the signal honor of being the only American, and one of three foreigners, to be elected to the National Convention. The *Rights of Man* (1791–92), reprinted in part below, was Paine's justification of that revolution against the bitter denunciations of Edmund Burke's *Reflections on the Revolution in France*. Paine, influenced by the ideas of Locke and Rousseau, argued for republicanism, natural rights, revolution, and against the conservative defense of precedence as the guide of law or hereditary monarchy as the principle of government.

Paine was not unmindful of the need for moderation in France and he opposed the death penalty for Louis XVI. Paine's own fortunes took a turn for the worse, and he was imprisoned for eleven months by Robespierre and the Jacobins during the "Reign of Terror." He was released (after the intervention of James Monroe) ill in health and spirit, convinced that George Washington and his American friends had abandoned him.

The first part of *The Age of Reason* (1793–95), a classic in freethinking, was finished hours before his arrest. The second part was written during and after his incarceration. Paine submitted to devastating criticism and satire both the Old and New Testaments, rejecting miracles, mysteries and prophecies, and claiming that the Scriptures were inconsistent and unsubstantiated. He looked upon Jesus as a moral individual, but Christianity as false. Instead he defended the principles of deism, or "rational religion." Sections from *The Age of Reason* are reprinted below.

Paine returned to America in 1802, revered for his work for the Revolutionary cause in America, but not for his French sojourn or his religious heresies. His later years were spent in defense of deism against the bitter attacks which his works aroused. A conservative reaction had set in; and Paine, earlier the darling of the liberals and radicals, now became a demon for the conservatives and reactionaries. He died, lonely and deserted by most of his erstwhile friends, not long after he had been denied the right to vote, on the ground that he was not an American citizen.

RIGHTS OF MAN

BEING AN ANSWER TO MR. BURKE'S ATTACK ON THE FRENCH REVOLUTION [1]

. . . Mr. Burke with his usual outrage, abused the *Declaration of the Rights of Man,* published by the National Assembly of France as the basis on which the constitution of France is built. This he calls "paltry and blurred sheets of paper about the rights of man." Does Mr. Burke mean to deny that *man* has any rights? If he does, then he must mean that there are no such things as rights anywhere, and that he has none himself; for who is there in the world but man? But if Mr. Burke means to admit that man has rights, the question then will be: What are those rights, and how man came by them originally?

The error of those who reason by precedents drawn from antiquity, respecting the rights of man, is that they do not go far enough into antiquity. They do not go the whole way. They stop in some of the intermediate stages of a hundred or a thousand years, and produce what was then done, as a rule for the present day. This is no authority at all. If we travel still farther into antiquity, we shall find a direct contrary opinion and practice prevailing; and if antiquity is to be authority, a thousand such authorities may be produced, successively contradicting each other; but if we proceed on, we shall at last come out right; we shall come to the time when man came from the hand of his Maker. What was he then? Man. Man was his high and only title, and a higher cannot be given him. But of titles I shall speak hereafter.

We are now got at the origin of man, and at the origin of his rights.

[1] First published in 1791.

As to the manner in which the world has been governed from that day to this, it is no farther any concern of ours than to make a proper use of the errors or the improvements which the history of it presents. Those who lived a hundred or a thousand years ago, were then moderns, as we are now. They had *their* ancients, and those ancients had others, and we also shall be ancients in our turn. If the mere name of antiquity is to govern in the affairs of life, the people who are to live a hundred or a thousand years hence, may as well take us for a precedent, as we make a precedent of those who lived a hundred or a thousand years ago. The fact is, that portions of antiquity, by proving everything, establish nothing. It is authority against authority all the way, till we come to the divine origin of the rights of man at the creation. Here our inquiries find a resting place, and our reason finds a home. If a dispute about the rights of man had arisen at the distance of a hundred years from the creation, it is to this source of authority they must have referred, and it is to this same source of authority that we must now refer.

Though I mean not to touch upon any sectarian principle of religion, yet it may be worth observing, that the genealogy of Christ is traced to Adam. Why then not trace the rights of man to the creation of man? I will answer the question. Because there have been upstart governments, thrusting themselves between, and presumptuously working to *un-make* man.

If any generation of men ever possessed the right of dictating the mode by which the world should be governed forever, it was the first generation that existed; and if that generation did it not, no succeeding generation can show any authority for doing it, nor can set any up. The illuminating and divine principle of the equal rights of man (for it has its origin from the Maker of man) relates, not only to the living individuals, but to generations of men succeeding each other. Every generation is equal in rights to generations which preceded it, by the same rule that every individual is born equal in rights with his contemporary.

Every history of the creation, and every traditionary account, whether from the lettered or unlettered world, however they may vary in their opinion or belief of certain particulars, all agree in establishing one point, *the unity of man;* by which I mean that men are all of *one degree,* and consequently that all men are born equal, and with equal natural right, in the same manner as if posterity had been continued by creation instead of generation, the latter being the only mode by which the former is carried forward; and consequently every child born into the world must be considered as deriving its existence from God. The world is as new to him as it was to the first man that existed, and his natural right in it is of the same kind.

The Mosaic account of the creation, whether taken as divine authority or merely historical, is full to this point, *the unity or equality of man.* The expression admits of no controversy. "And God said, Let us make man in our own image. In the image of God created he him; male and female created he them." The distinction of sexes is pointed out, but no other distinction is even implied. If this be not divine authority, it is at least historical authority, and shows that the equality of man, so far from being a modern doctrine, is the oldest upon record.

It is also to be observed that all the religions known in the world are founded, so far as they relate to man, on the *unity of man,* as being all of one degree. Whether in heaven or in hell, or in whatever state man may be supposed to exist hereafter, the good and the bad are the only distinctions. Nay, even the laws of governments are obliged to slide into this principle, by making degrees to consist in crimes and not in persons.

It is one of the greatest of all truths, and of the highest advantage to cultivate. By considering man in this light, and by instructing him to consider himself in this light, it places him in a close connection with all his duties, whether to his Creator or to the creation, of which he is a part; and it is only when he forgets his origin, or, to use a more fashionable phrase, his *birth and family,* that he becomes dissolute. It is not among the least of the evils of the present existing governments in all parts of Europe that man, considered as man, is thrown back to a vast distance from his Maker, and the artificial chasm filled up with a succession of barriers, or sort of turnpike gates, through which he has to pass. I will quote Mr. Burke's catalogue of barriers that he has set up between man and his Maker. Putting himself in the character of a herald, he says: "We fear God—we look with *awe* to kings—with affection to Parliaments—with duty to magistrates—with reverence to priests, and with respect to nobility." Mr. Burke has forgotten to put in "*chivalry.*" He has also forgotten to put in Peter.

The duty of man is not a wilderness of turnpike gates, through which he is to pass by tickets from one to the other. It is plain and simple, and consists but of two points. His duty to God, which every man must feel; and with respect to his neighbor, to do as he would be done by. If those to whom power is delegated do well, they will be respected: if not, they will be despised; and with regard to those to whom no power is delegated, but who assume it, the rational world can know nothing of them.

Hitherto we have spoken only (and that but in part) of the natural rights of man. We have now to consider the civil rights of man, and to show how the one originates from the other. Man did not enter into society to become *worse* than he was before, nor to have fewer rights than he had before, but to have those rights better secured. His natural rights are the foundation of all his civil rights. But in order to pursue this distinction with more precision, it will be necessary to mark the different qualities of natural and civil rights.

A few words will explain this. Natural rights are those which appertain to man in right of his existence. Of this kind are all the intellectual rights, or rights of the mind, and also all those rights of acting as an individual for his own comfort and happiness, which are not injurious to the natural rights of others. Civil rights are those which appertain to man in right of his being a member of society. Every civil right has for its foundation some natural right pre-existing in the individual, but to the enjoyment of which his individual power is not, in all cases, sufficiently competent. Of this kind are all those which relate to security and protection.

From this short review it will be easy to distinguish between that class of natural rights which man retains after entering into society and those which he throws into the common stock as a member of society.

The natural rights which he retains are all those in which the *power* to execute is as perfect in the individual as the right itself. Among this class, as is before mentioned, are all the intellectual rights, or rights of the mind; consequently religion is one of those rights. The natural rights which are not retained are all those in which, though the right is perfect in the individual, the power to execute them is defective. They answer not his purpose. A man, by natural right, has a right to judge in his own cause; and so far as the right of the mind is concerned, he never surrenders it. But what availeth it him to judge, if he has not power to redress? He therefore deposits this right in the common stock of society, and takes the arm of society, of which he is a part, in preference and in addition to his own. Society *grants* him nothing. Every man is a proprietor in society, and draws on the capital as a matter of right.

From these premises two or three certain conclusions will follow:

First, That every civil right grows out of a natural right; or, in other words, is a natural right exchanged.

Secondly, That civil power properly considered as such is made up of the aggregate of that class of the natural rights of man, which becomes defective in the individual in point of power, and answers not his purpose, but when collected to a focus becomes competent to the purpose of everyone.

Thirdly, That the power produced from the aggregate of natural rights, imperfect in power in the individual, cannot be applied to invade the natural rights which are retained in the individual, and in which the power to execute is as perfect as the right itself.

We have now, in a few words, traced man from a natural individual to a member of society, and shown, or endeavored to show, the quality of the natural rights retained, and of those which are exchanged for civil rights. . . .

THE AGE OF REASON [2]

PART THE FIRST. Being an Investigation of True and Fabulous Theology

Chapter I

It has been my intention, for several years past, to publish my thoughts upon religion; I am well aware of the difficulties that attend the subject, and, from that consideration, had reserved it to a more advanced period of life. I intended it to be the last offering I should make to my fellow citizens of all nations, and that at a time when the purity of the motive that induced me to it, could not admit of a question, even by those who might disapprove the work.

The circumstance that has now taken place in France of the total abolition of the whole national order of priesthood, and of everything appertaining to compulsive systems of religion, and compulsive articles of faith, has not only precipitated my intention, and rendered a work of this kind exceedingly necessary, lest, in the general wreck of superstition, of false systems of government, and false theology, we lose sight of morality, of humanity, and of the theology that is true.

As several of my colleagues, and others of my fellow citizens of France, have given me the example of making their voluntary and individual profession of faith, I also will make mine; and I do this with all that sincerity and frankness with which the mind of man communicates with itself.

I believe in one God, and no more; and I hope for happiness beyond this life.

I believe the equality of man; and I believe that religious duties consist in doing justice, loving mercy, and endeavoring to make our fellow creatures happy.

But, lest it should be supposed that I believe many other things in addition to these, I shall, in the progress of this work, declare the things I do not believe, and my reasons for not believing them.

I do not believe in the creed professed by the Jewish church, by the Roman church, by the Greek church, by the Turkish church, by the Protestant church, nor by any church that I know of. My own mind is my own church.

[2] First published in 1795.

All national institutions of churches, whether Jewish, Christian, or Turkish, appear to me no other than human inventions, set up to terrify and enslave mankind, and monopolize power and profit.

I do not mean by this declaration to condemn those who believe otherwise; they have the same right to their belief as I have to mine. But it is necessary to the happiness of man, that he be mentally faithful to himself. Infidelity does not consist in believing, or in disbelieving; it consists in professing to believe what he does not believe.

It is impossible to calculate the moral mischief, if I may so express it, that mental lying has produced in society. When a man has so far corrupted and prostituted the chastity of his mind, as to subscribe his professional belief to things he does not believe, he has prepared himself for the commission of every other crime. He takes up the trade of a priest for the sake of gain, and, in order to qualify himself for that trade, he begins with a perjury. Can we conceive anything more destructive to morality than this?

Soon after I had published the pamphlet, *Common Sense*, in America, I saw the exceeding probability that a revolution in the system of government would be followed by a revolution in the system of religion. The adulterous connection of church and state, wherever it had taken place, whether Jewish, Christian, or Turkish, had so effectually prohibited, by pains and penalties, every discussion upon established creeds, and upon first principles of religion, that until the system of government should be changed, those subjects could not be brought fairly and openly before the world; but that whenever this should be done, a revolution in the system of religion would follow. Human inventions and priestcraft would be detected; and man would return to the pure, unmixed, and unadulterated belief of one God, and no more.

Chapter II

Every national church or religion has established itself by pretending some special mission from God, communicated to certain individuals. The Jews have their Moses; the Christians their Jesus Christ, their apostles, and saints; and the Turks their Mohammed, as if the way to God was not open to every man alike.

Each of those churches show certain books, which they call *revelation*, or the word of God. The Jews say, that their word of God was given by God to Moses, face to face; the Christians say, that their word of God came by divine inspiration; and the Turks say, that their word of God (the Koran) was brought by an angel from heaven. Each of those churches accuse the other of unbelief; and, for my own part, I disbelieve them all.

As it is necessary to affix right ideas to words, I will, before I proceed further into the subject, offer some other observations on the word *revelation*. Revelation when applied to religion, means something communicated *immediately* from God to man.

No one will deny or dispute the power of the Almighty to make such a communication, if he pleases. But admitting, for the sake of a case, that something has been revealed to a certain person, and not revealed to any other person, it is revelation to that person only. When he tells it to a second person, a second to a third, a third to a fourth, and so on, it ceases to be a revelation to all those persons. It is revelation to the first person only, and *hearsay* to every other, and, consequently, they are not obliged to believe it.

It is a contradiction in terms and ideas, to call anything a revelation that comes to us at second-hand, either verbally or in writing. Revelation is necessarily limited to the first communication—after this, it is only an account of something which that person says was a revelation made to him; and though he may find himself obliged to believe it, it cannot be incumbent on me to believe it in the same manner, for it was not a revelation made to *me*, and I have only his word for it that it was made to him.

When Moses told the children of Israel that he received the two tables of the commandments from the hands of God, they were not obliged to believe him, because they had no other authority for it than his telling them so; and I have no other authority for it than some historian telling me so. The commandments carry no internal evidence of divinity with them; they contain some good moral precepts, such as any man qualified to be a lawgiver, or a moral legislator, could produce himself, without having recourse to supernatural intervention.[3]

When I was told that the Koran was written in heaven, and brought to Mohammed by an angel, the account comes too near the same kind of hearsay evidence and secondhand authority as the former. I did not see the angel myself, and, therefore, I have a right not to believe it.

When also I am told that a woman called the Virgin Mary said, or gave out, that she was with child without any cohabitation with a man, and that her betrothed husband, Joseph, said that an angel told him so, I have a right to believe them or not; such a circumstance required a much stronger evidence than their bare word for it; but we have not even this—for neither Joseph nor Mary wrote any such matter themselves; it is only reported by others that *they said so*—it is hearsay upon hearsay, and I do not choose to rest my belief upon such evidence.

It is, however, not difficult to account for the credit that was given

[3] It is, however, necessary to except the declaration which says that God *visits the sins of the fathers upon the children*; it is contrary to every principle of moral justice.—P.

to the story of Jesus Christ being the son of God. He was born when the heathen mythology had still some fashion and repute in the world, and mythology had prepared the people for the belief of such a story. Almost all the extraordinary men that lived under the heathen mythology were reputed to be the sons of some of the gods. It was not a new thing, at that time, to believe a man to have been celestially begotten; the intercourse of gods with women was then a matter of familiar opinion. Their Jupiter, according to their accounts, had cohabited with hundreds; the story therefore had nothing in it either new, wonderful or obscene; it was conformable to the opinions that then prevailed among the people called Gentiles, or Mythologists, and it was those people only that believed it. The Jews, who had kept strictly to the belief of one God, and no more, and who had always rejected the heathen mythology, never credited the story.

It is curious to observe how the theory of what is called the Christian Church, sprung out of the tail of heathen mythology. A direct incorporation took place in the first instance, by making the reputed founder to be celestially begotten. The trinity of gods that then followed was no other than a reduction of the former plurality, which was about twenty or thirty thousand; the statue of Mary succeeded the statue of Diana or Ephesus; the deification of heroes changed into the canonization of saints; the Mythologists had gods for everything; the Christian Mythologists had saints for everything; the church became as crowded with the one, as the pantheon had been with the other; and Rome was the place of both. The Christian theory is little else than the idolatry of the ancient Mythologists, accommodated to the purposes of power and revenue; and it yet remains to reason and philosophy to abolish the amphibious fraud.

Chapter III

Nothing that is here said can apply, even with the most distant disrespect, to the *real* character of Jesus Christ. He was a virtuous and an amiable man. The morality that he preached and practiced was of the most benevolent kind; and though similar systems of morality had been preached by Confucius, and by some of the Greek philosophers, many years before; by the Quakers since; and by many good men in all ages, it has not been exceeded by any.

Jesus Christ wrote no account of himself, of his birth, parentage, or anything else; not a line of what is called the New Testament is of his own writing. The history of him is altogether the work of other people; and as to the account given of his resurrection and ascension, it was the necessary counterpart to the story of his birth. His historians, having brought him into the world in a supernatural manner, were obliged to take him out again in the same manner, or the first part of the story must have fallen to the ground.

The wretched contrivance with which this latter part is told, exceeds everything that went before it. The first part, that of the miraculous conception, was not a thing that admitted of publicity; and therefore the tellers of this part of the story had this advantage, that though they might not be credited, they could not be detected. They could not be expected to prove it, because it was not one of those things that admitted of proof, and it was impossible that the person of whom it was told could prove it himself.

But the resurrection of a dead person from the grave, and his ascension through the air, is a thing very different as to the evidence it admits of, to the invisible conception of a child in the womb. The resurrection and ascension, supposing them to have taken place, admitted of public and ocular demonstration, like that of the ascension of a balloon, or the sun at noonday, to all Jerusalem at least. A thing which everybody is required to believe, requires that the proof and evidence of it should be equal to all, and universal; and as the public visibility of this last related act, was the only evidence that could give sanction to the former part, the whole of it falls to the ground, because that evidence never was given. Instead of this, a small number of persons, not more than eight or nine, are introduced as proxies for the whole world, to say they saw it, and all the rest of the world are called upon to believe it. But it appears that Thomas did not believe the resurrection; and, as they say, would not believe without having ocular and manual demonstration himself. So *neither will I*, and the reason is equally as good for me, and for every other person, as for Thomas.

It is in vain to attempt to palliate or disguise this matter. The story, so far as relates to the supernatural part, has every mark of fraud and imposition stamped upon the face of it. Who were the authors of it is as impossible for us now to know, as it is for us to be assured, that the books in which the account is related, were written by the persons whose names they bear; the best surviving evidence we now have respecting this affair is the Jews. They are regularly descended from the people who lived in the time this resurrection and ascension is said to have happened, and they say, *it is not true*. It has long appeared to me a strange inconsistency to cite the Jews as a proof of the truth of the story. It is just the same as if a man were to say, I will prove the truth of what I have told you, by producing the people who say it is false.

That such a person as Jesus Christ existed, and that he was crucified, which was the mode of execution at that day, are historical relations strictly within the limits of probability. He preached most excellent morality, and the equality of man; but he preached also against the corruptions and avarice of the Jewish priests, and this brought upon him the hatred and vengeance of the whole order of priesthood. The accusation which those priests brought against him was that of sedition and conspiracy against the Roman government, to which the Jews were then subject and tributary; and it is not improbable that the Roman government might have some secret apprehensions of the effects of his doctrine as well as the Jewish priests; neither is it improbable that Jesus Christ had in contemplation the delivery of the Jewish nation from the bondage of the Romans. Between the two, however, this virtuous reformer and revolutionist lost his life.

Chapter IV

It is upon this plain narrative of facts, together with another case I am going to mention, that the Christian Mythologists, calling themselves the Christian Church, have erected their fable, which for absurdity and extravagance, is not exceeded by anything that is to be found in the mythology of the ancients. . . .

Chapter VIII

. . . The Christian Mythologists tell us that Christ died for the sins of the world, and that he came on *purpose to die.* Would it not then have been the same if he had died of a fever or of the smallpox, of old age, or of anything else?

The declaratory sentence which, they say, was passed upon Adam, in case he ate of the apple, was not, that *thou shalt surely be crucified,* but, *thou shalt surely die.* The sentence was death, and not the *manner of dying.* Crucifixion, therefore, or any other particular manner of dying, made no part of the sentence that Adam was to suffer, and consequently, even upon their own tactic, it could make no part of the sentence that Christ was to suffer in the room of Adam. A fever would have done as well as a cross, if there was any occasion for either.

This sentence of death, which, they tell us, was thus passed upon Adam, must either have meant dying naturally, that is, ceasing to live, or have meant what these Mythologists call damnation; and consequently, the act of dying on the part of Jesus Christ, must, according to their system, apply as a prevention to one or other of these two things happening to Adam and to us.

That it does not prevent our dying is evident, because we all die; and if their accounts of longevity be true, men die faster since the crucifixion than before: and with respect to the second explanation (including with it the *natural death* of Jesus Christ as a substitute for the *eternal death or damnation* of all mankind), it is impertinently representing the Creator as coming off, or revoking the sentence, by a pun or a quibble upon the word *death*. That manufacturer of quibbles, Saint Paul, if he wrote the books that bear his name, has helped this quibble on by making another quibble upon the word *Adam*. He makes there to be two Adams; the one who sins in fact, and suffers by proxy; the other who sins by proxy, and suffers in fact. A religion thus interlarded with quibble, subterfuge, and pun, has a tendency to instruct its professors in the practice of these arts. They acquire the habit without being aware of the cause.

If Jesus Christ was the being which those Mythologists tell us he was, and that he came into this world *to suffer*, which is a word they sometimes use instead of *to die*, the only real suffering he could have endured would have been *to live*. His existence here was a state of exilement or transportation from heaven, and the way back to his original country was to die. In fine, everything in this strange system is the reverse of what it pretends to be. It is the reverse of truth, and I become so tired of examining into its inconsistencies and absurdities, that I hasten to the conclusion of it, in order to proceed to something better.

How much, or what parts of the books called the New Testament, were written by the persons whose names they bear, is what we can know nothing of, neither are we certain in what language they were originally written. The matters they now contain may be classed under two heads: anecdote, and epistolary correspondence.

The four books already mentioned, *Matthew, Mark, Luke*, and *John*, are altogether anecdotal. They relate events after they had taken place. They tell what Jesus Christ did and said, and what others did and said to him; and in several instances they relate the same event differently. Revelation is necessarily out of the question with respect to those books; not only because of the disagreement of the writers, but because revelation cannot be applied to the relating of facts by the persons who saw them done, nor to the relating or recording of any discourse or conversation by those who heard it. The book called the *Acts of the Apostles* (an anonymous work) belongs also to the anecdotal part.

All the other parts of the New Testament, except the book of enigmas, called the Revelations, are a collection of letters under the name of epistles; and the forgery of letters has been such a common practice in the world, that the probability is at least equal, whether they are genuine or forged. One thing, however, is much less equivocal, which is, that out of the matters contained in those books, together with the assistance of some old stories, the church has set up a system of religion very contradictory to the character of the person whose name it bears. It has set up a religion of pomp and of revenue in pretended imitation of a person whose life was humility and poverty.

The invention of a purgatory, and of the releasing of souls there-

from, by prayers, bought of the church with money; the selling of
pardons, dispensations, and indulgences, are revenue laws, without
bearing that name or carrying that appearance. But the case nevertheless is, that those things derive their origin from the proxysm of the
crucifixion, and the theory deduced therefrom, which was, that one
person could stand in the place of another, and could perform meri-
torious services for him. The probability, therefore, is, that the whole
theory or doctrine of what is called the redemption (which is said
to have been accomplished by the act of one person in the room of
another) was originally fabricated on purpose to bring forward and
build all those secondary and pecuniary redemptions upon; and that
the passages in the books upon which the idea of theory of redemption
is built, have been manufactured and fabricated for that purpose.
Why are we to give this church credit, when she tells us that those
books are genuine in every part, any more than we give her credit for
everything else she has told us; or for the miracles she says she has
performed? That she *could* fabricate writings is certain, because she
could write; and the composition of the writings in question, is of that
kind that anybody might do it; and that she *did* fabricate them is not
more inconsistent with probability, than that she should tell us, as she
has done, that she could and did work miracles.

Since, then, no external evidence can, at this long distance of time,
be produced to prove whether the church fabricated the doctrine
called redemption or not (for such evidence, whether for or against,
would be subject to the same suspicion of being fabricated), the case
can only be referred to the internal evidence which the thing carries
of itself; and this affords a very strong presumption of its being a
fabrication. For the internal evidence is, that the theory or doctrine
of redemption has for its basis an idea of pecuniary justice, and not
that of moral justice.

If I owe a person money, and cannot pay him, and he threatens to
put me in prison, another person can take the debt upon himself, and
pay it for me. But if I have committed a crime, every circumstance
of the case is changed. Moral justice cannot take the innocent for the
guilty even if the innocent would offer itself. To suppose justice to do
this, is to destroy the principle of its existence, which is the thing
itself. It is then no longer justice. It is indiscriminate revenge.

This single reflection will show that the doctrine of redemption is
founded on a mere pecuniary idea corresponding to that of a debt
which another person might pay; and as this pecuniary idea corresponds again with the system of second redemptions, obtained through
the means of money given to the church for pardons, the probability
is that the same persons fabricated both the one and the other of
those theories; and that, in truth, there is no such thing as redemption;
that it is fabulous; and that man stands in the same relative condition

with his Maker he ever did stand, since man existed; and that it is his greatest consolation to think so.

Let him believe this, and he will live more consistently and morally, than by any other system. It is by his being taught to contemplate himself as an outlaw, as an outcast, as a beggar, as a mumper, as one thrown as it were on a dunghill, at an immense distance from his Creator, and who must make his approaches by creeping, and cringing to intermediate beings, that he conceives either a contemptuous disregard for everything under the name of religion, or becomes indifferent, or turns what he calls devout. In the latter case, he consumes his life in grief, or the affectation of it. His prayers are reproaches. His humility is ingratitude. He calls himself a worm, and the fertile earth a dunghill; and all the blessings of life by the thankless name of vanities. He despises the choicest gift of God to man, the GIFT OF REASON; and having endeavored to force upon himself the belief of a system against which reason revolts, he ungratefully calls it *human reason,* as if man could give reason to himself.

Yet, with all this strange appearance of humility, and this contempt for human reason, he ventures into the boldest presumptions. He finds fault with everything. His selfishness is never satisfied; his ingratitude is never at an end. He takes on himself to direct the Almighty what to do, even in the government of the universe. He prays dictatorially. When it is sunshine, he prays for rain, and when it is rain, he prays for sunshine. He follows the same idea in everything that he prays for; for what is the amount of all his prayers, but an attempt to make the Almighty change his mind, and act otherwise than he does? It is as if he were to say—thou knowest not so well as I.

Chapter IX

But some perhaps will say, Are we to have no word of God, no revelation? I answer, Yes: there is a word of God; there is a revelation.

THE WORD OF GOD IS THE CREATION WE BEHOLD: And it is in *this word,* which no human invention can counterfeit or alter, that God speaketh universally to man.

Human language is local and changeable, and is therefore incapable of being used as the means of unchangeable and universal information. The idea that God sent Jesus Christ to publish, as they say, the glad tidings to all nations, from one end of the earth to the other, is consistent only with the ignorance of those who knew nothing of the extent of the world, and who believed, as those world-saviors believed, and continued to believe, for several centuries (and that in contradiction to the discoveries of philosophers and the experience of navigators), that the earth was flat like a trencher; and that a man might walk to the end of it.

But how was Jesus Christ to make anything known to all nations? He could speak but one language, which was Hebrew; and there are in the world several hundred languages. Scarcely any two nations speak the same language, or understand each other; and as to translations, every man who knows anything of languages, knows that it was impossible to translate from one language to another, not only without losing a great part of the original, but frequently of mistaking the sense; and besides all this, the art of printing was wholly unknown at the time Christ lived.

It is always necessary that the means that are to accomplish any end, be equal to the accomplishment of that end, or the end cannot be accomplished. It is in this, that the difference between finite and infinite power and wisdom discovers itself. Man frequently fails in accomplishing his ends, from a natural inability of the power to the purpose; and frequently from the want of wisdom to apply power properly. But it is impossible for infinite power and wisdom to fail as man faileth. The means it useth are always equal to the end; but human language, more especially as there is not a universal language, is incapable of being used as a universal means of unchangeable and uniform information, and therefore it is not the means that God useth in manifesting himself universally to man.

It is only in the CREATION that all our ideas and conceptions of a *word of God* can unite. The Creation speaketh a universal language, independently of human speech or human language, multiplied and various as they be. It is an ever-existing original, which every man can read. It cannot be forged; it cannot be counterfeited; it cannot be lost; it cannot be altered; it cannot be suppressed. It does not depend upon the will of man whether it shall be published or not; it publishes itself from one end of the earth to the other. It preaches to all nations and to all worlds; and this *word of God* reveals to man all that is necessary for man to know of God.

Do we want to contemplate his power? We see it in the immensity of the Creation. Do we want to contemplate his wisdom? We see it in the unchangeable order by which the incomprehensible whole is governed. Do we want to contemplate his munificence? We see it in the abundance with which he fills the earth. Do we went to contemplate his mercy? We see it in his not withholding that abundance even from the unthankful. In fine, do we want to know what God is? Search not the book called the Scripture, which any human hand might make, but the Scripture called the Creation.

Chapter X

The only idea man can affix to the name of God, is that of a *first cause,* the cause of all things. And, incomprehensible and difficult as it is for a man to conceive what a first cause is, he arrives at the belief of it, from the tenfold greater difficulty of disbelieving it. It is difficult beyond description to conceive that space can have no end; but it is more difficult to conceive an eternal duration of what we call time; but it is more impossible to conceive a time when there shall be no time.

In like manner of reasoning, everything we behold carries in itself the internal evidence that it did not make itself. Every man is an evidence to himself, that he did not make himself; neither could his father make himself, nor his grandfather, nor any of his race; neither could any tree, plant, or animal make itself; and it is the conviction arising from this evidence, that carries us on, as it were, by necessity, to the belief of a first cause eternally existing, of a nature totally different to any material existence we know of, and by the power of which all things exist; and this first cause man calls God.

It is only by the exercise of reason that man can discover God. Take away that reason, and he would be incapable of understanding any-thing; and, in this case it would be just as consistent to read even the book called the Bible to a horse as to a man. How then is it that those people pretend to reject reason? . . .

I recollect not a single passage in all the writings ascribed to the men called apostles, that convey any idea of what God is. Those writings are chiefly controversial; and the subject they dwell upon, that of a man dying in agony on a cross, is better suited to the gloomy genius of a monk in a cell, by whom it is not impossible they were written, than to any man breathing the open air of the Creation. The only passage that occurs to me, that has any reference to the works of God, by which only his power and wisdom can be known, is related to have been spoken by Jesus Christ, as a remedy against distrustful care. "Behold the lilies of the field, they toil not, neither do they spin." This, however, is far inferior to the allusions in Job and in the 19th Psalm; but it is similar in idea, and the modesty of the imagery is correspondent to the modesty of the man.

Chapter XI

As to the Christian system of faith, it appears to me as a species of atheism—a sort of religious denial of God. It professes to believe in a man rather than in God. It is a compound made up chiefly of manism with but little deism, and is as near to atheism as twilight is to dark-ness. It introduces between man and his Maker an opaque body, which it calls a Redeemer, as the moon introduces her opaque self between the earth and the sun, and it produces by this means a religious or an irreligious eclipse of light. It has put the whole orbit of reason into shade.

The effect of this obscurity has been that of turning everything upside down, and representing it in reverse; and among the revolutions it has thus magically produced, it has made a revolution in theology.

That which is now called natural philosophy, embracing the whole circle of science, of which astronomy occupies the chief place, is the study of the works of God, and of the power and wisdom of God in his works, and is the true theology.

As to the theology that is now studied in its place, it is the study of human opinions and of human fancies *concerning God.*[4] It is not the study of God himself in the works that he has made, but in the works or writings that man has made; and it is not among the least of the mischiefs that the Christian system has done to the world, that it has abandoned the original and beautful system of theology,[5] like a beautiful innocent, to distress and reproach, to make room for the hag of superstition.

The Book of Job and the 19th Psalm, which even the church admits to be more ancient than the chronological order in which they stand in the book called the Bible, are theological orations conformable to the original system of theology. The internal evidence of those orations proves to a demonstration that the study and contemplation of the works of creation, and of the power and wisdom of God revealed and manifested in those works, made a great part of the religious devotion of the times in which they were written; and it was this devotional study and contemplation that led to the discovery of the principles upon which what are now called Sciences are established; and it is to the discovery of these principles that almost all the Arts that contribute to the convenience of human life owe their existence. Every principal art has some science for its parent, though the person who mechanically performs that work does not always, and but very seldom, perceive the connection.[6]

It is a fraud[7] of the Christian system to call the sciences *human inventions;* it is only the application of them that is human. Every science has for its basis a system of principles as fixed and unalterable as those by which the universe is regulated and governed. Man cannot make principles, he can only discover them.

For example: Every person who looks at an almanac sees an account when an eclipse will take place, and he sees also that it never fails to

---

[4] French: "La suprême intelligence" instead of "God."

[5] French: "La théologie naturelle."

[6] In the French is added: "et que même, par l'ignorance que les gouvernements modernes ont répandue, il soit très-rare aujourd'hui, que ces personnes s'en doutent" ("and, such is the ignorance prevailing under modern governments, it is now even very rare for such persons to think about it").

[7] French: "C'est un mensonge, une *fraude pieuse.*"

take place according to the account there given. This shows that man is acquainted with the laws by which the heavenly bodies move. But it would be something worse than ignorance, were any church on earth to say that those laws are a human invention.

It would also be ignorance, or something worse, to say that the scientific principles, by the aid of which man is enabled to calculate and foreknow when an eclipse will take place, are a human invention. Man cannot invent anything that is eternal and immutable; and the scientific principles he employs for this purpose must, and are, of necessity, as eternal and immutable as the laws by which the heavenly bodies move, or they could not be used as they are to ascertain the time when, and the manner how, an eclipse will take place.

The scientific principles that man employs to obtain the foreknowledge of an eclipse, or of anything else relating to the motion of the heavenly bodies, are contained chiefly in that part of science that is called trigonometry, or the properties of a triangle, which, when applied to the study of the heavenly bodies, is called astronomy; when applied to direct the course of a ship on the ocean, it is called navigation; when applied to the construction of figures drawn by a rule and compass, it is called geometry; when applied to the construction of plans of edifices, it is called architecture; when applied to the measurement of any portion of the surface of the earth, it is called land-surveying. In fine, it is the soul of science. It is an eternal truth: it contains the *mathematical demonstration* of which man speaks, and the extent of its uses are unknown.

It may be said, that man can make or draw a triangle, and therefore a triangle is a human invention.

But the triangle, when drawn, is no other than the image of the principle: it is a delineation to the eye, and from thence to the mind, of a principle that would otherwise be imperceptible. The triangle does not make the principle, any more than a candle taken into a room that was dark, makes the chairs and tables that before were invisible. All the properties of a triangle exist independently of the figure, and existed before any triangle was drawn or thought of by man. Man had no more to do in the formation of those properties or principles, than he had to do in making the laws by which the heavenly bodies move; and therefore the one must have the same divine origin as the other.

In the same manner as, it may be said, that man can make a triangle, so also, may it be said, he can make the mechanical instrument called a lever. But the principle by which the lever acts, is a thing distinct from the instrument, and would exist if the instrument did not; it attaches itself to the instrument after it is made; the instrument, therefore, can act no otherwise than it does act; neither can all the efforts

of human invention make it act otherwise. That which, in all such
cases, man calls the *effect*, is no other than the principle itself rendered
perceptible to the senses.

Since, then, man cannot make principles, from whence did he gain
a knowledge of them, so as to be able to apply them, not only to things
on earth, but to ascertain the motion of bodies so immensely distant
from him as all the heavenly bodies are? From whence, I ask, *could*
he gain that knowledge, but from the study of the true theology?

It is the structure of the universe that has taught this knowledge
to man. That structure is an ever-existing exhibition of every principle
upon which every part of mathematical science is founded. The offspring of this science is mechanics; for mechanics is no other than the
principles of science applied practically. The man who proportions
the several parts of a mill uses the same scientific principles as if he
had the power of constructing a universe, but as he cannot give to
matter that invisible agency by which all the component parts of the
immense machine of the universe have influence upon each other,
and act in motional unison together, without any apparent contact,
and to which man has given the name of attraction, gravitation, and
repulsion, he supplies the place of that agency by the humble imitation
of teeth and cogs. All the parts of man's microcosm must visibly touch.
But could he gain a knowledge of that agency, so as to be able to
apply it in practice, we might then say that another *canonical book*
of the word of God had been discovered.

If man could alter the properties of the lever, so also could he alter
the properties of the triangle: for a lever (taking that sort of lever
which is called a steelyard, for the sake of explanation) forms, when
in motion, a triangle. The line it descends from (one point of that line
being in the fulcrum), the line it descends to, and the chord of the
arc, which the end of the lever describes in the air, are the three
sides of a triangle. The other arm of the lever describes also a triangle;
and the corresponding sides of those two triangles, calculated scientifically, or measured geometrically—and also the sines, tangents, and
secants generated from the angles, and geometrically measured—have
the same proportions to each other as the different weights have that
will balance each other on the lever, leaving the weight of the lever
out of the case.

It may also be said, that man can make a wheel and axis; that he
can put wheels of different magnitudes together, and produce a mill.
Still the case comes back to the same point, which is, that he did not
make the principle that gives the wheels those powers. This principle
is as unalterable as in the former cases, or rather it is the same principle
under a different appearance to the eye.

The power that two wheels of different magnitudes have upon each other is in the same proportion as if the semi-diameter of the two wheels were joined together and made into that kind of lever I have described, suspended at the part where the semi-diameters join; for the two wheels, scientifically considered, are no other than the two circles generated by the motion of the compound lever.

It is from the study of the true theology that all our knowledge of science is derived; and it is from that knowledge that all the arts have originated.

The Almighty lecturer, by displaying the principles of science in the structure of the universe, has invited man to study and to imitation. It is as if he had said to the inhabitants of this globe that we call ours, "I have made an earth for man to dwell upon, and I have rendered the starry heavens visible, to teach him science and the arts. He can now provide for his own comfort, AND LEARN FROM MY MUNIFICENCE TO ALL, TO BE KIND TO EACH OTHER."

Of what use is it, unless it be to teach man something, that his eye is endowed with the power of beholding, to an incomprehensible distance, an immensity of worlds revolving in the ocean of space? Or of what use is it that this immensity of worlds is visible to man? What has man to do with the Pleiades, with Orion, with Sirius, with the star he calls the north star, with the moving orbs he has named Saturn, Jupiter, Mars, Venus, and Mercury, if no uses are to follow from their being visible? A less power of vision would have been sufficient for man, if the immensity he now possesses were given only to waste itself, as it were, on an immense desert of space glittering with shows.

It is only by contemplating what he calls the starry heavens, as the book and school of science, that he discovers any use in their being visible to him, or any advantage resulting from his immensity of vision. But when he contemplates the subject in this light, he sees an additional motive for saying, that *nothing was made in vain;* for in vain would be this power of vision if it taught man nothing. . . .

Chapter XVII

Having shown the irreconcilable inconsistencies between the real word of God existing in the universe, and that which is called *the word of God* as shown to us in a printed book that any man might make, I proceed to speak of the three principal means that have been employed in all ages, and perhaps in all countries, to impose upon mankind.

Those three means are Mystery, Miracle, and Prophecy. The two first are incompatible with true religion, and the third ought always to be suspected.

With respect to mystery, everything we behold is, in one sense, a mystery to us. Our own existence is a mystery; the whole vegetable world is a mystery. We cannot account how it is that an acorn, when put into the ground, is made to develop itself, and become an oak. We know not how it is that the seed we sow unfolds and multiplies itself, and returns to us such an abundant interest for so small a capital.

The fact, however, as distinct from the operating cause, is not a mystery, because we see it; and we know also the means we are to use, which is no other than putting seed in the ground. We know, therefore, as much as is necessary for us to know; and that part of the operation that we do not know, and which if we did we could not perform, the Creator takes upon himself and performs it for us. We are, therefore, better off than if we had been let into the secret, and left to do it for ourselves.

But though every created thing is, in this sense, a mystery, the word mystery cannot be applied to moral truth, any more than obscurity can be applied to light. The God in whom we believe is a God of moral truth, and not a God of mystery or obscurity. Mystery is the antagonist of truth. It is a fog of human invention, that obscures truth, and represents it in distortion. Truth never envelops *itself* in mystery; and the mystery in which it is at any time enveloped, is the work of its antagonist, and never of itself.

Religion, therefore, being the belief of a God, and the practice of moral truth, cannot have connection with mystery. The belief of a God, so far from having anything of mystery in it, is of all beliefs the most easy, because it arises to us, as is before observed, out of necessity. And the practice of moral truth, or, in other words, a practical imitation of the moral goodness of God, is no other than our acting toward each other as he acts benignly toward all. We *cannot* serve God in the manner we serve those who cannot do without such service; and, therefore, the only idea we can have of serving God, is that of contributing to the happiness of the living creation that God has made. This cannot be done by retiring ourselves from the society of the world, and spending a recluse life in selfish devotion.

The very nature and design of religion, if I may so express it, prove, even to demonstration, that it must be free from everything of mystery, and unencumbered with everything that is mysterious. Religion, considered as a duty, is incumbent upon every living soul alike, and, therefore, must be on a level to the understanding and comprehension of all. Man does not learn religion as he learns the secrets and mysteries of a trade. He learns the theory of religion by reflection. It arises out of the action of his own mind upon the things which he sees, or upon what he may happen to hear or to read, and the practice joins itself thereto.

RECAPITULATION

Having now extended the subject to a greater length than I first intended, I shall bring it to a close by abstracting a summary from the whole.

First, That the idea or belief of a word of God existing in print, or in writing, or in speech, is inconsistent in itself for the reasons already assigned. These reasons, among many others, are the want of a universal language; the mutability of language; the errors to which translations are subject; the possibility of totally suppressing such a word; the probability of altering it, or of fabricating the whole, and imposing it upon the world.

Secondly, That the Creation we behold is the real and ever-existing word of God, in which we cannot be deceived. It proclaimeth his power, it demonstrates his wisdom, it manifests his goodness and beneficence.

Thirdly, That the moral duty of man consists in imitating the moral goodness and beneficence of God manifested in the creation toward all his creatures. That seeing as we daily do the goodness of God to all men, it is an example calling upon all men to practice the same toward each other; and, consequently, that everything of persecution and revenge between man and man, and everything of cruelty to animals, is a violation of moral duty.

I trouble not myself about the manner of future existence. I content myself with believing, even to positive conviction, that the power that gave me existence is able to continue it, in any form and manner he pleases, either with or without this body; and it appears more probable to me that I shall continue to exist hereafter than that I should have had existence, as I now have, before that existence began.

It is certain that, in one point, all nations of the earth and all religions agree. All believe in a God. The things in which they disagree are the redundancies annexed to that belief; and therefore, if ever a universal religion should prevail, it will not be believing anything new, but in getting rid of redundancies, and believing as man believed at first. Adam, if ever there was such a man, was created a Deist; but in the meantime, let every man follow, as he has a right to do, the religion and worship he prefers.

BIBLIOGRAPHY

PAINE, Thomas, *The Writings of Thomas Paine*, ed. by M.D. Conway. New York: G. P. Putnam's Sons, 1894–1896, 4 vols.

_____ *The Complete Writings of Thomas Paine*, ed. by Philip S. Foner. New York: Citadel Press, 1945, 2 vols.

_____ *The Selected Works of Tom Paine*, ed. by Howard Fast. New York: Duell, Sloan & Pearce, 1945.

_____ *The Living Thoughts of Tom Paine*, ed. by John Dos Passos. New York: Longmans, Green, 1940.

ALDRIDGE, Alfred O., *Man of Reason, The Life of Thomas Paine*. Philadelphia: Lippincott, 1959.

BEST, M. A., *Thomas Paine, Prophet and Martyr of Democracy*. New York: Harcourt, Brace, 1927.

CLARK, Harry Hayden, *Thomas Paine: Representative Selections*, with Introduction, Bibliography, and Notes. New York: American Book Co., 1944.

CONWAY, Moncure D., *The Life of Thomas Paine, With a History of His Literary, Political and Religious Career in America, France and England*. New York: G. P. Putnam's, 1892.

GIMBEL, Richard, *Thomas Paine: A Bibliographical Check List of Common Sense, With an Account of Its Publication*. New Haven: Yale U. Press, 1956.

LEWIS, Joseph, *Thomas Paine, Author of the Declaration of Independence*. New York: Free Thought Press, 1947.

PEARSON, Hesketh, *Tom Paine, a Friend of Mankind*. New York: Harpers, 1937.

RUSSELL, Bertrand, "The Fate of Thomas Paine," in *Why I Am Not a Christian and other Essays on Religion and Related Subjects*, ed. by Paul Edwards. New York: Simon & Schuster, 1957.

SMITH, Frank, *Thomas Paine, Liberator*. New York: Frederick A. Slater Co., 1938.

WAGNER, Donald I., ed. *Social Reformers, Adam Smith to John Dewey*. New York: Macmillan Co., 1934.

WOODWARD, W. E., *Thomas Paine, America's Godfather, 1737–1809*. New York: E. P. Dutton, 1945.

The Federalist

[1787–1788]

The Federalist papers (85 in all) first appeared in the New York press on October 27, 1787, and continued to appear throughout the following year under the pseudonym "Publius." They were written for the specific purpose of persuading the people of New York State to ratify the newly proposed Federal Constitution (in place of the Articles of Confederation). Although New York finally adopted the Constitution, the vote was close and in large part could be attributed to the persuasive talents of Alexander Hamilton at the New York State Convention. Hamilton was author of approximately fifty-one of the papers, the other authors being James Madison and John Jay.

Alexander Hamilton (1757–1804) was born in the British West Indies and came to America at the age of seventeen. He was educated at Kings College (now Columbia University) and was a distinguished lawyer before the age of thirty. He served on Washington's military staff during the Revolution and was a member of the Constitutional Convention. Subsequently he was appointed the first Secretary of the Treasury (1789–1795), in which post he became embroiled in numerous controversies. He was considered a conservative in his own day because of his antipathy to democracy, his defense of a strong centralized government and a National Bank. He was not entirely sympathetic to republican institutions, but he accepted the Constitution because he hated anarchy and thought that the upper classes might mold it to their design. Hamilton was a bitter critic of Jefferson, though he supported him instead of Aaron Burr for the Presidency in 1800. He later suffered a tragic and untimely death in a duel with Burr.

James Madison (1751–1836), a distinguished son of Virginia, was also involved in the politics of the Revolution and served in the Continental Congress. His scholarly knowledge of politics and history had a deep influence on the framers of the Constitution. Madison is sometimes called "the father of the Constitution." More liberal than Hamilton or Jay, he also helped to frame the Bill of Rights, enacted by the first session of Congress. Madison became Secretary of State and was elected President, serving from 1809 to 1817.

John Jay (1745–1829) wrote the smallest number of *The Federalist* papers, but his contribution was significant, for his prestige was much greater in 1787 than that of either Hamilton or Madison. With Franklin and John Adams he had negotiated the Treaty with Great Britain, and was President of the Continental Congress. Jay later became the first Chief Justice of the United States Supreme Court (1789–1795).

The Federalist has become a work of great significance and has been used to interpret the Constitution.

Translated into many languages, it is still widely read today in many parts of the world as a guide for newly liberated, formerly colonial, nations. Although the authors are concerned with particular points of government and law, they nonetheless express profound observations in political and social philosophy, and make important contributions to the theory of representative government.

The papers adhere closely to the intention which Hamilton announced in the first number: they discuss the necessity of the Union for political prosperity, the insufficiency of the Confederacy, the conformity of the proposed Constitution to the true principles of republican government, the guarantee such government would provide for liberty and property rights, and so on. In *No. 10* Madison distinguishes between republican government and a strict democracy, defending the former. He offers an economic interpretation of political history. Recognizing that distinctions of property may be a source of faction, he nonetheless expresses the hope that such factions may be overcome by means of republican government. In *No. 31* Hamilton argues for the recognition of first principles in morals and politics. He attempts to answer arguments against the central taxing power of the national government and to defend the Constitution. In *No. 47* Madison discusses the theory of checks and balances as propounded by the French philosopher, Montesquieu.

The writers of *The Federalist* papers were on the whole rather conservative in their attitudes toward democracy and propertied interests. The strongest exponents of democracy, Jefferson, Paine, and Samuel Adams, were not members of the Constitutional Convention. Although the first ten amendments, the Bill of Rights, were soon added, it was only much later that direct election of the Senate, *de jure* enfranchisement of the Negro, and woman suffrage provided a more democratic society.

THE FEDERALIST NO. 10 [1]

BY JAMES MADISON

Among the numerous advantages promised by a well-constructed Union, none deserves to be more accurately developed than its tendency to break and control the violence of faction. The friend of popular governments never finds himself so much alarmed for their character and fate as when he contemplates their propensity to this dangerous vice. He will not fail, therefore, to set a due value on any plan which, without violating the principles to which he is attached, provides a proper cure for it. The instability, injustice, and confusion introduced into the public councils, have, in truth, been the mortal

[1] From the *New York Packet,* November 23, 1787.

diseases under which popular governments have everywhere perished; as they continue to be the favorite and fruitful topics from which the adversaries to liberty derive their most specious declamations. The valuable improvements made by the American constitutions on the popular models, both ancient and modern, cannot certainly be too much admired; but it would be an unwarrantable partiality, to contend that they have as effectually obviated the danger on this side, as was wished and expected. Complaints are everywhere heard from our most considerate and virtuous citizens, equally the friends of public and private faith, and of public and personal liberty, that our governments are too unstable, that the public good is disregarded in the conflicts of rival parties, and that measures are too often decided, not according to the rules of justice and the rights of the minor party, but by the superior force of an interested and overbearing majority. However anxiously we may wish that these complaints had no foundation, the evidence of known facts will not permit us to deny that they are in some degree true. It will be found, indeed, on a candid review of our situation, that some of the distresses under which we labor have been erroneously charged on the operation of our governments; but it will be found, at the same time, that other causes will not alone account for many of our heaviest misfortunes; and, particularly, for that prevailing and increasing distrust of public engagements, and alarm for private rights, which are echoed from one end of the continent to the other. These must be chiefly, if not wholly, effects of the unsteadiness and injustice with which a factious spirit has tainted our public administrations.

By a faction, I understand a number of citizens, whether amounting to a majority or minority of the whole, who are united and actuated by some common impulse of passion, or of interest, adverse to the rights of other citizens, or to the permanent and aggregate interests of the community.

There are two methods of curing the mischiefs of faction: the one, by removing its causes; the other, by controlling its effects.

There are again two methods of removing the causes of faction: the one, by destroying the liberty which is essential to its existence; the other, by giving to every citizen the same opinions, the same passions, and the same interests.

It could never be more truly said than of the first remedy, that it was worse than the disease. Liberty is to faction what air is to fire, an aliment without which it instantly expires. But it could not be less folly to abolish liberty, which is essential to political life, because it nourishes faction, than it would be to wish the annihilation of air, which is essential to animal life, because it imparts to fire its destructive agency.

The second expedient is as impracticable as the first would be unwise. As long as the reason of man continues fallible, and he is at liberty to exercise it, different opinions will be formed. As long as the connection subsists between his reason and his self-love, his opinions and his passions will have a reciprocal influence on each other; and the former will be objects to which the latter will attach themselves. The diversity in the faculties of men, from which the rights of property originate, is not less an insuperable obstacle to a uniformity of interests. The protection of these faculties is the first object of government. From the protection of different and unequal faculties of acquiring property, the possession of different degrees and kinds of property immediately results; and from the influence of these on the sentiments and view of the respective proprietors, ensues a division of the society into different interests and parties.

The latent causes of faction are thus sown in the nature of man; and we see them everywhere brought into different degrees of activity, according to the different circumstances of civil society. A zeal for different opinions concerning religion, concerning government, and many other points, as well of speculation as of practice; an attachment to different leaders ambitiously contending for pre-eminence and power; or to persons of other descriptions whose fortunes have been interesting to the human passions, have, in turn, divided mankind into parties, inflamed them with mutual animosity, and rendered them much more disposed to vex and oppress each other than to co-operate for their common good. So strong is this propensity of mankind to fall into mutual animosities, that where no substantial occasion presents itself, the most frivolous and fanciful distinctions have been sufficient to kindle their unfriendly passions and excite their most violent conflicts. But the most common and durable source of factions has been the various and unequal distribution of property. Those who hold and those who are without property have ever formed distinct interests in society. Those who are creditors, and those who are debtors, fall under a like discrimination. A landed interest, a manufacturing interest, a mercantile interest, a moneyed interest, with many lesser interests, grow up of necessity in civilized nations, and divide them into different classes, actuated by different sentiments and views. The regulation of these various and interfering interests forms the principal task of modern legislation, and involves the spirit of party and faction in the necessary and ordinary operations of the government.

No man is allowed to be a judge in his own cause, because his interest would certainly bias his judgment, and, not improbably, corrupt his integrity. With equal, nay with greater reason, a body of men are unfit to be both judges and parties at the same time; yet what are many of the most important acts of legislation, but so many judicial determinations, not indeed concerning the rights of single persons, but concerning the rights of large bodies of citizens? And what are the different classes of legislators but advocates and parties to the causes which they determine? Is a law proposed concerning private debts? It is a question to which the creditors are parties on one side and the debtors on the other. Justice ought to hold the balance between them. Yet the parties are, and must be, themselves the judges; and the most numerous party, or, in other words, the most powerful faction, must be expected to prevail. Shall domestic manufactures be encouraged, and in what degree, by restrictions on foreign manufactures? are questions which would be differently decided by the landed and the manufacturing classes, and probably by neither with a sole regard to justice and the public good. The apportionment of taxes on the various descriptions of property is an act which seems to require the most exact impartiality; yet there is, perhaps, no legislative act in which greater opportunity and temptation are given to a predominant party to trample on the rules of justice. Every shilling with which they overburden the inferior number, is a shilling saved to their own pockets.

It is in vain to say that enlightened statesmen will be able to adjust these clashing interests, and render them all subservient to the public good. Enlightened statesmen will not always be at the helm. Nor, in many cases, can such an adjustment be made at all without taking into view indirect and remote considerations, which will rarely prevail over the immediate interest which one party may find in disregarding the rights of another or the good of the whole.

The inference to which we are brought is, that the *causes* of faction cannot be removed, and that relief is only to be sought in the means of controlling its *effects*.

If a faction consists of less than a majority, relief is supplied by the republican principle, which enables the majority to defeat its sinister views by regular vote. It may clog the administration, it may convulse the society; but it will be unable to execute and mask its violence under the forms of the Constitution. When a majority is included in a faction, the form of popular government, on the other hand, enables it to sacrifice to its ruling passion or interest both the public good and the rights of other citizens. To secure the public good and private rights against the danger of such a faction, and at the same time to preserve the spirit and the form of popular government, is then the great object to which our inquiries are directed. Let me add that it is the great desideratum by which this form of government can be rescued from the opprobrium under which it has so long labored, and be recommended to the esteem and adoption of mankind.

By what means is this object attainable? Evidently by one of two only. Either the existence of the same passion or interest in a majority at the same time must be prevented, or the majority, having such coexistent passion or interest, must be rendered, by their number and local situation, unable to concert and carry into effect schemes of oppression. If the impulse and the opportunity be suffered to coincide, we well know that neither moral nor religious motives can be relied on as an adequate control. They are not found to be such on the injustice and violence of individuals, and lose their efficacy in proportion to the number combined together, that is, in proportion as their efficacy becomes needful.

From this view of the subject it may be concluded that a pure democracy, by which I mean a society consisting of a small number of citizens, who assemble and administer the government in person, can admit of no cure for the mischiefs of faction. A common passion or interest will in almost every case, be felt by a majority of the whole; a communication and concert result from the form of government itself; and there is nothing to check the inducements to sacrifice the weaker party or an obnoxious individual. Hence it is that such democracies have ever been spectacles of turbulence and contention; have ever been found incompatible with personal security or the rights of property; and have in general been as short in their lives as they have been violent in their deaths. Theoretic politicians, who have patronized this species of government, have erroneously supposed that by reducing mankind to a perfect equality in their political rights, they would, at the same time, be perfectly equalized and assimilated in their possessions, their opinions, and their passions.

A republic, by which I mean a government in which the scheme of representation takes place, opens a different prospect, and promises the cure for which we are seeking. Let us examine the points in which it varies from pure democracy, and we shall comprehend both the nature of the cure and the efficacy which it must derive from the Union.

The two great points of difference between a democracy and a republic are: first, the delegation of the government, in the latter, to a small number of citizens elected by the rest; secondly, the greater number of citizens, and greater sphere of country, over which the latter may be extended.

The effect of the first difference is, on the one hand, to refine and enlarge the public views, by passing them through the medium of a chosen body of citizens, whose wisdom may best discern the true interest of their country, and whose patriotism and love of justice will be least likely to sacrifice it to temporary or partial considerations.

Under such a regulation, it may well happen that the public voice, pronounced by the representatives of the people, will be more consonant to the public good than if pronounced by the people themselves, convened for the purpose. On the other hand, the effect may be inverted. Men of factious tempers, of local prejudices, or of sinister designs, may, by intrigue, by corruption, or by other means, first obtain the suffrages, and then betray the interests, of the people. The question resulting is, whether small or extensive republics are more favorable to the election of proper guardians of the public weal; and it is clearly decided in favor of the latter by two obvious considerations:

In the first place, it is to be remarked that, however small the republic may be, the representatives must be raised to a certain number, in order to guard against the cabals of a few; and that, however large it may be, they must be limited to a certain number, in order to guard against the confusion of a multitude. Hence, the number of representatives in the two cases not being in proportion to that of the two constituents, and being proportionally greater in the small republic, it follows that, if the proportion of fit characters be not less in the large than in the small republic, the former will present a greater option, and consequently a greater probability of a fit choice.

In the next place, as each representative will be chosen by a greater number of citizens in the large than in the small republic, it will be more difficult for unworthy candidates to practice with success the vicious arts by which elections are too often carried; and the suffrages of the people being more free, will be more likely to center in men who possess the most attractive merit and the most diffusive and established characters.

It must be confessed that in this, as in most other cases, there is a mean, on both sides of which inconveniences will be found to lie. By enlarging too much the number of electors, you render the representative too little acquainted with all their local circumstances and lesser interests; as by reducing it too much, you render him unduly attached to these, and too little fit to comprehend and pursue great and national objects. The federal Constitution forms a happy combination in this respect; the great and aggregate interests being referred to the national, the local and particular to the State legislatures.

The other point of difference is, the greater number of citizens and extent of territory which may be brought within the compass of republican than of democratic government; and it is this circumstance principally which renders factious combinations less to be dreaded in the former than in the latter. The smaller the society, the fewer probably will be the distinct parties and interests composing it; the fewer the distinct parties and interests, the more frequently will a majority be found of the same party; and the smaller the number of individuals composing a majority, and the smaller the compass within which they are placed, the more easily will they concert and execute their plans of oppression. Extend the sphere, and you take in a greater variety of parties and interests; you make it less probable that a majority of the whole will have a common motive to invade the rights of other citizens; or if such a common motive exists, it will be more difficult for all who feel it to discover their own strength, and to act in unison with each other. Besides other impediments, it may be remarked that, where there is a consciousness of unjust or dishonorable purposes, communication is always checked by distrust in proportion to the number whose concurrence is necessary.

Hence, it clearly appears, that the same advantage which a republic has over a democracy, in controlling the effects of faction, is enjoyed by a large over a small republic—is enjoyed by the Union over the States composing it. Does the advantage consist in the substitution of representatives whose enlightened views and virtuous sentiments render them superior to local prejudices and to schemes of injustice? It will not be denied that the representation of the Union will be most likely to possess these requisite endowments. Does it consist in the greater security afforded by a greater variety of parties, against the event of any one party being able to outnumber and oppress the rest? In an equal degree does the increased variety of parties comprised within the Union increase this security? Does it, in fine, consist in the greater obstacles opposed to the concert and accomplishment of the secret wishes of an unjust and interested majority? Here, again, the extent of the Union gives it the most palpable advantage.

The influence of factious leaders may kindle a flame within their particular States, but will be unable to spread a general conflagration through the other States. A religious sect may degenerate into a political faction in a part of the Confederacy; but the variety of sects dispersed over the entire face of it must secure the national councils against any danger from that source. A rage for paper money, for an abolition of debts, for an equal division of property, or for any other improper or wicked project, will be less apt to pervade the whole body of the Union than a particular member of it; in the same proportion as such a malady is more likely to taint a particular county or district, than an entire State.

In the extent and proper structure of the Union, therefore, we behold a republican remedy for the diseases most incident to republican government. And according to the degree of pleasure and pride we feel in being republicans, ought to be our zeal in cherishing the spirit and supporting the character of Federalists.

THE FEDERALIST NO. 31 [2]

BY ALEXANDER HAMILTON

In disquisitions of every kind, there are certain primary truths, or first principles, upon which all subsequent reasonings must depend. These contain an internal evidence which, antecedent to all reflection or combination, commands the assent of the mind. Where it produces not this effect, it must proceed either from some defect or disorder in the ogans of perception, or from the influence of some strong interest, or passion, or prejudice. Of this nature are the maxims in geometry, that "the whole is greater than its parts; things equal to the same are equal to one another; two straight lines cannot enclose a space; and all right angles are equal to each other." Of the same nature are these other maxims in ethics and politics, that there cannot be an effect without a cause; that the means ought to be proportioned to the end; that every power ought to be commensurate with its object; that there ought to be no limitation of a power destined to effect a purpose which is itself incapable of limitation. And there are other truths in the two latter sciences which, if they cannot pretend to rank in the class of axioms, are yet such direct inferences from them, and so obvious in themselves, and so agreeable to the natural and unsophisticated dictates of common sense, that they challenge the assent of a sound and unbiased mind, with a degree of force and conviction almost equally irresistible.

The objects of geometrical inquiry are so entirely abstracted from those pursuits which stir up and put in motion the unruly passions of the human heart, that mankind, without difficulty, adopt not only the more simple theorems of the science, but even those abstruse paradoxes which, however they may appear susceptible of demonstration, are at variance with the natural conceptions which the mind, without the aid of philosophy, would be led to entertain upon the subject. The *infinite divisibility* of matter, or, in other words, the *infinite* divisibility of a *finite* thing, extending even to the minutest atom, is a point agreed among geometricians, though not less incomprehensible to common sense than any of those mysteries in religion, against which the batteries of infidelity have been so industriously levelled.

But in the sciences of morals and politics, men are found far less tractable. To a certain degree, it is right and useful that this should be the case. Caution and investigation are a necessary armor against error and imposition. But this untractableness may be carried too far,

[2] From the *New York Packet,* January 1, 1788.

and may degenerate into obstinacy, perverseness, or disingenuity. Though it cannot be pretended that the principles of moral and political knowledge have, in general, the same degree of certainty with those of mathematics, yet they have much better claims in this respect than, to judge from the conduct of men in particular situations, we should be disposed to allow them. The obscurity is much oftener in the passions and prejudices of the reasoner than in the subject. Men, upon too many occasions, do not give their own understandings fair play; but, yielding to some untoward bias, they entangle themselves in words and confound themselves in subtleties.

How else could it happen (if we admit the objectors to be sincere in their opposition), that positions so clear as those which manifest the necessity of a general power of taxation in the government of the Union, should have to encounter any adversaries among men of discernment? Though these positions have been elsewhere fully stated, they will perhaps not be improperly recapitulated in this place, as introductory to an examination of what may have been offered by way of objection to them. They are in substance as follows:

A government ought to contain in itself every power requisite to the full accomplishment of the objects committed to its care, and to the complete execution of the trusts for which it is responsible, free from every other control but a regard to the public good and to the sense of the people.

As the duties of superintending the national defense and of securing the public peace against foreign or domestic violence involve a provision for casualties and dangers to which no possible limits can be assigned, the power of making that provision ought to know no other bounds than the exigencies of the nation and the resources of the community.

As revenue is the essential engine by which the means of answering the national exigencies must be procured, the power of procuring that article in its full extent must necessarily be comprehended in that of providing for those exigencies.

As theory and practice conspire to prove that the power of procuring revenue is unavailing when exercised over the States in their collective capacities, the federal government must of necessity be invested with an unqualified power of taxation in the ordinary modes.

Did not experience evince the contrary, it would be natural to conclude that the propriety of a general power of taxation in the national government might safely be permitted to rest on the evidence of these propositions, unassisted by any additional arguments or illustrations. But we find, in fact, that the antagonists of the proposed Constitution, so far from acquiescing in their justness or truth, seem to make their principal and most zealous effort against this part of the plan. It may therefore be satisfactory to analyze the arguments with which they combat it.

Those of them which have been most labored with that view, seem in substance to amount to this: "It is not true, because the exigencies of the Union may not be susceptible of limitation, that its power of laying taxes ought to be unconfined. Revenue is as requisite to the purposes of the local administrations as to those of the Union; and the former are at least of equal importance with the latter to the happiness of the people. It is, therefore, as necessary that the State governments should be able to command the means of supplying their wants, as that the national government should possess the like faculty in respect to the wants of the Union. But an indefinite power of taxation in the *latter* might, and probably would in time, deprive the *former* of the means of providing for their own necessities; and would subject them entirely to the mercy of the national legislature. As the laws of the Union are to become the supreme law of the land, as it is to have power to pass all laws that may be *necessary* for carrying into execution the authorities with which it is proposed to vest it, the national government might at any time abolish the taxes imposed for State objects upon the pretense of an interference with its own. It might allege a necessity of doing this in order to give efficacy to the national revenues. And thus all the resources of taxation might by degrees become the subjects of federal monopoly, to the entire exclusion and destruction of the State governments."

This mode of reasoning appears sometimes to turn upon the supposition of usurpation in the national government; at other times it seems to be designed only as a deduction from the constitutional operation of its intended powers. It is only in the latter light that it can be admitted to have any pretensions to fairness. The moment we launch into conjectures about the usurpations of the federal government, we get into an unfathomable abyss, and fairly put ourselves out of the reach of all reasoning. Imagination may range at pleasure till it gets bewildered amidst the labyrinths of an enchanted castle, and knows not on which side to turn to extricate itself from the perplexities into which it has so rashly adventured. Whatever may be the limits or modifications of the powers of the Union, it is easy to imagine an endless train of possible dangers; and by indulging an excess of jealousy and timidity, we may bring ourselves to a state of absolute skepticism and irresolution. I repeat here what I have observed in substance in another place, that all observations founded upon the danger of usurpation ought to be referred to the composition and structure of the government, not to the nature or extent of its powers. The State governments, by their original constitutions, are invested with complete sovereignty. In what does our security consist against usurpation from that quarter? Doubtless in the manner of their formation, and in a due dependence of those who are to administer them upon the people. If the proposed construction of the federal government be found, upon an impartial examination of it, to be such as to afford, to a proper extent, the same species of security, all apprehensions on the score of usurpation ought to be discarded.

It should not be forgotten that a disposition in the State governments to encroach upon the rights of the Union is quite as probable as a disposition in the Union to encroach upon the rights of the State governments. What side would be likely to prevail in such a conflict, must depend on the means which the contending parties could employ toward insuring success. As in republics strength is always on the side of the people, and as there are weighty reasons to induce a belief that the State governments will commonly possess most influence over them, the natural conclusion is that such contests will be most apt to end to the disadvantage of the Union; and that there is a greater probability of encroachments by the members upon the federal head, than by the federal head upon the members. But it is evident that all conjectures of this kind must be extremely vague and fallible: and that it is by far the safest course to lay them altogether aside, and to confine our attention wholly to the nature and extent of the powers as they are delineated in the Constitution. Everything beyond this must be left to the prudence and firmness of the people; who, as they will hold the scale in their own hands, it is to be hoped, will always take care to preserve the constitutional equilibrium between the general and the State governments. Upon this ground, which is evidently the true one, it will not be difficult to obviate the objections which have been made to an indefinite power of taxation in the United States.

THE FEDERALIST NO. 47 [3]

BY JAMES MADISON

. . . One of the principal objections inculcated by the more respectable adversaries to the Constitution, is its supposed violation of the political maxim, that the legislative, executive, and judiciary departments ought to be separate and distinct. In the structure of the federal government, no regard, it is said, seems to have been paid to this essential precaution in favor of liberty. The several departments of power are distributed and blended in such a manner as at once to destroy all symmetry and beauty of form, and to expose some of the

[3] From the *New York Packet*, February 1, 1788.

essential parts of the edifice to the danger of being crushed by the disproportionate weight of other parts.

No political truth is certainly of greater intrinsic value, or is stamped with the authority of more enlightened patrons of liberty, than that on which the objection is founded. The accumulation of all powers, legislative, executive, and judiciary, in the same hands, whether of one, a few, or many, and whether hereditary, self-appointed, or elective, may justly be pronounced the very definition of tyranny. Were the federal Constitution, therefore, really chargeable with the accumulation of power, or with a mixture of powers, having a dangerous tendency to such an accumulation, no further arguments would be necessary to inspire a universal reprobation of the system. I persuade myself, however, that it will be made apparent to everyone, that the charge cannot be supported, and that the maxim on which it relies has been totally misconceived and misapplied. In order to form correct ideas on this important subject, it will be proper to investigate the sense in which the preservation of liberty requires that the three great departments of power should be separate and distinct.

The oracle who is always consulted and cited on this subject is the celebrated Montesquieu. If he be not the author of this invaluable precept in the science of politics, he has the merit at least of displaying and recommending it most effectually to the attention of mankind. Let us endeavor, in the first place, to ascertain his meaning on this point.

The British Constitution was to Montesquieu what Homer has been to the didactic writers on epic poetry. As the latter have considered the work of the immortal bard as the perfect model from which the principles and rules of the epic art were to be drawn, and by which all similar works were to be judged, so this great political critic appears to have viewed the Constitution of England as the standard, or to use his own expression, as the mirror of political liberty; and to have delivered, in the form of elementary truths, the several characteristic principles of that particular system. That we may be sure, then, not to mistake his meaning in this case, let us recur to the source from which the maxim was drawn.

On the slightest view of the British Constitution, we must perceive that the legislative, executive, and judiciary departments are by no means totally separate and distinct from each other. The executive magistrate forms an integral part of the legislative authority. He alone has the prerogative of making treaties with foreign sovereigns, which, when made, have, under certain limitations, the force of legislative acts. All the members of the judiciary department are appointed by him, can be removed by him on the address of the two Houses of Parliament, and form, when he pleases to consult them, one of his constitutional councils. One branch of the legislative department forms

also a great constitutional council to the executive chief, as, on another
hand, it is the sole depositary of judicial power in cases of impeachment, and is invested with the supreme appellate jurisdiction in all
other cases. The judges, again, are so far connected with the legislative department as often to attend and participate in its deliberations,
though not admitted to a legislative vote.

From these facts, by which Montesquieu was guided, it may clearly
be inferred that, in saying "There can be no liberty where the legislative and executive powers are united in the same person, or body of
magistrates," or, "if the power of judging be not separated from the
legislative and executive powers," he did not mean that these departments ought to have no *partial agency* in, or no *control* over, the acts
of each other. His meaning, as his own words import, and still more
conclusively as illustrated by the example in his eye, can amount to
no more than this, that where the *whole* power of one department is
exercised by the same hands which possess the *whole* power of another department, the fundamental principles of a free constitution
are subverted. This would have been the case in the constitution examined by him, if the king, who is the sole executive magistrate, had
possessed also the complete legislative power, or the supreme administration of justice; or if the entire legislative body had possessed the
supreme judiciary, or the supreme executive authority. This, however
is not among the vices of that constitution. The magistrate in whom
the whole executive power resides cannot of himself make a law,
though he can put a negative on every law; nor administer justice in
person, though he has the appointment of those who do administer it.
The judges can exercise no executive prerogative, though they are
shoots from the executive stock; nor any legislative function, though
they may be advised with by the legislative councils. The entire legislature can perform no judiciary act, though by the joint act of two of
its branches the judges may be removed from their offices, and though
one of its branches is possessed of the judicial power in the last resort.
The entire legislature, again, can exercise no executive prerogative,
though one of its branches constitutes the supreme executive magis-
tracy, and another, on the impeachment of a third, can try and condemn all the subordinate officers in the executive department.

The reasons on which Montesquieu grounds his maxim are a further
demonstration of his meaning. "When the legislative and executive
powers are united in the same person or body," says he, "there can be
no liberty, because apprehensions may arise lest *the same* monarch or
senate should *enact* tyrannical laws to *execute* them in a tyrannical
manner." Again: "Were the power of judging joined with the legislative, the life and liberty of the subject would be exposed to arbitrary
control, for *the judge* would then be *the legislator*. Were it joined to

the executive power, *the judge* might behave with all the violence of *an oppressor*." Some of these reasons are more fully explained in other passages; but briefly stated as they are here, they sufficiently establish the meaning which we have put on this celebrated maxim of this celebrated author. . . .

BIBLIOGRAPHY

ALEXANDER HAMILTON

HAMILTON, Alexander, JAY, John, MADISON, James, *The Federalist, A Commentary on The Constitution of the United States*. New York, 1788.

———— *Works*, ed. by H. C. Lodge. New York: G. P. Putnam's Sons, 1904, 12 vols.

———— *The Papers of Alexander Hamilton*, ed. by Harold C. Syrett. New York: Columbia U. Press, 1961, 2 vols.

———— *Industrial and Commercial Correspondence of Alexander Hamilton*, ed. by A. H. Cole. Chicago: A. W. Shaw, 1928.

———— *Papers on Public Credit, Commerce and Finance*, ed. by Samuel McKee, Jr. New York: Columbia U. Press, 1934.

———— *Selections Representing His Life, His Thought, and His Style*, ed. by Bower Aly. New York: The Liberal Arts Press, 1957.

BOWERS, Claude G., *Jefferson and Hamilton*. New York: Houghton, Mifflin, 1925.

FORD, Henry J., *Alexander Hamilton*. New York: Scribner's Sons, 1920.

KENYON, Cecelia M., "Alexander Hamilton: Rousseau of the Right." *Political Science Quarterly*, Vol. LXXIII, No. 2 (June, 1958), pp. 161–78.

MITCHELL, Broadus, *Alexander Hamilton. The National Adventure. 1788–1804*. New York: Macmillan Co., 1962.

OLIVER, Frederick S., *Alexander Hamilton*. London: A. Constable, 1906.

PADOVER, Saul K., ed., *The Mind of Alexander Hamilton*. New York: Harper, 1958.

TUGWELL, Rexford G., DORFMAN, Joseph, "Alexander Hamilton: Nation-Maker." *Columbia University Quarterly*, Vol. XXIX (1937), pp. 209–26; Vol. XXX (1938), pp. 59–72.

JAMES MADISON

MADISON, James, *Writings*. ed. by Guillard Hunt. New York: G. P. Putnam's Sons, 1900–10, 9 vols.

BRANT, Irving, *James Madison, Father of the Constitution*. Vol. III. New York: The Bobbs-Merrill Co., 1950. 6 vols.

BURNS, Edward M., *James Madison, Philosopher of the Constitution*. New Brunswick, N.J.: Rutgers U. Press, 1938.

GAY, Sydney H., *James Madison, American Statesman*. Boston: Houghton Mifflin, 1884.

HUNT, Guillard, *The Life of James Madison*. New York: Doubleday, Page & Co., 1902.

KOCH, Adrienne, *Jefferson and Madison: The Great Collaboration*. New York: Knopf, 1950.

RIVES, William C., *History of the Life and Times of James Madison*. Boston: Little, Brown, 1866–1873. 3 vols.

JOHN JAY

JAY, John, *The Correspondence and Public Papers of John Jay*, ed. by H. P. Johnston. New York: G. P. Putnam's Sons, 1890–93, 4 vols.

MONAGHAN, Frank, *John Jay*. New York: Bobbs-Merrill, 1935.

PELLEW, George, *John Jay*, Vol. IX. American Statesmen Series, ed. by J. T. Morse. New York: Houghton Mifflin, 1895.

FLANDERS, Henry, *The Lives and Times of the Chief Justices of the Supreme Court of the United States. First Series: John Jay and John Rutledge*, Vol. XXV. Philadelphia: Lippincott, Grambo & Co., 1855.

JAY, William, *The Life of John Jay: With Selections from His Correspondence and Miscellaneous Papers*. New York: J. & J. Harper, 1833, 2 vols.

STRINGER, George Alfred, *Life and Public Services of John Jay, Patriot, Jurist, Statesman, Diplomatist*. Buffalo: Buffalo Historical Society Publications, 1904.

Benjamin Rush

[1745–1813]

Although Benjamin Rush was primarily a medical man—he is sometimes called the father of psychiatry in America—he was also interested in questions of philosophical significance and was known as a philosophical materialist. The materialists attempted to apply generally what they had learned from Newtonian science and to explain all processes in physical terms. Thus, in *Three Lectures Upon Animal Life* (1799), Rush holds that the human body is a unit endowed with sensibility, and that life is the effect of stimuli acting upon that sensibility and extending throughout the body. In his essay, *The Influence of Physical Causes Upon the Moral Faculty* (1786), part of which is here reprinted, Rush argued that moral and immoral behavior may be explained by physical causes, and he enumerated a long list of material influences upon morality. In *Observations and Reasoning in Medicine* (1791), Rush advocated both empiricism and rationalism in medical inquiry. He held that medical science was in its infancy, and he urged continued and sober research.

Rush was born in Pennsylvania. He entered Princeton University as a very young man, graduating at the age of fifteen. He was awarded a medical degree from the University of Edinburgh (1768), was appointed Professor of Chemistry at the College and Academy of Philadelphia (the first medical school in America), and later, when the College became a University, he was appointed Professor of the Institutes and Practices of Medicine. Like so many others, Rush was involved with the struggle for Independence. He was a member of the Revolutionary Congress which passed the Declaration of Independence. He served in the war as Surgeon General. In 1797, he was appointed Treasurer of the United States Mint, a position he held until his death. Rush was a man of wide social interests and a truly democratic spirit. He was an advocate of free public schools, a foe of slavery and of capital punishment, the founder of the Philadelphia Dispensary, and a vehement critic of harsh penal laws. He also had a deep concern for the plight of the insane and worked for improvements in their conditions. Rush managed to reconcile his materialism with a belief in God and other key tenets of religion, and was indeed more orthodox than many other leading figures of the Revolutionary period.

THE INFLUENCE OF PHYSICAL CAUSES
UPON THE MORAL FACULTY [1]

. . . It has long been a question among metaphysicians, whether the conscience be seated in the will or in the understanding. The controversy can only be settled by admitting the will to be the seat of the moral faculty, and the understanding to be the seat of the conscience. The mysterious nature of the union of those two moral principles with the will and understanding is a subject foreign to the business of the present inquiry.

As I consider virtue and vice to consist in action, and not in opinion, and as this action has its seat in the will, and not in the conscience, I shall confine my inquiries chiefly to the influence of physical causes upon that moral power of the mind, which is connected with volition, although many of these causes act likewise upon the conscience, as I shall show hereafter. The state of the moral faculty is visible in actions, which affect the well-being of society. The state of the conscience is invisible, and therefore removed beyond our investigation.

The moral faculty has received different names from different authors. It is the "moral sense" of Dr. Hutchison; "the sympathy" of Dr. Adam Smith; the "moral instinct" of Rousseau; and "the light that lighteth every man that cometh into the world" of Saint John. I have adopted the term of moral faculty from Dr. Beattie, because I conceive it conveys, with the most perspicuity, the idea of a capacity in the mind of choosing good and evil.

Our books of medicine contain many records of the effects of physical causes upon the memory, the imagination, and the judgment. In some instances we behold their operation only on one, in others on two, and in many cases, upon the whole of these faculties. Their derangement has received different names, according to the number or nature of the faculties that are affected. The loss of memory has been called "amnesia"; false judgment upon one subject has been called "melancholia"; false judgment upon all subjects has been called "mania"; and a defect of all the three intellectual faculties that have been mentioned has received the name of "amentia." Persons who labor under the derangement, or want, of these faculties of the mind, are considered, very properly, as subjects of medicine; and there are many cases upon record, that prove that their diseases have yielded to the healing art.

[1] Delivered before the American Philosophical Society in 1786.

In order to illustrate the effects of physical causes upon the moral faculty, it will be necessary first to show their effects upon the memory, the imagination, and the judgment; and at the same time to point out the analogy between their operation upon the intellectual faculties of the mind and the moral faculty.

1. Do we observe a connection between the intellectual faculties and the degrees of consistency and firmness of the brain in infancy and childhood? The same connection has been observed between the strength, as well as the progress, of the moral faculty in children.

2. Do we observe a certain size of the brain, and a peculiar cast of features, such as the prominent eye, and the aquiline nose, to be connected with extraordinary portions of genius? We observe a similar connection between the figure and temperament of the body and certain moral qualities. Hence we often ascribe good temper and benevolence to corpulency, and irascibility to sanguineous habits. Caesar thought himself safe in the friendship of the "sleek-headed" Anthony and Dolabella, but was afraid to trust to the professions of the slender Cassius.

3. Do we observe certain degrees of the intellectual faculties to be hereditary in certain families? The same observation has been frequently extended to moral qualities. Hence we often find certain virtues and vices as peculiar to families, through all their degrees of consanguinity and duration, as a peculiarity of voice, complexion, or shape.

4. Do we observe instances of a total want of memory, imagination, and judgment, either from an original defect in the stamina of the brain, or from the influence of physical causes? The same unnatural defect is sometimes observed, and probably from the same causes, of a moral faculty. The celebrated Servin, whose character is drawn by the Duke of Sully, in his *Memoirs*, appears to be an instance of the total absence of the moral faculty, while the chasm produced by this defect, seems to have been filled up by a more than common extension of every other power of his mind. I beg leave to repeat the history of this prodigy of vice and knowledge. "Let the reader represent to himself a man of a genius so lively, and of an understanding so extensive, as rendered him scarce ignorant of anything that could be known; of so vast and ready a comprehension, that he immediately made himself master of whatever he attempted; and of so prodigious a memory, that he never forgot what he once learned. He possessed all parts of philosophy, and the mathematics, particularly fortification and drawing. Even in theology he was so well skilled, that he was an excellent preacher, whenever he had a mind to exert that talent, and an able disputant for and against the reformed religion, indifferently. He not only understood Greek,

Hebrew, and all the languages which we call learned, but also all the different jargons, or modern dialects. He accented and pronounced them so naturally, and so perfectly imitated the gestures and manners both of the several nations of Europe, and the particular provinces of France, that he might have been taken for a native of all, or any, of these countries: and this quality he applied to counterfeit all sorts of persons, wherein he succeeded wonderfully. He was, moreover, the best comedian, and the greatest droll that perhaps ever appeared. He had a genius for poetry, and had wrote many verses. He played upon almost all instruments, was a perfect master of music, and sang most agreeably and justly. He likewise could say mass, for he was of a disposition to do, as well as to know, all things. His body was perfectly well suited to his mind. He was light, nimble, and dexterous, and fit for all exercises. He could ride well, and in dancing, wrestling, and leaping, he was admired. There are not any recreative games that he did not know, and he was skilled in almost all mechanic arts. But now for the reverse of the medal. Here it appeared, that he was treacherous, cruel, cowardly, deceitful, a liar, a cheat, a drunkard, and a glutton, a sharper in play, immersed in every species of vice, a blasphemer, an atheist. In a word, in him might be found all the vices that are contrary to nature, honor, religion, and society, the truth of which he himself evinced with his latest breath; for he died in the flower of his age, in a common brothel, perfectly corrupted by his debaucheries, and expired with the glass in his hand, cursing and denying God."[2]

It was probably a state of the human mind such as has been described, that our Saviour alluded to in the disciple who was about to betray him, when he called him "a devil." Perhaps the essence of depravity, in infernal spirits, consists in their being wholly devoid of a moral faculty. In them the will has probably lost the power of choosing,[3] as well as the capacity of enjoying moral good. It is true, we read of their trembling in a belief of the existence of a God, and of their anticipating future punishment, by asking whether they were to be tormented before their time: but this is the effect of conscience, and hence arises another argument in favor of this judicial power of the mind being distinct from the moral faculty. It would seem as if the Supreme Being had preserved the moral faculty in man from the ruins of his fall, on purpose to guide him back again to Paradise, and at the same time had constituted the conscience, both

---

[2] Vol. iii. pp. 216, 217.—R.

[3] Milton seems to have been of this opinion. Hence, after ascribing repentance to Satan, he makes him declare,

> "Farewell remorse; all good to me is lost,
> Evil, be thou my good."_____

PARADISE LOST, Book IV.—R.

in men and fallen spirits, a kind of royalty in his moral empire, on purpose to show his property in all intelligent creatures, and their original resemblance to himself. Perhaps the essence of moral depravity in man consists in a total, but temporary, suspension of the power of conscience. Persons in this situation are emphatically said in the Scriptures to "be past feeling," and to have their consciences seared with a "hot iron"; they are likewise said to be "twice dead," that is, the same torpor, or moral insensibility, has seized both the moral faculty and the conscience.

5. Do we ever observe instances of the existence of only one of the three intellectual powers of the mind that have been named, in the absence of the other two? We observe something of the same kind with respect to the moral faculty. I once knew a man, who discovered no one mark of reason, who possessed the moral sense or faculty in so high a degree, that he spent his whole life in acts of benevolence. He was not only inoffensive (which is not always the case with idiots), but he was kind and affectionate to everybody. He had no ideas of time, but what were suggested to him by the returns of the stated periods for public worship, in which he appeared to take great delight. He spent several hours of every day in devotion, in which he was so careful to be private, that he was once found in the most improbable place in the world for that purpose, viz. in an oven.

6. Do we observe the memory, the imagination, and the judgment to be affected by diseases, particularly by madness? Where is the physician who has not seen the moral faculty affected from the same causes! How often do we see the temper wholly changed by a fit of sickness! And how often do we hear persons of the most delicate virtue utter speeches, in the delirium of a fever, that are offensive to decency or good manners! I have heard a well-attested history of a clergyman of the most exemplary moral character, who spent the last moments of a fever, which deprived him both of his reason and his life, in profane cursing and swearing. I once attended a young woman in a nervous fever, who discovered, after her recovery, a loss of her former habit of veracity. Her memory (a defect of which might be suspected of being the cause of this vice), was in every respect as perfect as it was before the attack of the fever.[4] The instances of immorality in maniacs, who were formerly distinguished for the opposite character, are so numerous and well-known that it will not be necessary to select any cases to establish the truth of the proposition contained under this head.

7. Do we observe any of the three intellectual faculties that have been named enlarged by diseases? Patients in the delirium of a fever

[4] I have selected this case from many others which have come under my notice, in which the moral faculty appeared to be impaired by diseases, particularly by the typhus of Dr. Cullen, and by those species of palsy which affect the brain.—R.

often discover extraordinary flights of imagination, and madmen often astonish us with their wonderful acts of memory. The same enlargement, sometimes, appears in the operations of the moral faculty. I have more than once heard the most sublime discourses of morality in the cell of a hospital; and who has not seen instances of patients in acute diseases discovering degrees of benevolence and integrity, that were not natural to them in the ordinary course of their lives?[5]

8. Do we ever observe a partial insanity or false perception on one subject, while the judgment is sound and correct upon all others? We perceive, in some instances, a similar defect in the moral faculty. There are persons who are moral in the highest degree as to certain duties, who nevertheless live under the influence of some one vice. I knew an instance of a woman, who was exemplary in her obedience to every command of the moral law, except one. She could not refrain from stealing. What made this vice the more remarkable was, that she was in easy circumstances, and not addicted to extravagance in anything. Such was her propensity to this vice, that when she could lay her hands upon nothing more valuable, she would often, at the table of a friend, fill her pockets secretly with bread. As a proof that her judgment was not affected by this defect in her moral faculty, she would both confess and lament her crime, when detected in it.

9. Do we observe the imagination in many instances to be affected with apprehensions of dangers that have no existence? In like manner we observe the moral faculty to discover a sensibility to vice, that is by no means proportioned to its degrees of depravity. How often do we see persons laboring under this morbid sensibility of the moral faculty refuse to give a direct answer to a plain question, that related perhaps only to the weather, or to the hour of the day, lest they should wound the peace of their minds by telling a falsehood!

10. Do dreams affect the memory, the imagination, and the judgment? Dreams are nothing but incoherent ideas, occasioned by partial or imperfect sleep. There is a variety in the suspension of the faculties and operations of the mind in this state of the system. In some cases the imagination only is deranged in dreams, in others the memory is affected, and in others the judgment. But there are cases in which the change that is produced in the state of the brain, by means of sleep, affects the moral faculty likewise; hence we sometimes dream of doing and saying things when asleep, which we shudder at as soon as we awake. This supposed defection from virtue exists frequently in dreams, where the memory and judgment are scarcely impaired.

---

[5] Xenophon makes Cyrus declare, in his last moments, "That the soul of man, at the hour of death, appears *most divine,* and then foresees something of future events."—R.

It cannot therefore be ascribed to an absence of the exercises of those two powers of the mind.

11. Do we read, in the accounts of travelers, of men, who, in respect of intellectual capacity and enjoyments, are but a few degrees above brutes? We read likewise of a similar degradation of our species, in respect to moral capacity and feeling. Here it will be necessary to remark, that the low degrees of moral perception, that have been discovered in certain African and Russian tribes of men, no more invalidate our proposition of the universal and essential existence of a moral faculty in the human mind, than the low state of their intellects prove, that reason is not natural to man. Their perceptions of good and evil are in exact proportion to their intellectual faculties. But I will go further, and admit, with Mr. Locke,[6] that some savage nations are totally devoid of the moral faculty, yet it will by no means follow, that this was the original constitution of their minds. The appetite for certain aliments is uniform among all mankind. Where is the nation and the individual, in their primitive state of health, to whom bread is not agreeable? But if we should find savages, or individuals, whose stomachs have been so disordered by intemperance as to refuse this simple and wholesome article of diet, shall we assert that this was the original constitution of their appetites? By no means. As well might we assert, because savages destroy their beauty by painting and cutting their faces, that the principles of taste do not exist naturally in the human mind. It is with virtue as with fire. It exists in the mind, as fire does in certain bodies, in a latent or quiescent state. As collision renders the one sensible, so education renders the other visible. It would be as absurd to maintain, because olives become agreeable to many people from habit, that we have no natural appetites for any other kind of food, as to assert that any part of the human species exists without a moral principle, because in some of them it has wanted causes to excite it into action, or has been perverted by example. There are appetites that are wholly artificial. There are tastes so entirely vitiated as to perceive beauty in deformity. There are torpid and unnatural passions. Why, under certain unfavorable circumstances, may there not exist also a moral faculty, in a state of sleep, or subject to mistakes?

The only apology I shall make, for presuming to differ from that justly celebrated oracle,[7] who first unfolded to us a map of the intellectual world, shall be, that the eagle eye of genius often darts its views beyond the notice of facts, which are accommodated to the slender organs of perception of men, who possess no other talent than that of observation.

[6] Essay concerning the Human Understanding, Book I, chap. 3.—R.

[7] Mr. Locke.—R.

It is not surprising, that Mr. Locke has confounded this moral principle with *reason*, or that Lord Shaftesbury has confounded it with *taste*, since all three of these faculties agree in the objects of their approbation, notwithstanding they exist in the mind independently of each other. The favorable influence, which the progress of science and taste has had upon the morals, can be ascribed to nothing else but to the perfect union that subsists in nature between the dictates of reason, of taste, and of the moral faculty. Why has the spirit of humanity made such rapid progress for some years past in the courts of Europe? It is because kings and their ministers have been taught to *reason* upon philosophical subjects. Why have indecency and profanity been banished from the stage in London and Paris? It is because immorality is an offense against the highly cultivated *taste* of the French and English nations.

It must afford great pleasure to the lovers of virtue, to behold the depth and extent of this moral principle in the human mind. Happily for the human race, the intimations of duty and the road to happiness are not left to the slow operations or doubtful inductions of reason, nor to the precarious decisions of taste. Hence we often find the moral faculty in a state of vigor in persons in whom reason and taste exist in a weak, or in an uncultivated state. It is worthy of notice, likewise, that while second thoughts are best in matters of judgment, first thoughts are always to be perferred in matters that relate to morality. Second thoughts, in these cases, are generally parleys between duty and corrupted inclinations. Hence Rousseau has justly said, that "a well regulated moral instinct is the surest guide to happiness."

It must afford equal pleasure to the lovers of virtue to behold, that our moral conduct and happiness are not committed to the determination of a single legislative power. The conscience, like a wise and faithful legislative council, performs the office of a check upon the moral faculty, and thus prevents the fatal consequences of immoral actions.

An objection, I foresee, will arise to the doctrine of the influence of physical causes upon the moral faculty, from its being supposed to favor the opinion of the *materiality* of the soul. But I do not see that this doctrine obliges us to decide upon the question of the nature of the soul, any more than the facts which prove the influence of physical causes upon the memory, the imagination, or the judgment. I shall, however, remark upon this subject, that the writers in favor of the *immortality* of the soul have done that truth great injury, by connecting it necessarily with its immateriality. The immortality of the soul depends upon the will of the Deity, and not upon the supposed properties of spirit. Matter is in its own nature as immortal as spirit.

It is resolvable by heat and mixture into a variety of forms; but it requires the same Almighty hand to annihilate it that it did to create it. I know of no arguments to prove the immortality of the soul, but such as are derived from the Christian revelation.[8] It would be as reasonable to assert that the basin of the ocean is immortal, from the greatness of its capacity to hold water; or that we are to live forever in this world, because we are afraid of dying; as to maintain the immortality of the soul, from the greatness of its capacity for knowledge and happiness, or from its dread of annihilation.

I remarked, in the beginning of this discourse, that persons who are deprived of the just exercise of memory, imagination, or judgment, were proper subjects of medicine; and that there are many cases upon record which prove that the diseases from the derangement of these faculties have yielded to the healing art.

It is perhaps only because the diseases of the moral faculty have not been traced to a connection with physical causes, that medical writers have neglected to give them a place in their systems of nosology, and that so few attempts have been hitherto made to lessen or remove them, by physical as well as rational and moral remedies.

I shall not attempt to derive any support to my opinions from the analogy of the influence of physical causes upon the temper and conduct of brute animals. The facts which I shall produce in favor of the action of these causes upon morals in the human species will, I hope, render unnecessary the arguments that might be drawn from that quarter.

I am aware that in venturing upon this subject I step upon untrodden ground. I feel as Æneas did, when he was about to enter the gates of Avernus, but without a sybil to instruct me in the mysteries that are before me. I foresee, that men who have been educated in the mechanical habits of adopting popular or established opinions will revolt at the doctrine I am about to deliver, while men of sense and genius will hear my propositions with candor, and if they do not adopt them, will commend that boldness of inquiry that prompted me to broach them.

I shall begin with an attempt to supply the defects of nosological writers, by naming the partial or weakened action of the moral faculty, "micronomia." The total absence of this faculty I shall call "anomia." By the law, referred to in these new genera of vesania, I mean the law of nature written in the human heart, and which I formerly quoted from the writings of Saint Paul.

In treating of the effects of physical causes upon the moral faculty, it might help to extend our ideas upon this subject, to reduce virtues

---

[8] "Life and immortality *are* brought to light *only* through the gospel."

2 Tim. i:10–R

and vices to certain species, and to point out the effects of particular species of virtue and vice; but this would lead us into a field too extensive for the limits of the present inquiry. I shall only hint at a few cases, and have no doubt but the ingenuity of my auditors will supply my silence, by applying the rest.

It is immaterial, whether the physical causes that are to be enumerated act upon the moral faculty through the medium of the senses, the passions, the memory, or the imagination. Their influence is equally certain, whether they act as remote, predisposing, or occasional causes.

1. The effects of CLIMATE upon the moral faculty claim our first attention. . . .

2. The effects of DIET upon the moral faculty are more certain, though less attended to, than the effects of climate. . . .

3. The effects of CERTAIN DRINKS upon the moral faculty are not less observable than upon the intellectual powers of the mind. . . .

4. EXTREME HUNGER produces the most unfriendly effects upon moral sensibility. . . .

5. I hinted formerly, in proving the analogy between the effects of DISEASES upon the intellects, and upon the moral faculty, that the latter was frequently impaired by fevers and madness. . . .

6. IDLENESS is the parent of every vice. . . . LABOR of all kinds favors and facilitates the practice of virtue. . . .

7. The effects of EXCESSIVE SLEEP are intimately connected with the effects of idleness upon the moral faculty. . . .

8. The effects of BODILY PAIN upon the moral, are not less remarkable than upon the intellectual powers of the mind. . . .

9. Too much cannot be said in favor of CLEANLINESS, as a physical means of promoting virtue. . . .

10. I hope I shall be excused in placing SOLITUDE among the physical causes which influence the moral faculty, when I add, that I confine its effects to persons who are irreclaimable by rational or moral remedies. . . .

11. Connected with solitude, as a mechanical means of promoting virture, SILENCE deserves to be mentioned in this place. . . .

12. The effects of MUSIC upon the moral faculty, have been felt and recorded in every country. . . .

13. The ELOQUENCE of the PULPIT is nearly allied to music in its effects upon the moral faculty. . . .

14. ODORS of various kinds have been observed to act in the most sensible manner upon the moral faculty. . . .

15. It will be sufficient only to mention LIGHT and DARKNESS, to suggest facts in favor of the influence of each of them upon moral sensibility. . . .

17. What shall we say of the effects of MEDICINES upon the moral faculty? That many substances in the materia medica act . . . upon the moral faculty? . . .

Thus have I enumerated the principal causes which act mechanically upon morals. If, from the combined action of physical powers that are opposed to each other, the moral faculty should become stationary, or if the virtue or vice produced by them should form a neutral quality, composed of both of them, I hope it will not call in question the truth of our general propositions. I have only mentioned the effects of physical causes in a simple state. . . .

BIBLIOGRAPHY

RUSH, Benjamin, *An Oration, Delivered Before the American Philosophical Society, Containing an Inquiry into the Influence of Physical Causes upon the Moral Faculty.* Philadelphia, 1786.

_____ *Essays: Literary, Moral and Philosophical.* Philadelphia, 1798.

_____ *An Inquiry into the Cause of Animal Life,* in *Medical Inquiries and Observations,* 3rd ed. Philadelphia, 1809, 4 vols.

_____ *Sixteen Introductory Lectures, to Courses of Lectures upon the Institutes and Practice of Medicine, with a Syllabus of the Latter. To Which Are Added Two Lectures upon the Pleasures of the Senses and of the Mind with an Inquiry into Their Proximate Cause.* Philadelphia, 1811.

_____ *Medical Inquiries and Observations upon the Diseases of the Mind.* Philadelphia, 1812.

_____ *The Selected Writings of Benjamin Rush,* ed. by Dagobert D. Runes. New York: Philosophical Library, 1947.

_____ *The Autobiography of Benjamin Rush,* ed. by G. W. Corner. Princeton, N.J.: Princeton U. Press, 1948.

BIDDLE, Louis A., ed., *A Memorial Containing Travels Through Life or Sundry Incident in the Life of Dr. Benjamin Rush.* Lanordie, Pa., 1905.

GOOD, Harry G., *Benjamin Rush and His Services to American Education.* Bluffton, Ohio: American Educator Co., 1918.

GOODMAN, Nathan G., *Benjamin Rush: Physician and Citizen (1746–1813).* Philadelphia: U. of Pennsylvania Press, 1934.

LETTSOM, John Coakley, *Recollection of Dr. Rush.* London, 1815.

Ethan Allen

[1737–1789]

Ethan Allen is best known as a patriot, having captured Fort Ticonderoga from the English, and having performed other military exploits during the War of Independence. Although he was born in Litchfield, Connecticut, he spent most of his adult life in Vermont, where he became Brigadier General of the militia and an acknowledged leader (especially in disputes that Vermont had with neighboring states). *Reason the Only Oracle of Man* (1784), whose authorship had been questioned by some of his detractors, is the first major deistic work published in the United States; and probably the first formal criticism of Christianity, appearing several years before Paine's more famous *Age of Reason*. Allen was bitterly attacked by President Dwight of Yale and others for being anti-Christian. In the "Preface," Allen writes: "I have generally been denominated a Deist, the reality of which I never disputed, being conscious I am no Christian . . . and as to being a Deist, I know not, strictly speaking, whether I am or not, for I have never read their writings." Whether Allen had been directly influenced by other deists is open to question. Like others of his age he condemned the traditional religion of revelation, miracles, and faith. He attacked Calvinism and the notion that reason was somehow depraved. *Reason the Only Oracle of Man* is throughout a forceful illustration of freethinking and of the independent frontier mind breaking away from the authority of tradition.

REASON THE ONLY ORACLE OF MAN [1]

Chapter I,

§ I. The Duty of Reforming Mankind from Superstition and Error, and the Good Consequences of It

The desire of knowledge has engaged the attention of the wise and curious among mankind of all ages, which has been productive of extending the arts and sciences far and wide in the several quarters of the globe, and excited the contemplative to explore nature's laws

[1] From *Reason the Only Oracle of Man*, first published in Bennington, Vermont, 1784.

in a gradual series of improvement, until philosophy, astronomy, geography and history, with many other branches of science, have arrived to a great degree of perfection.

It is nevertheless to be regretted that the bulk of mankind, even in those nations which are most celebrated for learning and wisdom, are still carried down the torrent of superstition, and entertain very unworthy apprehensions of the Being, Perfections, Creation, and Providence of God, and their duty to him, which lays an indispensable obligation on the philosophic friends of human nature, unanimously to exert themselves in every lawful, wise, and prudent method, to endeavor to reclaim mankind from their ignorance and delusion, by enlightening their minds in those great and sublime truths concerning God and his providence, and their obligations to moral rectitude, which in this world, and that which is to come, cannot fail greatly to affect their happiness and well-being.

Though "none by searching can find out God, or the Almighty to perfection," yet I am persuaded, that if mankind would dare to exercise their reason as freely on those divine topics, as they do in the common concerns of life, they would, in a great measure, rid themselves of their blindness and superstition, gain more exalted ideas of God and their obligations to him and one another, and be proportionably delighted and blessed with the views of his moral government, make better members of society, and acquire many powerful incentives to the practice of morality, which is the last and greatest perfection that human nature is capable of.

§ II. Of the Being of God

The Laws of Nature having subjected mankind to a state of absolute dependence on something out of, and manifestly beyond themselves, or the compound exertion of their natural powers, gave them the first conception of a superior principle of existing; otherwise they could have had no possible conception of a superintending power. But this sense of dependency, which results from experience and reasoning on the facts, which every day cannot fail to produce, has uniformly established the knowledge of our dependence to every individual of the species who are rational, which necessarily involves or contains in it the idea of a ruling power, or that there is a God, which ideas are synonymous.

The globe with its productions, the planets in their motions, and the starry heavens in their magnitudes, surprise our senses and confound our reason, in their munificent lessons of instruction concerning God, by means whereof we are apt to be more or less lost in our ideas of the object of divine adoration, though at the same time everyone is truly sensible that their being and preservation is from God. We are too apt to confound our ideas of God with his works, and take the latter for the former. Thus barbarous and unlearned nations have imagined that inasmuch as the sun in its influence is beneficial to them in bringing forth the spring of the year, causing the production of vegetation and food for their subsistence, that therefore it is their God: while others have located other parts of creation, and ascribe to them the prerogatives of God; and mere creatures and images have been substituted for gods by the wickedness or weakness of man, or both together. It seems that mankind in most ages and parts of the world have been fond of corporeal deities with whom their outward senses might be gratified, or as fantastically diverted from the just apprehension of the true God by a supposed supernatural intercourse with invisible and mere spiritual beings, to whom they ascribe divinity, so that through one means or other, the character of the true God has been much neglected, to the great detriment of truth, justice and morality in the world; nor is it possible, that mankind can be uniform in their religious opinions, or worship God according to knowledge, except they can form a consistent arrangement of ideas of the Divine character.

Although we extended our ideas retrospectively ever so far upon the succession, yet no one cause in the extended order of succession, which depends upon another prior to itself, can be the independent cause of all things: nor is it possible to trace the order of the succession of causes back to that self-existent cause, inasmuch as it is eternal and infinite, and therefore cannot be traced out by succession, which operates according to the order of time, consequently can bear no more proportion to the eternity of God than time itself may be supposed to do, which has no proportion at all; as the succeeding arguments respecting the eternity and infinity of God will evince. But notwithstanding the series of the succession of causes cannot be followed in a retrospective succession up to the self-existent or eternal cause, it is nevertheless a perpetual and conclusive evidence of a God. For a succession of causes considered collectively, can be nothing more than effects of the independent cause, and as much dependent on it as those dependent causes are upon one another; so that we may with certainty conclude that the system of nature, which we call by the name of natural causes, is as much dependent on a self-existent cause, as an individual of the species in the order of generation is dependent on its progenitors for existence. Such part of the series of nature's operations, which we understand has a regular and necessary connection with, and dependence on its parts, which we denominate by the names of cause and effect. From hence we are authorized from reason to conclude, that the vast system of causes and effects are thus necessarily connected (speaking of the natural world only), and the whole regularly and necessarily dependent on a self-existent cause; so that we are obliged to admit an independent cause, and ascribe self-existence to it, otherwise it would not be an independent cause, and consequently not a God. But the eternity or manner of the existence of a self-existent and independent being is to all finite capacities utterly incomprehensible; yet this is so far from an objection against the reality of such a being, that it is essentially necessary to support the evidence of it; for if we could comprehend that being whom we call God, he would not be God, but must have been finite, and that in the same degree as those may be supposed to be who could comprehend him; therefore, so certain as God is, we cannot comprehend his essence, eternity, or manner of existence. This should always be premised when we assay to reason on the being, perfection, eternity and infinity of God, or of his creation and providence. As far as we understand nature, we are become acquainted with the character of God, for the knowledge of nature is the revelation of God. If we form in our imagination a compendious idea of the harmony of the universe, it is the same as calling God by the name of harmony, for there could be no harmony without regulation, and no regulation without a regulator, which is expressive of the idea of a God. Nor could it be possible that there could be order or disorder, except we admit of such a thing as creation, and creation contains in it the idea of a creator, which is another appellation for the Divine Being, distinguishing God from his creation. Furthermore, there could be no proportion, figure or motion, without wisdom and power: wisdom to plan, and power to execute, and these are perfections, when applied to the works of nature, which signify the agency or superintendency of God. If we consider nature to be matter, figure and motion, we include the idea of God in that of motion; for motion implies a mover, as much as creation does a creator. If from the composition, texture and tendency of the universe in general, we form a complex idea of general good resulting therefrom to mankind, we implicitly admit a God by the name of good, including the idea of his providence to man. And from hence arises our obligations to love and adore God, because he provides for, and is beneficent to us: abstract the idea of goodness from the character of God, and it would cancel all our obligations to him, and excite us to hate and detest him as a tyrant; hence it is that ignorant people are superstitiously misled into a conceit that they hate God, when at the same time it is only the idol of their own imagination which they truly ought to hate and be ashamed of; but were such persons to connect the ideas of power, wisdom, goodness, and all possible perfection in the character of God, their hatred toward Him would be turned into love and adoration. . . .

By extending our ideas in a larger circle, we shall perceive our dependence on the earth and waters of the globe which we inhabit, and from which we are bountifully fed and gorgeously arrayed, and next extend our ideas to the sun, whose fiery mass darts its brilliant rays of light to our terraqueous ball with amazing velocity, and whose region of inexhaustible fire supplies it with fervent heat, which causes vegetation and gilds the various seasons of the year with ten thousand charms: this is not the achievement of man, but the workmanship and providence of God. But how the sun is supplied with materials, thus to perpetuate its kind influences, we know not. But will anyone deny the reality of those beneficial influences because we do not understand the manner of the perpetuality of that fiery world, or how it became such a body of fire; or will anyone deny the reality of nutrition by food because we do not understand the secret operation of the digesting powers of animal nature, or the minute particulars of its cherishing influence. None will be so stupid as to do it. Equally absurd would it be for us to deny the providence of God, by "whom we live, move, and have our being," because we cannot comprehend it.

We know that earth, water, fire and air, in their various compositions subserve us, and we also know that these elements are devoid of reflection, reason or design; from whence we may easily infer, that a wise, understanding, and designing being has ordained them to be thus subservient. Could blind chance constitute order and decorum, and consequently a providence?—That wisdom, order and design should be the production of nonentity, or of chaos, confusion and old night, is too absurd to deserve a serious confutation, for its supposeth that there may be effects without a cause, viz. produced by nonentity, or that chaos or confusion could produce the effects of power, wisdom and goodness; such absurdities as these we must assent to, or subscribe to the doctrine of a self-existent and providential being. . . .

Chapter V,

§ I. Argumentative Reflections on Supernatural and Mysterious Revelation in General

There is not anything which has contributed so much to delude mankind in religious matters as mistaken apprehensions concerning supernatural inspiration or revelation; not considering that all true religion originates from reason, and cannot otherwise be understood but by the exercise and improvement of it; therefore they are apt to confuse their minds with such inconsistencies. In the subsequent reasonings on this subject, we shall argue against supernatural revelation in general, which will comprehend the doctrine of inspiration or immediate illumination of the mind. And first—we will premise, that a revelation consists of an assemblage of rational ideas, intelligibly arranged and understood by those to whom it may be supposed to be revealed, for otherwise it could not exist in their minds as such. To suppose a revelation, void of rationality or understanding, or of communicating rational intelligence to those to whom it may be supposed to be given, would be a contradiction; for that it could contain nothing except it were unintelligibleness, which would be the same as to reveal and not to reveal; therefore, a revelation must consist of an assemblage of rational ideas, intelligibly communicated to those who are supposed to have been the partakers or receivers of it from the first supposed inspiration, down to this or any other period of time. But such a revelation as this could be nothing more or less than a transcript of the law of nature, predicated on reason, and would be no more supernatural than the reason of man may be supposed to be. The simple definition of supernatural is, that which is "beyond or above the powers of nature," which never was or can be understood by mankind; the first promulgators of revelation not excepted; for such revelation, doctrine, precept, or instruction only, as comes within the powers of our nature, is capable of being apprehended, contemplated or understood by us, and such as does not is to us incomprehensible and unknown, and consequently cannot for us compose any part of revelation.

The author of human nature impressed it with certain sensitive aptitudes and mental powers, so that apprehension, reflection or understanding could not otherwise be exerted or produced in the compound nature of man, but in the order prescribed by the creator. It would therefore be a contradiction in nature, and consequently impossible for God to inspire, infuse, or communicate the apprehension, reflection or understanding of anything whatever into human nature, out of, above, or beyond the natural aptitudes and mental powers of that nature, which was of his own production and constitution; for it would be the same as to inspire, infuse, or reveal apprehension, reflection or understanding, to that which is not; inasmuch as out of, beyond or above the powers of nature there could be nothing to operate upon, as a prerequisite principle to receive the inspiration or infusion of the revelation, which might therefore as well be inspired into, or revealed to nonentity as to man. For the essence of man is that which we denominate to be his nature, out of or above which he is as void of sensation, apprehension, reflection, and understanding, as nonentity may be supposed to be; therefore, such revelation as is adapted to the nature and capacity of man, and comes within his powers of perception and understanding, is the only revelation which he is able to receive from God or man. Supernatural revelation is as applicable to beasts, birds and fishes, as it is to us; for neither we nor they are capable of being acted upon supernaturally, as all the possible exertions and operations of nature, which respect the natural or moral world, are truly natural. Nor does God deviate from his rectitude of nature in matters of inspiration, revelation or instruction to the moral world, any more than in that of his government of the natural.

The infinitude of the wisdom of God's creation, providence and moral government will eternally remain supernatural to all finite capacities, and for that very reason we can never arrive to the comprehension of it in any state of being and improvement whatever; inasmuch as progression can never attain to that which is infinite, so that an eternal proficiency in knowledge could not be supernatural, but on the other hand would come within the limits and powers of our nature, for otherwise such proficiency would be impossible to us; nor is this infinite knowledge of God supernatural to Him, for that His perfection is also infinite. But if we could break over the limits of our capacity, so as to understand any one supernatural thing which is above or beyond the power of our natures, we might by that rule as well understand all things, and thus by breaking over the confines of finite nature and the rank of being which we hold in the universe, comprehend the knowledge of infinity. From hence we infer, that every kind and degree of apprehension, reflection and understanding, which we can attain to in any state of improvement whatever, is no more supernatural than the nature of man—from whence perception and understanding is produced—may be supposed to be so: nor has or could God Almighty ever have revealed himself to mankind in any other way or manner, but what is truly natural.

Chapter VII,
§ I. Of Miracles

Previous to the arguments concerning miracles, it is requisite that we give a definition of them, that the arguments may be clearly opposed to the doctrine of miracles, the reality of which we mean to negative; so that we do not dispute about matters in which we are all agreed, but that we may direct our speculations to the subject matter or essence of the controversy.

We will therefore premise, that miracles are opposed to, and counteract the laws of nature, or that they imply an absolute alteration in either a greater or less degree, to the eternal order, disposition and tendency of it; this, we conclude, is a just definition of miraculousness, and is that for which the advocates for miracles contend in their defining of miracles. For if they were supposed to make no alteration in the natural order of things, they could have no positive existence, but the laws of nature would produce their effects, which would preclude their reality, and render them altogether fictitious, inasmuch as their very existence is premised to consist in their opposition to, and alteration of the laws of nature: so that if this is not effected, miracles can have no positive existence, any more than nonentity itself; therefore, if in the course of the succeeding arguments, we should evince that the laws of nature have not and cannot be perverted, altered or suspended, it will foreclose miracles by making all things natural. Having thus defined miracles, and stated the dispute, we proceed to the arguments.

Should there ever have been a miraculous suspension and alteration of the laws of nature, God must have been the immediate author of it, as no finite beings may be supposed to be able to alter those laws or regulations, which were established by omnipotent power and infinite perfection, and which nothing short of such power and perfection can perpetuate. This then is the single point at issue, viz.: whether God has, or can, consistent with his nature as God, in any instance whatever, alter or deviate from the laws with which he has eternally impressed the universe, or not.

To suppose that God should subvert his laws (which is the same as changing them), would be to suppose him to be mutable; for that would necessarily imply, either that their eternal establishment was imperfect, or that a premised alteration thereof is so. To alter or change that which is absolutely perfect, would necessarily make it cease to be perfect, inasmuch as perfection could not be altered for the better, but for the worse, and consequently an alteration could not meet with the divine approbation; which terminates the issue of the matter in question against miracles, and authorizes us to deduce the following conclusive inference, to wit: that Almighty God, having eternally impressed the universe with a certain system of laws, for the same eternal reason that they were infinitely perfect and best, they could never admit of the least alteration, but are as unchangeable, in their nature, as God their immutable author. To form the foregoing argument into syllogisms, it would be thus:

God is perfect—the laws of nature were established by God; therefore, the laws of nature are perfect.

But admitting miracles, the syllogism should be thus:

The laws of nature were in their eternal establishment perfect— the laws of nature have been altered; therefore, the alteration of the laws of nature is imperfect.

Or thus: *the laws of nature have been altered—the alteration has been for the better; therefore, the eternal establishment thereof was imperfect.*

Thus it appears, from a syllogistical as well as other methods of reasoning, that provided we admit of miracles, which are synonymous to the alterations of nature, we by so doing derogate from the perfection of God, either in his eternal constitution of nature, or in a supposed subsequent miraculous alteration of it, so that take the argument either way, and it preponderates against miracles.

Furthermore, was it possible that the eternal order of nature should have been imperfect, there would be an end to all perfection. For God might be as imperfect in any supposed miraculous works, as in those of nature; nor could we ever have any security under His natural or moral government, if they were liable to change; for mutability is but another term for imperfection, or is inseparably connected with it.

God, the great architect of nature, has so constructed its machinery, that it never needs to be altered or rectified. In vain we endeavor to search out the hidden mystery of a perpetual motion, in order to copy nature, for after all our researches we must be contented with such mechanism as will run down and need rectification again; but the machine of the universe admits of no rectification, but continues its never-ceasing operations, under the unerring guidance of the providence of God. Human architects make and unmake things, and alter them as their invention may dictate and experience may determine to be most convenient and best. But that mind which is infinitely perfect gains nothing by experience, but surveys the immense universality of things, with all their possible relations, fitnesses and unfitnesses, of both a natural or moral kind, with one comprehensive view. . . .

Chapter XIII,

§ II. Of the Importance of the Exercise of Reason, and Practice of Morality, In Order to the Happiness of Mankind

The period of life is very uncertain, and at the longest is but short; a few years bring us from infancy to manhood, a few more to a dissolution; pain, sickness and death are the necessary consequences of animal life. Through life we struggle with physical evils, which eventually are certain to destroy our earthly composition; and well would it be for us did evils end here; but alas! moral evil has been more or less predominant in our agency, and though natural evil is unavoidable, yet moral evil may be prevented or remedied by the exercise of virtue. Morality is therefore of more importance to us than any or all other attainments; as it is a habit of mind which, from a retrospective consciousness of our agency in this life, we should carry with us into our succeeding state of existence, as an acquired appendage of our rational nature, and as the necessary means of our mental happiness. Virtue and vice are the only things in this world which, with our souls, are capable of surviving death; the former is the rational and only procuring cause of all intellectual happiness, and the latter of conscious guilt and misery; and therefore, our indispensable duty and ultimate interest is, to love, cultivate and improve the one as the means of our greatest good, and to hate and abstain from the other as productive of our greatest evil. And in order thereto, we should so far divest ourselves of the incumbrances of this world (which are too apt to engross our attention), as to inquire [investigate] a consistent system of the knowledge of religious duty, and make it our constant endeavor in life to act conformably to it. The knowledge of the being, perfections, creation, and providence of God, and of the immortality of our souls, is the foundation of religion. . . . And as the Pagan, Jewish, Christian and Mohammedan countries of the world have been overwhelmed with a multiplicity of revelations diverse from each other, and which, by their respective promulgators, are said to have been immediately inspired into their souls by the spirit of God, or immediately communicated to them by the intervening agency of angels (as in the instance of the invisible Gabriel to Mohammed) and as those revelations have been received and credited by far the greater part of the inhabitants of the several countries of the world (on whom they have been obtruded) as supernaturally revealed by God or angels, and which, in doctrine and discipline, are in the most respects repugnant to each other, it fully evinces their imposture, and authorizes us, without a lengthy course of arguing, to determine with certainty, that not one of them had their original from God; as they clash with each other, which is ground of high probability against the authenticity of each of them.

A revelation, that may be supposed to be really of the institution of God, must also be supposed to be perfectly consistent or uniform, and to be able to stand the test of truth; therefore such pretended revelations as are tendered to us as the contrivance of heaven, which do not bear that test, we may be morally certain, was either originally a deception, or has since by adulteration become spurious.

Reason therefore must be the standard by which we determine the respective claims of revelation; for otherwise we may as well subscribe to the divinity of the one as of the other, or to the whole of them, or to none at all. So likewise on this thesis; if reason rejects the whole of those revelations, we ought to return to the religion of nature and reason.

Undoubtedly it is our duty, and for our best good, that we occupy and improve the faculties with which our creator has endowed us, but so far as prejudice or prepossession of opinion prevails over our minds, in the same proportion, reason is excluded from our theory or practice.

Therefore, if we would acquire useful knowledge, we must first divest ourselves of those impediments; and sincerely endeavor to search out the truth: and draw our conclusions from reason and just argument, which will never conform to our inclination, interest or fancy; but we must conform to that if we would judge rightly. As certain as we determine contrary to reason, we make a wrong conclusion; therefore, our wisdom is, to conform to the nature and reason of things, as well in religious matters as in other sciences. Preposterously absurd would it be to negative the exercise of reason in religious concerns, and yet be actuated by it in all other and less occurrences of life. All our knowledge of things is derived from God, in and by the order of nature, out of which we cannot perceive, reflect or understand anything whatsoever; our external senses are natural; and those objects are also natural; so that ourselves, and all things about us, and our knowledge collected therefrom, is natural, and not supernatural; as argued in the fifth chapter.

An unjust composition never fails to contain error and falsehood. Therefore, an unjust connection of ideas is not derived from nature, but from the imperfect composition of man. Misconnection of ideas is the same as misjudging, and has no positive existence, being merely a creature of the imagination; but nature and truth are real and uniform; and the rational mind, by reasoning, discerns the uniformity and is thereby enabled to make a just composition of ideas, which will stand the test of truth. But the fantastical illuminations of the credulous and superstitious part of mankind, proceed from weakness, and, as far as they take place in the world, subvert the religion of REASON, NATURE and TRUTH.

BIBLIOGRAPHY

ALLEN, Ethan, *Reason the Only Oracle of Man; or a Compenduous System of Natural Religion. Alternately Adorned with Confutations of a variety of Doctrines incompatible to it; Deduced from the most exalted Ideas which we are able to form of the Divine and Human Characters, and from the Universe in General.* Bennington, Vt., 1784. Abridged editions, New York, 1836; Boston, 1854.

——— "An Essay on the Universal Plenitude of Being and on the Nature and Immortality of the Human Soul and Its Agency" (written about 1787), *The Historical Magazine, and Notes and Queries Concerning the Antiquities, History and Biography of America.* Third series. Vol. I (1872–73), pp. 193–96, 274–82, 330–33; Vol. II (1873), pp. 29–32, 76–82.

ANDERSON, George P., "Who Wrote Ethan Allen's Bible?" *New England Quarterly,* 10 (1937), pp. 685–96.

CONWAY, Moncure D., "Ethan Allen's Oracles of Reason." *Open Court*, Vol. VI (1892), pp. 3119–21.

DOTEN, Dana, "Ethan Allen's 'Original Something.'" *New England Quarterly*, Vol. XI (1938), pp. 361–66.

GOHDES, Clarence, "Ethan Allen and His Magnum Opus." *Open Court*, Vol. XLIII (1929), pp. 129–51.

HALL, Henry, *Ethan Allen, the Robin Hood of Vermont*. New York: D. Appleton, 1892.

KOCH, G. Adolf, *Republican Religion: The American Revolution and the Cult of Reason*. New York: Henry Holt, 1933. Esp. Chap. 1, "Ethan Allen, Freethinking Revolutionist."

PELL, John, *Ethan Allen*. Boston: Houghton Mifflin, 1929.

———— "Ethan Allen's Literary Career." *New England Quarterly*, Vol. II (1929), pp. 585–602.

RIFE, Clarence W., "Ethan Allen, an Interpretation." *New England Quarterly*, Vol. II (1929), 561–84.

SCHANTZ, B.T., "Ethan Allen's Religious Ideas." *Journal of Religion*, Vol. XVIII (1938), pp. 183–217.

SPARKS, Jared, *Life of Ethan Allen*. Vol. 1, *The Library of American Biography*. Boston, 1834.

Elihu Palmer

[1764–1806]

Elihu Palmer was born in Canterbury, Connecticut. He studied divinity and became a minister, but was removed from his pulpit on charges of heresy. Later in life he turned to the legal profession. But his outspoken views as a freethinker constantly provoked vigorous and violent opposition. He joined John Fitch's controversial "Universal Society." Eventually he helped organize deistic societies, especially "The Deistical Society of the State of New York." He also edited the deistic journal, *The Prospect; or View of the Moral World.* Interested in "republican religion," he joined Thomas Paine in founding a non-Christian deistic church. Palmer's judgment of Paine was exceedingly high, claiming that he was "probably the most useful man that ever existed on the face of the earth."

Palmer's religious radicalism originally stemmed from his reaction to Calvinism. This was transformed into a militant anti-Christianity and anti-clericalism. He attacked institutionalized religion for hypocrisy and immorality. Palmer defended a religion of nature, in which the universe was ordered and harmonious and the divine being One. Human nature was not corrupt or evil, but capable of improvement by the destruction of superstition and the application of education, liberty and science to human institutions. The brief piece which follows is a summary statement of much of the deism of the period.

PRINCIPLES OF THE DEISTICAL SOCIETY OF THE STATE OF NEW YORK [1]

Proposals for forming a society for the promotion of moral science and the religion of nature—having in view the destruction of superstition and fanaticism—tending to the development of the principles of a genuine natural morality—the practice of a pure and uncorrupted virtue—the cultivation of science and philosophy—the resurrection of reason—and the renovation of the intelligent world.

[1] Elihu Palmer, "Principles of the Deistical Society of the State of New York," *Posthumous Pieces*, London, 1826, pp. 10–11.

At a time when the political despotism of the earth is disappearing, and man is about to reclaim and enjoy the liberties of which for ages he has been deprived, it would be unpardonable to neglect the important concerns of intellectual and moral nature. The slavery of the mind has been the most destructive of all slavery; and the baneful effects of a dark and gloomy superstition have suppressed all the dignified efforts of the human understanding, and essentially circumscribed the sphere of intellectual energy. It is only by returning to the laws of nature, which man has so frequently abandoned, that happiness is to be acquired. And, although the efforts of a few individuals will be inadequate to the sudden establishment of moral and mental felicity; yet, they may lay the foundation on which a superstructure may be reared incalculably valuable to the welfare of future generations. To contribute to the accomplishment of an object so important, the members of this association do approve of the following fundamental principles:

1. That the universe proclaims the existence of one supreme Deity, worthy the adoration of intelligent beings.

2. That man is possessed of moral and intellectual faculties sufficient for the improvement of his nature, and the acquisition of happiness.

3. That the religion of nature is the only universal religion; that it grows out of the moral relations of intelligent beings, and that it stands connected with the progressive improvement and common welfare of the human race.

4. That it is essential to the true interest of man that he love truth and practice virtue.

5. That vice is everywhere ruinous and destructive to the happiness of the individual and of society.

6. That a benevolent disposition, and beneficent actions, are fundamental duties of rational beings.

7. That a religion mingled with persecution and malice cannot be of divine origin.

8. That education and science are essential to the happiness of man.

9. That civil and religious liberty is equally essential to his true interests.

10. That there can be no human authority to which man ought to be amenable for his religious opinions.

11. That science and truth, virtue and happiness, are the great objects to which the activity and energy of the human faculties ought to be directed.

Every member admitted into this association shall deem it his duty, by every suitable method in his power, to promote the cause of nature and moral truth, in opposition to all schemes of superstition and fanaticism, claiming divine origin.

BIBLIOGRAPHY

PALMER, Elihu, *The Examiners Examined: Being a Defense of the Age of Reason.* New York, 1794.

———— *The Principles of Nature: or, A Development of the Moral Causes of Happiness and Misery Among the Human Species.* New York, 1802.

———— *An Enquiry Relative to the Moral and Political Improvement of the Human Species.* New York, 1797.

———— *Political Miscellany.* New York, 1793.

———— *Posthumous Pieces.* London, 1826.

———— *The Political Happiness of Nations.* New York, 1800.

———— ed., *Prospect; or, View of the Moral World,* Vols. I–II, no. 13 (Dec. 10, 1803; Mar. 30, 1805).

KOCH, G. Adolf, *Republican Religion: The American Revolution and the Cult of Reason.* New York: Henry Holt, 1933.

PART THREE

Conservatism in Political Theory and Philosophy (1800-1850)

John C. Calhoun

[1782–1850]

Calhoun was the outstanding political philosopher of the South in the first half of the nineteenth century, and was recognized as its preeminent spokesman. Deeply involved in the political affairs of the day, he was a man of action as well as a thinker. Calhoun was born in South Carolina, a member of the Southern plantation aristocracy. He studied briefly at Litchfield, Connecticut, and at Yale. His positions were numerous: a member of the state legislature (1808–10), Congressman (1810–17), Secretary of War under James Monroe (1817–25), Vice-President under John Quincy Adams and Andrew Jackson (1825–32), Senator (1832–43, 1845–50), Secretary of State under Tyler (1844–45), and candidate for the Presidency many times (1822–50).

Calhoun's career was spent in defending Southern agricultural interests against the commercial interests of the North. He argued that the Constitution was based upon a compact of Sovereign States, and that it established a government of "concurrent majorities" composed of two elements: the state governments and the federal government. The several states, he thought, preserved the right of veto, could nullify legislation inimical to their interests, and possessed the right of secession from the Union. Nullification was an important issue in the 1830's, and although a compromise was reached by Henry Clay and Andrew Jackson, the larger issue of States' Rights (which Calhoun dramatically debated with Daniel Webster) continued to enflame the Union. As abolitionists grew stronger in the North, Calhoun became an outspoken apologist for slavery. To ensure continuation of the balance of political power between North and South, he opposed any prohibition of the spread of slavery to newly-admitted states.

His major work, *A Disquisition on Government and a Discourse on the Constitution and Government of the United States*, published posthumously in 1851, crystallized his political philosophy. Calhoun repudiated the doctrines of natural rights, natural liberty, and human equality. He held instead that man was by nature social, that government was a natural and organic outgrowth of human instincts, and that inequality was essential to human progress. Calhoun feared the "tyranny of the majority," which he proposed to check by means of a concurrent rather than a numerical majority.

Although aspects of Calhoun's thought were similar to those of Aristotle, he was an independent thinker in American life, and stood opposed to the democratic equalitarianism of Jefferson (and later of Lincoln). Analytic and philosophic in outlook, Calhoun attempted to reduce all ideas to their basic principles and to organize them into a

systematic unity. But his first principles and his philosophic system were
not consonant with the moral idealism of the majority of Americans—
and the issues of slavery and secession were to be resolved, in the
decade after his death, by the Civil
War.

A DISQUISITION ON GOVERNMENT [1]

In order to have a clear and just conception of the nature and object
of government, it is indispensable to understand correctly what that
constitution or law of our nature is, in which government originates;
or, to express it more fully and accurately: that law, without which
government would not, and with which, it must necessarily exist. Without this, it is as impossible to lay any solid foundation for the science
of government, as it would be to lay one for that of astronomy, without
a like understanding of that constitution or law of the material world,
according to which the several bodies composing the solar system
mutually act on each other, and by which they are kept in their
respective spheres. The first question, accordingly, to be considered is:
What is that constitution or law of our nature, without which government would not exist, and with which its existence is necessary?

In considering this, I assume, as an incontestable fact, that man is so
constituted as to be a social being. His inclinations and wants, physical
and moral, irresistibly impel him to associate with his kind; and he has,
accordingly, never been found, in any age or country, in any state
other than the social. In no other, indeed, could he exist; and in no
other—were it possible for him to exist—could he attain to a full development of his moral and intellectual faculties, or raise himself, in
the scale of being, much above the level of the brute creation.

I next assume, also, as a fact not less incontestable that, while man
is so constituted as to make the social state necessary to his existence
and the full development of his faculties, this state itself cannot exist
without government. The assumption rests on universal experience.
In no age or country has any society or community ever been found,
whether enlightened or savage, without government of some description.

Having assumed these, as unquestionable phenomena of our nature,
I shall, without further remark, proceed to the investigation of the
primary and important question: What is that constitution of our
nature, which, while it impels man to associate with his kind, renders
it impossible for society to exist without government?

[1] *The Works of John C. Calhoun*, Charleston, S. C., 1851; Vol. I, *A Disquisition
on Government and a Discourse on the Constitution and Government of the
United States*, pp. 1–59.

The answer will be found in the fact—not less incontestable than either of the others—that, while man is created for the social state, and is accordingly so formed as to feel what affects others, as well as what affects himself, he is, at the same time, so constituted as to feel more intensely what affects him directly, than what affects him indirectly through others; or, to express it differently, he is so constituted that his direct or individual affections are stronger than his sympathetic or social feelings. I intentionally avoid the expression, *selfish* feelings, as applicable to the former; because, as commonly used, it implies an unusual excess of the individual over the social feelings, in the person to whom it is applied; and, consequently, something depraved and vicious. My object is, to exclude such inference, and to restrict the inquiry exclusively to facts in their bearings on the subject under consideration, viewed as mere phenomena appertaining to our nature, constituted as it is; and which are as unquestionable as is that of gravitation, or any other phenomenon of the material world.

In asserting that our individual, are stronger than our social feelings, it is not intended to deny that there are instances, growing out of peculiar relations—as that of a mother and her infant—or resulting from the force of education and habit over peculiar constitutions, in which the latter have overpowered the former; but these instances are few, and always regarded as something extraordinary. The deep impression they make, whenever they occur, is the strongest proof that they are regarded as exceptions to some general and well-understood law of our nature; just as some of the minor powers of the material world are apparently to gravitation.

I might go farther and assert this to be a phenomenon, not of our nature only, but of all animated existence throughout its entire range, so far as our knowledge extends. It would, indeed, seem to be essentially connected with the great law of self-preservation which pervades all that feels, from man down to the lowest and most insignificant reptile or insect. In none is it stronger than in man. His social feelings may, indeed, in a state of safety and abundance, combined with high intellectual and moral culture, acquire great expansion and force; but not so great as to overpower this all-pervading and essential law of animated existence.

But that constitution of our nature which makes us feel more intensely what affects us directly than what affects us indirectly through others, necessarily leads to conflict between individuals. Each, in consequence, has a greater regard for his own safety or happiness than for the safety or happiness of others; and, where these come in opposition, is ready to sacrifice the interests of others to his own. And hence, the tendency to a universal state of conflict between individual and individual; accompanied by the connected passions of suspicion, jealousy, anger and revenge, followed by insolence, fraud and cruelty;

and, if not prevented by some controlling power, ending in a state of universal discord and confusion, destructive of the social state and the ends for which it is ordained. This controlling power, wherever vested, or by whomsoever exercised, is GOVERNMENT.

It follows, then, that man is so constituted, that government is necessary to the existence of society, and society to his existence, and the perfection of his faculties. It follows, also, that government has its origin in this twofold constitution of his nature; the sympathetic or social feelings constituting the remote, and the individual or direct, the proximate cause.

If man had been differently constituted in either particular: if, instead of being social in his nature, he had been created without sympathy for his kind, and independent of others for his safety and existence; or if, on the other hand, he had been so created as to feel more intensely what affected others than what affected himself (if that were possible), or even had this supposed interest been equal— it is manifest that, in either case, there would have been no necessity for government, and that none would ever have existed. But, although society and government are thus intimately connected with and dependent on each other—of the two, society is the greater. It is the first in the order of things, and in the dignity of its object; that of society being primary, to preserve and perfect our race; and that of government secondary and subordinate, to preserve and perfect society. Both are, however, necessary to the existence and well-being of our race, and equally of Divine ordination.

I have said—if it were possible for man to be so constituted as to feel what affects others more strongly than what affects himself, or even as strongly—because, it may well be doubted, whether the stronger feeling or affection of individuals for themselves, combined with a feebler and subordinate feeling or affection for others, is not, in beings of limited reason and faculties, a constitution necessary to their preservation and existence. If reversed, if their feelings and affections were stronger for others than for themselves, or even as strong, the necessary result would seem to be that all individuality would be lost; and boundless and remediless disorder and confusion would ensue. For each, at the same moment, intensely participating in all the conflicting emotions of those around him, would, of course, forget himself and all that concerned him immediately, in his officious intermeddling with the affairs of all others; which, from his limited reason and faculties, he could neither properly understand nor manage. Such a state of things would, as far as we can see, lead to endless disorder and confusion, not less destructive to our race than a state of anarchy. It would, besides, be remediless—for government would be impossible; or, if it could possibly exist, its object would be reversed. Selfishness would have to be encouraged, and benevolence discouraged. Individuals would have to be encouraged, by rewards, to become more selfish, and deterred, by punishments, from being too benevolent; and this, too, by a government, administered by those who, on the supposition, would have the greatest aversion for selfishness and the highest admiration for benevolence.

To the Infinite Being, the Creator of all, belongs exclusively the care and superintendence of the whole. He, in his infinite wisdom and goodness, has allotted to every class of animated beings its condition and appropriate functions; and has endowed each with feelings, instincts, capacities, and faculties, best adapted to its allotted condition. To man, he has assigned the social and political state, as best adapted to develop the great capacities and faculties, intellectual and moral, with which he has endowed him; and has, accordingly, constituted him so as not only to impel him into the social state, but to make government necessary for his preservation and well-being.

But government, although intended to protect and preserve society, has itself a strong tendency to disorder and abuse of its powers, as all experience and most every page of history testify. The cause is to be found in the same constitution of our nature which makes government indispensable. The powers which it is necessary for government to possess, in order to repress violence and preserve order, cannot execute themselves. They must be administered by men in whom, like others, the individual are stronger than the social feelings. And hence, the powers vested in them to prevent injustice and oppression on the part of others will, if left unguarded, be by them converted into instruments to oppress the rest of the community. That by which this is prevented, by whatever name called, is what is meant by CONSTITUTION, in its most comprehensive sense, when applied to GOVERNMENT.

Having its origin in the same principle of our nature, *constitution* stands to *government*, as *government* stands to *society*; and, as the end for which society is ordained would be defeated without government, so that for which government is ordained would, in a great measure, be defeated without constitution. But they differ in this striking particular. There is no difficulty in forming government. It is not even a matter of choice whether there shall be one or not. Like breathing, it is not permitted to depend on our volition. Necessity will force it on all communities in some one form or another. Very different is the case as to constitution. Instead of a matter of necessity, it is one of the most difficult tasks imposed on man to form a constitution worthy of the name; while, to form a perfect one—one that would completely counteract the tendency of government to oppression and abuse, and hold it strictly to the great ends for which it is ordained—has thus far exceeded human wisdom, and possibly ever will. From this, another striking difference results. Constitution is the contrivance of man, while government is of Divine ordination. Man is left to perfect what the wisdom of the Infinite ordained as necessary to preserve the race.

With these remarks, I proceed to the consideration of the important and difficult question: How is this tendency of government to be counteracted? Or, to express it more fully: How can those who are invested with the powers of government be prevented from employing them as the means of aggrandizing themselves, instead of using them to protect and preserve society? . . .

In answering the important question under consideration, it is not necessary to enter into an examination of the various contrivances adopted by these celebrated governments to counteract this tendency to disorder and abuse, nor to undertake to treat of constitution in its most comprehensive sense. What I propose is far more limited: to explain on what principles government must be formed in order to resist, by its own interior structure—or, to use a single term, *organism*— the tendency to abuse of power. This structure, or organism, is what is meant by constitution, in its strict and more usual sense; and it is this which distinguishes what are called constitutional governments from absolute. It is in this strict and more usual sense that I propose to use the term hereafter.

How government, then, must be constructed, in order to counter-act through its organism this tendency on the part of those who make and execute the laws to oppress those subject to their operation, is the next question which claims attention.

There is but one way in which this can possibly be done; and that is, by such an organism as will furnish the ruled with the means of resisting successfully this tendency on the part of the rulers to oppression and abuse. Power can only be resisted by power—and tendency by tendency. Those who exercise power and those subject to its exer-cise—the rulers and the ruled—stand in antagonistic relations to each other. The same constitution of our nature which leads rulers to oppress the ruled—regardless of the object for which government is ordained—will, with equal strength, lead the ruled to resist when possessed of the means of making peaceable and effective resistance. Such an organism, then, as will furnish the means by which resistance may be systematically and peaceably made on the part of the ruled, to oppression and abuse of power on the part of the rulers, is the first and indispensable step toward forming a constitutional government. And as this can only be effected by or through the right of suffrage— the right on the part of the ruled to choose their rulers at proper intervals, and to hold them thereby responsible for their conduct— the responsibility of the rulers to the ruled, through the right of suffrage, is the indispensable and primary principle in the foundation of a constitutional government. . . .

. . . The right of suffrage, by placing the control of the government in the community must, from the same constitution of our nature which makes government necessary to preserve society, lead to conflict among its different interests: each striving to obtain possession of its powers, as the means of protecting itself against the others; or of advancing its respective interests, regardless of the interests of others. For this purpose, a struggle will take place between the various interests to obtain a majority, in order to control the government. If no one interest be strong enough, of itself, to obtain it, a combination will be formed between those whose interests are most alike—each conceding something to the others, until a sufficient number is obtained to make a majority. The process may be slow, and much time may be required before a compact, organized majority can be thus formed; but formed it will be in time, even without preconcert or design, by the sure workings of that principle or constitution of our nature in which government itself originates. When once formed, the community will be divided into two great parties—a major and minor—between which there will be incessant struggles on the one side to retain, and on the other to obtain the majority—and, thereby, the control of the government and the advantages it confers. . . .

The necessary result, then, of the unequal fiscal action of the government is to divide the community into two great classes; one consisting of those who, in reality, pay the taxes and, of course, bear exclusively the burden of supporting the government; and the other, of those who are the recipients of their proceeds, through disbursements, and who are, in fact, supported by the government; or, in fewer words, to divide it into tax-payers and tax-consumers.

But the effect of this is to place them in antagonistic relations, in reference to the fiscal action of the government, and the entire course of policy therewith connected. For, the greater the taxes and disbursements, the greater the gain of the one and the loss of the other, and vice versa; and consequently, the more the policy of the government is calculated to increase taxes and disbursements, the more it will be favored by the one and opposed by the other. . . .

As, then, the right of suffrage, without some other provision, cannot counteract this tendency of government, the next question for consideration is: What is that other provision? This demands the most serious consideration; for of all the questions embraced in the science of government, it involves a principle, the most important, and the least understood—and when understood, the most difficult of application in practice. It is, indeed, emphatically, that principle which makes the constitution, in its strict and limited sense.

From what has been said, it is manifest, that this provision must be of a character calculated to prevent any one interest, or combination of interests, from using the powers of government to aggrandize itself at the expense of the others. Here lies the evil: and just in proportion as it shall prevent, or fail to prevent it, in the same degree it will effect, or fail to effect the end intended to be accomplished. There is but one certain mode in which this result can be secured; and that is, by the adoption of some restriction or limitation which shall so effectually prevent any one interest, or combination of interests, from obtaining the exclusive control of the government, as to render hopeless all attempts directed to that end. There is, again, but one mode in which this can be effected; and that is, by taking the sense of each interest or portion of the community, which may be unequally and injuriously affected by the action of the government, separately, through its own majority, or in some other way by which its voice may be fairly expressed; and to require the consent of each interest, either to put or to keep the government in action. This, too, can be accomplished only in one way; and that is, by such an organism of the government—and, if necessary for the purpose, of the community also— as will, by dividing and distributing the powers of government, give to each division or interest, through its appropriate organ, either a concurrent voice in making and executing the laws, or a veto on their execution. It is only by such an organism that the assent of each can be made necessary to put the government in motion; or the power made effectual to arrest its action, when put in motion; and it is only by the one or the other that the different interests, orders, classes, or portions, into which the community may be divided, can be protected, and all conflict and struggle between them prevented—by rendering it impossible to put or to keep it in action, without the concurrent consent of all.

Such an organism as this, combined with the right of suffrage, constitutes, in fact, the elements of constitutional government. The one, by rendering those who make and execute the laws responsible to those on whom they operate, prevents the rulers from oppressing the ruled; and the other, by making it impossible for any one interest or combination of interests or class, or order, or portion of the community, to obtain exclusive control, prevents any one of them from oppressing the other. It is clear that oppression and abuse of power must come, if at all, from the one or the other quarter. From no other can they come. It follows, that the two, suffrage and proper organism combined, are sufficient to counteract the tendency of government to oppression and abuse of power; and to restrict it to the fulfillment of the great ends for which it is ordained. . . .

It results, from what has been said, that there are two different modes in which the sense of the community may be taken; one, simply by the right of suffrage, unaided; the other, by the right through a proper organism. Each collects the sense of the majority. But one regards numbers only, and considers the whole community as a unit, having but one common interest throughout; and collects the sense of the greater number of the whole, as that of the community. The other, on the contrary, regards interests as well as numbers—considering the community as made up of different and conflicting interests, as far as the action of the government is concerned; and takes the sense of each, through its majority or appropriate organ, and the united sense of all, as the sense of the entire community. The former of these I shall call the numerical, or absolute majority; and the latter, the concurrent, or constitutional majority. I call it the constitutional majority because it is an essential element in every constitutional government—be its form what it may. So great is the difference, politically speaking, between the two majorities, that they cannot be confounded without leading to great and fatal errors; and yet the distinction between them has been so entirely overlooked, that when the term *majority* is used in political discussions, it is applied exclusively to designate the numerical—as if there were no other. Until this distinction is recognized, and better understood, there will continue to be great liability to error in properly constructing constitutional governments, especially of the popular form, and of preserving them when properly constructed. Until then, the latter will have a strong tendency to slide, first, into the government of the numerical majority, and, finally, into absolute government of some other form. . . .

If the two be compared, in reference to the ends for which government is ordained, the superiority of the government of the concurrent majority will not be less striking. These . . . are twofold; to protect, and to perfect society. But to preserve society, it is necessary to guard the community against injustice, violence, and anarchy within, and against attacks from without. If it fail in either, it would fail in the primary end of government, and would not deserve the name.

To perfect society, it is necessary to develop the faculties, intellectual and moral, with which man is endowed. But the mainspring to their development and, through this, to progress, improvement and civilization, with all their blessings, is the desire of individuals to better their condition. For this purpose, liberty and security are indispensable. Liberty leaves each free to pursue the course he may deem best to promote his interest and happiness, as far as it may be compatible with the primary end for which government is ordained—while security gives assurance to each, that he shall not be deprived of the fruits of his exertions to better his condition. These combined, give to this desire the strongest impulse of which it is susceptible. For, to extend liberty beyond the limits assigned would be to weaken the government and to render it incompetent to fulfill its primary end—the protection of society against dangers, internal and external. The effect of this would be, insecurity; and, of insecurity, to weaken the impulse of individuals to better their condition, and thereby retard progress and improvement. On the other hand, to extend the powers of the government so as to contract the sphere assigned to liberty, would have the same effect, by disabling individuals in their efforts to better their condition. . . .

Liberty, indeed, though among the greatest of blessings, is not so great as that of protection; inasmuch as the end of the former is the progress and improvement of the race, while that of the latter is its preservation and perpetuation. And hence, when the two come into conflict, liberty must, and ever ought, to yield to protection; as the existence of the race is of greater moment than its improvement.

It follows from what has been stated that it is a great and dangerous error to suppose that all people are equally entitled to liberty. It is a reward to be earned, not a blessing to be gratuitously lavished on all alike; a reward reserved for the intelligent, the patriotic, the virtuous and deserving; and not a boon to be bestowed on a people too ignorant, degraded and vicious, to be capable either of appreciating or of enjoying it. Nor is it any disparagement to liberty that such is, and ought to be the case. On the contrary, its greatest praise—its proudest distinction—is that an all-wise Providence has reserved it as the noblest and highest reward for the development of our faculties, moral and intellectual. A reward more appropriate than liberty could not be conferred on the deserving—nor a punishment inflicted on the undeserving more just, than to be subject to lawless and despotic rule. This dispensation seems to be the result of some fixed law; and every effort to disturb or defeat it, by attempting to elevate a people in the scale of liberty, above the point to which they are entitled to rise, must ever prove abortive, and end in disappointment. The progress of a people rising from a lower to a higher point in the scale of liberty is necessarily slow; and by attempting to precipitate, we either retard, or permanently defeat it.

There is another error, not less great and dangerous, usually associated with the one which has just been considered. I refer to the opinion that liberty and equality are so intimately united, that liberty cannot be perfect without perfect equality.

That they are united to a certain extent, and that equality of citizens, in the eyes of the law, is essential to liberty in a popular government, is conceded. But to go further, and make equality of *condition* essential to liberty, would be to destroy both liberty and progress. The reason is, that inequality of condition, while it is a necessary consequence of liberty, is, at the same time, indispensable to progress. In order to understand why this is so, it is necessary to bear in mind that the mainspring to progress is the desire of individuals to better their condition; and that the strongest impulse which can be given to it is, to leave individuals free to exert themselves in the manner they may deem best for that purpose—as far at least as it can be done consistently with the ends for which government is ordained—and to secure to all the fruits of their exertions. Now, as individuals differ greatly from each other—in intelligence, sagacity, energy, perseverance, skill, habits of industry and economy, physical power, position and opportunity—the necessary effect of leaving all free to exert themselves to better their condition, must be a corresponding inequality between those who may possess these qualities and advantages in a high degree, and those who may be deficient in them. The only means by which this result can be prevented are, either to impose such restrictions on the exertions of those who may possess them in a high degree as will place them on a level with those who do not; or to deprive them of the fruits of their exertions. But to impose such restrictions on them would be destructive of liberty; while, to deprive them of the fruits of their exertions, would be to destroy the desire of bettering their condition. It is, indeed, this inequality of condition between the front and rear ranks, in the march of progress, which gives so strong an impulse to the former to maintain their position, and to the latter to press forward into their files. This gives to progress its greatest impulse. To force the front rank back to the rear, or attempt to push forward the rear into line with the front by the interposition of the government, would put an end to the impulse, and effectually arrest the march of progress.

These great and dangerous errors have their origin in the prevalent opinion that all men are born free and equal—than which nothing can be more unfounded and false. It rests upon the assumption of a fact which is contrary to universal observation, in whatever light it may be regarded. It is, indeed, difficult to explain how an opinion so destitute of all sound reason ever could have been so extensively entertained, unless we regard it as being confounded with another, which has some semblance of truth—but which, when properly understood, is not less false and dangerous. I refer to the assertion that all men are equal in the state of nature; meaning, by a state of nature, a state of individuality, supposed to have existed prior to the social and political state; and in which men lived apart and independent of each other. If such a state ever did exist, all men would have been, indeed, free and equal in it; that is, free to do as they pleased, and exempt from the authority or control of others—as, by supposition, it existed anterior to society and government. But such a state is purely hypothetical. It never did, nor can exist; as it is inconsistent with the preservation and perpetuation of the race. It is, therefore, a great misnomer to call it *the state of nature*. Instead of being the natural state of man, it is, of all conceivable states, the most opposed to his nature—most repugnant to his feelings, and most incompatible with his wants. His natural state is the social and political—the one for which his Creator made him, and the only one in which he can preserve and perfect his race. As, then, there never was such a state as the so called state of nature, and never can be, it follows that men, instead of being born in it, are born in the social and political state; and of course, instead of being born free and equal, are born subject, not only to parental authority, but to the laws and institutions of the country where born, and under whose protection they draw their first breath. . . .

It follows, from all that has been said, that the more perfectly a government combines power and liberty—that is, the greater its power and the more enlarged and secure the liberty of individuals—the more perfectly it fulfills the ends for which government is ordained. . . .

The concurrent majority, then, is better suited to enlarge and secure the bounds of liberty, because it is better suited to prevent government from passing beyond its proper limits, and to restrict it to its primary end, the protection of the community. . . .

BIBLIOGRAPHY

CALHOUN, John C., *Life of John C. Calhoun: Presenting a Condensed History of Political Events from 1811 to 1843*. New York: Harper and Bros., 1843.
_____ *The Works of John C. Calhoun*, ed. by Richard K. Cralle. Charleston, S.C., 1851, 6 vols.

BANCROFT, Frederick, *Calhoun and the South Carolina Nullification Movement*. Baltimore: John Hopkins U. Press, 1928.

COIT, Margaret L., *John C. Calhoun: American Portrait*. Boston: Houghton Mifflin, 1950.

HUNT, Gaillard, *John C. Calhoun*. Philadelphia: George W. Jacobs, 1908.

MEIGS, William M., *The Life of John Caldwell Calhoun*. New York: Neale Publishing Co., 1917, 2 vols.

MERRIAM, Charles E., "The Political Philosophy of John C. Calhoun," in *Studies in Southern History and Politics Inscribed to William Archibald Dunning*. New York: Columbia U. Press, 1914, pp. 319–38.

SPAIN, A.O., *The Political Theory of John C. Calhoun*. New York: Bookman Assoc., 1951.

STYRON, Arthur, *The Cast-Iron Man: John C. Calhoun and American Democracy*. New York: Longmans, Green, 1935.

WILTSE, C.M., *John C. Calhoun: Nationalist, 1782–1828*. New York: Bobbs-Merrill, 1944.

_____ *John C. Calhoun, Nullifier, 1829–1839*. New York: Bobbs-Merrill, 1949.

_____ *John C. Calhoun, Sectionalist, 1840–1850*. New York: Bobbs-Merrill, 1951.

James McCosh

[1811-1894]

McCosh was invited to America in 1868, at the age of fifty-seven, to become President of the College of New Jersey (Princeton), where he remained for the next twenty years. Whether he should be classified as an American philosopher is debatable. The reason for including him in an anthology of American thought is that he well represents the kind of conservative academic philosophy— Scottish realism—that was widely taught and flourished in the United States throughout a good part of the nineteenth century. Interestingly, McCosh, like Edwards before, summed up the meaning of a movement at the very time that it had lost its primacy in influence. Born in Scotland in 1811, McCosh studied at the Universities of Glasgow and Edinburgh, where he came under the influence of the common sense philosophy of Thomas Reid and Sir William Hamilton. Later he became a minister and a Professor of Philosophy of Queens College, Belfast.

McCosh's published writings are usually expository rather than original. He was, however, one of the ablest defenders of Scottish realism. His most influential book, *The Intuitions of the Mind, Inductively Investigated* (1860), was a systematic statement of the main principles of realism. In *The Scottish Philosophy, Bibliographical, Expository, and Critical, from Hutcheson to Hamilton* (1875), McCosh expressed the

hope that realistic philosophy might find a responsive hearing in America. In *Realistic Philosophy* (1882), Mc-Cosh observed that the time had come for America to develop its independence in philosophy, and he believed that if there was to be an American philosophy, it must be realistic. The two selections reprinted below—"Characteristics of the Scottish School and Comparison of It With the Critical Philosophy of Kant" and "First and Fundamental Truths"—are taken from *Realistic Philosophy*.

McCosh found the prevailing transcendental idealism or materialistic psychology unsatisfactory and wished to avoid both Kantian idealism and Humean skepticism. Although Emerson's fame was at its peak, McCosh maintained that he was not a philosopher: "Though his thoughts were insightful, they were like strung pearls, without system and connection." Skeptical empiricism offered no guide either. Mc-Cosh held instead that there were intuitions of the mind, simple and immediate perceptions of a real and objective order. The mind seized its objects directly, whether these objects were sensory, relational, or abstract. We have truth only when our ideas conform to things; this means that we must employ the inductive method and pay close heed to the facts. Among the facts observed are causation, the uniformity of nature, mathematical forms, and mind and bodies as perceived in space and time. In ethics, McCosh defended self-evident certitudes of moral obligation. In religion, realism provided an intuition of God and a defense of Protestant orthodoxy. Intuition then was used by McCosh to justify the existing structure of ideas and values.

REALISTIC PHILOSOPHY

CHARACTERISTICS OF THE SCOTTISH SCHOOL
AND COMPARISON OF IT
WITH THE CRITICAL PHILOSOPHY OF KANT [1]

I. *It proceeds throughout by observation.* It has all along professed a profound reverence for Bacon, and in its earliest works it attempted to do for metaphysics what Newton had done for physics. It begins with facts and ends with facts. Between, it has analyses, generalizations, and reasonings; but all upon the actual operations of the mind. Its laws are suggested by facts and are verified by facts. It sets out, as Bacon recommends, with the necessary "rejections and exclusions," with what Whewell calls the "decomposition of facts," but all to get at the exact facts it means to examine. Its generalizations are formed by observing the points in which the operations of the mind agree, and it proceeds gradually—*gradatim,* as Bacon expresses it—rising from particulars to generals, and from lower to higher laws. It is afraid of rapid and high speculation, lest it carry us like a balloon, not into the heavens, but into a cloud, where it will explode sooner or later. It is suspicious of long and complicated ratiocinations like those of Spinoza and Hegel, for it is sure—such is human fallibility—that there will lurk in them some error or defect in the premise, or some oversight or weak link in the process, weakening the whole chain. Thomas Reid was not sure whether Samuel Clarke's demonstration of the existence of God was more distinguished for ingenuity than sublimity.

II. *It observes the operations of the mind by the inner sense—that is, consciousness.* In this philosophy consciousness, the perception of self in its various states, comes into greater prominence than it had ever done before. Bacon did not appreciate its importance; he recommended in the study of the human mind the gathering of instances, to be arranged in tables, of memory, judgment, and the like. Descartes appealed to consciousness, but only to get a principle such as *cogito,* to be used in deduction, *ergo sum;* in which *sum* there is an idea of an

[1] From *Realistic Philosophy,* Vol. II, *Historical and Critical,* N. Y., Macmillan, 1887, pp. 181–86, 239–44.

infinite, a perfect. Locke was ever appealing to internal observation, but it was to support a preconceived theory that all our ideas are derived from sensation and reflection. Turnbull and Hutcheson and Reid were the first to avow and declare that the laws of the human mind were to be discovered only by internal observation, and that mental philosophy consisted solely in the construction of these. They held that consciousness, the internal sense, was as much to be trusted as the external senses; and that as we can form a natural philosophy out of the facts furnished by the one, we can construct a mental philosophy by the facts furnished by the other. They held resolutely that the eye cannot see our thoughts and feelings even when aided by the microscope or telescope. They were sure that no man ever grasped an idea by his muscular power, tasted the beauty of a rose or lily, smelt an emotion, or heard the writhings of the conviction of conscience. But they thought that the mind could observe the world within by consciousness more directly and quite as accurately as it could observe the world without by sight, touch, and the other senses, and could in the one case as in the other make a scientific arrangement of its observations and construct a science.

III. *By observation principles are discovered which are above observation, universal and eternal.* All the genuine masters and followers proceed on this principle, and apply it more or less successfully. I am not sure that they have expressly avowed it and explicitly stated it. I am responsible for the form which is given it at the head of this paragraph. No man can understand or appreciate or do justice to the philosophy of Scotland who does not notice it as running through and through their whole investigations and conclusions. It was in this way that Reid opposed Hume. It was in this way that Dugald Stewart, and indeed the whole school, sought to lay a foundation on which all truth might be built. They were fond of representing the principles as fundamental, and they guarded against all erroneous, against all extravagant and defective statements and applications of them, by insisting that they be shown to be in the constitution of the mind, and that their nature be ascertained before they are employed in speculation of any kind. By insisting on this restriction, their mode of procedure has been described as timid, and their results as mean and poor, by those speculators who assume a principle without a previous induction, and mount up with it, wishing to reach the sky, but stayed in the clouds. By thus holding that there are truths above and prior to our observation of them, they claim and have a place in the brotherhood of our higher philosophers, such as Plato and Aristotle in ancient times, Descartes, Leibnitz, and Kant in modern times.

They present these principles in the mind under various aspects and in different names. Reid called them principles of common sense in the mind itself, and common to all men. Hamilton defended the use of the phrase common sense. I am not sure it is the best one, as it includes two meanings: one, good sense, of mighty use in the practical affairs of life, and the other, first principles in the minds of all men, in which latter sense alone it can be legitimately employed in philosophy. He also calls them, happily, reason in the first degree, which discerns truth at once, as distinguished from reason in the second degree, which discovers truth by arguing. Stewart represented them as "fundamental laws of human thought and belief," and is commended for this by Sir James Mackintosh, who is so far a member of the school. Thomas Brown represented them as intuitions, a phrase I am fond of, as it presents the mind as looking into the nature of things. Perhaps the phrase "intuitive reason," used by Milton when he talks of "reason intuitive and discursive," might be as good a phrase as any by which to designate these primary principles. Hamilton, who sought to add the philosophy of Kant to that of Reid, often without his being able to make them cohere, sometimes uses the Scotch phrases, and at other times the favorite Kantian designation, a priori. . . .

But it is asked, How do you reconcile your one element with the other—your observation with your truth anterior to observation? I do hold with the whole genuine Scottish school, that there are principles in the mind called common sense, primary reason, intuition, prior to and independent of our observation of them. But I also hold, and this in perfect consistency, that it is by observation we discover them, that they exist, and what they are. I have found it difficult to make some people understand and fall in with this distinction. Historians and critics of philosophy are apt to divide all philosophies into two grand schools, the a priori and a posteriori, or in other words, the rational and the experiential. They are utterly averse to call in a third school, which would disturb all their classifications, and thus trouble them, and require the authors among them, especially the followers of Kant or Cousin, to rewrite all they have written. They do not know very well what to make of the Scottish school, and I may add of the great body of American thinkers, who will not just fall into either one or other of their grand trunk-divisions. In particular, when they condescend to notice the author of this paper they feel as if they do not know what to make of him. "Are you," they ask, "of the a posteriori or empirical school? You seem as if you are so, you are constantly appealing to facts and experience. If so, you have no right to appeal to or call in a priori principles, which can never be established by a limited observation. But you are inconsistently ever bringing in necessary and universal principles, such as those of cause and effect, and moral good." Or they attack me at the other horn of the dilemma. "You hold rather by a priori principles; you are ever falling back on principles, self-evident, necessary, and universal, on personality, on identity, on substance and quality, causation, on the good and the infinite." I have sometimes felt as if I were placed between two contending armies, exposed to the fire of both. Yet I believe I am able to keep and defend my position. Now I direct a shot at the one side, say at John S. Mill, and at other times a shot at the other side, say at Kant—not venturing to attack Hegel, who is in a region which my weapons can never reach. They pay little attention to me, being so engrossed with fighting each other. But I do cherish the hope that when each of the sides finds it impossible to extinguish the other they may become weary of the fight, look for the *juste-milieu*, and turn a favorable look toward the independent place which the Scotch and the great body of the Americans who think on these subjects are occupying. We invite you to throw down your arms, and come up to the peaceful height which we occupy. Hither you may bring all the wealth you have laid up in your separate positions, and here it will be safe. You have here primitive rocks strong and deep as the granite on which to rest it, and here you may add to it riches gathered from as wide regions as your ken can reach, and establish a city which can never be moved or shaken. . . .

Sir James Mackintosh and Dr. Chalmers, who were trained in the Scottish school, upon becoming somewhat acquainted in mature life with the German system, were greatly interested to notice the points of resemblance between the two philosophies. The two—the Scotch and the German—agree, and they differ. Each has a fitting representative: the one in Thomas Reid and the other in Immanuel Kant. The one was a careful observer, guided by common sense—with the meaning of good sense—suspicious of high speculations as sure to have error lurking in them, and shrinking from extreme positions; the other was a powerful logician, a great organizer and systematizer, following his principles to their consequences, which he was ever ready to accept, avow, and proclaim. The two have very important points of agreement. Reid and Kant both lived to oppose Hume, the great skeptic, or, as he would be called in the present day, agnostic. Both met him by calling in great mental principles, which reveal and guarantee truth, which can never be set aside, and which have foundations deep as the universe. Both appeal to reason, which Reid called reason in the first degree, and the other pure reason. The one presents this reason to us under the name of common sense—that is, the powers of intelligence common to all men; the other, as principles necessary and universal. The one pointed to laws, native and fundamental; the other, to forms in the mind. The one carefully observed these by consciousness and sought to unfold their nature; the other determined their existence by a criticism, and professes to give an inventory of them. All students should note these agreements as confirmatory of the truth of both.

The Scotch and German people do so far agree, while they also differ. Both have a considerable amount of broad sense, and, I may add, of humor; but the Scotch have greater clearness of thinking, and the Germans of attractive idealism. Scotland and Germany, in the opinion of foreigners, are not very far distant from each other. But between them there roars an ocean which is often very stormy. I proceed to specify the differences of the two philosophies.

First, they differ in their method. The Scotch follows the inductive method as I have endeavored to explain it. The German has created and carried out the critical method, which has never been very clearly explained and examined. It maintains that things are not to be accepted as they appear; they are to be searched and sifted. Pure reason, according to Kant, can criticize itself. But every criticism ought to have some principles on which it proceeds. Kant, a professor of logic, fortunately adopted the forms of logic which I can show had been carefully inducted by Aristotle, and hence has reached much truth. Others have adopted other principles, and have reached very different conclusions. The philosophies that have followed that of Kant in Germany have been a series of criticisms, each speculator setting out with his own favorite principle—say with the universal ego, or intuition, or identity, or the absolute—and, carrying it out to its consequences, it has become so inextricably entangled, that the cry among young men is, "Out of this forest, and back to the clearer ground occupied by Kant." The Scottish philosophy has not been able to form such lofty speculations as the Germans, but the soberer inductions it has made may contain quite as much truth.

Secondly, the one starts with facts, internal and external, revealed by the senses, inner and outer. It does not profess to prove these by mediate reasoning: it assumes them, and shows that it is entitled to assume them; it declares them as self-evident. The other, the German school, starts with phenomena—not meaning facts to be explained (as physicists understand the phrase), but appearances. The phrase was subtly introduced by Hume, and was unfortunately accepted by Kant. Let us, he said, or at least thought, accept, what Hume grants, phenomena, and guard the truth by mental forms—forms of sense, understanding, and reason. Our knowledge of bodies and their actions, our knowledge even of our minds and their operations, is phenomenal. Having assumed only phenomena, he never could rise to anything else. Having only phenomena in his premises he never could reach realities in his conclusions except by a palpable paralogism, which he himself saw and acknowledged. We human beings are phenomena in the unknown and unknowable of Herbert Spencer, implying no doubt a known, but which never can be known by us. We all know that Locke, though himself a most determined realist, laid down principles which led logically to the idealism of Berkeley. In like manner, Kant, though certainly no agnostic, has laid down a principle in his phenomenal theory which has terminated logically in agnosticism. We meet all this by showing that appearances properly understood are things appearing, and not appearances without things.

Thirdly, the two differ in that the one supposes that our perceptive powers reveal to us things as they are, whereas the other supposes that they add to things. According to Reid and the Scottish school, our consciousness and our senses look at once on real things; not discovering all that is in them, but perceiving them under the aspect in which they are presented—say this table as a colored surface perceived by a perceiving mind. According to Kant and the German school, the mind adds to the things by its own forms. Kant said we perceive appearances under the forms of space and time superimposed by the mind, and judge by categories, and reach higher truth by ideas of pure reason, all of them subjective. Fichte gave consistency to the whole by making these same forms create things.

Our thinking youth in the English and French speaking countries having no very influential philosophy at this present time, and no names to rule them, are taking longing looks toward Germany. When circumstances admit, they go a year or two to a German university—to Berlin or to Leipzig. There they get into a labyrinth of showy and binding forms, and have to go on in the paths opened to them. They return with an imposing nomenclature, and clothed with an armor formidable as the panoply of the middle ages. They write papers and deliver lectures which are read and listened to with the profoundest reverence—some, however, doubting whether all these distinctions are as correct as they are subtle, whether these speculations are as sound as they are imposing. All students may get immeasurable good from the study of the German philosophy. I encourage my students to go to Germany for a time to study. But let them meanwhile maintain their independence. They may be the better for a clue to help them out of the labyrinth when they are wandering. The children of Israel got vast good in the wilderness as they wandered: saw wonders in the pillar of cloud and fire, in the waters issuing from the rock, and the manna on the ground; but they longed all the while to get into a land of rest, with green fields and living rivers. We may all get incalculable good from German speculation, but let us bring it all to the standard of consciousness and of fact, which alone can give us security and rest.

I am quite aware that a large body of speculators will look down with contempt on the sober views I have been expounding, and not think it worth their while to examine them. Metaphysical youths from Britain and America, who have passed a year or two at a German university, and have there been listening to lectures in which the speaker passed along so easily, and without allowing a word of cross-examination, such phrases as subject and object, form and matter, a priori and a posteriori, real and phenomenon and noumenon, will wonder that anyone should be satisfied to stay on such low ground as I have done, while they themselves are on such elevated heights. But I can bear their superciliousness without losing my temper, and I make no other retort than that of Kant on one occasion, "that their master is milking the he-goat while they are holding the sieve." I am sure that the agnostics, whether of the philosophical or physiological schools, will resent my attempt to give knowledge so firm a foundation. I may not have influence myself to stop the crowd which is moving on so exultingly; I may be thrown down by the advancing cavalcade; but I am sure I see the right road to which men will have to return sooner or later; and I am satisfied if only I have opened a gate ready for those who come to discover that the end of their present broad path is darkness and nihilism.

FIRST AND FUNDAMENTAL TRUTHS[2]

The mind must start with something. There are things which it knows at once. I know pleasure and pain. I do more: I know myself as feeling pleasure and pain. I know that I am surrounded with material objects extended and exercising properties. I know by barely contemplating them that these two straight lines cannot contain a space. These are called first truths. There must be first truths before there can be secondary ones; original before there can be derivative ones. Can we discover and enunciate these? I believe we can.

We are not at liberty, indeed, to appeal to a first principle when we please, or because it suits our purpose. When we are left without evidence, we are not therefore allowed to allege that we need no evidence. When we are defeated in argument, we are not to be permitted to escape by falling back on what is unproved and unprovable. It is true that we cannot prove everything, for this would imply an infinite chain of proofs every link of which would hang on another, while the whole would hang on nothing—that is, be incapable of proof. We cannot prove everything by mediate evidence, but we can show that we are justified in assuming certain things. We cannot prove that two straight lines cannot enclose a space, but we can show that

[2] From *Realistic Philosophy*, Vol. I, *Expository*, pp. 33–41.

we are justified in saying so. We can do so by the application of certain tests.

SELF-EVIDENCE is the primary test of that kind of truth which we are entitled to assume without mediate proof. We perceive the object to exist by simply looking at it. The truth shines in its own light, and in order to see we do not require light to shine upon it from any other quarter. We are conscious directly of self as understanding, as thinking, or as feeling, and we need no indirect evidence. Thus, too, we perceive by the eye a colored surface, and by the muscular touch a resisting object, and by the moral sense the evil of hypocrisy. The proof is seen by the contemplative mind in the things themselves. We are convinced that we need no other proof. A proffered probation from any other quarter would not add to the strength of our conviction. We do not seek any external proof, and if any were pressed upon us we would feel it to be unnecessary—nay, to be an encumbrance, and almost an insult to our understanding.

But let us properly understand the nature of this self-evidence. It has constantly been misunderstood and misrepresented. It is not a mere feeling or an emotion belonging to the sensitive part of our nature. It is not a blind instinct or a belief in what we cannot see. It is not above reason or below reason; it is an exercise of primary reason prior, in the nature of things, to any derivative exercises. It is not, as Kant represents it, of the nature of a form in the mind imposed on objects contemplated and giving them a shape and color. It is a perception, it is an intuition of the object. We inspect these two straight lines, and perceive them to be such in their nature that they cannot enclose a space. If two straight lines go on for an inch without coming nearer each other, we are sure they will be no nearer if lengthened millions of miles as straight lines. On contemplating deceit we perceive the act to be wrong in its very nature. It is not a mere sentiment, such as we feel on the contemplation of pleasure and pain; it is a knowledge of an object. It is not the mind imposing or superinducing on the thing what is not in the thing; it is simply the mind perceiving what is in the thing. It is not merely subjective, it is also objective—to use phrases very liable to be misunderstood; or, to speak clearly, the perceiving mind (subject) perceives the thing (object). This is the most satisfactory of all evidence; and this because in it we are immediately cognizant of the thing. There is no evidence so ready to carry conviction. We cannot so much as conceive or imagine any evidence stronger.

NECESSITY is a secondary criterion. It has been represented by Leibnitz and many metaphysicians as the first and the essential test. This I regard as a mistake. Self-evidence comes first, and the other follows and is derived from it. We perceive an object before us

and we know so much of its nature; and we cannot be made to believe
that there is no such object, or that it is not what we know it to be.
I demur to the idea so often pressed upon us that we are to believe
a certain proposition because we are necessitated to believe in it.
This sounds too much like fatality to be agreeable to the free spirit
of man. It is because we are conscious of self that we cannot be made
to believe that we do not exist. The account given of the principle
by Herbert Spencer is a perverted and a vague one: all propositions are to be accepted as unquestionable whose negative is inconceivable. This does not give us a direct criterion, as self-evidence
does, and the word inconceivable is very ambiguous. But necessity,
while it is not the primary, is a potent secondary test. The self-evidence
convinces us; the necessity prevents us from holding any different conviction.

UNIVERSALITY is the tertiary test. By this is meant that it is
believed by all men. It is the argument from catholicity, or common
consent—the *sensus communis*. All men are found to assent to the
particular truth when it is fairly laid before them, as, for instance,
that the shortest distance between two points is a straight line. It
would not be wise nor safe to make this the primary test, as some
of the ancients did. For, in the complexity of thought, in the constant
actual mixing up of experiential with immediate evidence, it is difficult
to determine what all men believe. It is even conceivable that all
men might be deceived by reason of the deceitfulness of the faculties
and the illusive nature of things. But this tertiary comes in to corrobo-
rate the primary test, or rather to show that the proposition can stand
the primary test which proceeds on the observation of the very thing,
in which it is satisfactory to find that all men are agreed.

Combine these and we have a perfect means of determining what
are first truths. The first gives us a personal assurance of which we
can never be deprived; the second secures that we cannot conquer
it; the third that we can appeal to all men as having the same conviction. The first makes known realities; the second restrains us from
breaking off from them; the third shows that we are surrounded with
a community of beings to whom we can address ourselves in the
assurance of meeting with a response.

But in order to be able to apply these criteria properly we must
carry along with us certain explanations and limitations.

1. It should be noticed of intuitive truths that they are, in the
first instance, individual or singular, and that we need to generalize
the single perceptions in order to reach general maxims. In them we
begin with contemplating a single object, say an external object, and
know it to be extended and solid, or an act of benevolence and know
it to be good, or an act of cruelty and proclaim it to be evil. But we

can generalize the individual perceptions, and then we have general maxims or axioms, which we can apply to an infinite number of cases. We perceive that these two parallel lines will never meet; and we are sure that we should affirm the same of every other set of parallel lines, and hence we reach the general maxim that parallel lines will never meet. We perceive, on the bare contemplation of this deed of deceit, that it is base, but we would feel the same of every other deed of deceit, and hence the maxim deceit is evil. But it should be observed that in the formation of these general principles there is a discursive act, in the shape of a generalizing process, involved. It is here that there may creep in error, which is not in the intuitive but in the discursive process; for we may form a partial, a one-sided, or exaggerated generalization. Thus, on discovering a particular effect we at once judge or decide that it has a cause. But when we would make the principle universal we may fall into a mistake, and declare that "everything has a cause," which would require an infinite series of causes and make it necessary to hold that God himself has a cause. In such a case our generalization is wrong. But let the maxim take the form that "everything which begins to be has a cause," and we perceive that on a thing presenting itself to us as beginning we should proclaim it to have had a producing power. We thus see that there may be both truth and error in our metaphysical or moral maxims: truth in the primitive perception at the basis of the whole, while there may be hastiness leading to mutilation in the expression. Hence the wrangling in metaphysics. Thus, everybody acknowledges that two parallel lines can never meet, but there may be disputes as to the fit form in which to put the axiom. So, in regard to the generalized principles that every effect has a cause, that every quality implies a substance, that virtue is commendable, there may be a difficulty in expressing exactly what is meant by cause and effect, what by substance and quality, and what by virtue and moral good; and we may find that when we would make the expressions definite we fall into grievous mistakes, and this while we are certain that there is a self-evident, necessary, and universal truth if only we can seize it.

2. First truths are of various kinds, which we shall endeavor to classify. Some of them are

Primitive Cognitions. In these the object is now before us, and is perceived by us. We perceive that this body has three dimensions in space, and cannot be made to believe otherwise. We decide that this thing, material or mental, cannot be and not be at the same time; that these two things, being each equal to the same thing, are equal to one another. In these cases the object is perceived at once and immediately. But there are others in which the object is not present, and the convictions may be regarded as

Primitive Beliefs. Here there is still an object. It is not present, but still it is contemplated. We have known the object somehow, and on conceiving it beliefs become attached to it. Thus, we know time in the concrete, and in regarding it we believe that time is continuous, that time past has run into time present, and that time present will run into time to come. A number of such faiths gather round our primitive cognitions and widen them indefinitely. We see two points in space; we are sure there is space between, and that the shortest line between the two is a straight line. We can rise to still higher faiths. We believe of certain objects, say space and time, and God—when we come to know him—that they are infinite, that is, that they are always beyond our widest image or concept and such that nothing can be added to or taken from them. The senses cannot give us these beliefs, nor can the understanding construct them out of the materials supplied by the senses. Some of them, such as the idea of the infinite, the perfect, lift us above our immediate experience into a higher sphere. We begin in all such cases with realities perceived or apprehended; and we are sure, if we proceed legitimately, that we end with realities. It should be remarked that in order to our having these cognitions and beliefs it is not necessary to express them or even put them in the shape of propositions. It is necessary first to have cognitions or beliefs regarding them before we form comparisons of them or affirm that they exist or possess certain properties. But out of these we can form

Primitive Judgments, in which we predicate—that is, make affirmations or denials—or discover certain properties or relations, as when we say space and time are without bounds and exist independent of the contemplative mind. In order that these judgments may be primitive they must be pronounced as to objects which have been perceived by intuition.

I ought here to add that the mind is capable of perceiving at once certain moral qualities, and we have

Moral Cognitions, Beliefs, and Judgments. On contemplating an act as self-sacrifice done for a friend or a good cause we know it at once to be good, or an act of selfishness we perceive it to be evil. When these acts are done by our neighbors we cannot notice them directly, but we are sure that they are good or evil; and these may be regarded as beliefs. When we put them in propositions we exercise judgment, as when we declare that sin deserves punishment.

But it will be asked, do we perceive the good and evil to be a reality, to be in the very thing. It might be allowed, it is urged, that intuitively we perceive matter to be extended and that two straight lines cannot enclose a space; for the matter and the straight lines are before us. But moral excellence and depravity have no such reality, they exist only in our conceptions. To all this I reply that we have the acts before us in the one case as in the other; we have before us every day a deed and an implied affection of benevolence or of cruelty, and in it we perceive the morally good or the morally evil. The benevolence in this act of charity has a reality quite as much as the hand that bestows the alms or the alms bestowed. The malevolence in this calumny is a reality, quite as much as the tongue that uttered it or the newspaper that published it. The reality is of a different kind, no doubt, but it is of a kind which all acknowledge when they approve of the charity and disapprove of the scandal, and perhaps impose a penalty upon the person who has been guilty of it.

It is of vast moment, to ourselves and to the community, that we and all others should acknowledge, theoretically and practically, that there are other realities besides those of sense, and these higher and more enduring. It is the worst influence of the prevailing agnosticism that while it can have little power to keep us from believing in the things that are seen, it may have a mighty influence in keeping us from believing in and realizing the things that are spiritual, and therefore unseen, but eternal. The idealist errs when he denies the reality of a material world which, though temporal, is real. But the sensualist errs far more egregiously when he denies the existence of a spiritual world, which is real and eternal. It should be the aim of the highest philosophy to carry us up, as Plato endeavored to do, to this high and pure region which has as high an existence as the heavens, which are its special dwelling place. We should train ourselves, and especially train the young, to retreat from time to time into the higher world, that they may there hold communion with all that is great and good and elevating.

BIBLIOGRAPHY

MC COSH, James, *The Method of the Divine Government, Physical and Moral.* Edinburgh, 1850.

———— *Typical Forms and Special Ends in Creation.* London, 1855.

———— *The Supernatural in Relation to the Natural.* New York, 1862.

———— *An Examination of Mr. J. S. Mill's Philosophy: Being a Defence of Fundamental Truth.* London, 1866.

———— *The Scottish Philosophy: Biographical, Expository, and Critical, from Hutcheson to Hamilton.* New York, 1875.

———— *The Development Hypothesis: Is It Sufficient?* New York, 1876.

———— *The Intuitions of the Mind Inductively Investigated,* first ed., London, 1860; rev. ed., New York, 1882.

_____ *Development: What It Can Do and What It Cannot Do.* New York: Charles Scribner's Sons, 1883.

_____ *Realistic Philosophy.* New York: Charles Scribner's Sons, 1887, 2 vols. First published, 1882.

_____ *Christianity and Positivism: A Series of Lectures to the Times on Natural Theology and Apologetics.* New York: Robert Carter & Bros., 1871.

_____ *Psychology: The Cognitive Powers.* New York: Charles Scribner's Sons, 1886.

ROBINSON, Daniel Sommer, *The Story of Scottish Philosophy.* New York: Exposition-University Book, 1961. Esp. "James McCosh. The Man and His Work," pp. 265–71.

SLOANE, William M., ed., *The Life of James McCosh.* New York, 1896.

PART FOUR

Transcendentalism
(1820-1860)

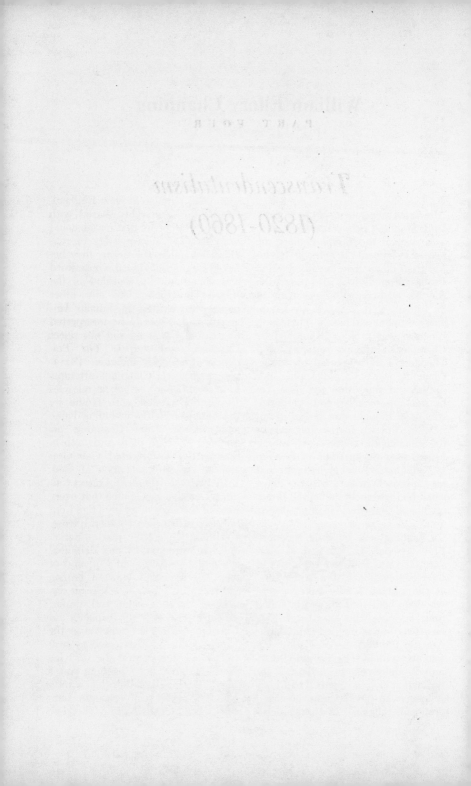

William Ellery Channing

[1780–1842]

Channing has often been called "the great awakener" of New England. Standing between two periods, as a man of the Enlightenment, he helped to redeem the heirs of Calvinism from dogmatism and to develop Unitarianism. But he also paved the way for transcendentalism; many of its leaders were inspired by Channing's sermons and essays. The young Emerson was profoundly moved by Channing's "sublime sermons" and Theodore Parker revered his name. Channing was not a philosopher, nor did he add much that was new. Yet he was able to grasp and synthesize strands of thought that began to appear in America in the first half of the nineteenth century. Channing helped lead the attempt to develop an "enlightened" religious faith; and his approach was attractive to a small but extremely influential group of liberal ministers in the Boston area.

Channing was born in Newport, Rhode Island. He studied at Harvard, and was ordained a minister of the Congregational Church of Boston at the age of twenty-three, a post which he held until his death. Channing became "the apostle of Unitarianism," and helped found the American Unitarian Association. His famous sermon "Unitarian Christianity," delivered in 1819 at the ordination of Jared Sparks, had great influence. In it Channing defends a "rational religion." Extreme deism was never popular in New England, though the Unitarians shared with the deists the belief that reason could bring man to a knowledge of religion. But unlike the deists, they believed in a personal God whose word was supernaturally revealed in the Bible. The Bible, like any other book, was written in human language, and it was to be interpreted by reason. Channing did not reject Christian revelation. In *The Evidences of Revealed Religion* (1821), here reprinted, Channing attempts to answer Hume's attack on miracles (a position shared with Hume by the American deists, including Paine and Allen). Thus Channing attempted to relate piety and faith to reason. But he rejected Calvinism and its austere conception of God. In *The Moral Argument Against Calvinism* (1820) he claimed that every item of theology must be judged not only by reason but by moral sense. Channing rejected predestination and natural depravity and defended the moral perfection of God and of man, an Arminian view of human virtue. In his view there was no distinction between saint and sinner; all men possessed the capacity for Christian virtue. He believed in the Unity of God, and rejected as irrational and unscriptural the doctrine of the Trinity. But Channing was a liberal in religion, rather than a radical, and never really thought himself a transcendentalist. Theodore

Parker's rejection of the miraculous element in religion in favor of an absolute religion, for example, offended him. Although Channing consistently defended reason, there was still a perceptible romantic thread running through his work, especially in his attitude toward sentiment and his feeling toward nature. Channing was also a humanitarian and in the forefront of reform projects. He was sympathetic to the social and political ideals of Godwin and Rousseau. His book, *Slavery* (1835), was a stirring defense of the rights of man and contributed to the awakening of abolitionism.

Channing's reputation was enhanced by his critical essays (on Milton, Napoleon, Fénelon, and so on) and by his essay, "Remarks on National Literature" (1830), in which he called for the cultural independence of the American people. His *Works*, published in 1841–43, went through some twenty-two editions within twelve years after his death, a testament to his wide popularity and influence.

THE EVIDENCES OF REVEALED RELIGION [1]

. . . The great objection to Christianity—the only one which has much influence at the present day—meets us at the very threshold. We cannot, if we would, evade it, for it is founded on a primary and essential attribute of this religion. The objection is oftener felt than expressed, and amounts to this, that miracles are incredible, and that the supernatural character of an alleged fact is proof enough of its falsehood. So strong is this propensity to doubt of departures from the order of nature that there are sincere Christians who incline to rest their religion wholly on its internal evidence and to overlook the outward extraordinary interposition of God by which it was at first established. But the difficulty cannot in this way be evaded; for Christianity is not only confirmed by miracles, but is in itself, in its very essence, a miraculous religion. It is not a system which the human mind might have gathered in the ordinary exercise of its powers from the ordinary course of nature. Its doctrines, especially those which relate to its Founder, claim for it the distinction of being a supernatural provision for the recovery of the human race. So that the objection which I have stated still presses upon us, and, if it be well grounded, it is fatal to Christianity.

It is proper, then, to begin the discussion with inquiring whence the disposition to discredit miracles springs, and how far it is rational. A preliminary remark of some importance is that this disposition is not

[1] Lecture delivered March 14, 1821. Reprinted in *The Works of William E. Channing*, Boston, 1886.

a necessary part or principle of our mental constitution, like the disposition to trace effects to adequate causes. We are indeed so framed as to expect a continuance of that order of nature which we have uniformly experienced; but not so framed as to revolt at alleged violations of that order and to account them impossible or absurd. On the contrary, men at large discover a strong and incurable propensity to believe in miracles. Almost all histories, until within the two last centuries, reported, seriously, supernatural facts. Skepticism as to miracles is comparatively a new thing, if we except the Epicurean or atheistical sect among the ancients; and so far from being founded in human nature, it is resisted by an almost infinite preponderance of belief on the other side.

Whence, then, has this skepticism sprung? It may be explained by two principal causes. (1) It is now an acknowledged fact among enlightened men that in past times and in our own a strong disposition has existed, and still exists, to admit miracles without examination. Human credulity is found to have devoured nothing more eagerly than reports of prodigies. Now it is argued that we discover here a principle of human nature, namely, the love of the supernatural and marvelous, which accounts sufficiently for the belief of miracles wherever we find it; and that it is, consequently, unnecessary and unphilosophical to seek for other causes, and especially to admit that most improbable one—the actual existence of miracles. This sweeping conclusion is a specimen of that rash habit of generalizing which rather distinguishes our times, and shows that philosophical reasoning has made fewer advances than we are apt to boast. It is true that there is a principle of credulity as to prodigies in a considerable part of society, a disposition to believe without due scrutiny. But this principle, like every other in our nature, has its limits; acts according to fixed laws; is not omnipotent—cannot make the eyes see and the ears hear and the understanding credit delusions under all imaginable circumstances; but requires the concurrence of various circumstances and of other principles of our nature in order to its operation. For example, the belief of spectral appearances has been very common; but under what circumstances and in what state of mind has it occurred? Do men see ghosts in broad day and amidst cheerful society? Or in solitary places; in graveyards; in twilights or mists, where outward objects are so undefined as easily to take a form from imagination; and in other circumstances favorable to terror and associated with the delusion in question? The principle of credulity is as regular in its operation as any other principle of the mind; and is so dependent on circumstances and so restrained and checked by other parts of human nature, that sometimes the most obstinate incredulity is found in that very class of people whose easy belief on other occasions moves our contempt. It is well known, for example, that the efficacy of the vaccine inoculation has been encountered with much more unyielding skepticism among the vulgar than among the improved; and in general it may be affirmed that the credulity of the ignorant operates under the control of their strongest passions and impressions, and that no class of society yields a slower assent to positions which manifestly subvert their old modes of thinking and most settled prejudices. It is, then, very unphilosophical to assume this principle as an explanation of all miracles whatever. I grant that the fact that accounts of supernatural agency so generally prove false is a reason for looking upon them with peculiar distrust. Miracles ought on this account to be sifted more than common facts. But if we find that a belief in a series of supernatural works has occurred under circumstances very different from those under which false prodigies have been received, under circumstances most unfavorable to the operation of credulity, then this belief cannot be resolved into the common causes which have blinded men in regard to supernatural agency. We must look for other causes, and if none can be found but the actual existence of the miracles, then true philosophy binds us to believe them. I close this head with observing that the propensity of men to believe in what is strange and miraculous, though a presumption against particular miracles, is not a presumption against miracles universally, but rather the reverse; for great principles of human nature have generally a foundation in truth, and one explanation of this propensity so common to mankind is obviously this: that in the earlier ages of the human race, miraculous interpositions, suited to man's infant state, were not uncommon, and, being the most striking facts of human history, they spread through all future times a belief and expectation of miracles.

I proceed now to the second cause of the skepticism in regard to supernatural agency which has grown up, especially among the more improved, in later times. These later times are distinguished, as you well know, by successful researches into nature; and the discoveries of science have continually added strength to that great principle, that the phenomena of the universe are regulated by general and permanent laws, or that the Author of the universe exerts his power according to an established order. Nature, the more it is explored, is found to be uniform. We observe an unbroken succession of causes and effects. Many phenomena, once denominated irregular and ascribed to supernatural agency, are found to be connected with preceding circumstances as regularly as the most common events. The comet, we learn, observes the same attraction as the sun and planets. When a new phenomenon now occurs, no one thinks it miraculous, but believes that, when better understood, it may be reduced to laws already known, or is an example of a law not yet investigated.

Now this increasing acquaintance with the uniformity of nature begets a distrust of alleged violations of it, and a rational distrust, too; for, while many causes of mistake in regard to alleged miracles may be assigned, there is but one adequate cause of real miracles, that is, the power of God; and the regularity of nature forms a strong presumption against the miraculous exertion of this power, except in extraordinary circumstances and for extraordinary purposes to which the established laws of the creation are not competent. But the observation of the uniformity of nature produces, in multitudes, not merely this rational distrust of alleged violations of it, but a secret feeling as if such violations were impossible. That attention to the powers of nature which is implied in scientific research tends to weaken the practical conviction of a higher power; and the laws of the creation, instead of being regarded as the modes of Divine operation, come insensibly to be considered as fetters on His agency—as too sacred to be suspended even by their Author. This secret feeling, essentially atheistical and at war with all sound philosophy, is the chief foundation of that skepticism which prevails in regard to miraculous agency, and deserves our particular consideration.

To a man whose belief in God is strong and practical, a miracle will appear as possible as any other effect, as the most common event in life; and the argument against miracles, drawn from the uniformity of nature, will weigh with him only as far as this uniformity is a pledge and proof of the Creator's disposition to accomplish his purposes by a fixed order or mode of operation. Now it is freely granted that the Creator's regard or attachment to such an order may be inferred from the steadiness with which He observes it; and a strong presumption lies against any violation of it on slight occasions, or for purposes to which the established laws of nature are adequate. But this is the utmost which the order of nature authorizes us to infer respecting its Author. It forms no presumption against miracles universally, in all imaginable cases, but may even furnish a presumption in their favor.

We are never to forget that God's adherence to the order of the universe is not necessary and mechanical but intelligent and voluntary. He adheres to it, not for its own sake or because it has a sacredness which compels Him to respect it, but because it is most suited to accomplish His purposes. It is a means, and not an end; and, like all other means, must give way when the end can best be promoted without it. It is the mark of a weak mind to make an idol of order and method to cling to established forms of business when they clog instead of advancing it. If, then, the great purposes of the universe can best be accomplished by departing from its established laws, these laws will undoubtedly be suspended; and though broken in the letter, they will be observed in their spirit, for the ends for which they were first instituted will be advanced by their violation. Now the question arises, For what purposes were nature and its order appointed? And there is no presumption in saying that the highest of these is the improvement of intelligent beings. Mind (by which we mean both moral and intellectual powers) is God's first end. The great purpose for which an order of nature is fixed is plainly the formation of mind. In a creation without order, where events would follow without any regular succession, it is obvious that mind must be kept in perpetual infancy; for, in such a universe, there could be no reasoning from effects to causes, no induction to establish general truths, no adaptation of means to ends; that is, no science relating to God, or matter, or mind; no action; no virtue. The great purpose of God, then, I repeat it, in establishing the order of nature, is to form and advance the mind; and if the case should occur in which the interests of the mind could best be advanced by departing from this order, or by miraculous agency, then the great purpose of the creation, the great end of its laws and regularity, would demand such departure; and miracles, instead of warring against, would concur with nature.

Now we Christians maintain that such a case has existed. We affirm that, when Jesus Christ came into the world, nature had failed to communicate instructions to men in which, as intelligent beings, they had the deepest concern, and on which the full development of their highest faculties essentially depended; and we affirm that there was no prospect of relief from nature; so that an exigence had occurred in which additional communications, supernatural lights, might rationally be expected from the Father of spirits. Let me state two particulars out of many in which men needed intellectual aids not given by nature. I refer to the doctrine of one God and Father, on which all piety rests; and to the doctrine of immortality, which is the great spring of virtuous effort. Had I time to enlarge on the history of that period, I might show you under what heaps of rubbish and superstition these doctrines were buried. But I should repeat only what you know familiarly. The works of ancient genius, which form your studies, carry on their front the brand of polytheism, and of debasing error on subjects of the first and deepest concern. It is more important to observe that the very uniformity of nature had some tendency to obscure the doctrines which I have named, or at least to impair their practical power, so that a departure from this uniformity was needed to fasten them on men's minds.

That a fixed order of nature, though a proof of the One God to reflecting and enlarged understandings, has yet a tendency to hide him from men in general, will appear if we consider, first, that as the human mind is constituted, what is regular and of constant occurrence excites it feebly; and benefits flowing to it through fixed, unchanging laws seem to come by a kind of necessity and are apt to be traced up to natural causes alone. Accordingly, religious convictions and feelings, even in the present advanced condition of society, are excited not so much by the ordinary course of God's providence as by sudden, unexpected events which rouse and startle the mind and speak of a Power higher than nature. There is another way in which a fixed order of nature seems unfavorable to just impressions respecting its Author. It discovers to us in the Creator a regard to general good rather than an affection to individuals. The laws of nature, operating as they do with an inflexible steadiness, never varying to meet the cases and wants of individuals, and inflicting much private suffering in their stern administration for the general weal, give the idea of a distant, reserved sovereign much more than of a tender parent; and yet this last view of God is the only effectual security from superstition and idolatry. Nature, then, we fear, would not have brought back the world to its Creator. And as to the doctrine of immortality, the order of the natural world had little tendency to teach this, at least with clearness and energy. The natural world contains no provisions or arrangements for reviving the dead. The sun and the rain, which cover the tomb with verdure, send no vital influences to the moldering body. The researches of science detect no secret processes for restoring the lost powers of life. If man is to live again, he is not to live through any known laws of nature, but by a power higher than nature; and how, then, can we be assured of this truth but by a manifestation of this power, that is, by miraculous agency, confirming a future life?

I have labored in these remarks to show that the uniformity of nature is no presumption against miraculous agency when employed in confirmation of such a religion as Christianity. Nature, on the contrary, furnishes a presumption in its favor. Nature clearly shows to us a power above itself, so that it proves miracles to be possible. Nature reveals purposes and attributes in its Author with which Christianity remarkably agrees. Nature, too, has deficiencies, which show that it was not intended by its Author to be his whole method of instructing mankind; and in this way it gives great confirmation to Christianity, which meets its wants, supplies its chasms, explains its mysteries, and lightens its heart-oppressing cares and sorrows.

Before quitting the general consideration of miracles, I ought to take some notice of Hume's celebrated argument on this subject; not that it merits the attention which it has received, but because it is specious and has derived weight from the name of its author.[2] The argument is briefly this: "That belief is founded upon and regulated by experience. Now we often experience testimony to be false, but

<hr />

[2] David Hume made his case against miracles in Section X of *An Inquiry Concerning Human Understanding* (1748).

never witness a departure from the order of nature. That men may deceive us when they testify to miracles is therefore more accordant with experience than that nature should be irregular; and hence there is a balance of proof against miracles, a presumption so strong as to outweigh the strongest testimony." The usual replies to this argument I have not time to repeat. Dr. Campbell's work, which is accessible to all, will show you that it rests on an equivocal use of terms, and will furnish you with many fine remarks on testimony and on the conditions or qualities which give it validity.[3] I will only add a few remarks which seem to me worthy of attention.

1. This argument affirms that the credibility of facts or statements is to be decided by their accordance with the established order of nature, and by this standard only. Now, if nature comprehended all existences and all powers, this position might be admitted. But if there is a Being higher than nature, the origin of all its powers and motions, and whose character falls under our notice and experience as truly as the creation, then there is an additional standard to which facts and statements are to be referred; and works which violate nature's order will still be credible if they agree with the known properties and attributes of its Author; because for such works we can assign an adequate cause and sufficient reasons, and these are the qualities and conditions on which credibility depends.

2. This argument of Hume proves too much, and therefore proves nothing. It proves too much: for if I am to reject the strongest testimony to miracles because testimony has often deceived me while nature's order has never been found to fail, then I ought to reject a miracle even if I should see it with my own eyes and if all my senses should attest it; for all my senses have sometimes given false reports, while nature has never gone astray; and, therefore, be the circumstances ever so decisive or inconsistent with deception, still I must not believe what I see and hear and touch—what my senses, exercised according to the most deliberate judgment, declare to be true. All this the argument requires; and it proves too much; for disbelief in the case supposed is out of our power and is instinctively pronounced absurd; and what is more, it would subvert that very order of nature on which the argument rests; for this order of nature is learned only by the exercise of my senses and judgment, and if these fail me in the most unexceptionable circumstances, then their testimony to nature is of little worth.

Once more, this argument is built on an ignorance of the nature of testimony. Testimony, we are told, cannot prove a miracle. Now the truth is that testimony, of itself and immediately, proves no facts whatever, not even the most common. Testimony can do nothing more than

[3] George Campbell, Scottish theologian whose *Dissertation on Miracles* (1763) was written to refute Hume.

show us the state of another's mind in regard to a given fact. It can only show us that the testifier has a belief, a conviction, that a certain phenomenon or event has occurred. Here testimony stops; and the reality of the event is to be judged altogether from the nature and degree of this conviction and from the circumstances under which it exists. This conviction is an effect, which must have a cause and needs to be explained; and if no cause can be found but the real occurrence of the event, then this occurrence is admitted as true. Such is the extent of testimony. Now a man who affirms a miraculous phenomenon or event may give us just as decisive proofs, by his character and conduct, of the strength and depth of his conviction as if he were affirming a common occurrence. Testimony, then, does just as much in the case of miracles as of common events; that is, it discloses to us the conviction of another's mind. Now this conviction in the case of miracles requires a cause, an explanation, as much as in every other; and if the circumstances be such that it could not have sprung up and been established but by the reality of the alleged miracle, then that great and fundamental principle of human belief, namely, that every effect must have a cause, compels us to admit the miracle.

It may be observed of Hume and of other philosophical opposers of our religion that they are much more inclined to argue against miracles in general than against the particular miracles on which Christianity rests. And the reason is obvious. Miracles, when considered in a general abstract manner—that is, when divested of all circumstances and supposed to occur as disconnected facts, to stand alone in history, to have no explanations or reasons in preceding events and no influence on those which follow—are indeed open to great objection, as wanton and useless violations of nature's order; and it is accordingly against miracles, considered in this naked, general form, that the arguments of infidelity are chiefly urged. But it is great disingenuity to class under this head the miracles of Christianity. They are palpably different. They do not stand alone in history, but are most intimately incorporated with it. They were demanded by the state of the world which preceded them, and they have left deep traces on all subsequent ages. In fact, the history of the whole civilized world, since their alleged occurrence, has been swayed and colored by them, and is wholly inexplicable without them. Now such miracles are not to be met and disposed of by general reasonings which apply only to insulated, unimportant, uninfluential prodigies.

I have thus considered the objections to miracles in general; and I would close this head with observing that these objections will lose their weight just in proportion as we strengthen our conviction of God's power over nature and of His parental interest in His creatures. The great repugnance to the belief of miraculous agency is founded in a lurking atheism, which ascribes supremacy to nature and which, while it professes to believe in God, questions his tender concern for the improvement of men. To a man who cherishes a sense of God, the great difficulty is, not to account for miracles, but to account for their rare occurrence. One of the mysteries of the universe is this, that its Author retires so continually behind the veil of his works, that the great and good Father does not manifest himself more distinctly to his creatures. There is something like coldness and repulsiveness in instructing us only by fixed, inflexible laws of nature. The intercourse of God with Adam and the patriarchs suits our best conceptions of the relation which He bears to the human race, and ought not to surprise us more than the expression of a human parent's tenderness and concern toward his offspring.

After the remarks now made to remove the objection to revelation in general, I proceed to consider the evidences of the Christian religion in particular; and these are so numerous that should I attempt to compress them into the short space which now remains, I could give but a syllabus—a dry and uninteresting index. It will be more useful to state to you, with some distinctness, the general principle into which all Christian evidences may be resolved and on which the whole religion rests, and then to illustrate it in a few striking particulars.

All the evidences of Christianity may be traced to this great principle—that every effect must have an adequate cause. We claim for our religion a divine original because no adequate cause for it can be found in the powers or passions of human nature, or in the circumstances under which it appeared; because it can only be accounted for by the interposition of that Being to whom its first preachers universally ascribed it, and with whose nature it perfectly agrees.

Christianity, by which we mean not merely the doctrines of the religion but everything relating to it, its rise, its progress, the character of its Author, the conduct of its propagators—Christianity, in this broad sense, can only be accounted for in two ways. It either sprang from the principles of human nature, under the excitements, motives, impulses of the age in which it was first preached, or it had its origin in a higher and supernatural agency. To which of these causes the religion should be referred is not a question beyond our reach; for, being partakers of human nature, and knowing more of it than of any other part of creation, we can judge with sufficient accuracy of the operation of its principles and of the effects to which they are competent. It is indeed true that human powers are not exactly defined, nor can we state precisely the bounds beyond which they cannot pass; but still, the disproportion between human nature and an effect ascribed to it may be so vast and palpable as to satisfy us at once that the effect is inexplicable by human power. I know not precisely what advances may be made by the intellect of an unassisted savage, but that a savage in the woods could not compose the *Principia* of Newton is about as plain as that he could not create the world. I know not the point at which bodily strength must stop, but that a man cannot carry Atlas or Andes on his shoulders is a safe position. The question, therefore, whether the principles of human nature, under the circumstances in which it was placed at Christ's birth, will explain his religion, is one to which we are competent, and is the great question on which the whole controversy turns.

Now we maintain that a great variety of facts belonging to this religion—such as the character of its Founder; its peculiar principles; the style and character of its records; its progress; the conduct, circumstances, and sufferings of its first propagators; the reception of it from the first on the ground of miraculous attestations; the prophecies which it fulfilled and which it contains; its influence on society, and other circumstances connected with it—are utterly inexplicable by human powers and principles, but accord with, and are fully explained by, the power and perfections of God. . . .

BIBLIOGRAPHY

CHANNING, William Ellery, *The Works of William E. Channing, D. D.*, ed. by William Henry Channing. Boston: American Unitarian Assn., 1886.

———— *Works.* Boston, 1841–43. 6 vols.

———— *Unitarian Christianity and Other Essays*, ed. by Irving H. Bartlett. New York: Liberal Arts Press, 1957.

———— *Dr. Channing's Notebook: Passages from the Unpublished Manuscripts of William Ellery Channing*, ed. by Grace Ellery Channing. Boston: Houghton Mifflin, 1887.

EDGELL, David P., *William Ellery Channing: An Intellectual Portrait*. Boston: Beacon Press, 1955.

LADU, Arthur I., "Channing and Transcendentalism." *American Literature*, Vol. XI (1939), pp. 129–37.

PATTERSON, Robert Leet, *The Philosophy of William Ellery Channing*. New York: Bookman Assoc., 1952.

PEABODY, Elizabeth, *Reminiscences of Rev. Wm. Ellery Channing, D. D.* Boston, 1880.

SCHNEIDER, Herbert W., "The Intellectual Background of William Ellery Channing." *Church History*, Vol. VII (1938), pp. 3–23.

SPILLER, Robert E., "A Case for W. E. Channing." *New England Quarterly*, Vol. III (1930), pp. 55–81.

WRIGHT, Conrad, *The Beginnings of Unitarianism in America*. Boston: Starr King Press, 1955.

Ralph Waldo Emerson

[1803–1882]

The writings of Emerson do not present systematic analyses or philosophical questions—they are intuitive excursions in imagination, emotion, and poetry. Yet many of America's outstanding philosophers—Santayana, James, Dewey, Royce—have claimed profit from reading him; and Harvard University honored Emerson during the golden age of American philosophy by naming its new philosophy hall after him. It is difficult to say whether Emerson was a "philosopher"; he did not make such a claim, regarding himself as essentially a poet. His writings, however, are sprinkled throughout with philosophical ideas derived from Plato, Proclus, Plotinus, Kant, Coleridge, and the German idealists of his day. Transcendentalism, the movement which Emerson helped to further, and which restored to New England some of the intellectual predominance it had lost during the Age of Reason, was in some sense a philosophical movement. Emerson greatly influenced the young men who grew up in the middle of the nineteenth century, and his leadership may be attributed not only to his literary attainments, but to the religious, moral, and philosophical outlook which he awakened.

Ralph Waldo Emerson was a product of "America's Athens"—Boston. The son of a minister, he entered Harvard at the age of fourteen, and was graduated in 1821.

His famous introspective *Journals* (ten volumes), which contain his sundry views, were begun there. Emerson was ordained Unitarian minister of Old North Church in Boston in 1829. But three years later, disagreeing with his Congregation about the Sacraments of the Lord's Supper, he left this post, resigned from the Church, and moved to Concord where he lived the rest of his life. His relations with established religion were further strained after his delivery of a lecture at the Harvard Divinity School in 1838, a lecture in which he asserted that one could find redemption only in one's own soul, and not in historical or institutionalized Christianity, and in which he urged men to find God and live in the present. This was interpreted as a radical repudiation of Christianity. He was not welcomed back to Harvard for twenty-eight years.

Emerson's famous Phi Beta Kappa Lecture, "The American Scholar" (1837), called for the independence of America from European cultural leadership. Moreover one finds in it pragmatic overtones not often associated with Emerson. Thought was not simply speculative, but had an experimental relation to the present. In "Self-Reliance" (1841), he urged the individual to turn to himself. Many took this to be a defense of material success and rugged individualism, although Emerson was, on the contrary, defending spiritual development, which only solitude and speculation could give. He was, indeed, attacking social institutions and property where they prevented a man from experiencing his own intuitions.

In 1840 a small group of transcendentalists founded a magazine, *The Dial*, which Emerson later edited for two years. Transcendentalism began with a criticism of Locke's sensation philosophy (on which both deism and Unitarianism were based), and went beyond understanding (*Verstand*) to reason (*Vernuft*). Emerson's address, *The Transcendentalist* (1842), is perhaps the best single expression of the key ideas of that movement, which is seen to be not only a defense of epistemological intuition and metaphysical idealism, but a moral attitude toward nature and society.

Nature (1836) is Emerson's most sustained effort at philosophical composition and expresses his faith in the individual. "To what end is nature?" he asks. There are the direct

uses which nature is found to fulfill: "Commodity," "Beauty," "Language," "Discipline." But the noblest role of nature is to express the unity of existence: "Idealism" and "Spirit." The "Prospects" for man are to go beyond the ordinary mode of sensation and understanding to intuition and reason—with fuller insight into the depths of reality. Here, as in "Oversoul" (1841), Emerson ends up using a quasi-mystical language of emanation reminiscent of Plotinus.

Emerson became virtually a divine oracle to many of his followers. He did not present us with a body of truths, so much as with an intuitive method by means of which he thought we might discover "reality." Like others in Boston at that time, he became allied with liberal causes.

Emerson preferred to reform the individual from within rather than from without. He presented the case for the "representative man" who believed that the nobility of humanity resides in the "spiritual" part of each man, which stands ready to be awakened.

THE TRANSCENDENTALIST [1]

The first thing we have to say respecting what are called new views here in New England at the present time, is, that they are not new, but the very oldest of thoughts cast into the mold of these new times. The light is always identical in its composition, but falls on a great variety of objects, and by so falling is first revealed to us, not in its own form, for it is formless, but in theirs; in like manner, thought only appears in the objects it classifies. What is popularly called Transcendentalism among us, is idealism; idealism as it appears in 1842. As thinkers, mankind have ever divided into two sects, materialists

[1] A lecture read in the Masonic Temple, Boston, Jan., 1842. Reprinted in *The Works of Ralph Waldo Emerson*, Boston, Houghton Mifflin, 1883, Vol. I, pp. 311–39.

and idealists; the first class founding on experience, the second on consciousness; the first class beginning to think from the data of the senses, the second class perceive that the senses are not final, and say, The senses give us representations of things—but what are the things themselves they cannot tell. The materialist insists on facts, on history, on the force of circumstances and the animal wants of man; the idealist on the power of Thought and of Will, on inspiration, on miracle, on individual culture. These two modes of thinking are both natural, but the idealist contends that his way of thinking is in higher nature. He concedes all that the other affirms, admits the impressions of sense, admits their coherency, their use and beauty, and then asks the materialist for his grounds of assurance that things are as his senses represent them. But I, he says, affirm facts not affected by the illusions of sense, facts which are of the same nature as the faculty which reports them, and not liable to doubt; facts which in their first appearance to us assume a native superiority to material facts, degrading these into a language by which the first are to be spoken; facts which it only needs a retirement from the senses to discern. Every materialist will be an idealist; but an idealist can never go backward to be a materialist.

The idealist, in speaking of events, sees them as spirits. He does not deny the sensuous fact: by no means; but he will not see that alone. He does not deny the presence of this table, this chair, and the walls of this room, but he looks at these things as the reverse side of the tapestry, as the *other end,* each being a sequel or completion of a spiritual fact which nearly concerns him. This manner of looking at things transfers every object in nature from an independent and anomalous position without there, into the consciousness. Even the materialist Condillac, perhaps the most logical expounder of materialism, was constrained to say, "Though we should soar into the heavens, though we should sink into the abyss, we never go out of ourselves; it is always our own thought that we perceive." What more could an idealist say?

The materialist, secure in the certainty of sensation, mocks at fine-spun theories, at stargazers and dreamers, and believes that his life is solid, that he at least takes nothing for granted, but knows where he stands and what he does. Yet how easy it is to show him that he also is a phantom walking and working amid phantoms, and that he need only ask a question or two beyond his daily questions to find his solid universe growing dim and impalpable before his sense. The sturdy capitalist, no matter how deep and square on blocks of Quincy granite he lays the foundations of his banking house or Exchange, must set it, at last, not on a cube corresponding to the angles of his structure, but on a mass of unknown materials and solidity, red-hot or white-hot perhaps at the core, which rounds off to an almost perfect sphericity, and lies floating in soft air, and goes spinning away, dragging bank and banker with it at a rate of thousands of miles the hour, he knows not whither—a bit of bullet, now glimmering, now darkling through a small cubic space on the edge of an unimaginable pit of emptiness. And this wild balloon, in which his whole venture is embarked, is a just symbol of his whole state and faculty. One thing at least, he says, is certain, and does not give me the headache, that figures do not lie; the multiplication table has been hitherto found unimpeachable truth; and, moreover, if I put a gold eagle in my safe, I find it again tomorrow—but for these thoughts, I know not whence they are. They change and pass away. But ask him why he believes that a uniform experience will continue uniform, or on what grounds he founds his faith in his figures, and he will perceive that his mental fabric is built up on just as strange and quaking foundations as his proud edifice of stone.

In the order of thought, the materialist takes his departure from the external world, and esteems a man as one product of that. The idealist takes his departure from his consciousness, and reckons the world an appearance. The materialist respects sensible masses, society, government, social art and luxury, every establishment, every mass, whether majority of numbers, or extent of space, or amount of objects, every social action. The idealist has another measure, which is metaphysical, namely the *rank* which things themselves take in his consciousness; not at all the size or appearance. Mind is the only reality, of which men and all other natures are better or worse reflectors. Nature, literature, history, are only subjective phenomena. Although in his action overpowered by the laws of action, and so, warmly co-operating with men, even preferring them to himself, yet when he speaks scientifically, or after the order of thought, he is constrained to degrade persons into representatives of truths. He does not respect labor, or the products of labor, namely property, otherwise than as a manifold symbol, illustrating with wonderful fidelity of details the laws of being; he does not respect government, except as far as it reiterates the law of his mind; nor the church, nor charities, nor arts, for themselves; but hears, as at a vast distance, what they say, as if his consciousness would speak to him through a pantomimic scene. His thought—that is the Universe. His experience inclines him to behold the procession of facts you call the world as flowing perpetually outward from an invisible unsounded center in himself, center alike of him and of them, and necessitating him to regard all things as having a subjective or relative existence, relative to that aforesaid Unknown Center of him.

From this transfer of the world into the consciousness, this beholding of all things in the mind, follow easily his whole ethics. It is simpler to be self-dependent. The height, the deity of man is to be self-sustained, to need no gift, no foreign force. Society is good when it does not violate me, but best when it is likest to solitude. Everything real is self-existent. Everything divine shares the self-existence of Deity. All that you call the world is the shadow of that substance which you are, the perpetual creation of the powers of thought, of those that are dependent and of those that are independent of your will. Do not cumber yourself with fruitless pains to mend and remedy remote effects; let the soul be erect, and all things will go well. You think me the child of my circumstances: I make my circumstance. Let any thought or motive of mine be different from that they are, the difference will transform my condition and economy. I—this thought which is called I—is the mold into which the world is poured like melted wax. The mold is invisible, but the world betrays the shape of the mold. You call it the power of circumstance, but it is the power of me. Am I in harmony with myself? my position will seem to you just and commanding. Am I vicious and insane? my fortunes will seem to you obscure and descending. As I am, so shall I associate, and so shall I act; Cæsar's history will paint out Cæsar. Jesus acted so, because he thought so. I do not wish to overlook or to gainsay any reality; I say I make my circumstance; but if you ask me, Whence am I? I feel like other men my relation to that fact which cannot be spoken, or defined, nor even thought, but which exists, and will exist.

The Transcendentalist adopts the whole connection of spiritual doctrine. He believes in miracle, in the perpetual openness of the human mind to new influx of light and power; he believes in inspiration and in ecstasy. He wishes that the spiritual principle should be suffered to demonstrate itself to the end, in all possible applications to the state of man, without the admission of anything unspiritual; that is, anything positive, dogmatic, personal. Thus the spiritual measure of inspiration is the depth of the thought, and never—who said it? And so he resists all attempts to palm other rules and measures on the spirit than its own.

In action he easily incurs the charge of antinomianism by his avowal that he, who has the lawgiver, may with safety not only neglect, but even contravene every written commandment. . . .

. . . If there is anything grand and daring in human thought or virtue, any reliance on the vast, the unknown, any presentiment, any extravagance of faith, the spiritualist adopts it as most in nature. The oriental mind has always tended to this largeness. Buddhism is an expression of it. The Buddhist, who thanks no man, who says "Do not flatter your benefactors," but who, in his conviction that every good deed can by no possibility escape its reward, will not deceive the benefactor by pretending that he has done more than he should, is a Transcendentalist.

You will see by this sketch that there is no such thing as a Transcendental party; that there is no pure Transcendentalist; that we know of none but prophets and heralds of such a philosophy; that all who by strong bias of nature have leaned to the spiritual side in doctrine have stopped short of their goal. We have had many harbingers and forerunners; but of a purely spiritual life, history has afforded no example. I mean we have yet no man who has leaned entirely on his character, and eaten angels' food; who, trusting to his sentiments, found life made of miracles; who, working for universal aims, found himself fed, he knew not how; clothed, sheltered, and weaponed, he knew not how, and yet it was done by his own hands. Only in the instinct of the lower animals we find the suggestion of the methods of it, and something higher than our understanding. The squirrel hoards nuts and the bee gathers honey without knowing what they do, and they are thus provided for without selfishness or disgrace.

Shall we say then that Transcendentalism is the Saturnalia or excess of Faith; the presentiment of a faith proper to man in his integrity, excessive only when his imperfect obedience hinders the satisfaction of his wish? Nature is transcendental, exists primarily, necessarily, ever works and advances, yet takes no thought for the morrow. Man owns the dignity of the life which throbs around him, in chemistry, and tree, and animal, and in the involuntary functions of his own body; yet he is balked when he tries to fling himself into this enchanted circle, where all is done without degradation. Yet genius and virtue predict in man the same absence of private ends and of condescension to circumstances, united with every trait and talent of beauty and power.

This way of thinking, falling on Roman times, made Stoic philosophers; falling on despotic times, made patriot Catos and Brutuses; falling on superstitious times, made prophets and apostles; on popish times, made Protestants and ascetic monks, preachers of Faith against the preachers of Works; on prelatical times, made Puritans and Quakers; and falling on Unitarian and commercial times, makes the peculiar shades of idealism which we know.

It is well known to most of my audience that the idealism of the present day acquired the name of Transcendental from the use of that term by Immanuel Kant, of Königsberg, who replied to the skeptical philosophy of Locke, which insisted that there was nothing in the intellect which was not previously in the experience of the senses, by showing that there was a very important class of ideas or imperative forms, which did not come by experience, but through which experience was acquired; that these were intuitions of the mind itself; and he denominated them *Transcendental* forms. The extraordinary profoundness and precision of that man's thinking have given vogue to his nomenclature, in Europe and America, to that extent that whatever belongs to the class of intuitive thought is popularly called at the present day *Transcendental*.

Although, as we have said, there is no pure Transcendentalist, yet the tendency to respect the intuitions and to give them, at least in our creed, all authority over our experience, has deeply colored the conversation and poetry of the present day; and the history of genius and of religion in these times, though impure, and as yet not incarnated in any powerful individual, will be the history of this tendency.

It is a sign of our times, conspicuous to the coarsest observer, that many intelligent and religious persons withdraw themselves from the common labors and competitions of the market and the caucus, and betake themselves to a certain solitary and critical way of living, from which no solid fruit has yet appeared to justify their separation. . . .

. . . But their solitary and fastidious manners not only withdraw them from the conversation, but from the labors of the world; they are not good citizens, not good members of society; unwillingly they bear their part of the public and private burdens; they do not willingly share in the public charities, in the public religious rites, in the enterprises of education, of missions foreign and domestic, in the abolition of the slave trade, or in the temperance society. They do not even like to vote. The philanthropists inquire whether Transcendentalism does not mean sloth: they had as lief hear that their friend is dead as that he is a Transcendentalist; for then is he paralyzed, and can never do anything for humanity. What right, cries the good world, has the man of genius to retreat from work, and indulge himself? The popular literary creed seems to be, "I am a sublime genius; I ought not therefore to labor." But genius is the power to labor better and more availably. Deserve thy genius: exalt it. The good, the illuminated, sit apart from the rest, censuring their dullness and vices, as if they thought that by sitting very grand in their chairs, the very brokers, attorneys, and congressmen would see the error of their ways, and flock to them. But the good and wise must learn to act, and carry salvation to the combatants and demagogues in the dusty arena below.

On the part of these children it is replied that life and their faculty seem to them gifts too rich to be squandered on such trifles as you propose to them. What you call your fundamental institutions, your great and holy causes, seem to them great abuses, and, when nearly seen, paltry matters. Each "cause" as it is called—say Abolition, Temperance, say Calvinism, or Unitarianism—becomes speedily a little shop, where the article, let it have been at first never so subtle and ethereal, is now made up into portable and convenient cakes, and retailed in small quantities to suit purchasers. You make very free use of these words "great" and "holy," but few things appear to them such.

Few persons have any magnificence of nature to inspire enthusiasm, and the philanthropies and charities have a certain air of quackery. As to the general course of living, and the daily employments of men, they cannot see much virtue in these, since they are parts of this vicious circle; and as no great ends are answered by the men, there is nothing noble in the arts by which they are maintained. No, they have made the experiment and found that from the liberal professions to the coarsest manual labor, and from the courtesies of the academy and the college to the conventions of the cotillion room and the morning call, there is a spirit of cowardly compromise and seeming which intimates a frightful skepticism, a life without love, and an activity without an aim.

Unless the action is necessary, unless it is adequate, I do not wish to perform it. I do not wish to do one thing but once. I do not love routine. Once possessed of the principle, it is equally easy to make four or forty thousand applications of it. A great man will be content to have indicated in any the slightest manner his perception of the reigning idea of his time, and will leave to those who like it the multiplication of examples. . . .

But this class are not sufficiently characterized if we omit to add that they are lovers and worshippers of Beauty. In the eternal trinity of Truth, Goodness, and Beauty, each in its perfection including the three, they prefer to make Beauty the sign and head. Something of the same taste is observable in all the moral movements of the time, in the religious and benevolent enterprises. They have a liberal, even an aesthetic spirit. A reference to Beauty in action sounds, to be sure, a little hollow and ridiculous in the ears of the old church. In politics, it has often sufficed, when they treated of justice, if they kept the bounds of selfish calculation. If they granted restitution, it was prudence which granted it. But the justice which is now claimed for the black, and the pauper, and the drunkard, is for Beauty—is for a necessity to the soul of the agent, not of the beneficiary. I say this is the tendency, not yet the realization. Our virtue totters and trips, does not yet walk firmly. Its representatives are austere; they preach and denounce; their rectitude is not yet a grace. They are still liable to that slight taint of burlesque which in our strange world attaches to the zealot. A saint should be as dear as the apple of the eye. Yet we are tempted to smile, and we flee from the working to the speculative reformer, to escape that same slight ridicule. Alas for these days of derision and criticism! We call the Beautiful the highest, because it appears to us the golden mean, escaping the dowdiness of the good and the heartlessness of the true. They are lovers of nature also, and find an indemnity in the inviolable order of the world for the violated order and grace of man.

. . . Amidst the downward tendency and proneness of things, when every voice is raised for a new road or another statute or a subscription of stock; for an improvement in dress, or in dentistry; for a new house or a larger business; for a political party, or the division of an estate—will you not tolerate one or two solitary voices in the land speaking for thoughts and principles not marketable or perishable? Soon these improvements and mechanical inventions will be superseded; these modes of living lost out of memory; these cities rotted, ruined by war, by new inventions, by new seats of trade, or the geologic changes: all gone, like the shells which sprinkle the seabeach with a white colony today, forever renewed to be forever destroyed. But the thoughts which these few hermits strove to proclaim by silence as well as by speech, not only by what they did, but by what they forebore to do, shall abide in beauty and strength, to reorganize themselves in nature, to invest themselves anew in other, perhaps higher endowed and happier mixed clay than ours, in fuller union with the surrounding system.

NATURE [2]

INTRODUCTION

Our age is retrospective. It builds the sepulchres of the fathers. It writes biographies, histories, and criticism. The foregoing generations beheld God and nature face to face; we, through their eyes. Why should not we also enjoy an original relation to the universe? Why should not we have a poetry and philosophy of insight and not of tradition, and a religion by revelation to us, and not the history of theirs? Embosomed for a season in nature, whose floods of life stream around and through us and invite us by the powers they supply to action proportioned to nature, why should we grope among the dry bones of the past, or put the living generation into masquerade out of its faded wardrobe? The sun shines today also. There is more wool and flax in the fields. There are new lands, new men, new thoughts. Let us demand our own works and laws and worship.

Undoubtedly we have no questions to ask which are unanswerable. We must trust the perfection of the creation so far as to believe that whatever curiosity the order of things has awakened in our minds, the order of things can satisfy. Every man's condition is a solution in hieroglyphic to those inquiries he would put. He acts it as life, before

[2] *Works*, Vol. I, pp. 9–80.

he apprehends it as truth. In like manner, nature is already, in its forms and tendencies, describing its own design. Let us interrogate the great apparition that shines so peacefully around us. Let us inquire, to what end is nature?

All science has one aim, namely, to find a theory of nature. We have theories of races and of functions, but scarcely yet a remote approach to an idea of creation. We are now so far from the road to truth, that religious teachers dispute and hate each other, and speculative men are esteemed unsound and frivolous. But to a sound judgment, the most abstract truth is the most practical. Whenever a true theory appears, it will be its own evidence. Its test is, that it will explain all phenomena. Now, many are thought not only unexplained but inexplicable; as language, sleep, madness, dreams, beasts, sex.

Philosophically considered, the universe is composed of Nature and the Soul. Strictly speaking, therefore, all that is separate from us, all which philosophy distinguishes as the *not me,* that is, both nature and art, all other men and my own body, must be ranked under this name, *Nature.* In enumerating the values of nature and casting up their sum, I shall use the word in both senses—in its common and in its philosophical import. In inquiries so general as our present one, the inaccuracy is not material; no confusion of thought will occur. *Nature,* in the common sense, refers to essences unchanged by man; space, the air, the river, the leaf. *Art* is applied to the mixture of his will with the same things, as in a house, a canal, a statue, a picture. But his operations taken together are so insignificant, a little chipping, baking, patching, and washing, that in an impression so grand as that of the world on the human mind, they do not vary the result.

NATURE

To go into solitude, a man needs to retire as much from his chamber as from society. I am not solitary whilst I read and write, though nobody is with me. But if a man would be alone, let him look at the stars. The rays that come from those heavenly worlds will separate between him and what he touches. One might think the atmosphere was made transparent with this design, to give man, in the heavenly bodies, the perpetual presence of the sublime. Seen in the streets of cities, how great they are! If the stars should appear one night in a thousand years, how would men believe and adore; and preserve for many generations the remembrance of the city of God which had been shown! But every night come out these envoys of beauty, and light the universe with their admonishing smile.

The stars awaken a certain reverence, because though always present, they are inaccessible; but all natural objects make a kindred impression, when the mind is open to their influence. Nature never wears a mean appearance. Neither does the wisest man extort her secret, and lose his curiosity by finding out all her perfection. Nature never became a toy to a wise spirit. The flowers, the animals, the mountains, reflected the wisdom of his best hour, as much as they had delighted the simplicity of his childhood.

When we speak of nature in this manner, we have a distinct but most poetical sense in the mind. We mean the integrity of impression made by manifold natural objects. It is this which distinguishes the stick of timber of the woodcutter from the tree of the poet. The charming landscape which I saw this morning is indubitably made up of some twenty or thirty farms. Miller owns this field, Locke that, and Manning the woodland beyond. But none of them owns the landscape. There is a property in the horizon which no man has but he whose eye can integrate all the parts, that is, the poet. This is the best part of these men's farms, yet to this their warranty-deeds give no title.

To speak truly, few adult persons can see nature. Most persons do not see the sun. At least they have a very superficial seeing. . . .

COMMODITY

Whoever considers the final cause of the world will discern a multitude of uses that enter as parts into that result. They all admit of being thrown into one of the following classes: Commodity; Beauty; Language; and Discipline.

Under the general name of commodity, I rank all those advantages which our senses owe to nature. This, of course, is a benefit which is temporary and mediate, not ultimate, like its service to the soul. Yet although low, it is perfect in its kind, and is the only use of nature which all men apprehend. The misery of man appears like childish petulance when we explore the steady and prodigal provision that has been made for his support and delight on this green ball which floats him through the heavens. What angels invented these splendid ornaments, these rich conveniences, this ocean of air above, this ocean of water beneath, this firmament of earth between, this zodiac of lights, this tent of dropping clouds, this striped coat of climates, this fourfold year? . . .

BEAUTY

A nobler want of man is served by nature; namely, the love of Beauty. . . .

For better consideration, we may distribute the aspects of Beauty in a threefold manner.

1. First, the simple perception of natural forms is a delight. The influence of the forms and actions in nature is so needful to man, that, in its lowest functions, it seems to lie on the confines of commodity and beauty. To the body and mind which have been cramped by noxious work or company, nature is medicinal and restores their tone. The tradesman, the attorney comes out of the din and craft of the street and sees the sky and the woods, and is a man again. In their eternal calm, he finds himself. The health of the eye seems to demand a horizon. We are never tired, so long as we can see far enough. . . .

2. The presence of a higher—namely, of the spiritual—element is essential to its perfection. The high and divine beauty which can be loved without effeminacy, is that which is found in combination with the human will. Beauty is the mark God sets upon virtue. . . .

3. There is still another aspect under which the beauty of the world may be viewed; namely, as it becomes an object of the intellect. Beside the relation of things to virtue, they have a relation to thought. The intellect searches out the absolute order of things as they stand in the mind of God, and without the colors of affection. The intellectual and the active powers seem to succeed each other, and the exclusive activity of the one generates the exclusive activity of the other. There is something unfriendly in each to the other, but they are like the alternate periods of feeding and working in animals; each prepares and will be followed by the other. Therefore does beauty, which, in relation to actions, as we have seen, comes unsought, and comes because it is unsought, remain for the apprehension and pursuit of the intellect; and there again, in its turn, of the active power. Nothing divine dies. All good is eternally reproductive. The beauty of nature re-forms itself in the mind, and not for barren contemplation, but for new creation. . . .

LANGUAGE

Language is a third use which Nature subserves to man. Nature is the vehicle of thought, and in a simple, double, and threefold degree.

1. Words are signs of natural facts.
2. Particular natural facts are symbols of particular spiritual facts.
3. Nature is the symbol of spirit.

1. Words are signs of natural facts. The use of natural history is to give us aid in supernatural history; the use of the outer creation, to give us language for the beings and changes of the inward creation. Every word which is used to express a moral or intellectual fact, if traced to its root, is found to be borrowed from some material appearance. *Right* means *straight; wrong* means *twisted. Spirit* primarily means *wind; transgression,* the crossing of a *line; supercilious,* the

raising of the eyebrow. We say the *heart* to express emotion, the *head* to denote thought; and *thought* and *emotion* are words borrowed from sensible things, and now appropriated to spiritual nature. Most of the process by which this transformation is made is hidden from us in the remote time when language was framed; but the same tendency may be daily observed in children. Children and savages use only nouns or names of things, which they convert into verbs, and apply to analogous mental acts.

2. But this origin of all words that convey a spiritual import—so conspicuous a fact in the history of language—is our least debt to nature. It is not words only that are emblematic; it is things which are emblematic. Every natural fact is a symbol of some spiritual fact. Every appearance in nature corresponds to some state of the mind, and that state of the mind can only be described by presenting that natural appearance as its picture. An enraged man is a lion, a cunning man is a fox, a firm man is a rock, a learned man is a torch. A lamb is innocence; a snake is subtle spite; flowers express to us the delicate affections. Light and darkness are our familiar expression for knowledge and ignorance; and heat for love. Visible distance behind and before us, is respectively our image of memory and hope.

Who looks upon a river in a meditative hour and is not reminded of the flux of all things? Throw a stone into the stream, and the circles that propagate themselves are the beautiful type of all influence. Man is conscious of a universal soul within or behind his individual life, wherein, as in a firmament, the natures of Justice, Truth, Love, Freedom, arise and shine. This universal soul he calls Reason: it is not mine, or thine, or his, but we are its; we are its property and men. And the blue sky in which the private earth is buried, the sky with its eternal calm, and full of everlasting orbs, is the type of Reason. That which intellectually considered we call Reason, considered in relation to nature, we call Spirit. Spirit is the Creator. Spirit hath life in itself. And man in all ages and countries embodies it in his language as the FATHER.

It is easily seen that there is nothing lucky or capricious in these analogies, but that they are constant, and pervade nature. These are not the dreams of a few poets, here and there; but man is an analogist, and studies relations in all objects. He is placed in the center of beings, and a ray of relation passes from every other being to him. And neither can man be understood without these objects, nor these objects without man. All the facts in natural history taken by themselves, have no value, but are barren, like a single sex. But marry it to human history, and it is full of life. Whole floras, all Linnaeus' and Buffon's volumes, are dry catalogues of facts; but the most trivial of these facts, the habit of a plant, the organs, or work, or noise of an insect, applied to the illustration of a fact in intellectual philosophy, or in any way associated to human nature, affects us in the most lively and agreeable manner. The seed of a plant—to what affecting analogies in the nature of man is that little fruit made use of, in all discourse, up to the voice of Paul, who calls the human corpse a seed—: "It is sown a natural body; it is raised a spiritual body." The motion of the earth around its axis and around the sun, makes the day and the year. These are certain amounts of brute light and heat. But is there no intent of an analogy between man's life and the seasons? And do the seasons gain no grandeur or pathos from that analogy? The instincts of the ant are very unimportant considered as the ant's; but the moment a ray of relation is seen to extend from it to man, and the little drudge is seen to be a monitor, a little body with a mighty heart, then all its habits, even that said to be recently observed, that it never sleeps, become sublime.

Because of this radical correspondence between visible things and human thoughts, savages, who have only what is necessary, converse in figures. As we go back in history, language becomes more picturesque, until its infancy, when it is all poetry; or all spiritual facts are represented by natural symbols. The same symbols are found to make the original elements of all languages. It has moreover been observed, that the idioms of all languages approach each other in passages of the greatest eloquence and power. And as this is the first language, so is it the last. This immediate dependence of language upon nature, this conversion of an outward phenomenon into a type of somewhat in human life, never loses its power to affect us. It is this which gives that piquancy to the conversation of a strong-natured farmer or backwoodsman, which all men relish.

A man's power to connect his thought with its proper symbol, and so to utter it, depends on the simplicity of his character, that is, upon his love of truth and his desire to communicate it without loss. The corruption of man is followed by the corruption of language. When simplicity of character and the sovereignty of ideas is broken up by the prevalence of secondary desires—the desire of riches, of pleasure, of power, and of praise,—and duplicity and falsehood take place of simplicity and truth, the power over nature as an interpreter of the will is in a degree lost; new imagery ceases to be created, and old words are perverted to stand for things which are not; a paper currency is employed when there is no bullion in the vaults. In due time the fraud is manifest, and words lose all power to stimulate the understanding or the affections. Hundreds of writers may be found in every long-civilized nation who for a short time believe and make others believe that they see and utter truths, who do not of themselves clothe one thought in its natural garment, but who feed unconsciously on the language created by the primary writers of the country; those, namely, who hold primarily on nature.

But wise men pierce this rotten diction and fasten words again to visible things; so that picturesque language is at once a commanding certificate that he who employs it is a man in alliance with truth and God. The moment our discourse arises above the ground line of familiar facts and is inflamed with passion or exalted by thought, it clothes itself in images. A man conversing in earnest, if he watch his intellectual processes, will find that a material image more or less luminous arises in his mind, contemporaneous with every thought, which furnishes the vestment of the thought. Hence, good writing and brilliant discourse are perpetual allegories. This imagery is spontaneous. It is the blending of experience with the present action of the mind. It is proper creation. It is the working of the Original Cause through the instruments he has already made.

These facts may suggest the advantage which the country life possesses, for a powerful mind, over the artificial and curtailed life of cities. We know more from nature than we can at will communicate. Its light flows into the mind evermore, and we forget its presence. The poet, the orator, bred in the woods, whose senses have been nourished by their fair and appeasing changes, year after year, without design and without heed, shall not lose their lesson altogether, in the roar of cities or the broil of politics. Long hereafter, amidst agitation and terror in national councils—in the hour of revolution—these solemn images shall reappear in their morning luster, as fit symbols and words of the thoughts which the passing events shall awaken. At the call of a noble sentiment, again the woods wave, the pines murmur, the river rolls and shines, and the cattle low upon the mountains, as he saw and heard them in his infancy. And with these forms, the spells of persuasion, the keys of power are put into his hands.

3. We are thus assisted by natural objects in the expression of particular meanings. But how great a language to convey such peppercorn informations! Did it need such noble races of creatures, this profusion of forms, this host of orbs in heaven, to furnish man with the dictionary and grammar of his municipal speech? Whilst we use this grand cipher to expedite the affairs of our pot and kettle, we feel that we have not yet put it to its use, neither are we able. We are like travelers using the cinders of a volcano to roast their eggs. Whilst we see that it always stands ready to clothe what we would say, we cannot avoid the question whether the characters are not significant for themselves. Have mountains, and waves, and skies, no significance but what we consciously give them when we employ them as emblems of our thoughts? The world is emblematic. Parts of speech are metaphors, because the whole of nature is a metaphor of the human mind. The laws of moral nature answer to those of matter as face to face in a glass. "The

visible world and the relation of its parts, is the dial plate of the invisible." The axioms of physics translate the laws of ethics. Thus, "the whole is greater than its part"; "reaction is equal to action"; "the smallest weight may be made to lift the greatest, the difference of weight being compensated by time"; and many the like propositions, which have an ethical as well as physical sense. These propositions have a much more extensive and universal sense when applied to human life, than when confined to technical use.

In like manner, the memorable words of history and the proverbs of nations consist usually of a natural fact, selected as a picture or parable of a moral truth. Thus; A rolling stone gathers no moss; A bird in the hand is worth two in the bush; A cripple in the right way will beat a racer in the wrong; Make hay while the sun shines; 'Tis hard to carry a full cup even; Vinegar is the son of wine; The last ounce broke the camel's back; Long-lived trees make roots first— and the like. In their primary sense these are trivial facts, but we repeat them for the value of their analogical import. What is true of proverbs is true of all fables, parables, and allegories.

This relation between the mind and matter is not fancied by some poet, but stands in the will of God, and so is free to be known by all men. It appears to men, or it does not appear. When in fortunate hours we ponder this miracle, the wise man doubts if at all other times he is not blind and deaf;

> Can such things be,
> And overcome us like a summer's cloud,
> Without our special wonder?

for the universe becomes transparent, and the light of higher laws than its own shines through it. It is the standing problem which has exercised the wonder and the study of every fine genius since the world began; from the era of the Egyptians and the Brahmins to that of Pythagoras, of Plato, of Bacon, of Leibnitz, of Swedenborg. There sits the Sphinx at the roadside, and from the age to age, as each prophet comes by, he tries his fortune at reading her riddle. There seems to be a necessity in spirit to manifest itself in material forms; and day and night, river and storm, beast and bird, acid and alkali, preexist in necessary ideas in the mind of God, and are what they are by virtue of preceding affections in the world of spirit. A fact is the end or last issue of spirit. The visible creation is the terminus or the circumference of the invisible world. "Material objects," said a French philosopher, "are necessarily kinds of scoriae of the substantial thoughts of the Creator, which must always preserve an exact relation to their first origin; in other words, visible nature must have a spiritual and moral side."

This doctrine is abstruse, and though the images of "garment," "scoriae," "mirror," etc., may stimulate the fancy, we must summon the aid of subtler and more vital expositors to make it plain. "Every scripture is to be interpreted by the same spirit which gave it forth" —is the fundamental law of criticism. A life in harmony with Nature, the love of truth and of virtue, will purge the eyes to understand her text. By degrees we may come to know the primitive sense of the permanent objects of nature, so that the world shall be to us an open book, and every form significant of its hidden life and final cause.

A new interest surprises us, whilst, under the view now suggested, we contemplate the fearful extent and multitude of objects; since "every object rightly seen, unlocks a new faculty of the soul." That which was unconscious truth, becomes, when interpreted and defined in an object, a part of the domain of knowledge—a new weapon in the magazine of power.

DISCIPLINE

In view of the significance of nature, we arrive at once at a new fact— that nature is a discipline. This use of the world includes the preceding uses, as parts of itself.

Space, time, society, labor, climate, food, locomotion, the animals, the mechanical forces, give us sincerest lessons, day by day, whose meaning is unlimited. They educate both the Understanding and the Reason. Every property of matter is a school for the understanding— its solidity or resistance, its inertia, its extension, its figure, its divisi- bility. The understanding adds, divides, combines, measures, and finds nutriment and room for its activity in this worthy scene. Mean- time, Reason transfers all these lessons into its own world of thought, by perceiving the analogy that marries Matter and Mind.

1. Nature is a discipline of the understanding in intellectual truths. Our dealing with sensible objects is a constant exercise in the necessary lessons of difference, of likeness, of order, of being and seeming, of progressive arrangement; of ascent from particular to general; of combination to one end of manifold forces. Proportioned to the im- portance of the organ to be formed, is the extreme care with which its tuition is provided—a care pretermitted in no single case. What tedious training, day after day, year after year, never ending, to form the common sense; what continual reproduction of annoyances, in- conveniences, dilemmas; what rejoicing over us of little men; what disputing of prices, what reckonings of interest—and all to form the Hand of the mind—to instruct us that "good thoughts are no better than good dreams, unless they be executed!"

The same good office is performed by Property and its filial systems of debt and credit. Debt, grinding debt, whose iron face the widow, the orphan, and the sons of genius fear and hate; debt, which consumes so much time, which so cripples and disheartens a great spirit with cares that seem so base, is a preceptor whose lessons cannot be foregone, and is needed most by those who suffer from it most. Moreover, property which has been well compared to snow—"if it fall level today, it will be blown into drifts tomorrow"—is the surface action of internal machinery, like the index on the face of a clock. Whilst now it is the gymnastics of the understanding, it is hiving, in the foresight of the spirit, experience in profounder laws.

The whole character and fortune of the individual are affected by the least inequalities in the culture of the understanding; for example, in the perception of differences. Therefore is Space, and therefore Time, that man may know that things are not huddled and lumped, but sundered and individual. A bell and a plow have each their use, and neither can do the office of the other. Water is good to drink, coal to burn, wool to wear; but wool cannot be drunk, nor water spun, nor coal eaten. The wise man shows his wisdom in separation, in gradation, and his scale of creatures and of merits is as wide as nature. The foolish have no range in their scale, but suppose every man is as every other man. What is not good they call the worst, and what is not hateful, they call the best.

In like manner, what good heed Nature forms in us! She pardons no mistakes. Her yea is yea, and her nay, nay.

The first steps in agriculture, astronomy, zoology (those first steps which the farmer, the hunter, and the sailor take), teach that Nature's dice are always loaded; that in her heaps and rubbish are concealed sure and useful results.

How calmly and genially the mind apprehends one after another the laws of physics! What noble emotions dilate the mortal as he enters into the councils of the creation, and feels by knowledge the privilege to Be! His insight refines him. The beauty of nature shines in his own breast. Man is greater that he can see this, and the universe less, because Time and Space relations vanish as laws are known.

Here again we are impressed and even daunted by the immense Universe to be explored. "What we know is a point to what we do not know." Open any recent journal of science, and weigh the problems suggested concerning light, heat, electricity, magnetism, physiology, geology, and judge whether the interest of natural science is likely to be soon exhausted. . . .

2. Sensible objects conform to the premonitions of Reason and reflect the conscience. All things are moral; and in their boundless changes have an unceasing reference to spiritual nature. Therefore is nature

glorious with form, color, and motion; that every globe in the remotest heaven, every chemical change from the rudest crystal up to the laws of life, every change of vegetation from the first principle of growth in the eye of a leaf, to the tropical forest and antediluvian coal-mine, every animal function from the sponge up to Hercules, shall hint or thunder to man the laws of right and wrong, and echo the Ten Commandments. Therefore is Nature ever the ally of Religion: lends all her pomp and riches to the religious sentiment. Prophet and priest, David, Isaiah, Jesus, have drawn deeply from this source. This ethical character so penetrates the bone and marrow of nature, as to seem the end for which it was made. Whatever private purpose is answered by any member or part, this is its public and universal function, and is never omitted. Nothing in nature is exhausted in its first use. When a thing has served an end to the uttermost, it is wholly new for an ulterior service. In God, every end is converted into a new means. Thus the use of commodity, regarded by itself, is mean and squalid. But it is to the mind an education in the doctrine of Use; namely, that a thing is good only so far as it serves; that a conspiring of parts and efforts to the production of an end is essential to any being. The first and gross manifestation of this truth is our inevitable and hated training in values and wants, in corn and meat.

It has already been illustrated that every natural process is a version of a moral sentence. The moral law lies at the center of nature and radiates to the circumference. It is the pith and marrow of every substance, every relation, and every process. . . .

Herein is especially apprehended the unity of Nature—the unity in variety—which meets us everywhere. All the endless variety of things make an identical impression. Xenophanes complained in his old age, that look where he would, all things hastened back to Unity. He was weary of seeing the same entity in the tedious variety of forms. The fable of Proteus has a cordial truth. A leaf, a drop, a crystal, a moment of time, is related to the whole, and partakes of the perfection of the whole. Each particle is a microcosm, and faithfully renders the likeness of the world. . . .

IDEALISM

Thus is the unspeakable but intelligible and practicable meaning of the world conveyed to man, the immortal pupil, in every object of sense. To this one end of Discipline, all parts of Nature conspire.

A noble doubt perpetually suggests itself—whether this end be not the Final Cause of the Universe; and whether Nature outwardly exists. It is a sufficient account of that appearance we call the World, that

God will teach a human mind, and so make it the receiver of a certain number of congruent sensations, which we call sun and moon, man and woman, house and trade. In my utter impotence to test the authenticity of the report of my senses, to know whether the impressions they make on me correspond with outlying objects, what difference does it make, whether Orion is up there in heaven, or some god paints the image in the firmament of the soul? The relations of parts and the end of the whole remaining the same, what is the difference, whether land and sea interact, and worlds revolve and intermingle without number or end—deep yawning under deep, and galaxy balancing galaxy throughout absolute space—or whether, without relations of time and space, the same appearances are inscribed in the constant faith of man? Whether Nature enjoy a substantial existence without, or is only in the apocalypse of the mind, it is alike useful and alike venerable to me. Be it what it may, it is ideal to me so long as I cannot try the accuracy of my senses.

The frivolous make themselves merry with the ideal theory, as if its consequences were burlesque; as if it affected the stability of Nature. It surely does not. God never jests with us, and will not compromise the end of Nature by permitting any inconsequence in its procession. Any distrust of the permanence of laws would paralyze the faculties of man. Their permanence is sacredly respected, and his faith therein is perfect. The wheels and springs of man are all set to the hypothesis of the permanence of Nature. We are not built like a ship to be tossed, but like a house to stand. It is a natural consequence of this structure, that so long as the active powers predominate over the reflective, we resist with indignation any hint that Nature is more short-lived or mutable than Spirit. The broker, the wheelwright, the carpenter, the tollman are much displeased at the intimation.

But whilst we acquiesce entirely in the permanence of natural laws, the question of the absolute existence of Nature still remains open. It is the uniform effect of culture on the human mind, not to shake our faith in the stability of particular phenomena, as of heat, water, azote; but to lead us to regard Nature as phenomenon, not a substance; to attribute necessary existence to spirit; to esteem nature as an accident and an effect.

To the senses and the unrenewed understanding, belongs a sort of instinctive belief in the absolute existence of Nature. In their view, man and Nature are indissolubly joined. Things are ultimates, and they never look beyond their sphere. The presence of Reason mars this faith. The first effort of thought tends to relax this despotism of the senses which binds us to Nature as if we were a part of it, and shows us Nature aloof, and, as it were, afloat. Until this higher agency intervened, the animal eye sees, with wonderful accuracy, sharp out-

lines and colored surfaces. When the eye of Reason opens, to outline and surface are at once added grace and expression. These
proceed from imagination and affection, and abate somewhat of the
angular distinctness of objects. If the reason be stimulated to more
earnest vision, outlines and surfaces become transparent, and are no
longer seen; causes and spirits are seen through them. The best
moments of life are these delicious awakenings of the higher powers,
and the reverential withdrawing of nature before its God.

Let us proceed to indicate the effects of culture.

1. Our first institution in the ideal philosophy is a hint from Nature
herself.

Nature is made to conspire with spirit to emancipate us. Certain
mechanical changes, a small alteration in our local position, apprises
us of a dualism. We are strangely affected by seeing the shore from
a moving ship, from a balloon, or through the tints of an unusual sky.
The least change in our point of view gives the whole world a pictorial
air. A man who seldom rides, needs only to get into a coach and
traverse his own town to turn the street into a puppet show. The
men, the women—talking, running, bartering, fighting—the earnest
mechanic, the lounger, the beggar, the boys, the dogs, are unrealized
at once, or, a least, wholly detached from all relation to the observer,
and seen as apparent, not substantial beings. What new thoughts
are suggested by seeing a face of country quite familiar, in the rapid
movement of the railroad car! Nay, the most wonted objects (make
a very slight change in the point of vision) please us most. In a camera
obscura, the butcher's cart, and the figure of one of our own family
amuse us. So a portrait of a well-known face gratifies us. Turn the eyes
upside down, by looking at the landscape through your legs, and
how agreeable is the picture, though you have seen it any time these
twenty years!

In these cases, by mechanical means, is suggested the difference
between the observer and the spectacle—between man and Nature.
Hence arises a pleasure mixed with awe; I may say, a low degree of
the sublime is felt, from the fact, probably, that man is hereby
apprised that whilst the world is a spectacle, something in himself
is stable.

2. In a higher manner the poet communicates the same pleasure.
By a few strokes he delineates, as on air, the sun, the mountain,
the camp, the city, the hero, the maiden, not different from what we
know them, but only lifted from the ground and afloat before the
eye. He unfixes the land and the sea, makes them revolve around the
axis of his primary thought, and disposes them anew. Possessed himself by a heroic passion, he uses matter as symbols of it. The sensual
man conforms thoughts to things; the poet conforms things to his

thoughts. The one esteems nature as rooted and fast; the other, as fluid, and impresses his being thereon. To him, the refractory world is ductile and flexible; he invests dust and stones with humanity, and makes them the words of the Reason. The Imagination may be defined to be the use which Reason makes of the material world. . . .

3. Whilst thus the poet animates Nature with his own thoughts, he differs from the philosopher only herein; that the one proposes Beauty as his main end, the other Truth. But the philosopher, not less than the poet, postpones the apparent order and relations of things to the empire of thought. "The problem of philosophy," according to Plato, "is, for all that exists conditionally, to find a ground unconditioned and absolute." It proceeds on the faith that a law determines all phenomena, which being known, the phenomena can be predicted. That law, when in the mind, is an idea. Its beauty is infinite. The true philosopher and the true poet are one, and a beauty which is truth, and a truth which is beauty, is the aim of both. Is not the charm of one of Plato's or Aristotle's definitions strictly like that of the *Antigone* of Sophocles? It is, in both cases, that a spiritual life has been imparted to nature; that the solid-seeming block of matter has been pervaded and dissolved by a thought; that this feeble human being has penetrated the vast masses of nature with an informing soul, and recognized itself in their harmony; that is, seized their law. In physics, when this is attained, the memory disburdens itself of its cumbrous catalogues of particulars, and carries centuries of observation in a single formula.

Thus, even in physics, the material is degraded before the spiritual. The astronomer, the geometer, rely on their irrefragable analysis, and disdain the results of observation. The sublime remark of Euler on his law of arches, "This will be found contrary to all experience, yet is true," had already transferred nature into the mind, and left matter like an outcast corpse.

4. Intellectual science has been observed to beget invariably a doubt of the existence of matter. Turgot said, "He that has never doubted the existence of matter, may be assured he has no aptitude for metaphysical inquiries." It fastens the attention upon immortal, necessary, uncreated natures; that is, upon ideas; and in their presence we feel that the outward circumstance is a dream and a shade. Whilst we wait in this Olympus of gods, we think of Nature as an appendix to the soul. We ascend into their region, and know that these are the thoughts of the Supreme Being. "These are they who were set up from everlasting, from the beginning, or ever the earth was. When he prepared the heavens, they were there; when he established the clouds above, when he strengthened the fountains of the deep. Then they were by him, as one brought up with him. Of them took he counsel."

Their influence is proportionate. As objects of science they are accessible to few men. Yet all men are capable of being raised by piety or by passion, into their region. And no man touches these Divine Natures without becoming, in some degree, himself Divine. Like a new soul, they renew the body. We become physically nimble and lightsome; we tread on air; life is no longer irksome, and we think it will never be so. No man fears age or misfortune or death in their serene company, for he is transported out of the district of change. Whilst we behold unveiled the nature of Justice and Truth, we learn the difference between the absolute and the conditional or relative. We apprehend the absolute. As it were, for the first time, *we exist*. We become immortal, for we learn that time and space are relations of matter; that with a perception of truth or a virtuous will they have no affinity.

5. Finally, religion and ethics, which may be fitly called the practice of ideas, or the introduction of ideas into life, have an analogous effect with all lower culture in degrading nature and suggesting its dependence on spirit. Ethics and religion differ herein; that the one is the system of human duties commencing from man; the other, from God. Religion includes the personality of God; ethics does not. They are one to our present design. They both put nature underfoot. The first and last lesson of religion is, "The things that are seen, are temporal; the things that are unseen, are eternal." It puts an affront upon nature. It does that for the unschooled which philosophy does for Berkeley and Viasa. The uniform language that may be heard in the churches of the most ignorant sects is—"Contemn the unsubstantial shows of the world; they are vanities, dreams, shadows, unrealities; seek the realities of religion." The devotee flouts nature. Some theosophists have arrived at a certain hostility and indignation towards matter, as the Manichean and Plotinus. They distrusted in themselves any looking back to those fleshpots of Egypt. Plotinus was ashamed of his body. In short, they might all say of matter, what Michelangelo said of external beauty: "It is the frail and weary weed, in which God dresses the soul which he has called into time."

It appears that motion, poetry, physical and intellectual science, and religion, all tend to affect our convictions of the reality of the external world. But I own there is something ungrateful in expanding too curiously the particulars of the general proposition, that all culture tends to imbue us with idealism. I have no hostility to nature, but a child's love to it. I expand and live in the warm day like corn and melons. Let us speak her fair. I do not wish to fling stones at my beautiful mother, nor soil my gentle nest. I only wish to indicate the true position of nature in regard to man, wherein to establish man all right education tends; as the ground which to attain is the object of human life; that is, of man's connection with nature. Culture inverts the vulgar views of nature, and brings the mind to call that apparent which it uses to call real, and that real which it uses to call visionary. Children, it is true, believe in the external world. The belief that it appears only, is an afterthought, but with culture this faith will as surely arise on the mind as did the first.

The advantage of the ideal theory over the popular faith is this; that it presents the world in precisely that view which is most desirable to the mind. It is, in fact, the view which Reason, both speculative and practical, that is, philosophy and virtue, take. For seen in the light of thought, the world always is phenomenal; and virtue subordinates it to the mind. Idealism sees the world in God. It beholds the whole circle of persons and things, of actions and events, of country and religion, not as painfully accumulated, atom after atom, act after act, in an aged creeping Past, but as one vast picture which God paints on the instant eternity for the contemplation of the soul. Therefore, the soul holds itself off from a too trivial and microscopic study of the universal tablet. It respects the end too much to immerse itself in the means. It sees something more important in Christianity than the scandals of ecclesiastical history or the niceties of criticism; and, very incurious concerning persons or miracles, and not at all disturbed by chasms of historical evidence, it accepts from God the phenomenon, as it finds it, as the pure and awful form of religion in the world. It is not hot and passionate at the appearance of what it calls its own good or bad fortune, at the union or opposition of other persons. No man is its enemy. It accepts whatsoever befalls, as part of its lesson. It is a watcher more than a doer, and it is a doer only that it may the better watch.

SPIRIT

It is essential to a true theory of Nature and of man, that it should contain something progressive. Uses that are exhausted or that may be, and facts that end in the statement, cannot be all that is true of this brave lodging wherein man is harbored, and wherein all his faculties find appropriate and endless exercise. And all the uses of nature admit of being summed in one, which yields the activity of man an infinite scope. Through all its kingdoms, to the suburbs and outskirts of things, it is faithful to the cause whence it had its origin. It always speaks of Spirit. It suggests the absolute. It is a perpetual effect. It is a great shadow pointing always to the sun behind us.

The aspect of Nature is devout. Like the figure of Jesus, she stands with bent head, and hands folded upon the breast. The happiest man is he who learns from Nature the lesson of worship.

Of that ineffable essence which we call Spirit, he that thinks most

will say least. We can foresee God in the coarse, and, as it were,
distant phenomena of matter; but when we try to define and describe
Himself, both language and thought desert us, and we are as helpless
as fools and savages. That essence refuses to be recorded in propositions, but when man has worshiped him intellectually, the noblest
ministry of nature is to stand as the apparition of God. It is the organ
through which the universal spirit speaks to the individual, and strives
to lead back the individual to it.

When we consider Spirit, we see that the views already presented
do not include the whole circumference of man. We must add some
related thoughts.

Three problems are put by Nature to the mind: What is matter?
Whence is it? and Whereto? The first of these questions only, the ideal
theory answers. Idealism saith: Matter is a phenomenon, not a substance. Idealism acquaints us with the total disparity between the
evidence of our own being and the evidence of the world's being.
The one is perfect; the other, incapable of any assurance; the mind
is a part of the nature of things; the world is a divine dream, from
which we may presently awake to the glories and certainties of day.
Idealism is an hypothesis to account for Nature by other principles
than those of carpentry and chemistry. Yet, if it only deny the existence
of matter, it does not satisfy the demands of the spirit. It leaves God
out of me. It leaves me in the splendid labyrinth of my perceptions, to
wander without end. Then the heart resists it, because it balks the
affections in denying substantive being to men and women. Nature is
so pervaded with human life that there is something of humanity
in all and in every particular. But this theory makes nature foreign
to me, and does not account for that consanguinity which we acknowledge to it.

Let it stand then, in the present state of our knowledge, merely as
a useful introductory hypothesis, serving to apprise us of the eternal
distinction between the soul and the world.

But when, following the invisible steps of thought, we come to inquire, Whence is matter? and Whereto? many truths arise to us out
of the recesses of consciousness. We learn that the highest is present
to the soul of man; that the dread Universal Essence, which is not
wisdom, or love, or beauty, or power, but all in one, and each
entirely, is that for which all things exist, and that by which they
are; that Spirit creates; that behind Nature, throughout Nature, Spirit
is present; one and not compound it does not act upon us from without, that is, in space and time, but spiritually, or through ourselves;
therefore, that spirit, that is, the Supreme Being, does not build up
Nature around us, but puts it forth through us, as the life of the tree
puts forth new branches and leaves through the pores of the old. As

a plant upon the earth, so a man rests upon the bosom of God; he is nourished by unfailing fountains, and draws at his need inexhaustible power. Who can set bounds to the possibilities of man? Once inhale the upper air, being admitted to behold the absolute natures of justice and truth, and we learn that man has access to the entire mind of the Creator, is himself the creator in the finite. This view, which admonishes me where the sources of wisdom and power lie, and points to virtue as to

> The golden key
> Which opes the palace of eternity,

carries upon its face the highest certificate of truth, because it animates me to create my own world through the purification of my soul.

The world proceeds from the same spirit as the body of man. It is a remoter and inferior incarnation of God, a projection of God in the unconscious. But it differs from the body in one important respect. It is not, like that, now subjected to the human will. Its serene order is inviolable by us. It is, therefore, to us, the present expositor of the divine mind. It is a fixed point whereby we may measure our departure. As we degenerate, the contrast between us and our house is more evident. We are as much strangers in Nature as we are aliens from God. We do not understand the notes of birds. The fox and the deer run away from us; the bear and tiger rend us. We do not know the uses of more than a few plants, as corn and the apple, the potato and the vine. Is not the landscape, every glimpse of which hath a grandeur, a face of him? Yet this may show us what discord is between man and Nature, for you cannot freely admire a noble landscape if laborers are digging in the field hard by. The poet finds something ridiculous in his delight until he is out of the sight of men.

PROSPECTS

In inquiries respecting the laws of the world and the frame of things, the highest reason is always the truest. That which seems faintly possible, it is so refined, is often faint and dim because it is deepest seated in the mind among the eternal verities. Empirical science is apt to cloud the sight, and by the very knowledge of functions and processes to bereave the student of the manly contemplation of the whole. The savant becomes unpoetic. But the best-read naturalist who lends an entire and devout attention to truth, will see that there remains much to learn of his relation to the world, and that it is not to be learned by any addition or subtraction or other comparison of known quantities, but is arrived at by untaught sallies of the spirit, by a continual self-recovery, and by entire humility. He will perceive that there are far more excellent qualities in the student than preciseness and infallibility; that a guess is often more fruitful than an indisputable affirmation, and that a dream may let us deeper into the secret of Nature than a hundred concerted experiments.

For the problems to be solved are precisely those which the physiologist and the naturalist omit to state. . . .

. . . We accept the sentence of Plato, that "poetry comes nearer to vital truth than history." Every surmise and vaticination of the mind is entitled to a certain respect, and we learn to prefer imperfect theories, and sentences, which contain glimpses of truth, to digested systems which have no one valuable suggestion. A wise writer will feel that the ends of study and composition are best answered by announcing undiscovered regions of thought, and so communicating, through hope, new activity to the torpid spirit.

. . . At present, man applies to Nature but half his force. He works on the world with his understanding alone. He lives in it, and masters it by a penny wisdom; and he that works most in it, is but a halfman, and whilst his arms are strong and his digestion good, his mind is imbruted, and he is a selfish savage. His relation to nature, his power over it, is through the understanding; as by manure; the economic use of fire, wind, water, and the mariner's needle; steam, coal, chemical agriculture; the repairs of the human body by the dentist and the surgeon. This is such a resumption of power, as if a banished king should buy his territories inch by inch, instead of vaulting at once to his throne. Meantime, in the thick darkness, there are not wanting gleams of a better light—occasional examples of the action of man upon Nature with his entire force—with Reason as well as understanding. Such examples are: the traditions of miracles in the earliest antiquity of all nations; the history of Jesus Christ; the achievements of a principle, as in religious and political revolutions, and in the abolition of the slave trade; the miracles of enthusiasm, as those reported of Swedenborg, Hohenlohe, and the Shakers; many obscure and yet contested facts, now arranged under the name of animal magnetism; prayer, eloquence, self-healing; and the wisdom of children. These are examples of Reason's momentary grasp of the scepter; the exertions of a power which exists not in time or space, but an instantaneous instreaming causing power. The difference between the actual and the ideal force of man is happily figured by the schoolmen, in saying that the knowledge of man is an evening knowledge, *vespertina cognitio*, but that of God is a morning knowledge, *matutina cognitio*.

The problem of restoring to the world original and eternal beauty, is solved by the redemption of the soul. The ruin or the blank, that we see when we look at nature, is in our own eye. The axis of vision

is not coincident with the axis of things, and so they appear not transparent but opaque. The reason why the world lacks unity, and lies
broken and in heaps, is, because man is disunited with himself. He
cannot be a naturalist, until he satisfies all the demands of the spirit.
Love is as much its demand as perception. Indeed, neither can be
perfect without the other. In the uttermost meaning of the words,
thought is devout, and devotion is thought. Deep calls unto deep.
But in actual life, the marriage is not celebrated. There are innocent
men who worship God after the tradition of their fathers, but their
sense of duty has not yet extended to the use of all their faculties.
And there are patient naturalists, but they freeze their subject under
the wintry light of the understanding. Is not prayer also a study of
truth—a sally of the soul into the unfound infinite? No man ever
prayed heartily, without learning something. But when a faithful
thinker, resolute to detach every object from personal relations, and
see it in the light of thought, shall, at the same time, kindle science
with the fire of the holiest affections, then will God go forth anew into
the creation.

It will not need, when the mind is prepared for study, to search
for objects. The invariable mark of wisdom is to see the miraculous
in the common. What is a day? What is a year? What is summer?
What is woman? What is a child? What is sleep? To our blindness,
these things seem unaffecting. We make fables to hide the baldness of
the fact and conform it, as we say, to the higher law of the mind.
But when the fact is seen under the light of an idea, the gaudy fable
fades and shrivels. We behold the real higher law. To the wise, therefore, a fact is true poetry, and the most beautiful of fables. These
wonders are brought to our own door. You also are a man. Man and
woman, and their social life, poverty, labor, sleep, fear, fortune, are
known to you. Learn that none of these things is superficial, but that
each phenomenon has its roots in the faculties and affections of the
mind. Whilst the abstract question occupies your intellect, nature
brings it in the concrete to be solved by your hands. It were a wise
inquiry for the closet, to compare, point by point, especially at remarkable crises in life, our daily history, with the rise and progress
of ideas in the mind.

So shall we come to look at the world with new eyes. It shall
answer the endless inquiry of the intellect—What is truth? and of the
affections—What is good? by yielding itself passive to the educated
will: Then shall come to pass what my poet said: "Nature is not fixed
but fluid. Spirit alters, molds, makes it. The immobility or bruteness
of nature, is the absence of spirit; to pure spirit, it is fluid, it is volatile,
it is obedient. Every spirit builds itself a house; and beyond its house
a world; and beyond its world, a heaven. Know then, that the world

exists for you. For you is the phenomenon perfect. What we are, that only can we see. All that Adam had, all that Caesar could, you have and can do. Adam called his house, heaven and earth; Caesar called his house Rome; you perhaps call yours a cobbler's trade; a hundred acres of plowed land; or a scholar's garret. Yet line for line and point for point, your dominion is as great as theirs, though without fine names. Build, therefore, your own world. As fast as you conform your life to the pure idea in your mind, that will unfold its great proportions. A correspondent revolution in things will attend the influx of the spirit. So fast will disagreeable appearances, swine, spiders, snakes, pests, madhouses, prisons, enemies, vanish; they are temporary and shall be no more seen. The sordor and filths of nature the sun shall dry up, and the wind exhale. As when the summer comes from the south, the snowbanks melt, and the face of the earth becomes green before it, so shall the advancing spirit create its ornaments along its path, and carry with it the beauty it visits, and the song which enchants it; it shall draw beautiful faces, warm hearts, wise discourse, and heroic acts, around its way, until evil is no more seen. The kingdom of man over nature, which cometh not with observation—a dominion such as now is beyond his dream of God—he shall enter without more wonder than the blind man feels who is gradually restored to perfect sight."

THE AMERICAN SCHOLAR [1]

. . . There goes in the world a notion that the scholar should be a recluse, a valetudinarian—as unfit for any handiwork or public labor as a penknife for an ax. The so-called "practical men" sneer at speculative men, as if, because they speculate or *see*, they could do nothing. I have heard it said that the clergy—who are always, more universally than any other class, the scholars of their day—are addressed as women; that the rough, spontaneous conversation of men they do not hear, but only a mincing and diluted speech. They are often virtually disfranchised; and indeed there are advocates for their celibacy. As far as this is true of the studious classes, it is not just and wise. Action is with the scholar subordinate, but it is essential. Without it he is not yet man. Without it thought can never ripen into truth. Whilst the world hangs before the eye as a cloud of beauty, we cannot even see its beauty. Inaction is cowardice, but there can be no scholar without the heroic mind. The preamble of thought, the transition through

[1] *Works,* Vol. I, pp. 83–115.

which it passes from the unconscious to the conscious, is action. Only so much do I know as I have lived. Instantly we know whose words are loaded with life and whose not.

The world—this shadow of the soul, or *other me*—lies wide around. Its attractions are the keys which unlock my thoughts and make me acquainted with myself. I run eagerly into this resounding tumult. I grasp the hands of those next me, and take my place in the ring to suffer and to work, taught by an instinct that so shall the dumb abyss be vocal with speech. I pierce its order; I dissipate its fear; I dispose of it within the circuit of my expanding life. So much only of life as I know by experience, so much of the wilderness have I vanquished and planted, or so far have I extended my being, my dominion. I do not see how any man can afford, for the sake of his nerves and his nap, to spare any action in which he can partake. It is pearls and rubies to his discourse. Drudgery, calamity, exasperation, want, are instructors in eloquence and wisdom. The true scholar grudges every opportunity of action passed by, as a loss of power. It is the raw material out of which the intellect molds her splendid products. A strange process too, this by which experience is converted into thought, as a mulberry leaf is converted into satin. The manufacture goes forward at all hours.

The actions and events of our childhood and youth are now matters of calmest observation. They lie like fair pictures in the air. Not so with our recent actions—with the business which we now have in hand. On this we are quite unable to speculate. Our affections as yet circulate through it. We no more feel or know it than we feel the feet, or the hand, or the brain of our body. The new deed is yet a part of life— remains for a time immersed in our unconscious life. In some contemplative hour it detaches itself from the life like a ripe fruit, to become a thought of the mind. Instantly it is raised, transfigured; the corruptible has put on incorruption. Henceforth it is an object of beauty, however base its origin and neighborhood. Observe too the impossibility of antedating this act. In its grub state, it cannot fly, it cannot shine, it is a dull grub. But suddenly, without observation, the selfsame thing unfurls beautiful wings, and is an angel of wisdom. So is there no fact, no event, in our private history, which shall not, sooner or later, lose its adhesive, inert form, and astonish us by soaring from our body into the empyrean. Cradle and infancy, school and playground, the fear of boys, and dogs, and ferules, the love of little maids and berries, and many another fact that once filled the whole sky, are gone already; friend and relative, profession and party, town and country, nation and world, must also soar and sing.

Of course, he who has put forth his total strength in fit actions has the richest return of wisdom. I will not shut myself out of this globe of action, and transplant an oak into a flowerpot, there to hunger and pine; nor trust the revenue of some single faculty, and exhaust one vein of thought, much like those Savoyards, who, getting their livelihood by carving shepherds, shepherdesses, and smoking Dutchmen, for all Europe, went out one day to the mountain to find stock, and discovered that they had whittled up the last of their pine trees. Authors we have, in numbers, who have written out their vein, and who, moved by a commendable prudence, sail for Greece or Palestine, follow the trapper into the prairie, or ramble round Algiers, to replenish their merchantable stock.

If it were only for a vocabulary, the scholar would be covetous of action. Life is our dictionary. Years are well-spent in country labors; in town; in the insight into trades and manufactures; in frank intercourse with many men and women; in science; in art; to the one end of mastering in all their facts a language by which to illustrate and embody our perceptions. I learn immediately from any speaker how much he has already lived, through the poverty or the splendor of his speech. Life lies behind us as the quarry from whence we get tiles and copestones for the masonry of today. This is the way to learn grammar. Colleges and books only copy the language which the field and the workyard made.

But the final value of action, like that of books, and better than books, is that it is a resource. That great principle of Undulation in Nature, that shows itself in the inspiring and expiring of the breath; in desire and satiety; in the ebb and flow of the sea; in day and night; in heat and cold; and, as yet more deeply ingrained in every atom and every fluid, is known to us under the name of Polarity—these "fits of easy transmission and reflection," as Newton called them, are the law of nature because they are the law of spirit.

The mind now thinks, now acts, and each fit reproduces the other. When the artist has exhausted his materials, when the fancy no longer paints, when thoughts are no longer apprehended and books are a weariness—he has always the resource *to live*. Character is higher than intellect. Thinking is the function. Living is the functionary. The stream retreats to its source. A great soul will be strong to live, as well as strong to think. Does he lack organ or medium to impart his truths? He can still fall back on this elemental force of living them. This is a total act. Thinking is a partial act. Let the grandeur of justice shine in his affairs. Let the beauty of affection cheer his lowly roof. Those "far from fame," who dwell and act with him, will feel the force of his constitution in the doings and passages of the day better than it can be measured by any public and designed display. Time shall teach him that the scholar loses no hour which the man lives. Herein he unfolds the sacred germ of his instinct, screened from influence. What is lost in seemliness is gained in strength. Not out of those on whom systems of education have exhausted their culture, comes the helpful giant to destroy the old or to build the new, but out of unhandselled savage nature; out of terrible Druids and Berserkers come at last Alfred and Shakespeare.

I hear therefore with joy whatever is beginning to be said of the dignity and necessity of labor to every citizen. There is virtue yet in the hoe and the spade, for learned as well as for unlearned hands. And labor is everywhere welcome; always we are invited to work; only be this limitation observed, that a man shall not for the sake of wider activity sacrifice any opinion to the popular judgments and modes of action.

BIBLIOGRAPHY

EMERSON, Ralph Waldo, *The Works of Ralph Waldo Emerson.* Boston: Houghton Mifflin, 1883, 14 vols.

———— *Journals.* Boston: Houghton Mifflin, 1909–14, 10 vols.

———— *Letters.* New York: Columbia U. Press, 1939, 6 vols.

———— *Young Emerson Speaks, Unpublished Discourses on Many Subjects,* ed. by Arthur Cushman McGiffert, Jr. Boston: Houghton Mifflin, 1938.

BEACH, Joseph Warren, "Emerson and Evolution." *U. of Toronto Quarterly,* Vol. III (1933–34), pp. 474–97.

BROWN, Stewart G., "Emerson's Platonism." *New England Quarterly,* Vol. XVIII (1945), pp. 325–45.

CABOT, James Elliot, *A Memoir of Ralph Waldo Emerson.* Boston: Houghton Mifflin, 1887, 2 vols.

CAMERON, Kenneth W., *Emerson, the Essayist; An Outline of His Philosophical Development Through 1836.* Raleigh, N. C.: Thistle Press, 1945, 2 vols.

CAPONIGRI, A. Robert, "Brownson and Emerson: Nature and History." *New England Quarterly,* Vol. XVIII (1945), pp. 368–90.

CARPENTER, Frederic Ives, *Emerson and Asia.* Cambridge: Harvard U. Press, 1930.

———— *Ralph Waldo Emerson.* Representative Selections, with Introduction, Bibliography and Notes. Cincinnati: American Book Co., 1934.

———— *Emerson Handbook.* New York: Hendricks House, 1953.

DAVIS, Merrell R., "Emerson's 'Reason' and the Scottish Philosophers." *New England Quarterly,* Vol. XVII (1944), pp. 209–28.

DEWEY, John, "Emerson—The Philosopher of Democracy." *International Journal of Ethics,* Vol. XIII (1902–03), pp. 405–13.

FIRKINS, Oscar W., *Ralph Waldo Emerson.* Boston: Houghton Mifflin, 1915.

FROTHINGHAM, Octavius, *Transcendentalism in New England; A History.* New York: G.P. Putnam's Sons, 1876; New York: Harpers, 1959.

GAY, Robert M., *Emerson: A Study of the Poet as Seer.* Garden City, N.Y.: Doubleday, Doran & Co., 1928.

GRAY, Henry David, *Emerson: A Statement of New England Transcendentalism as Expressed in the Philosophy of its Chief Exponent.* Stanford U., Cal.: The University, 1917.

HARRIS, William Torrey, "The Dialectic Unity in Emerson's Prose." *Journal of Speculative Philosophy*, Vol. XVIII (1884), pp. 195–202.

HARRISON, John Smith, *The Teachers of Emerson.* New York: Sturgis & Walton, 1910.

HOTSON, Clarence Paul, "Sampson Reed, A Teacher of Emerson." *New England Quarterly*, Vol. II (1929), pp. 249–77.

HUTCHINSON, William R., *The Transcendentalist Ministers.* New Haven: Yale U. Press, 1959.

JAMES, William, *Memories and Studies.* New York: Longmans, Green, 1911. Chap. 2, "Address at the Emerson Centenary."

KRUTCH, Joseph Wood, *Henry David Thoreau.* New York: Wm. Sloan, Assoc., 1948.

PADOVER, Saul K., "Ralph Waldo Emerson: The Moral Voice in Politics." *Political Science Quarterly*, Vol. LXXIV, No. 3 (Sept., 1959), pp. 334–50.

PAUL, Sherman, *Emerson's Angle of Vision: Man and Nature in American Experience.* Cambridge: Harvard U. Press, 1952.

PERRY, Bliss, *Emerson Today.* Princeton: Princeton U. Press, 1931.

RUSK, Ralph L., *The Life of Ralph Waldo Emerson.* New York: Charles Scribner's Sons, 1949.

SANTAYANA, George, *Interpretations of Poetry and Religion.* New York: Charles Scribner's Sons, 1900. Chap. 8, "Emerson."

WELLECK, Rene, "Emerson and German Philosophy." *New England Quarterly*, Vol. XVI, 1943, pp. 41–62.

WHICHER, Stephen E., *Freedom and Fate: An Inner Life of Ralph Waldo Emerson.* Philadelphia: U. of Pennsylvania Press, 1953.

WOODBERRY, George Edward, *Ralph Waldo Emerson. English Men of Letters Series.* New York: Macmillan Co., 1907.

Henry David Thoreau

[1817–1862]

Thoreau stands out in American life as the nonconforming individual par excellence. Born in Concord, Massachusetts (the only one of the Concord Group of transcendentalists born there) and graduated from Harvard College, he pursued thereafter an independent life: reading widely (he was conversant with the Greek classics) and expressing his convictions in his writings. He possessed little visible means of support and was considered iconoclastic and eccentric by his neighbors. His independence and originality in thought and temper, and his devotion to the cause of individual liberty, have few parallels in our history. Thoreau defended the utility of freedom as an aid to happiness and self-fulfillment. He asserted the need of liberty of thought and action for each man to be himself. In *Walden* (1854), Thoreau's most famous work, he dramatized the possibilities of a life free from coercion, originating from within one's own daily necessities. Here the portrayal is of a simple life with a parsimony of needs, yet close to nature and the world of bounty and delight which she offers. In *Civil Disobedience* (1849), a remarkable piece which influenced many libertarians and pacifists (such as Gandhi), Thoreau defends the freedom of the individual against coercion from others, from the state or society. He was not opposed to all social institutions, but he detested the legal sanctioning of injustice. Thus, when Thoreau was arrested for refusing to pay a poll tax to the State of Massachusetts, he was expressing his impassioned objections to the Fugitive Slave Law, which was passed by Congress, and which required, under penalty of law, citizens, North and South, to capture and return runaway slaves to their masters. Thoreau did not fear unpopularity, and he was not merely unconventional for the sake of being unconventional; but he thought that a man had to stand by the dictates of his inner voice and conscience. He was not given to ordered philosophical speculation and his philosophy was intuitive rather than analytic. Yet his letters, journals, and literary pieces reveal a profound philosophical temperament.

CIVIL DISOBEDIENCE [1]

I heartily accept the motto, "That government is best which governs least"; and I should like to see it acted up to more rapidly and systematically. Carried out, it finally amounts to this, which also I believe, "That government is best which governs not at all"; and when men are prepared for it, that will be the kind of government which they will have. Government is at best but an expedient; but most governments are usually, and all governments are sometimes inexpedient. The objections which have been brought against a standing army, and they are many and weighty, and deserve to prevail, may also at last be brought against a standing government. The standing army is only an arm of the standing government. The government itself, which is only the mode which the people have chosen to execute their will, is equally liable to be abused and perverted before the people can act through it. Witness the present Mexican War, the work of comparatively a few individuals using the standing government as their tool; for, in the outset, the people would not have consented to this measure.

This American government—what is it but a tradition, though a recent one, endeavoring to transmit itself unimpaired to posterity, but each instant losing some of its integrity? It has not the vitality and force of a single living man; for a single man can bend it to his will. It is a sort of wooden gun to the people themselves. But it is not the less necessary for this; for the people must have some complicated machinery or other, and hear its din, to satisfy that idea of government which they have. Governments show thus how successfully men can be imposed on, even impose on themselves, for their own advantage. It is excellent, we must all allow. Yet this government never of itself furthered any enterprise, but by the alacrity with which it got out of its way. *It* does not keep the country free. *It* does not settle the West. *It* does not educate. The character inherent in the American people has done all that has been accomplished; and it would have done somewhat more, if the government had not sometimes got in its way. For government is an expedient by which men would fain succeed in letting one another alone; and, as has been said, when it is most expedient, the governed are most let alone by it. Trade and commerce, if they were not made of India rubber, would never manage to bounce over the obstacles which legislators are continually putting in their way; and, if one were to judge these men wholly by the effects of their

[1] First printed under the title "Resistance to Civil Government" in 1849 in the first number of *Æsthetic Papers*, edited by Miss Elizabeth Peabody. Reprinted in *The Writings of Henry David Thoreau*, Boston: Houghton Mifflin, 1906.

actions and not partly by their intentions, they would deserve to be classed and punished with those mischievous persons who put obstructions on the railroads.

But, to speak practically and as a citizen, unlike those who call themselves no-government men, I ask for, not at once no government, but *at once* a better government. Let every man make known what kind of government would command his respect, and that will be one step toward obtaining it.

After all, the practical reason why, when the power is once in the hands of the people, a majority are permitted, and for a long period continue, to rule is not because they are most likely to be in the right, nor because this seems fairest to the minority, but because they are physically the strongest. But a government in which the majority rule in all cases cannot be based on justice, even as far as men understand it. Can there not be a government in which majorities do not virtually decide right and wrong, but conscience?—in which majorities decide only those questions to which the rule of expediency is applicable? Must the citizen ever for a moment, or in the least degree, resign his conscience to the legislator? Why has every man a conscience, then? I think that we should be men first, and subjects afterward. It is not desirable to cultivate a respect for the law, so much as for the right. The only obligation which I have a right to assume is to do at any time what I think right. It is truly enough said, that a corporation has no conscience; but a corporation of conscientious men is a corporation *with* a conscience. Law never made men a whit more just; and, by means of their respect for it, even the well-disposed are daily made the agents of injustice. A common and natural result of an undue respect for law is, that you may see a file of soldiers, colonel, captain, corporal, privates, powdermonkeys, and all, marching in admirable order over hill and dale to the wars, against their wills, ay, against their common sense and consciences, which makes it very steep marching indeed, and produces a palpitation of the heart. They have no doubt that it is a damnable business in which they are concerned; they are all peaceably inclined. Now, what are they? Men at all? or small movable forts and magazines, at the service of some unscrupulous man in power? Visit the navy yard and behold a marine, such a man as an American government can make, or such as it can make a man with its black arts—a mere shadow and reminiscence of humanity, a man laid out alive and standing, and already, as one may say, buried under arms with funeral accompaniments, though it may be—

> Not a drum was heard, not a funeral note,
> As his corse to the rampart we hurried;
> Not a soldier discharged his farewell shot
> O'er the grave where our hero we buried.

The mass of men serve the state thus, not as men mainly, but as machines, with their bodies. They are the standing army, and the militia, jailers, constables, *posse comitatus,* etc. In most cases there is no free exercise whatever of the judgment or of the moral sense; but they put themselves on a level with wood and earth and stones; and wooden men can perhaps be manufactured that will serve the purpose as well. Such command no more respect than men of straw or a lump of dirt. They have the same sort of worth only as horses and dogs. Yet such as these even are commonly esteemed good citizens. Others— as most legislators, politicians, lawyers, ministers, and officeholders— serve the state chiefly with their heads; and, as they rarely make any moral distinctions, they are as likely to serve the Devil, without *in-tending* it, as God. A very few, as heroes, patriots, martyrs, reformers in the great sense, and *men,* serve the state with their consciences also, and so necessarily resist it for the most part; and they are commonly treated as enemies by it. A wise man will only be useful as a man, and will not submit to be "clay," and "stop a hole to keep the wind away," but leave that office to his dust at least:

> I am too high-born to be propertied,
> To be a secondary at control,
> Or useful serving-man and instrument
> To any sovereign state throughout the world.

He who gives himself entirely to his fellow men appears to them useless and selfish; but he who gives himself partially to them is pronounced a benefactor and philanthropist.

How does it become a man to behave toward this American government today? I answer, that he cannot without disgrace be associated with it. I cannot for an instant recognize that political organization as *my* government which is the *slave's* government also.

All men recognize the right of revolution; that is, the right to refuse allegiance to, and to resist, the government, when its tyranny or its inefficiency are great and unendurable. But almost all say that such is not the case now. But such was the case, they think, in the Revolution of '75. If one were to tell me that this was a bad government because it taxed certain foreign commodities brought to its ports, it is most probable that I should not make an ado about it, for I can do without them. All machines have their friction; and possibly this does enough good to counterbalance the evil. At any rate, it is a great evil to make a stir about it. But when the friction comes to have its machine, and oppression and robbery are organized, I say, let us not have such a machine any longer. In other words, when a sixth of the population of a nation which has undertaken to be the refuge of liberty are slaves, and a whole country is unjustly overrun and conquered by a foreign army, and subjected to military law, I think that it is not too soon for honest men to rebel and revolutionize. What makes this duty the more urgent is the fact that the country so overrun is not our own, but ours is the invading army.

Paley, a common authority with many on moral questions, in his chapter on the "Duty of Submission to Civil Government," resolves all civil obligation into expediency; and he proceeds to say, "that so long as the interest of the whole society requires it, that is, so long as the established government cannot be resisted or changed without public inconveniency, it is the will of God that the established government be obeyed, and no longer. . . . This principle being admitted, the justice of every particular case of resistance is reduced to a computation of the quantity of the danger and grievance on the one side, and of the probability and expense of redressing it on the other." Of this, he says, every man shall judge for himself. But Paley appears never to have contemplated those cases to which the rule of expediency does not apply, in which a people, as well as an individual, must do justice, cost what it may. If I have unjustly wrested a plank from a drowning man, I must restore it to him though I drown myself. This, according to Paley, would be inconvenient. But he that would save his life, in such a case, shall lose it. This people must cease to hold slaves, and to make war on Mexico, though it cost them their existence as a people.

In their practice, nations agree with Paley; but does anyone think that Massachusetts does exactly what is right at the present crisis?

A drab of state, a cloth-o'-silver slut,
To have her train borne up, and her soul trail in the dirt.

Practically speaking, the opponents to a reform in Massachusetts are not a hundred thousand politicians at the South, but a hundred thousand merchants and farmers here, who are more interested in commerce and agriculture than they are in humanity, and are not prepared to do justice to the slave and to Mexico, *cost what it may*. I quarrel not with far-off foes, but with those who, near at home, co-operate with and do the bidding of those far away, and without whom the latter would be harmless. We are accustomed to say that the mass of men are unprepared; but improvement is slow, because the few are not materially wiser or better than the many. It is not so important that many should be as good as you, as that there be some absolute goodness somewhere; for that will leaven the whole lump. There are thousands who are *in opinion* opposed to slavery and to the war, who yet in effect do nothing to put an end to them; who, esteeming themselves children of Washington and Franklin, sit down with their hands in their pockets, and say that they know not what to do, and do nothing; who ever postpone the question of freedom to the question of free trade, and quietly read the prices current along with the latest advices from Mexico, after dinner, and, it may be, fall asleep over them both. What is the price current of an honest man and patriot today? They hesitate, and they regret, and sometimes they petition; but they do nothing in earnest and with effect. They will wait, well disposed, for others to remedy the evil, that they may no longer have it to regret. At most, they give only a cheap vote, and a feeble countenance and Godspeed, to the right, as it goes by them. There are nine hundred and ninety-nine patrons of virtue to one virtuous man. But it is easier to deal with the real possessor of a thing than with the temporary guardian of it.

All voting is a sort of gaming, like checkers or backgammon, with a slight moral tinge to it, a playing with right and wrong, with moral questions; and betting naturally accompanies it. The character of the voters is not staked. I cast my vote, perchance, as I think right; but I am not vitally concerned that that right should prevail. I am willing to leave it to the majority. Its obligation, therefore, never exceeds that of expediency. Even voting *for the right* is *doing* nothing for it. It is only expressing to men feebly your desire that it should prevail. A wise man will not leave the right to the mercy of chance, nor wish it to prevail through the power of majority. There is but little virtue in the action of masses of men. When the majority shall at length vote for the abolition of slavery, it will be because they are indifferent to slavery, or because there is but little slavery left to be abolished by their vote. *They* will then be the only slaves. Only *his* vote can hasten the abolition of slavery who asserts his own freedom by his vote.

I hear of a convention to be held at Baltimore, or elsewhere, for the selection of a candidate for the Presidency, made up chiefly of editors, and men who are politicians by profession; but I think, what is it to any independent, intelligent, and respectable man what decision they may come to? Shall we not have the advantage of his wisdom and honesty, nevertheless? Can we not count upon some independent votes? Are there not many individuals in the country who do not attend conventions? But no: I find that the respectable man, so-called, has immediately drifted from his position, and despairs of his country, when his country has more reason to despair of him. He forthwith adopts one of the candidates thus selected as the only *available* one, thus proving that he is himself *available* for any purposes of the demagogue. His vote is of no more worth than that of any unprincipled foreigner or hireling native, who may have been bought. O for a man who is a *man*, and, as my neighbor says, has a bone in his back which you cannot pass your hand through! Our statistics are at fault: the population has been returned too large. How many *men* are there to a square thousand miles in this country? Hardly one. Does not America offer any inducement for men to settle here? The American has dwindled into an Odd Fellow—one who may be known by the development of his organ of gregariousness, and a manifest lack of intellect and cheerful self-reliance; whose first and chief concern, on coming into the world, is to see that the almshouses are in good repair; and, before yet he has lawfully donned the virile garb, to collect a fund for the support of the widows and orphans that may be; who, in short, ventures to live only by the aid of the mutual insurance company, which has promised to bury him decently.

It is not a man's duty, as a matter of course, to devote himself to the eradication of any, even the most enormous wrong; he may still properly have other concerns to engage him; but it is his duty, at least, to wash his hands of it, and, if he gives it no thought longer, not to give it practically his support. If I devote myself to other pursuits and contemplations, I must first see, at least, that I do not pursue them sitting upon another man's shoulders. I must get off him first, that he may pursue his contemplations too. See what gross inconsistency is tolerated. I have heard some of my townsmen say, "I should like to have them order me out to help put down an insurrection of the slaves, or to march to Mexico—see if I would go"; and yet these very men have each, directly by their allegiance, and so indirectly at least by their money, furnished a substitute. The soldier is applauded who refuses to serve in an unjust war by those who do not refuse to sustain the unjust government which makes the war; is applauded by those whose own act and authority he disregards and sets at naught; as if the State were penitent to that degree that it hired one to scourge it while it sinned, but not to that degree that it left off sinning for a moment. Thus, under the name of Order and Civil Government, we are all made at last to pay homage to and support our own meanness. After the first blush of sin comes its indifference; and from immoral it becomes, as it were, *un*moral, and not quite unnecessary to that life which we have made.

The broadest and most prevalent error requires the most disinterested virtue to sustain it. The slight reproach to which the virtue of patriotism is commonly liable, the noble are most likely to incur. Those who, while they disapprove of the character and measures of a government, yield to it their allegiance and support are undoubtedly its most conscientious supporters, and so frequently the most serious obstacles to reform. Some are petitioning the State to dissolve the Union, to disregard the requisitions of the President. Why do they not dissolve it themselves—the union between themselves and the State—and refuse to pay their quota into its treasury? Do not they stand in the same relation to the State that the State does to the Union? And have not the same reasons prevented the State from resisting the Union which have prevented them from resisting the State?

How can a man be satisfied to entertain an opinion merely, and enjoy it? Is there any enjoyment in it, if his opinion is that he is aggrieved? If you are cheated out of a single dollar by your neighbor, you do not rest satisfied with knowing that you are cheated, or with saying that you are cheated, or even with petitioning him to pay you your due; but you take effectual steps at once to obtain the full amount, and see that you are never cheated again. Action from principle, the perception and the performance of right, changes things and relations; it is essentially revolutionary, and does not consist wholly with anything which was. It not only divides States and Churches, it divides families; aye, it divides the *individual,* separating the diabolical in him from the divine.

Unjust laws exist: shall we be content to obey them, or shall we endeavor to amend them, and obey them until we have succeeded, or shall we transgress them at once? Men generally, under such a government as this, think that they ought to wait until they have persuaded the majority to alter them. They think that, if they should resist, the remedy would be worse than the evil. But it is the fault of the government itself that the remedy *is* worse than the evil. *It* makes it worse. Why is it not more apt to anticipate and provide for reform? Why does it not cherish its wise minority? Why does it cry and resist before it is hurt? Why does it not encourage its citizens to be on the alert to point out its faults, and *do* better than it would have them? Why does it always crucify Christ, and excommunicate Copernicus and Luther, and pronounce Washington and Franklin rebels?

One would think that a deliberate and practical denial of its authority was the only offense never contemplated by government; else, why has it not assigned its definite, its suitable and proportionate penalty? If a man who has no property refuses but once to earn nine shillings for the State, he is put in prison for a period unlimited by any law that I know, and determined only by the discretion of those who placed him there; but if he should steal ninety times nine shillings from the State, he is soon permitted to go at large again.

If the injustice is part of the necessary friction of the machine of government, let it go, let it go: perchance it will wear smooth—certainly the machine will wear out. If the injustice has a spring, or a pulley, or a rope, or a crank, exclusively for itself, then perhaps you may consider whether the remedy will not be worse than the evil; but if it is of such a nature that it requires you to be the agent of injustice to another, then, I say, break the law. Let your life be a counter-friction to stop the machine. What I have to do is to see, at any rate, that I do not lend myself to the wrong which I condemn.

As for adopting the ways which the State has provided for remedying the evil, I know not of such ways. They take too much time, and a man's life will be gone. I have other affairs to attend to. I came into this world, not chiefly to make this a good place to live in, but to live in it, be it good or bad. A man has not everything to do, but something; and because he cannot do *everything*, it is not necessary that he should do *something* wrong. It is not my business to be petitioning the governor or the legislature any more than it is theirs to petition me; and if they should not hear my petition, what should I do then? But in this case the State has provided no way: its very Constitution is the evil. This may seem to be harsh and stubborn and unconciliatory; but it is to treat with the utmost kindness and consideration the only spirit that can appreciate or deserves it. So is all change for the better, like birth and death, which convulse the body.

I do not hesitate to say, that those who call themselves abolitionists should at once effectually withdraw their support, both in person and property, from the government of Massachusetts, and not wait till they constitute a majority of one before they suffer the right to prevail through them. I think that it is enough if they have God on their side, without waiting for that other one. Moreover, any man more right than his neighbors constitutes a majority of one already.

I meet this American government, or its representative, the State government, directly and face to face, once a year—no more—in the person of its taxgatherer; this is the only mode in which a man situated as I am necessarily meets it; and it then says distinctly, Recognize me; and the simplest, the most effectual, and, in the present posture of affairs, the indispensablest mode of treating with it on this head, of expressing your little satisfaction with and love for it, is to deny it then. My civil neighbor, the taxgatherer, is the very man I have to deal with—for it is, after all, with men and not with parchment that I quarrel—and he has voluntarily chosen to be an agent of the government. How shall he ever know well what he is and does as an officer of the government, or as a man, until he is obliged to consider whether he shall treat me, his neighbor, for whom he has respect, as a neighbor and well-disposed man, or as a maniac and disturber of the peace, and see if he can get over this obstruction to his neighborliness without a ruder and more impetuous thought or speech corresponding with his action. I know this well, that if one thousand, if one hundred, if ten men whom I could name—if ten *honest* men only—aye, if *one* HONEST man, in this State of Massachusetts, *ceasing to hold slaves,* were actually to withdraw from this copartnership, and be locked up in the county jail therefor, it would be the abolition of slavery in America. For it matters not how small the beginning may seem to be: what is once well done is done forever. But we love better to talk about it: that we say is our mission. Reform keeps many scores of newspapers in its service, but not one man. If my esteemed neighbor, the State's ambassador, who will devote his days to the settlement of the question of human rights in the council chamber, instead of being threatened with the prisons of Carolina, were to sit down the prisoner of Massachusetts, that State which is so anxious to foist the sin of slavery upon her sister—though at present she can discover only an act of inhospitality to be the ground of a quarrel with her—the legislature would not wholly waive the subject the following winter.

Under a government which imprisons any unjustly, the true place for a just man is also a prison. The proper place today, the only place which Massachusetts has provided for her freer and less desponding spirits, is in her prisons, to be put out and locked out of the State by her own act, as they have already put themselves out by their principles. It is there that the fugitive slave, and the Mexican prisoner on parole, and the Indian come to plead the wrongs of his race should find them; on that separate, but more free and honorable ground, where the State places those who are not *with* her, but *against* her—the only house in a slave State in which a free man can abide with honor. If any think that their influence would be lost there, and their voices no longer afflict the ear of the State, that they would not be as an enemy within its walls, they do not know by how much truth is stronger than error, nor how much more eloquently and effectively he can combat injustice who has experienced a little in his own person. Cast your whole vote, not a strip of paper merely, but your whole influence. A minority is powerless while it conforms to the majority; it is not even a minority then; but it is irresistible when it clogs by its whole weight. If the alternative is to keep all just men in prison, or give up war and slavery, the State will not hesitate which to choose. If a thousand men were not to pay their tax bills this year, that would not be a violent and bloody measure, as it would be to pay them, and enable the State to commit violence and shed innocent blood. This is, in fact, the definition of a peaceable revolution, if any such is possible. If the taxgatherer, or any other public officer, asks me, as one has done, "But what shall I do?" my answer is, "If you really wish to do anything, resign your office." When the subject has refused allegiance, and the officer has resigned his office, then the revolution is accomplished. But even suppose blood should flow. Is there not a sort of bloodshed when the conscience is wounded? Through this wound a man's real manhood and immortality flow out, and he bleeds to an everlasting death. I see this blood flowing now.

I have contemplated the imprisonment of the offender, rather than the seizure of his goods—though both will serve the same purpose—because they who assert the purest right, and consequently are most dangerous to a corrupt State, commonly have not spent much time in accumulating property. To such the State renders comparatively small service, and a slight tax is wont to appear exorbitant, particularly if they are obliged to earn it by special labor with their hands. If there were one who lived wholly without the use of money, the State itself would hesitate to demand it of him. But the rich man—not to make any invidious comparison—is always sold to the institution which makes him rich. Absolutely speaking, the more money, the less virtue; for money comes between a man and his objects, and obtains them for him; and it was certainly no great virtue to obtain it. It puts to rest many questions which he would otherwise be taxed to answer; while the only new question which it puts is the hard but superfluous one, how to spend it. Thus his moral ground is taken from under his feet. The opportunities of living are diminished in proportion as what are called the "means" are increased. The best thing a man can do for his culture when he is rich is to endeavor to carry out those schemes which he entertained when he was poor. Christ answered the Herodians according to their condition. "Show me the tribute money," said he; and one took a penny out of his pocket; if you use money which has the image of Caesar on it, and which he has made current and valuable, that is, *if you are men of the State*, and gladly enjoy the advantages of Caesar's government, then pay him back some of his own when he demands it. "Render therefore to Caesar that which is Caesar's, and to God those things which are God's," leaving them no wiser than before as to which was which; for they did not wish to know.

When I converse with the freest of my neighbors, I perceive that, whatever they may say about the magnitude and seriousness of the question and their regard for the public tranquillity, the long and short of the matter is, that they cannot spare the protection of the existing government, and they dread the consequences to their property and families of disobedience to it. For my own part, I should not like to think that I ever rely on the protection of the State. But, if I deny the authority of the State when it presents its tax bill, it will soon take and waste all my property, and so harass me and my children without end. This is hard. This makes it impossible for a man to live honestly, and at the same time comfortably, in outward respects. It will not be worth the while to accumulate property; that would be sure to go again. You must hire or squat somewhere, and raise but a small crop, and eat that soon. You must live within yourself, and depend upon yourself always tucked up and ready for a start, and not have many affairs. A man may grow rich in Turkey even, if he will be in all respects a good subject of the Turkish government. Confucius said: "If a state is governed by the principles of reason, poverty and misery are subjects of shame; if a state is not governed by the principles of reason, riches and honors are the subjects of shame." No: until I want the protection of Massachusetts to be extended to me in some distant Southern port where my liberty is endangered, or until I am bent solely on building up an estate at home by peaceful enterprise, I can afford to refuse allegiance to Massachusetts, and her right to my property and life. It costs me less in every sense to incur the penalty of disobedience to the State than it would to obey. I should feel as if I were worth less in that case.

Some years ago, the State met me in behalf of the Church, and commanded me to pay a certain sum toward the support of a clergyman whose preaching my father attended, but never I myself. "Pay," it said, "or be locked up in the jail." I declined to pay. But, unfortunately, another man saw fit to pay it. I did not see why the schoolmaster should be taxed to support the priest, and not the priest the schoolmaster; for I was not the State's schoolmaster, but I supported myself by voluntary subscription. I did not see why the lyceum should not present its tax bill, and have the State to back its demand, as well as the Church. However, at the request of the selectmen, I condescended to make some such statement as this in writing: "Know all men by these presents, that I, Henry Thoreau, do not wish to be regarded as a member of any incorporated society which I have not joined." This I gave to the town clerk; and he has it. The State, having thus learned that I did not wish to be regarded as a member of that Church, has never made a like demand on me since; though it said that it must adhere to its original presumption that time. If I had known how to name them, I should then have signed off in detail from all the societies which I never signed onto; but I did not know where to find a complete list.

I have paid no poll tax for six years. I was put into a jail once on this account, for one night; and, as I stood considering the walls of solid stone, two or three feet thick, the door of wood and iron, a foot thick, and the iron grating which strained the light, I could not help being struck with the foolishness of that institution which treated me as if I were mere flesh and blood and bones, to be locked up. I wondered that it should have concluded at length that this was the best use it could put me to, and had never thought to avail itself of my services in some way. I saw that, if there was a wall of stone between me and my townsmen, there was a still more difficult one to climb or break through before they could get to be as free as I was. I did not for a moment feel confined, and the walls seemed a great waste of stone and mortar. I felt as if I alone of all my townsmen had paid my tax. They plainly did not know how to treat me, but behaved like persons who are underbred. In every threat and in every compliment there was a blunder; for they thought that my chief desire was to stand the other side of that stone wall. I could not but smile to see how industriously they locked the door on my meditations, which followed them out again without let or hindrance, and *they* were really all that was dangerous. As they could not reach me, they had resolved to punish my body; just as boys, if they cannot come at some person against whom they have a spite, will abuse his dog. I saw that the State was half-witted, that it was timid as a lone woman with her silver spoons, and that it did not know its friends from its foes, and I lost all my remaining respect for it, and pitied it.

Thus the State never intentionally confronts a man's sense, intellectual or moral, but only his body, his senses. It is not armed with superior wit or honesty, but with superior physical strength. I was not born to be forced. I will breathe after my own fashion. Let us see who is the strongest. What force has a multitude? They only can force me who obey a higher law than I. They force me to become like themselves. I do not hear of *men* being *forced* to live this way or that by masses of men. What sort of life were that to live? When I meet a government which says to me, "Your money or your life," why should I be in haste to give it my money? It may be in a great strait, and not know what to do: I cannot help that. It must help itself; do as I do. It is not worth the while to snivel about it. I am not responsible for the successful working of the machinery of society. I am not the son of the engineer. I perceive that, when an acorn and a chestnut fall side by side, the one does not remain inert to make way for the other, but both obey their own laws, and spring and grow and flourish as best they can, till one, perchance, overshadows and destroys the other. If a plant cannot live according to its nature, it dies; and so a man.

. . . When I came out of prison—for someone interfered and paid that tax—I did not perceive that great changes had taken place on the common, such as he observed who went in a youth and emerged a tottering and gray-headed man; and yet a change had to my eyes come over the scene—the town, and State, and country—greater than any that mere time could effect. I saw yet more distinctly the State in which I lived. I saw to what extent the people among whom I lived could be trusted as good neighbors and friends; that their friendship was for summer weather only; that they did not greatly propose to do right; that they were a distinct race from me by their prejudices and superstitions, as the Chinese and Malays are; that in their sacrifices to humanity they ran no risks, not even to their property; that after all they were not so noble but they treated the thief as he had treated them, and hoped, by a certain outward observance and a few prayers, and by walking in a particular straight though useless path from time to time, to save their souls. This may be to judge my neighbors harshly; for I believe that many of them are not aware that they have such an institution as the jail in their village.

It was formerly the custom in our village, when a poor debtor came out of jail, for his acquaintances to salute him, looking through their fingers, which were crossed to represent the grating of a jail window, "How do ye do?" My neighbors did not thus salute me, but first looked at me, and then at one another, as if I had returned from a long journey. I was put into jail as I was going to the shoemaker's to get a shoe which was mended. When I was let out the next morning, I proceeded to finish my errand, and, having put on my mended shoe, joined a huckleberry party, who were impatient to put themselves under my conduct; and in half an hour—for the horse was soon tackled—was in the midst of a huckleberry field, on one of our highest hills, two miles off, and then the State was nowhere to be seen.

This is the whole history of "My Prisons."

I have never declined paying the highway tax, because I am as desirous of being a good neighbor as I am of being a bad subject; and as for supporting schools, I am doing my part to educate my fellow countrymen now. It is for no particular item in the tax bill that I refuse to pay it. I simply wish to refuse allegiance to the State, to withdraw and stand aloof from it effectually. I do not care to trace the course of my dollar, if I could, till it buys a man or a musket to shoot one with—the dollar is innocent—but I am concerned to trace the effects of my allegiance. In fact, I quietly declare war with the State, after my fashion, though I will still make what use and get what advantage of her I can, as is usual in such cases.

If others pay the tax which is demanded of me, from a sympathy with the State, they do but what they have already done in their own case, or rather they abet injustice to a greater extent than the State requires. If they pay the tax from a mistaken interest in the individual taxed, to save his property, or prevent his going to jail, it is because they have not considered wisely how far they let their private feelings interfere with the public good.

This, then, is my position at present. But one cannot be too much on his guard in such a case, lest his action be biased by obstinacy or an undue regard for the opinions of men. Let him see that he does only what belongs to himself and to the hour.

I think sometimes, Why, this people mean well, they are only ignorant; they would do better if they knew how: why give your neighbors this pain to treat you as they are not inclined to? But I think again, This is no reason why I should do as they do, or permit others to suffer much greater pain of a different kind. Again, I sometimes say to myself, When many millions of men, without heat, without ill will, without personal feeling of any kind, demand of you a few shillings only, without the possibility, such is their constitution, of retracting or altering their present demand, and without the possibility, on your side, of appeal to any other millions, why expose yourself to this over-whelming brute force? You do not resist cold and hunger, the winds and the waves, thus obstinately; you quietly submit to a thousand similar necessities. You do not put your head into the fire. But just in proportion as I regard this as not wholly a brute force, but partly a human force, and consider that I have relations to those millions as to so many millions of men, and not of mere brute or inanimate things, I see that appeal is possible, first and instantaneously, from them to the Maker of them, and, secondly, from them to themselves. But if I put my head deliberately into the fire, there is no appeal to fire or to the Maker of fire, and I have only myself to blame. If I could convince myself that I have any right to be satisfied with men as they are, and to treat them accordingly, and not according, in some respects, to my requisitions and expectations of what they and I ought to be, then, like a good Mussulman and fatalists, I should endeavor to be satisfied with things as they are, and say it is the will of God. And, above all, there is this difference between resisting this and a purely brute or natural force, that I can resist this with some effect; but I cannot expect, like Orpheus, to change the nature of the rocks and trees and beasts.

I do not wish to quarrel with any man or nation. I do not wish to split hairs, to make fine distinctions, or set myself up as better than my neighbors. I seek rather, I may say, even an excuse for conforming to the laws of the land. I am but too ready to conform to them. Indeed, I have reason to suspect myself on this head; and each year, as the taxgatherer comes round, I find myself disposed to review the acts and position of the general and State governments, and the spirit of the people, to discover a pretext for conformity.

> We must affect our country as our parents,
> And if at any time we alienate
> Our love or industry from doing it honor,
> We must respect effects and teach the soul
> Matter of conscience and religion,
> And not desire of rule or benefit.

I believe that the State will soon be able to take all my work of this sort out of my hands, and then I shall be no better a patriot than my fellow countrymen. Seen from a lower point of view, the Constitution, with all its faults, is very good; the law and the courts are very re-spectable; even this State and this American government are, in many respects, very admirable and rare things, to be thankful for, such as a great many have described them; but seen from a point of view a little higher, they are what I have described them; seen from higher still, and the highest, who shall say what they are, or that they are worth looking at or thinking of at all?

However, the government does not concern me much, and I shall bestow the fewest possible thoughts on it. It is not many moments that I live under a government, even in this world. If a man is thought-free, fancy-free, imagination-free, that which *is not* never for a long time appearing *to be* to him, unwise rulers or reformers cannot fatally interrupt him.

I know that most men think differently from myself; but those whose lives are by profession devoted to the study of these or kindred subjects content me as little as any. Statesmen and legislators, standing so completely within the institution, never distinctly and nakedly behold it. They speak of moving society, but have no resting place without it. They may be men of a certain experience and discrimination, and have no doubt invented ingenious and even useful systems, for which we sincerely thank them; but all their wit and usefulness lie within certain not very wide limits. They are wont to forget that the world is not governed by policy and expediency. Webster never goes behind government, and so cannot speak with authority about it. His words are wisdom to those legislators who contemplate no essential reform in the existing government; but for thinkers, and those who legislate for all time, he never once glances at the subject. I know of those whose serene and wise speculations on this theme would soon reveal the limits of his mind's range and hospitality. Yet, compared with the cheap professions of most reformers, and the still cheaper wisdom and eloquence of politicians in general, his are almost the only sensible and valuable words, and we thank Heaven for him. Comparatively, he is always strong, original, and, above all, practical. Still, his quality is not wisdom, but prudence. The lawyer's truth is not Truth, but consistency or a consistent expediency. Truth is always in harmony with herself, and is not concerned chiefly to reveal the justice that may consist with wrongdoing. He well deserves to be called, as he has been called, the Defender of the Constitution. There are really no blows to be given by him but defensive ones. He is not a leader, but a follower. His leaders are the men of '87. "I have never made an effort," he says, "and never propose to make an effort; I have never countenanced an effort, and never mean to countenance an effort, to disturb the arrangement as originally made, by which the various States came into the Union." Still thinking of the sanction which the Constitution gives to slavery, he says, "Because it was a part of the original compact—let it stand." Notwithstanding his special acuteness and ability, he is unable to take a fact out of its merely political relations, and behold it as it lies absolutely to be disposed of by the intellect—what, for instance, it behooves a man to do here in America today with regard to slavery—but ventures, or is driven, to make some such desperate answer as the following, while professing to speak absolutely, and as a private man—from which what new and singular code of social duties might be inferred? "The manner," says he, "in which the governments of those States where slavery exists are to regulate it is for their own consideration, under their responsibility to their constituents, to the general laws of propriety, humanity, and justice, and to God. Associations formed elsewhere, springing from a feeling of humanity, or any other cause, have nothing whatever to do with it. They have never received any encouragement from me, and they never will."

They who know of no purer sources of truth, who have traced up its stream no higher, stand, and wisely stand, by the Bible and the Constitution, and drink at it there with reverence and humility; but they who behold where it comes trickling into this lake or that pool, gird up their loins once more, and continue their pilgrimage toward its fountainhead.

No man with a genius for legislation has appeared in America. They are rare in the history of the world. There are orators, politicians, and eloquent men, by the thousand; but the speaker has not yet opened his mouth to speak who is capable of settling the much-vexed questions of the day. We love eloquence for its own sake, and not for any truth which it may utter, or any heroism it may inspire. Our legislators have not yet learned the comparative value of free trade and of freedom, of union, and of rectitude, to a nation. They have no genius or talent for comparatively humble questions of taxation and finance, commerce and manufactures and agriculture. If we were left solely to the wordy wit of legislators in Congress for our guidance, uncorrected by the reasonable experience and the effectual complaints of the people, America would not long retain her rank among the nations. For eighteen hundred years, though perchance I have no right to say it, the New Testament has been written; yet where is the legislator who has wisdom and practical talent enough to avail himself of the light which it sheds on the science of legislation?

The authority of government, even such as I am willing to submit to—for I will cheerfully obey those who know and can do better than I, and in many things even those who neither know nor can do so well—is still an impure one: to be strictly just, it must have the sanction and consent of the governed. It can have no pure right over my person and property but what I concede to it. The progress from an absolute to a limited monarchy, from a limited monarchy to a democracy, is a progress toward a true respect for the individual. Even the Chinese philosopher was wise enough to regard the individual as the basis of the empire. Is a democracy, such as we know it, the last improvement possible in government? Is it not possible to take a step further toward recognizing and organizing the rights of man? There will never be a really free and enlightened State until the State comes to recognize the individual as a higher and independent power, from which all its own power and authority are derived, and treats him accordingly. I please myself with imagining a State at last which can afford to be just to all men, and to treat the individual with respect as a neighbor; which even would not think it inconsistent with its own repose if a few were to live aloof from it, not meddling with it, nor embraced by it, who fulfilled all the duties of neighbors and fellow men. A State which bore this kind of fruit, and suffered it to drop off as fast as it ripened, would prepare the way for a still more perfect and glorious State, which also I have imagined, but not yet anywhere seen.

BIBLIOGRAPHY

THOREAU, Henry David, *The Writings of Henry David Thoreau*. Boston: Houghton Mifflin, 1906, 20 vols.

———— *The Correspondence of Henry David Thoreau*, ed. by Carl Bode and Walter Harding. New York: N.Y.U. Press, 1959.

———— *The Heart of Thoreau's Journals*, ed. by Odell Shepard. Boston: Houghton Mifflin, 1927.

———— *Consciousness in Concord*, ed. by Perry Miller. Boston: Houghton Mifflin, 1958.

CANBY, Henry S., *Thoreau*. Boston: Houghton Mifflin, 1939.

CRAWFORD, Bartholow V., *Henry David Thoreau: Representative Selections, with Introduction, Bibliography, and Notes*. New York: American Book Co., 1934.

KRUTCH, Joseph Wood, *Henry David Thoreau*. New York: W. Sloane Assoc., 1948.

KWIAT, Joseph L., "Thoreau's Philosophical Apprenticeship." *New England Quarterly*, Vol. XVII (1945), pp. 51–69.

MACKAYE, James, ed., *Thoreau: Philosopher of Freedom; Writings on Liberty*. New York: Vanguard Press, 1930.

MADISON, Charles A., "Henry David Thoreau: Transcendental Individualist." *Ethics*, Vol. LIV (1943–44), pp. 110–23.

PAUL, Sherman, *The Shores of America: Thoreau's Inward Exploration*. Urbana: U. of Illinois Press, 1958.

SANBORN, Franklin B., *Henry D. Thoreau*. Boston: Houghton Mifflin, 1889.

PART FIVE

Speculative and Absolute Idealism
(1860-1900)

William Torrey Harris

[1835–1909]

Harris was the founder and editor of America's first philosophical journal, *The Journal of Speculative Philosophy* (1867–93). This journal allowed many different writers to express their views and contributed much to the development of philosophy as a distinct field of scholarship. Harris's own ideas were largely speculative and idealistic and were influenced by New England transcendentalism and Hegel. Indeed, through the efforts of Harris and others, the works of Hegel and other German idealists were translated into English and began to exert some influence in America, especially in the Middle West. In no small sense Harris was responsible for the prominence of idealism in America in the late nineteenth century, and for the fact that it became the "official" philosophy of many professors of philosophy, the most important of whom was to be Josiah Royce.

Harris was not an original thinker, but rather, a devoted advocate of classical philosophical idealism—its method and metaphysics. The arti-

cle, *The Concrete and the Abstract* (1871), reprinted below, is a brief statement of the differences between speculative and positivistic philosophy and a defense of the former.

Harris was born in the East, but he moved to St. Louis, where he became a teacher and subsequently superintendent of public schools. Here Harris was instrumental in helping to form—along with some recently arrived German intellectuals, especially Henry C. Brokmeyer (1828–1906)—the St. Louis Philosophical Society, which was devoted to the study of philosophical idealism. Harris also helped to organize, along with Bronson Alcott in New England, the famous Concord School of Philosophy and Literature (1879). Harris was later appointed to the post of Commissioner of Education for the United States (1889–1906). This provided him with a platform from which to disseminate his pedagogical philosophy. For nearly forty years he addressed himself to teachers' groups, with both pen and voice.

THE CONCRETE AND THE ABSTRACT [1]

It is a prevalent error to confound the speculative with the abstract, and to suppose that the concrete is a realm which philosophy does not reach.

[1] *The Journal of Speculative Philosophy*, Vol. V (1871), pp. 1–5.

The abstract in its usual signification includes whatever is the product of analysis. Separation, isolation, has been at work, and what is cut off from the living reality is "abstract."

Metaphysics is supposed to deal with abstractions—ideal essences or phases that have been sundered from concrete wholes by analytic reflection.

Taking one step further in the same direction, one may say that the total or the whole is concrete, and that the partial or incomplete is abstract. Anyone who represents to himself a partial phase of something as a true conception of it, deals only with abstractions, and deserves to be called "visionary." So, on the contrary, one who deals with things as wholes or takes them exhaustively, has a concrete mind, and is, in a proper sense of the term, "speculative."

For it must be noted that the speculative philosopher claims synthetic thought as his province. His object is to return from the abstract to the concrete. His instrument and method is the dialetic. All partial and incomplete somewhats exhibit in their defects their presuppositions. In order to be just what they seem to be, other existences are involved, and when we trace out these implications we find that things exist only through the agency of a system or organism. This ascent from what is directly given, or immediate to the whole of which it is a part or phase, is the dialectic movement, and is the occupation of speculative philosophy. It is twofold.

ABSTRACTIONS OF SENSE

It has to deal with the abstractions of the senses. The senses cannot attain of themselves to concrete wholes. Mere properties and qualities, mere effects and results, the external realm of manifestation—if we concede that these are sensuous, yet they are not united by the senses. The isolated multiplicity is not the concrete and true. Those who are immersed in sensuous consciousness, and who reflect least, are the people to regard as existing separately and independently things which are known by reflecting people to be dependent on relations. They are prone to ignore the realm of law or "essential relation," and to give wide validity to chance in their world-scheme. Their conceptions of the world and of the real things in it are very crude, very partial, and incomplete; and we may well call them *abstract*, for they leave out essential elements, and cling to one or more phases which they have accidentally seized.

ABSTRACTIONS OF REFLECTION

The first activity of thought awakens in the mind of the individual as the perception of relations; at first mere external, accidental relations, not affecting the nature of the objects he perceives; afterward, essential relations.

Sensuous objects that before seemed to be independent and complete in themselves, now are found to be composite, and to relate on all hands to outlying spheres of being. The gravity of the stone is its assertion of dependence upon all the rest of the universe. Blot out of existence the smallest piece of matter on the farthest star, and the weight of this stone would be at once changed.

Analytic reflection occupies itself with noting and recording these relations. It forms a world of abstractions for itself—abstract ideas. These abstract ideas are truer than the sensuous ideas which they supplant—truer in that they underlie those sensuous ideas as their logical conditions. The physicist who deals with such abstractions as *matter, force,* and *law,* is a deeper and truer thinker than the one who only knows that this fossil was found in that layer of rocks, or that the explosion of the powder heated the gun, etc. "Law" states the essential relation, and hence is universal and abides, while the particular instance of the senses begins and ceases. That things exist in relation—otherwise stated—means: things are partial phases of a systematic organic totality. To seize things in this totality should be the highest object of thought, and it is this which science attempts.

The Speculative

The abstract ideas of reflection when examined and sifted, or when placed in the crucible of the dialectic, exhibit their lack of universality, and hence their dependence upon more concrete or synthetic ideas. To find an idea which is sufficient for itself is the problem of speculative philosophy. Spinoza has very happily stated this problem at the commencement of his *Ethics.* His "substance" as that which is "self-comprised and conceived by and through itself alone" is this adequate or concrete idea which speculative thought must reach as its goal.

Philosophy versus Poetry

One who knows Plato, Aristotle, or Spinoza, in their deepest thoughts, does not need to be told that philosophy is not engaged "merely with the anatomy of thought." The formal logic, perhaps, might justly be accused of this; not so speculative philosophy.

Poetry or art in general seeks to clothe the living idea of the whole in sensuous shapes of one sort or another: a divine function—dealing with "the splendor of the Eternal Verities." As compared with the mere analytic thinker, the poet may claim great precedence. His task is a creative one, while the abstract or metaphysical thinker is manipulating dead results, the *caput mortuum* of analysis and reflection. But certainly in this respect the poet has no prestige over the speculative thinker. Both have the same task so far as creative activity is concerned. The philosopher elevates to concreteness the abstractions of reflection, while the poet performs the same functions for the abstractions of sense. The common mind sees the world as isolated prose realities, bereft of spiritual truth and wholeness; the poet comes and presents his kaleidoscope, wherein everything is seen in its threefold relation with the totality. Beauty is the result. Reflection sees the world as abstract relations, isolated spectral nonentities—all the juice of sensuous life squeezed out, and none of the transparency of spiritual life attained; the philosopher's stone (which is the dialectic) transmutes these into gold; makes these dead abstractions living processes of arrival at the Truth. Thus the poet and the philosopher seek to replace the part by the whole, the imperfect by the perfect. And the extraordinary tribute which Goethe pays to Spinoza, Dante to Aristotle, and Emerson to Plato, is a recognition of this identity of function, though on different planes. The abstractions of sense are transcended and elevated into eternal verities in the poet's version; the abstractions of reflection are transcended and complemented by speculative insight, and thus become archetypal, demiurgic, "creative with the whole."

Speculative versus "Positive" Philosophy

If one examines the materialistic philosophies of the day, he will find them fast gathering into one flock around the banner of "positivism." This stage of thought is best characterized as a confusion of perception and inference—a mingling of immediateness and mediation. The French materialism of the eighteenth century confounds the abstractions "matter and force" with sensuous reality. Our Comtians, the positivists of today, mix up the vague idea of Law with immediate concrete things. They do not see that the logical outcome of their doctrine is an abstract idealism. (1) They set up Law as the absolute; (2) but Law is a mere abstract form that abides under the change of phenomena; (3) the phenomena begin and cease, and there is nothing of them but this beginning and ceasing—nothing that stops or stays even for a moment, except the form of this abstract law. (4) Hence, Law acts negatively on all that exists in the world, reducing each and every thing to something else and destroying its identity. (5) The real world accordingly cannot be the world of the senses, for that which destroys the world of the senses is more real than it. Law is, therefore, more real than the world spread out before the senses. (6) But Law is a generalization, an abstraction, hence an ideality (no one would contend that it is a physical thing); and hence the ground for calling the positivist an abstract idealist.

Positivism as abstract idealism is repugnant to all sound thinking. Its naïve, half-conscious asseverations of utter devotion to "positive science" are amusing when compared with immediately subsequent utterances, in which it sets up some half a dozen abstract categories of reflection, and proceeds to measure out the world on these as indisputable concrete truths. The atomic theory—a remote inference of reflection—is handled as though identical in directness with the perception of qualitative differences. Its supreme doctrine of Humanity swallows up the individual—his immortality and freedom—at one gulp.

The depth of a system of thought has an infallible test in the manner it disposes of institutions. When one man, or set of men, get up on the housetops and proclaim a new doctrine for all mankind, Civilization answers back: "What do you make of my creations—the institutions of realized intelligence—the family, society, the state, and religion?" If the answer comes again, "Try my experiment of doing away with all these, or of substituting contrivances of individualism for them," no heed is given to the pseudo-prophetic voice. For the forms of civilization—the laws and usages which constitute the warp and woof of its institutions—are not the vain thought of abstract theorists, but the grim necessity in which the human will has made possible the exercise of its freedom. For necessity and freedom are harmonized in institutions alone, and without institutions man is a savage and nothing more. The form of freedom is to the child and uncultured adult a constraining necessity; to the partly cultured man it becomes an ethical or moral law; to the clearest insight and highest culture it becomes spontaneous, independent choice and volition, what Spinoza and the mystics call Love.

BIBLIOGRAPHY

HARRIS, William Torrey, *Hegel's Logic: A Book on the Genesis of the Categories of the Mind: A Critical Exposition.* Chicago: S. C. Griggs and Co., 1890.

———— *Introduction to the Study of Philosophy.* Comprising Passages from his Writings, Selected and Arranged with Commentary and Illustrations by Marietta Kies. New York: D. Appleton and Co., 1899.

———— *The Spiritual Sense of Dante's "Divina Commedia,"* rev. ed., Boston: Houghton Mifflin, 1896; first ed. 1889.

———— "The Philosophy of Bronson Alcott and the Transcendentalists," in Sanborn, F. B., and Harris, William T., *A. Bronson Alcott: His Life and Philosophy.* Boston: Roberts Brothers, 1893, pp. 544–664.

_____ *Psychologic Foundations of Education: An Attempt to Show the Genesis of the Higher Faculties of the Mind.* New York: D. Appleton & Co., 1898.

CURTI, Merle, *The Social Ideas of American Educators.* New York: Charles Scribner's Sons, 1935. Chap. 9, "William T. Harris, The Conservator."

HARMON, Francis B., *The Social Philosophy of the St. Louis Hegelians.* New York: Columbia U. Press, 1943.

LEIDECKER, Kurt F., *Yankee Teacher: The Life of William Torrey Harris.* New York: Philosophical Library, 1946.

PERRY, Charles M., ed., *The St. Louis Movement in Philosophy: Some Source Material.* Norman: U. of Oklahoma Press, 1930. Contains a list of 479 writings of Harris, chronologically arranged, with subject index.

POCHMANN, Henry A., *New England Transcendentalism and St. Louis Hegelianism.* Philadelphia: Carl Schurz Memorial Foundation, 1948.

SCHAUB, Edward L., ed., *William Torrey Harris, 1835–1935.* Chicago: Open Court Pub. Co., 1936.

The Journal of Speculative Philosophy. Vols. I–XXII, 1867 to 1893.

Laurens Perseus Hickok

[1798–1888]

Hickok is a relatively unknown figure in the main stream of American thought; he left few, if any, disciples. Yet Morris R. Cohen claims that "For sheer intellectual power . . . and for comprehensive grasp of technical philosophy, Hickok is easily the foremost figure in American philosophy between the time of Jonathan Edwards and the period of the Civil War."[1] Herbert W. Schneider says, "Hickok expounded by far the most elaborate, extravagant, and ambitious system of philosophy ever conceived by an American philosopher."[2] Whether Hickok's philosophical attainments were due to superior philosophical power or to the fact that there were still few competitors in technical philosophy at that time is an issue which we do not here seek to resolve. At any rate, in his books we find a dedication to reason which Schneider believes is at times quite "unreasonable." Hickok deftly attempted to unite Revelation (Scriptural and Calvinistic), Virtue (the common moral sense of mankind), and Science (rationalism) under the aegis of Absolute Reason. Every cause in the universe, he believed, must have an ultimate reason for its being, and this reason he traced back to God. Hickok's philosophy is one of the purest examples that we have of a priori speculative system-building—one, indeed, that out-Hegels Hegel. From a few basic principles Hickok virtually deduces the universe, including the basic laws of physics and biology.

Born in Bethel, Connecticut, Hickok was graduated from Union College in 1820. After graduation, Hickok entered the Presbyterian ministry and became professor of theology, first at Western Reserve College, then at Auburn Theological Seminary. Called back to Union College by President Eliphalet Nott as his prospective successor, Hickok became Vice-President and Professor of Mental and Moral Philosophy, then President for two short and inglorious years (1866–68).[3] The last two decades of his life were spent in retirement at Amherst.

Hickok was a frequent contributor to *The Journal of Speculative Philosophy*, and shared most of its aims and conceptions. His transcendental metaphysics was influenced by German idealism, though unlike Emersonian transcendentalism, it was opposed to romanticism and mysticism. Hickok's early works, *Rational Psychology* (1849) and *A System of Moral Science* (1853), were Kantian in tone, the first in its use of the transcendental and a priori method

---

[1] *Cambridge History of American Literature*, Vol. 3, p. 229.

[2] *Union Worthies*, No. 29, Schenectady, 1947, p. 11.

[3] See the account by Harold A. Larrabee, *Ibid.*, No. 2, p. 9.

in analyzing the presuppositions of experience, and the second in relating the moral life to practical reason. In *Rational Cosmology* (1858), Hickok argued that there was need to construct a comprehensive and rational cosmological system of the universe. *The Logic of Reason* (1875), Hickok's last work, a portion of which is reprinted below, traces the role of reason in all of its senses, and culminates in a defense of the "Absolute."

THE LOGIC OF REASON, UNIVERSAL AND ETERNAL [4]

. . . What is commonly meant by "The Absolute," when taken as an abstraction from human experience, is the conception of pure being from whence all attributes have been taken. The abstraction has been carried to an edge so thin and a point so fine that nothing can be predicated of it, and such negation of all positive possession is the ultimate which abstract logic can find and retain as its Author of the universe. No thinking can get any judgment from it, nor find any meaning in it. But the Absolute, when taken as Eternal Reason, is a concrete of infinite possession, having in itself all that is essential to the overt production and manifested existence of the universe, with all its mechanical, instinctive, sensitive, and responsible agencies. There is not merely negative absolution from universal coercion, but positive resources for free origination, sustentation, and consummation of the universe essentially within itself. Not by any abstraction expanded to so broad a generalization can we attain any satisfactory conception of an Author of the universe, nor any intelligent comprehension of the universe itself in its connections and dependencies. We must apply the same insight of reason to the Source, by the method of a concrete and integrant logic, that has brought us to the knowledge of the being of universal nature in its forces and vitalities. Not by any abstract "searching can we find out God," but by the reason-insight we can, "from the creation of the world, clearly see the eternal power and Godhead." Embodied reason can never enter within the conscious experience of the Deity, but in the knowledge of itself the human spirit can know more than merely what is not, even positively what is, the essence of the Divine Spirit.

Human reason, though allied to sentient life, yet knows itself in distinction from all sensation. Force is a new existence as static contest of original energies, and life is new existence as original urgency possessing and using force, and sensation is new existence as irritable nerve center, bringing outer impression and inner affection to conscious

[4] Boston, Lee and Shepard, 1875, pp. 179–92.

feeling; but human reason is an impartation from its uncreated source of that in man, which ever was and ever is in unchanged likeness to its original. It is ever reason, both in its source and in its imparted individualization; and what only is new is individual sentient life endowed with and possessed by imparted rationality, in which sentient individuality is made personal, and rational personality is made individual. There is no individualizing out of the uncreated source of reason but by some incorporation of rationality in individualized sentiency. Whether human or conceived angelic existence is in question, neither can be known as individual personal existence out from its unmanifested source, except as imparted reason to some substantial corporeity. This makes the man and the angel to be in, and portions of, the universe, while the unembodied Reason is Absolute Spirit, independent of the universe. Both the measure of the reason and the manner of substantial force embodied may differ in human or in supposed angelic beings, but rationality, in some mode of individualized substantial embodying, is conditional for knowing any personal spirit as within the universe, and a component portion of it. The unembodied "Father of Spirits" is above the universe, and independent Creator and upholder of it. The sentient portion of the human being is the animal soul, the rational portion of humanity is the personal spirit, and what in the mere animal is brute sentiency only, standing in the nervous organism, and lost in its dissolution, becomes in the human person immortal soul in the right and claim of the responsible spirit; and as joint participants in probationary disposition, soul and spirit must stand together in unity in the retributive future experience of every individual personality.

Taking, thus, the distinctive human reason as coming in its measure to man from the uncreated and unembodied Absolute Source, and whose urgencies to activity are the imperative claims of either beauty, truth, or goodness—i. e., either taste in art, science in philosophy, or righteousness in morals and piety—we may put its insight directly to itself to come to the knowledge of what is the essence, and what the attributes of its Absolute Source.

A number of steps, consequential one upon another, taken with careful precision, will lead to as many particulars, which human reason may see must necessarily be in the Absolute Source of all being.

Finite reason already is, and knows both itself and its dependence on a higher source for its individuality of existence. What is not subject to reason is against it, and therefore reason cannot come from unreason; and thus above the finite must be the Absolute Reason, which must stand independent in its own essence. Absolute Reason is *self-essential*.

This Absolute Reason, purely as reason, must know all that itself is, and all that its knowledge urges its activity to accomplish, and must thus be thoroughly self-conscious. Absolute Reason is essentially *self-intelligent*.

This conscious urgency to activity must be competent to accomplish its ends and fulfil its own behests, or the inward disagreement between known claims and conscious performance must make the unsatisfied reason to become unreason. Absolute Reason is *self-sufficient*.

The urgencies to activity in reason are ever imperative, and never appetitive as in sense; and in Absolute Reason the imperatives are behests springing out of conscious intrinsic worth and excellency, and can come from no extrinsic authority, and thus the Absolute is ever self-law; and as efficient to execute all its urgencies, Absolute Reason is also self-determining; and in this is the dignity of independent self-hood. The self only makes claims, and what the self demands the self alone accomplishes. The Absolute is ever in full *self-possession*.

This perpetual self-possession secures a persistent disposition to the end of its own honor, and in which is the continual satisfying of the claims of conscious intrinsic worth by a voluntarily attained worth; and such persistent disposing is will in liberty, and also will in constant integrity. The Absolute Reason is *free-agency in full self-approbation*.

Free Intelligence can act executively only in the subjective possession of clear ideas, and for the proposing to himself such ideas the Absolute must have working within him the three following associated activities, viz., that of holding the manifold elements as promiscuous content for all ideas; the sorting from the manifold the particulars necessary for the specific idea; and the combination of these sorted elements in the self-consistency of the individual idea; and without such threefold agency, no complete idea can be made to stand in any reason-consciousness. The activities must be readily distinguishable, though they are in perfect concert. Neither the apprehensions of the manifold, nor the sorting of the needed particulars can be sufficient, and full knowing can be secured only as the arranged particulars are made indissoluble in the grasp of the reason, in which is accomplished literally the individuality of the manifold elements. In proposing practical ideas to himself, the Absolute Reason is essentially *threefold activity in concert*.

Human reason is shut within its own organism, and can use for expressing its inner ideas to others only the already made forces in which itself is embodied. But Absolute Reason is unembodied, and must himself make the forces that shall manifest his hidden idea. The clear practical idea ever urges reason to its expressed communication, and whether in the aspect of beauty, truth, or goodness, the concerted ideal plans of the Absolute will lovingly press to their execution, in which will necessarily be involved a literal creation. The thought-out plan must also become wrought-out substance, and the secret idea must "stand fast" in open fact, in order to which the activities thinking in concert must supplement the thought-result by a solid environment which shall impress the sense. Absolute Reason will pass from ideal constructions to *substantial force-creation.*

To manifest the full idea in substantial force requires an authoritative control by a persistent proposing of the ideal plan, an answering expression of each particular element in substantial appropriate force, and a combination of the joint particulars in thought and substance into a consistent individuality. No created thing can be either intelligently expressed or intelligently apprehended except in a complete fulfillment of these requisitions, and the holding of the idea in authoritative control is necessarily the part of a distinct voluntary agency, while also the energizing in the particular force-expressing is necessarily the part of another voluntary agency, and the putting the substantial particular forces into a consistent whole is the necessary part of still another voluntary agency, all being distinct while all are active together. Each must also do its work in consciousness for itself, and also in consciousness of what is done by the others, and therefore each must have a self-appropriation of, and a joint communion in, the one consciousness of the One Absolute Reason. The three agencies are in this way three personalities in will, while they are joint-participants in the one being and consciousness of the absolute. One creative Reason has controlled in a paternal will, and also expressed substantially in a filial obedient will, and also fashioned in consistency substance and idea in a spiritual will, the last executing the processes of both the former. The Absolute Creator is *one Being in three-fold personality.*

Some portions of creation will be subsidiary to others, but an ultimate end must have been proposed comprehensive of all subordinate ones, and this can be found only in the Creator himself, since he alone was ere that which was to come from him was yet unmanifested within him. As Absolute Reason he knows himself and his own intrinsic excellency and worth of being, and so is conscious of what is due to himself, and consequently this claim to act for his own honor and dignity must be his ultimate and most comprehensive urgency. This identical object of attainment can be foreknown only to himself and to others but just as the executive work progresses, yet without any speculative particularity through what thing it is to be gained, it is sufficient here to say, in the gross, that God created, and thus gave outer expression to his inner idea, that he might please himself. He has no appetites to gratify, and hence the pleasing was purely spiritual, and fulfilled in his own approbation of his work. He looked and saw all was good. For this the most orthodox statement is the best —*"He created all things for his own glory."*

What Absolute Reason has created, he must overrule for the attainment of his final end. Mechanical force as material substance, and vital power as instinctive or sensitive being, are but physical products, and cannot be satisfactory as ultimate ends in reason. To permit activity to terminate here, would be the absurdity that reason should be unreasonable, and so the physical can be but as instrumentally subservient to the spiritual. Both matter and vegetable and animal life are means only for ministration to reason. Their end is in man, and man as rational personality finds his end in communion with the Absolute personality. Hence the necessary grades in divine government. Force can only push and pull in mechanical necessity. Vegetable life can only act from instinctive want. Sentient life acts from appetitive gratification, and has necessary determination to the end of highest happiness. The Maker, thus, must govern matter by force, and mere life by instinct, and animal life by sense; but man is spiritual, and God's government of him must be by appeals to that which is reasonable. Reason can check and control sense by holding to imperatives rather than appetites, and all moral government is in this, that it holds the subject to the duty of spiritual approbation before all sense-gratification. It is more to be personally worthy than to be sentiently happy, and God approves that man the best who honors himself the most; for the greatest dishonor man can do to God is in debasing and dishonoring his own spirit in his sight. All inorganic matter and organic life is *nature*, and God governs it by its own *necessitated connections;* and all rational existence is *supernatural*, which God governs by *moral and religious interests in reason itself.*

Nature works with no alternatives, whether in its mechanical forces, instinctive wants, or sentient appetites. If an intended ultimate end is to be consummated by nature, it must be set at first in preestablished harmony to such end, and have no subsequent interferences, since of itself nature can do no other than run through its necessitated successions to its necessitated point of ultimate balanced rest. But nature has the supernatural rational spirit working in it in human personality, and initiating its own interfering changes; and the intended ultimate end, then, cannot be consummated except by superhuman interpositions guiding the human activity in accordance with the ultimate intent, or correcting any untoward changes humanly introduced in nature. Such superhuman interference with human will in itself, or in its introduced changes in nature, is miracle, and in a universe where rational individuals act there must be supernatural and superhuman interventions. Miracles are not merely rational expectancies, but necessary incidentals to free human agency and divine ultimate results. Besides all this, there are the occasions for superhuman interpositions in nature in attestation of the presence and pleasure of the absolute sovereignty. If a revelation is to be made in anything beyond nature's teaching, nothing but a supernatural interference can adequately attest the supernatural communication. As providential and moral Governor of the universe, the Absolute Reason will take his own occasions to make *absolute miraculous interventions.*

Miraculous interpositions in the ongoing of nature must be wholly within the determination and control of the Absolute Reason, and as persistently reason-restrained as reason-prompted. The ultimate end is to be reached not only in guiding nature, but in consistency with, and even by, the direct procurance of human reason in human liberty. No miraculous interventions can contravene the true prerogatives of reason, either in finite individualities or in the Absolute. The Absolute Reason urges to overt manifestation, and which must reach intelligences that can apprehend the communication. To give individuality to such intelligence, reason must take possession of specific substantial forces, and hold them in unity, and hold such individuality also in connection with, and yet in personal distinction from, the other universal forces. Such individuality necessitates the finite personality to be in some way sense *and* spirit, and so necessarily tries and tests the spiritual disposing. Opportunity to dignify himself and honor God, necessarily gives possibility to the finite individual to reproach God in debasing himself. The virtue of the human individual cannot, from the nature of the case, be acquired and retained but at the hazard of a vicious inclination and sinful disposing. The Absolute Reason requires the opportunity for the virtue even at the hazard of the vice, and having put the individual in the fairest position for his probation, it behooves him, for his reason's sake, to let the individual decide the issue on his own responsibility. The virtue itself that could not endure hardness and contradictory influence would be of little excellency. God does what Absolute Reason may for virtue and against sin, but on no account can physical interposition miraculously confirm in virtue and exclude vice, and so when sin enters, God is, in his own sight and openly before the intelligent universe, in full self-integrity, and competent fairly to judge the demerit of the sinner, and subject to reasonable retribution both the righteous and the wicked. He may reasonably do no more and nothing other than he has in the making and proving the individual persons, and the sin the individual commits is by God's *reasonable permission.*

Sin stains and defiles the finite personality only, never the Absolute Reason. The individual sinning has no reason for his wickedness, but all reason has been against it. The sin is in the renouncing of reason and espousing sense. Appetite has been the occasion, gratification of appetite the motive, but in this there has been no reason, and only sin from the exclusion of reason. If the gratification had been truly for a reason, it would not have been vicious but virtuous. To ask a reason for sin is folly and absurdity, since to find a reason is to take away all sinfulness from any action; and to plead the urgency of appetite which was its occasion, or the intensity of gratification which was its motive, as any extenuation or excuse, is but to pronounce the sinner's self-condemnation, for the essence of guilt is in this very thing, that the act was from appetite not reason, and the motive gratification not approbation.

And all the sinfulness of the act is at the expense of the sinning person, while the personality of Absolute Reason in all connection with the guilty transaction has neither done anything nor omitted anything to which reason did not prompt and which it does not fully approve. It is neither to his self-reproach, nor to any reproach in the sight of the universe toward God, that any sin, or that so much sin, has been introduced; and though grieved and angry, yet is God's grief and anger on account of sin only to just the measure and of just the kind that is perfectly reasonable. All sin, notwithstanding, the Absolute Reason has his own justification, and the approval of reason in every individual who knows his action toward it. It is reason only, and not sense, that can approve or disapprove, respect or abhor, congratulate or commiserate, in anything. Joy and sadness are from the reason and in the spirit, and not from sense and in the flesh in any matter, and in no case is the reason-susceptibility of the Absolute ever unreasonably excited. Sadness in its place is as reasonable in God as is gladness in its place, and the self-sufficiency and persistent integrity of the Absolute exclude the possibility of any unreasonable disturbance. Absolute Reason is conscious of *perpetual and eternal tranquillity and serenity.*

We have then, at last, Absolute Reason in its Absolute fullness. It has not come from aught above itself, and does not pass on to aught beyond itself, and is ever self-sufficient to execute its own purposes. Its energies produce and perpetuate the universal forces, and put the proper forces in the possession and use of their respective life-activities. It raises sense to consciousness in the brute-organism, and gives manly dignity to the human body by the inspiration of a rational spirit. It peoples the worlds in its wisdom, and holds them all in one space and one time by their universal connections. It originates its ideal plans in the accordant counsel of its threefold agencies, and these agencies, with wills distinct in personality permanently abiding in the one being and consciousness of reason, give overt expression to the ideal plan in steadfast universal substance. It is itself above the universe it creates and upholds, and guides its movements in consummation of an original design, and to the intent of a final purpose.

Within the universe are individual personalities, who have yielded to sentient appetites against the conscious imperatives of reason, and have thus become sinful by consenting to become unreasonable; but the dishonor to reason by the creature has carried no impeachment of integrity or derogation of dignity over to the Absolute Creator. Individual reason in some cases within the universe has become debased by its prostitution to appetitive indulgence, but above the universe is no unreason, and only Reason in absolute wholeness and fullness, and holding all finite personalities to such eternal retributions as both satisfy the claim and magnify the honor of all reason, finite and absolute. Reason is here fully known to be *absolutely universal and eternal.*

In such process of excluded doubt, with universal existence known as under the control of one Absolute Being, concrete logic has found both its triumph and its termination.

BIBLIOGRAPHY

HICKOK, Laurens Perseus, *Theology as a Science*. Inaugural Address, Auburn Theological Seminary, Auburn, 1845.

———— *Rational Psychology; or, The Subjective Idea and the Objective Law of All Intelligence*. Auburn, 1849; rev. ed., New York, 1870.

———— *A System of Moral Science*. Schenectady, 1853; rev. ed., Boston, 1880.

———— *Empirical Psychology; or, The Human Mind as Given in Consciousness*. Schenectady, 1854; rev. ed., Boston, 1882.

———— *Rational Cosmology; or, The Eternal Principles and the Necessary Laws of the Universe*. New York, 1858.

———— *Creator and Creation; or, The Knowledge in the Reason of God and His Work*. New York, 1872.

———— *Humanity Immortal; or, Man Tried, Fallen and Redeemed*. Boston, 1872.

———— *The Logic of Reason, Universal and Eternal*. Boston, 1875.

BASCOM, John, "Laurens Perseus Hickok." *American Journal of Psychology*, Vol. XIX, pp. 359–73.

BATES, E. S., "Laurens Perseus Hickok," in the *Dictionary of American Biography*, Vol. IX, pp. 5–6.

"Dr. Hickok's Philosophy." *Bibliotheca Sacra*, Vol. XVI (1859), pp. 253–78 (an unsigned article).

SCHNEIDER, H. W., *A History of American Philosophy*. New York: Columbia U. Press, 1946. Chap. 35.

Union Worthies, No. 2. Schenectady, N.Y.: Union College, 1947.

Josiah Royce

[1855–1916]

Josiah Royce is usually considered to be the greatest defender of Absolute Idealism in America. He lived and wrote at Harvard during the first part of the golden age of American philosophy, and he was deeply affected by his contemporaries and affected them. Thus while Kant, the romantics, Schopenhauer, and Hegel all had an impact on Royce's philosophy, so did Peirce and James. Indeed, Peirce's advice to Royce: "Royce, you ought to study logic, you need it so much," led Royce, relatively late in his career, to a study of mathematical logic and to the incorporation of many of Peirce's ideas in his general position. Similarly, James was Royce's closest friend at Harvard—though the two were locked in continual intellectual battle. And it was no doubt James' voluntarism and pragmatism that led Royce to assert that meaning was related to internal purposes and that he, Royce, was an "absolute pragmatist."

In his own day Royce inspired a whole generation of students and disciples. Royce's stand was probably the last great stand of idealism in America. As has frequently been the case in the past, a philosophical movement may come to be summed up only when it is about to die or has already done so. This was true, for example, of the systems of both Aristotle and Aquinas. In any case,

the newer winds of doctrine that began to blow strong—pragmatism, realism, and naturalism—proved to be too much for Royce's brand of idealism; and for many philosophers Royce became the straw man to attack. In spite of this, Royce's valiant defense of idealism, his dialectical power, historical scholarship and erudition, literary eloquence, and moral righteousness have made lasting impressions on American thought.

Royce was born of pioneering stock in a mining camp in the High Sierras of California, and was educated by his mother. He went on, in 1871, to the University of California and was one of its first graduates. He so impressed a group of wealthy Californians that he was given a grant to study for a year in Germany. Later he took his Ph.D. at Johns Hopkins (1878). Unable to locate a job in philosophy, he began his career by teaching rhetoric and logic at the University of California; but he was soon invited to replace James for a year at Harvard (1882–83) while the latter was abroad. And the following year George Herbert Palmer took a year off, allowing Royce to continue at Harvard. His impact at Harvard was so great that he remained there until his death.

Royce's first book in philosophy, *The Religious Aspect of Philosophy* (1885), outlined his basic position. Royce was interested in religious questions, but he thought little of blind or sectarian faith, and he labeled himself "a born nonconformist." Is there any real thing in the universe, he asks, of "infinite worth?" And he replies that an individual's life, his ends and purposes, are purely partial and fragmentary, unless they are related to an inclusive and higher purpose. This Absolute Purpose is a standard of value, in terms of which all our partial moral ideals, indeed the problem of evil, find ultimate resolution. Is there an "infinite reality?" Royce asks. Yes, he replies, the very possibility of error necessitated the existence of an all-inclusive standard of thought, an "Absolute Thought" or "Absolute Truth," and all reality must be present to this Unity of Infinite Thought.

Why must all reality be a Unity of Infinite Thought? His argument is simple: the world must be either through and through of the same character as mind, or else completely unknowable; but to affirm the unknowable x is to suggest that it has an intelligible structure, and that it is therefore like mind. Thus the self has meaning only in relation to a "Larger Self."

What is an idea? asks Royce, and how is it related to reality? In terms of both its "internal" purpose (interest, desire, or volition) and its "external" reference (to an object), he answers, and both are related to the Absolute. Royce was a pragmatist and voluntarist in the sense that truth was related to human needs and purposes. But he was an absolutist in the sense that needs were universal and that there was a timeless or eternal basis to truth.

Royce elaborated these themes throughout the rest of his writings— in *The Spirit of Modern Philosophy*

(1892), *The Conception of God* (1892), *The World and the Individual* (Royce's Gifford Lectures, 1900–01), *The Sources of Religious Insight* (1912), *The Problem of Christianity* (1913), and *Lectures on Modern Idealism* (1919). Royce continually maintained that experience would be limited unless it were interpreted by reference to an all-encompassing Absolute Experience. The lecture on *Reality and Idealism*, taken from *The Spirit of Modern Philosophy* and reprinted below, sets forth Royce's fundamental philosophic position. It illustrates Royce's pursuit of philosophy in its classic sense, his devotion to reason, and his attempt to suggest a synoptic vision of the universe. For Royce, idealism provided such a comprehensive explanation. Matter was only appearance and mind was the ultimate reality. But reality was not to be identified with subjective solipsism. Absolute Mind was the true reality, and this was greater than individual mind, comprising the total structure of the universe.

Royce later used the idea of infinity, derived from his study of mathematics, to argue anew for the Infinite Mind—logic was related by Royce to the concept of order. Royce also claimed, with Peirce, that interpretation was triadic in relationship, but he used this again to proceed to a community of interpretation. In *The Philosophy of Loyalty* (1908), a portion of which is reprinted below, Royce considered loyalty to a cause, whatever the cause, as a moral virtue, since it took an individual beyond his own narrow aims. Is there one cause, he asks, that unites the diversity of causes? Yes, he replies, the greater cause which provides a basis for a larger community is the cause of *loyalty to loyalty* itself. In his later writings, the idea of community becomes increasingly important; and Royce at the end of his life observed in retrospect that his deepest motives and problems centered about this "idea of community."

REALITY AND IDEALISM [1]

. . . Idealism has two aspects. It is, for the first, a kind of analysis of the world, an analysis which so far has no absolute character about it, but which undertakes, in a fashion that might be acceptable to any skeptic, to examine what you mean by all the things, whatever they are, that you believe in or experience. This idealistic analysis consists merely in a pointing out, by various devices, that the world of your knowledge, whatever it contains, is through and through such stuff as ideas are made of, that you never in your life believed in anything definable *but* ideas, that, as Berkeley put it, "this whole choir of heaven and furniture of earth" is nothing for any of us but a system of ideas which govern our belief and conduct. Such idealism has numerous statements, interpretations, embodiments: forms part of the most various systems and experiences, is consistent with Berkeley's theism, with Fichte's ethical absolutism, with Professor Huxley's agnostic empiricism, with Clifford's mind-stuff theory, with countless other theories that have used such idealism as a part of their scheme. In this aspect idealism is already a little puzzling to our natural consciousness, but it becomes quickly familiar, in fact almost commonplace, and seems after all to alter our practical faith or to solve our deeper problems very little.

The other aspect of idealism is the one which gives us our notion of the absolute Self. To it the first is only preparatory. This second aspect is the one which from Kant, until the present time, has formed the deeper problem of thought. Whenever the world has become more conscious of its significance, the work of human philosophy will be, not nearly ended (Heaven forbid an end!), but for the first time fairly begun. For then, in critically estimating our passions, we shall have some truer sense of whose passions they are.

I begin with the first and the less significant aspect of idealism. Our world, I say, whatever it may contain, is such stuff as ideas are made of. This preparatory sort of idealism is the one that, as I just suggested,

[1] From Josiah Royce, *The Spirit of Modern Philosophy.* New York: Houghton Mifflin Co., 1892, Chap. 11, "Reality and Idealism, The Inner World and Its Meaning," pp. 341–80.

Berkeley made prominent, and, after a fashion, familiar. I must state it in my own way, although one in vain seeks to attain novelty in illustrating so frequently described a view.

Here, then, is our so real world of the senses, full of light and warmth and sound. If anything could be solid and external, surely, one at first will say it is this world. Hard facts, not mere ideas, meet us on every hand. Ideas anyone can mold as he wishes. Not so facts. In idea, socialists can dream out Utopias, disappointed lovers can imagine themselves successful, beggars can ride horses, wanderers can enjoy the fireside at home. In the realm of facts, society organizes itself as it must, rejected lovers stand for the time defeated, beggars are alone with their wishes, oceans roll drearily between home and the wanderer. Yet this world of fact is, after all, not entirely stubborn, not merely hard. The strenuous will can mold facts. We can form our world, in part, according to our ideas. Statesmen influence the social order, lovers woo afresh, wanderers find the way home. But thus to alter the world we must work, and just because the laborer is worthy of his hire, it is well that the real world should thus have such fixity of things as enables us to anticipate what facts will prove lasting, and to see of the travail of our souls when it is once done. This, then, is the presupposition of life, that we work in a real world, where house-walls do not melt away as in dreams, but stand firm against the winds of many winters, and can be felt as real. We do not wish to find facts wholly plastic; we want them to be stubborn, if only the stubbornness be not altogether unmerciful. Our will makes constantly a sort of agreement with the world, whereby, if the world will continually show some respect to the will, the will shall consent to be strenuous in its industry. Interfere with the reality of my world, and you therefore take the very life and heart out of my will.

The reality of the world, however, when thus defined in terms of its stubbornness, its firmness as against the will that has not conformed to its laws, its kindly rigidity in preserving for us the fruits of our labors—such reality, I say, is still something wholly unanalyzed. In what does this stubbornness consist? Surely, many different sorts of reality, as it would seem, may be stubborn. Matter is stubborn when it stands in hard walls against us, or rises in vast mountain ranges before the pathfinding explorer. But minds can be stubborn also. The lonely wanderer, who watches by the seashore the waves that roll between him and his home, talks of cruel facts, material barriers that, just because they *are* material, and not ideal, shall be the irresistible foes of his longing heart. "In wish," he says, "I am with my dear ones, but alas, wishes cannot cross oceans! Oceans are material facts, in the cold outer world. Would that the world of the heart were all!" But alas! to the rejected lover the world of the heart *is* all, and that is just his woe. Were the barrier between him and his beloved only made of those stubborn material facts, only of walls or of oceans, how lightly might his will erelong transcend them all! Matter stubborn! Outer nature cruelly the foe of ideas! Nay, it is just an idea that now opposes him—just an idea, and that, too, in the mind of the maiden he loves. But in vain does he call this stubborn bit of disdain a merely ideal fact. No flint was ever more definite in preserving its identity and its edge than this disdain may be. Place me for a moment, then, in an external world that shall consist wholly of ideas—the ideas, namely, of other people about me, a world of maidens who shall scorn me, of old friends who shall have learned to hate me, of angels who shall condemn me, of God who shall judge me. In what piercing north winds, amidst what fields of ice, in the labyrinths of what tangled forests, in the depths of what thick-walled dungeons, on the edges of what tremendous precipices, should I be more genuinely in the presence of stubborn and unyielding facts than in that conceived world of ideas! So, as one sees, I by no means deprive my world of stubborn reality, if I merely call it a world of ideas. On the contrary, as every teacher knows, the ideas of the people are often the most difficult of facts to influence. We were wrong, then, when we said that while matter was stubborn, ideas could be molded at pleasure. Ideas are often the most implacable of facts. Even my own ideas, the facts of my own inner life, may cruelly decline to be plastic to my wish. The wicked will that refuses to be destroyed—what rock has often more consistency for our senses than this will has for our inner consciousness! The king, in his soliloquy in *Hamlet*—in what an unyielding world of hard facts does he not move! and yet they are now only inner facts. The fault is past; he is alone with his conscience:

> What rests?
> Try what repentance can. What can it not?
> Yet what can it, when one cannot repent?
> O wretched state! O bosom black as death!
> O limèd soul, that, struggling to be free,
> Art more engaged!

No, here are barriers worse than any material chains. The world of ideas has its own horrible dungeons and chasms. Let those who have refuted Bishop Berkeley's idealism by the wonder why he did not walk over every precipice or into every fire if these things existed only in his idea, let such, I say, first try some of the fires and the precipices of the inner life, before they decide that dangers cease to be dangers as soon as they are called ideal, or even subjectively ideal in me.

Many sorts of reality, then, may be existent at the heart of any world of facts. But this bright and beautiful sense-world of ours—

what, amongst these many possible sorts of reality, does that embody? Are the stars and the oceans, the walls and the pictures, real as the maiden's heart is real, embodying the ideas of somebody, but none the less stubbornly real for that? Or can we make something else of their reality? For, of course, that the stars and the oceans, the walls and the pictures have *some* sort of stubborn reality, just as the minds of our fellows have, our analysis so far does not for an instant think of denying. Our present question is, what sort of reality? Consider, then, in detail, certain aspects of the reality that seems to be exemplified in our sense-world. The sublimity of the sky, the life and majesty of the ocean, the interest of a picture—to what sort of real facts do these belong? Evidently here we shall have no question. So far as the sense-world is beautiful, is majestic, is sublime, this beauty and dignity exist only for the appreciative observer. If they exist beyond him, they exist only for some other mind, or as the thought and embodied purpose of some universal soul of nature. A man who sees the same world, but who has no eye for the fairness of it, will find all the visible facts, but will catch nothing of their value. At once, then, the sublimity and beauty of the world are thus truths that one who pretends to insight ought to see, and they are truths which have no meaning except for such a beholder's mind, or except as embodying the thought of the mind of the world. So here, at least, is so much of the outer world that is ideal, just as the coin or the jewel or the bank note or the bond has its value not alone in its physical presence, but in the idea that it symbolizes to a beholder's mind, or to the relatively universal thought of the commercial world. But let us look a little deeper. Surely, if the objects yonder are unideal and outer, odors and tastes and temperatures do not exist in these objects in just the way in which they exist in us. Part of the being of these properties, at least, if not all of it, is ideal and exists for us, or at best is once more the embodiment of the thought or purpose of some world-mind. About tastes you cannot dispute, because they are not only ideal but personal. For the benumbed tongue and palate of diseased bodily conditions, all things are tasteless. As for temperatures, a well-known experiment will show how the same water may seem cold to one hand and warm to the other. But even so, colors and sounds are at least in part ideal. Their causes may have some other sort of reality; but colors themselves are not in the things, since they change with the light that falls on the things, vanish in the dark (while the things remained unchanged), and differ for different eyes. And as for sounds, both the pitch and the quality of tones depend for us upon certain interesting peculiarities of our hearing organs, and exist in nature only as voiceless sound waves trembling through the air. All such sense qualities, then, are ideal. The world yonder may—yes, must—have attributes that give reasons why these qualities are thus felt by us; for so we assume. The world yonder may even be a mind that thus expresses its will to us. But these qualities need not, nay, cannot resemble the ideas that are produced in us, unless, indeed, that is because these qualities have placed as ideas in some world-mind. Sound waves in the air are not like our musical sensations; nor is the symphony as we hear it and feel it any physical property of the strings and the wind instruments; nor are the ether vibrations that the sun sends us like our ideas when we see the sun; nor yet is the flashing of moonlight on the water as we watch the waves a direct expression of the actual truths of fluid motion as the water embodies them.

Unless, then, the real physical world yonder is itself the embodiment of some world-spirit's ideas, which he conveys to us, unless it is real only as the maiden's heart is real, namely, as itself a conscious thought, then we have so far but one result: that real world (to repeat one of the commonplaces of modern popular science) is in itself, apart from somebody's eyes and tongue and ears and touch, neither colored nor tasteful, neither cool nor warm, neither light nor dark, neither musical nor silent. All these qualities belong to our ideas, being indeed none the less genuine facts for that, but being in so far ideal facts. We must see colors when we look, we must hear music when there is playing in our presence; but this *must* is a must that consists in a certain irresistible presence of an idea in us under certain conditions. That this idea must come is, indeed, a truth as unalterable, once more, as the king's settled remorse in Hamlet. But like this remorse, again, it exists as an ideal truth, objective, but through and through objective *for* somebody, and not *apart from* anybody. What this truth implies we have yet to see. So far it is only an ideal truth for the beholder, with just the bare possibility that behind it all there is the thought of a world-spirit. And, in fact, *so* far we must all go together if we reflect.

But now, at this point, the Berkeleyan idealist goes one step further. The real outside world that is still left unexplained and unanalyzed after its beauty, its warmth, its odors, its tastes, its colors, and its tones have been relegated to the realm of ideal truths, what do you now *mean* by calling it real? No doubt it *is* known as somehow real, but *what* is this reality *known as* being? If you know that this world is still there and outer, as by hypothesis you know, you are bound to say *what* this outer character implies for your thought. And here you have trouble. Is the outer world, as it exists outside of your ideas, or of anybody's ideas, something having shape, filling space, possessing solidity, full of moving things? That would in the first place seem evident. The sound is not outside of me, but the sound waves, you say, are. The colors are ideal facts; but the ether waves do not need a mind to know them. Warmth is ideal, but the physical fact called heat, this playing to and fro of molecules, is real, and is there apart from any mind. But once more, *is* this so evident? What do I *mean* by the shape of anything, or by the size of anything? Do I not mean just the idea of shape or of size that I am obliged to get under certain circumstances? What is the meaning of any property that I give to the real outer world? How can I express that property except in case I think it in terms of my ideas? As for the sound waves and the ether waves, what are they but things ideally conceived to explain the facts of nature? The conceptions have doubtless their truth, but it is an ideal truth. What I mean by saying that the things yonder have shape and size and trembling molecules, and that there is air with sound waves, and ether with light waves in it—what I *mean* by all this is that experience forces upon me, directly or indirectly, a vast system of ideas, which may indeed be founded in truth beyond me, which in fact *must* be founded in such truth if my experience has any sense, but which, like my ideas of color and of warmth, are simply expressions of how the world's order must appear to me, and to anybody constituted like me. Above all, is this plain about space. The real things, I say, outside of me, fill space, and move about in it. But what do I mean by space? Only a vast system of ideas which experience and my own mind force upon me. Doubtless these ideas have a validity. They have *this* validity, that I, at all events, when I look upon the world, am bound to see it in space, as much bound as the king in Hamlet was, when he looked within, to see himself as guilty and unrepentant. But just as his guilt was an idea—a crushing, an irresistible, an overwhelming idea, but still just an idea—so, too, the space in which I place my world is one great formal idea of mine. That is just why I can describe it to other people. "It has three dimensions," I say, "length, breadth, depth." I describe each. I form, I convey, I construct an idea of it through them. I know space, as an idea, very well. I can compute all sorts of unseen truths about the relations of its parts. I am sure that you, too, share this idea. But, then, for all of us alike it is just an idea; and when we put our world into space, and call it real there, we simply think one idea into another idea, not voluntarily, to be sure, but inevitably, and yet without leaving the realm of ideas.

Thus, all the reality that *we* attribute to our world, in so far as *we* know and can tell what we mean thereby, becomes ideal. There is, in fact, a certain system of ideas, forced upon us by experience, which we have to use as the guide of our conduct. This system of ideas we cannot change by our wish; it is for us as overwhelming a fact as guilt, or as the bearing of our fellows toward us, but we know it only *as* such a system of ideas. And we call it the world of matter. John Stuart Mill very well expressed the puzzle of the whole thing, as we have now reached the statement of this puzzle, when he called matter a mass of "permanent possibilities of experience" for each of us. Mill's definition has its faults, but is a very fair beginning. You know matter as something that either now gives you this idea or experience, or that would give you some other idea or experience under other circumstances. A fire, while it burns, is for you a permanent possibility of either getting the idea of an agreeable warmth, or of getting the idea of a bad burn, and you treat it accordingly. A precipice amongst mountains is a permanent possibility of your experiencing a fall, or of your getting a feeling of the exciting or of the sublime in mountain scenery. You have no experience just now of the tropics or of the poles, but both tropical and polar climates exist in your world as permanent possibilities of experience. When you call the sun 92,000,000 miles away, you mean that between you and the sun (that is, between your present experience and the possible experience of the sun's surface) there would inevitably lie the actually inaccessible, but still numerically conceivable series of experiences of distance expressed by the number of miles in question. In short, your whole attitude toward the real world may be summed up by saying: "I have experiences now which I seem bound to have, experiences of color, sound, and all the rest of my present ideas; and I am also bound by experience to believe that in case I did certain things (for instance, touched the wall, traveled to the tropics, visited Europe, studied physics), I then should get, in a determinate order, dependent wholly upon *what* I have done, certain other experiences (for instance, experiences of the wall's solidity, or of a tropical climate, or of the scenes of a European tour, or of the facts of physics)." And this acceptance of actual experience, this belief in possible experience, constitutes all that you mean by your faith in the outer world.

But, you say, Is not, then, all this faith of ours after all well-founded? Is not there really something yonder that corresponds in fact to this series of experiences in us? Yes, indeed, there no doubt is. But what if this, which so shall correspond without us to the ideas within us, what if this hard and fast reality should itself be a system of ideas, outside of our minds but not outside of every mind? As the maiden's disdain is outside the rejected lover's mind, unchangeable so far for him, but not on that account the less ideal, not the less a fact in a mind, as, to take afresh a former fashion of illustration, the price of a security or the objective existence of this lecture is an ideal fact, but real and external for the individual person—even so why might not this world beyond us, this "permanent possibility of experience," be in essence itself a system of ideal experiences of some standard thought of which ours is only the copy? Nay, must it not be such a system in case it has any reality at all? For, after all, is not this precisely what our analysis brings us to? Nothing whatever can I say about my world yonder that I do not express in terms of mind. *What* things are, extended, moving, colored, tuneful, majestic, beautiful, holy, *what* they are in any aspect of their nature, mathematical, logical, physical, sensuously pleasing, spiritually valuable, all this must mean for me only something that I have to express in the fashion of ideas. The more I am to know my world, the more of a mind I must have for the purpose. The closer I come to the truth about the things, the more ideas I get. Is not it plain, then, that *if* my world yonder is anything knowable at all, it must be in and for itself essentially a mental world? Are my ideas to *resemble* in any way the world? Is the truth of my thought to consist in its *agreement* with reality? And am I thus capable, as common sense supposes, of *conforming* my ideas to things? Then reflect. What can, after all, so well agree with an idea as another idea? To what can things that go on in my mind conform unless it be to another mind? If the more my mind grows in mental clearness, the nearer it gets to the nature of reality, then surely the reality that my mind thus resembles must be in itself mental.

After all, then, would it deprive the world here about me of reality, nay, would it not rather save and assure the reality and the knowableness of my world of experience, if I said that this world, as it exists outside of my mind, and of any other human minds, exists in and for a standard, an universal mind, whose system of ideas simply constitutes the world? Even if I fail to prove that there is such a mind, do I not at least thus make plausible that, as I said, our world of common sense has no fact in it which we cannot interpret in terms of ideas, so that this world is throughout such stuff as ideas are made of? To say this, as you see, in no wise deprives our world of its due share of reality. If the standard mind knows now that its ideal fire has the quality of burning those who touch it, and if I in my finitude am bound to conform in my experiences to the thoughts of this standard mind, then in case I touch that fire I shall surely get the idea of a burn. The standard mind will be at least as hard and fast and real in its ideal consistency as is the maiden in her disdain for the rejected lover; and I, in presence of the ideal stars and the oceans, will see the genuine realities of fate as certainly as the lover hears his fate in the voice that expresses her will.

I need not now proceed further with an analysis that will be more or less familiar to many of you, especially after our foregoing historical lectures. What I have desired thus far is merely to give each of you, as it were, the sensation of being an idealist in this first and purely analytical sense of the word idealism. The sum and substance of it all is, you see, this: you know your world in fact as a system of ideas about things, such that from moment to moment you find this system forced upon you by experience. Even matter you know just as a mass of coherent ideas that you cannot help having. Space and time, as you think them, are surely ideas of yours. Now, what more natural than to say that *if* this be so, the real world beyond you must in itself be a system of somebody's ideas? If it is, then you can comprehend what its existence means. If it isn't, then since all you can know of it is ideal, the real world must be utterly unknowable, a bare *x*. Minds I can understand, because I myself am a mind. An existence that has no mental attribute is wholly opaque to me. So far, however, from such a world of ideas, existent beyond me in another mind, seeming to coherent thought essentially *un*real, ideas and minds and their ways, are, on the contrary, the hardest and stubbornest facts that we can name. *If* the external world is in itself mental, then, be this reality a standard and universal thought, or a mass of little atomic minds constituting the various particles of matter, in any case one can comprehend what it is, and will have at the same time to submit to its stubborn authority as the lover accepts the reality of the maiden's moods. If the world *isn't* such an ideal thing, then indeed all our science, which is through and through concerned with our mental interpretations of things, can neither have objective validity, nor make satisfactory progress toward truth. For as science is concerned with ideas, the world beyond all ideas is a bare *x*.

But with this bare *x*, you will say, this analytical idealism after all leaves me, as with something that, in spite of all my analyses and interpretations, may after all be there beyond me as the real world, which my ideas are vainly striving to reach, but which eternally flees before me. So far, you will say, what idealism teaches is that the real world can only be interpreted by treating it as if it were somebody's thought. So regarded, the idealism of Berkeley and of other such thinkers is very suggestive; yet it does not tell us what the true world is, but only that *so much* of the true world as we ever get into our comprehension has to be conceived in ideal terms. Perhaps, however, while neither beauty, nor majesty, nor odor, nor warmth, nor tone, nor color, nor form, nor motion, nor space, nor time (all these being but ideas of ours), can be said to belong to the extra-mental world— perhaps, after all, there does exist there yonder an extra-mental world, which has nothing to do, except by accident, with *any* mind, and which is through and through just extra-mental, something unknowable, inscrutable, the basis of experience, the source of ideas, but itself never experienced as it is in itself, never adequately represented by any idea in us. Perhaps it is there. Yes, you will say, *must* it not be there? Must not one accept our limitations once for all, and say, "What reality is, we can never hope to make clear to ourselves. That which has been made clear becomes an idea in us. But always there is the beyond, the mystery, the inscrutable, the real, the *x*. To be sure, perhaps we cannot even know so much as that this x after all does exist. But then we feel bound to regard it as existent; or even if we doubt or deny it, may it not be there all the same?" In such doubt and darkness, then, this first form of idealism closes. If that were all there were to say, I should indeed have led you a long road in vain. Analyzing what the known world is for you, in case there is haply any world known to you at all—this surely is not proving that there is any real world, or that the real world can be known. Are we not just where we started?

No; there lies now just ahead of us the goal of a synthetic idealistic conception, which will not be content with this mere analysis of the colors and forms of things, and with the mere discovery that all these are for us nothing but ideas. In this second aspect, idealism grows bolder, and fears not the profoundest doubt that may have entered your mind as to whether there is any world at all, or as to whether it is in any fashion knowable. State in full the deepest problem, the hardest question about the world that your thought ever conceived. In this new form idealism offers you a suggestion that indeed will not wholly answer nor do away with every such problem, but that certainly will set the meaning of it in a new light. What this new light is, I must in conclusion seek to illustrate.

Note the point we have reached. *Either,* as you see, your real world yonder is through and through a world of ideas, an outer mind that you are more or less comprehending through your experience; *or else,* in so far as it is real and outer it is unknowable, an inscrutable x, an absolute mystery. The dilemma is perfect. There is no third alternative. Either a mind yonder, or else the unknowable; that is your choice. Philosophy loves such dilemmas, wherein all the mightiest interests of the spirit, all the deepest longings of human passion, are at stake, waiting as for the fall of a die. Philosophy loves such situations, I say, and loves, too, to keep its scrutiny as cool in the midst of them as if it were watching a game of chess, instead of the great world-game. Well, try the darker choice that the dilemma gives you. The world yonder shall be an x, an unknowable something, outer, problematic, foreign, opaque. And you—you shall look upon it and believe in it. Yes, you shall for argument's sake first put on an air of resigned confidence, and say, "I do not only fancy it to be an extra-mental and unknowable something there, an impenetrable x, but I know it to be such. I cannot help it. I did not make it unknowable. I regret the fact, but there it is. I have to admit its existence. But I know that I shall never solve the problem of its nature." Ah, its nature is a *problem,* then. But what do you mean by this *"problem"*? Problems are, after a fashion, rather familiar things—that is, in the world of ideas. There are problems soluble and problems insoluble in that world of ideas. It is a soluble problem if one asks what whole number is the square root of 64. The answer is 8. It is an insoluble problem if one asks me to find what whole number is the square root of 65. There is, namely, no such whole number. If one asks me to name the length of a straight line that shall be equal to the circumference of a circle of a known radius, that again, in the world of ideas, is an insoluble problem, because, as can be proved, the circumference of a circle is a length that cannot possibly be exactly expressed in terms of any statable number when the radius is of a stated length. So in the world of ideas, problems are definite questions which can be asked in knowable terms. Fair questions of this sort either may be fairly answered in our present state of knowledge, or else they could be answered if we knew a little or a good deal more, or, finally, they could not possibly be answered. But in the latter case, if they could not possibly be answered, they always must resemble the problem how to square the circle. They then always turn out, namely, to be absurdly stated questions, and it is their absurdity that makes these problems absolutely insoluble. Any fair question could be answered by one who knew enough. No fair question has an unknowable answer. But now, *if* your unknowable world out there is a thing of wholly, of absolutely problematic and inscrutable nature, is it so because you do not *yet* know enough about it, or because in its very nature and essence it is an absurd thing, an *x* that *would* answer a question, which actually it is nonsense to ask? Surely one must choose the former alternative. The real world may be unknown; it cannot be essentially unknowable.

This subtlety is wearisome enough, I know, just here, but I shall not dwell long upon it. Plainly *if* the unknowable world out there is through and through in its nature a really inscrutable problem, this must mean that in nature it resembles such problems as, What is the whole number that is the square root of 65? Or, what two adjacent hills are there that have no valley between them? For in the world of thought such are the *only* insoluble problems. All others either may now be solved, or would be solved if we knew more than we now do. But, once more, *if* this unknowable is only just the real world as now unknown to us, but capable some time of becoming known, then remember that, as we have just seen, only a mind can ever become an object known to a mind. If I know you as external to me, it is only because you are minds. If I can come to know *any* truth, it is only in so far as this truth is essentially mental, is an idea, is a thought, that I can ever come to know it. Hence, if that so-called unknowable, that unknown outer world there, ever could, by any device, come within our ken, then it is already an ideal world. For just that is what our whole idealistic analysis has been proving. Only ideas are knowable. And nothing absolutely unknowable can exist. For the absolutely unknowable, the *x* pure and simple, the Kantian thing in itself, simply cannot be admitted. The notion of it is nonsense. The assertion of it is a contradiction. Round-squares, and sugar-salt-lumps, and Snarks, and Boojums, and Jabberwocks, and abracadabras; such, I insist, are the only unknowables there are. The unknown, that which our human and finite selfhood has not grasped, exists spread out before us in a boundless world of truth; but the unknowable is essentially, confessedly, *ipso facto* a fiction.

The nerve of our whole argument in the foregoing is now pretty fairly exposed. We have seen that the outer truth must be, if anything, a "possibility of experience." But we may now see that a *bare* "possibility" as such, is, like the unknowable, something meaningless. That which, whenever I come to know it, turns out to be through and through an idea, an experience, must be in itself, before I know it, either somebody's idea, somebody's experience, or it must be nothing. What is a "possibility" of experience that is outside of me, and that is still nothing *for* anyone else than myself? Is it not a bare x, a nonsense phrase? Is it not like an unseen color, an untasted taste, an unfelt feeling? In proving that the world is one of "possible" experience, we have proved that in so far as it is real it is one of actual experience.

Once more, then, to sum up here, *if*, however vast the world of the unknown, only the essentially knowable can exist, and *if* everything knowable is an idea, a mental somewhat, the content of some mind, then once for all we are the world of ideas. Your deepest doubt proves this. Only the nonsense of that inscrutable x, of that abracadabra, of that Snark, the unknowable of whose essence you make your real world, prevents you from seeing this.

To return, however, to our dilemma. *Either* idealism, we said, *or* the unknowable. What we have now said is that the absolutely unknowable is essentially an absurdity, a nonexistent. For any fair and statable problem admits of an answer. *If* the world exists yonder, its essence is then already capable of being known by some mind. If capable of being known by a mind, this essence is then already essentially ideal and mental. A mind that knew the real world would, for instance, find it a something possessing qualities. But qualities are ideal existences, just as much as are the particular qualities called odors or tones or colors. A mind knowing the real world would again find in it relations, such as equality and inequality, attraction and repulsion, likeness and unlikeness. But such relations have no meaning except as objects of a mind. In brief, then, the world as known would be found to be a world that had all the while been ideal and mental, even before it became known to the particular mind that we are to conceive as coming into connection with it. Thus, then, we are driven to the second alternative. The real world must be a mind, or else a group of minds.

But with this result we come in presence of a final problem. All this, you say, depends upon my assurance that there is after all a real and therefore an essentially knowable and rational world yonder. Such a world would have to be in essence a mind, or a world of minds. But after all, how does one ever escape from the prison of the inner life? Am I not in all this merely wandering amidst the realm of my own ideas? *My* world, of course, is not and cannot be a mere *x*, an essentially unknowable thing, just because it *is my* world, and I have an idea of it. But then does not this mean that *my* world is, after all, forever just *my* world, so that I never get to any truth beyond myself? Is not this result very disheartening? My world is thus a world of ideas, but alas! how do I then ever reach those ideas of the minds beyond me?

The answer is a simple, but in one sense a very problematic one. You, in one sense, namely, never *do* or can get beyond your own ideas, nor ought you to wish to do so, because in truth all those other minds that constitute your outer and real world are in essence one with your own self. This whole world of ideas is essentially *one* world, and so it is essentially the world of one self and *That art Thou.*

The truth and meaning of this deepest proposition of all idealism is now not at all remote from us. The considerations, however, upon which it depends are of the dryest possible sort, as commonplace as they are deep.

Whatever objects you may think about, whether they are objects directly known to you, or objects infinitely far removed, objects in the distant stars, or objects remote in time, or objects near and present—such objects, then, as a number with fifty places of digits in it, or the mountains on the other side of the moon, or the day of your death, or the character of Cromwell, or the law of gravitation, or a name that you are just now trying to think of and have forgotten, or the meaning of some mood or feeling or idea now in your mind—all such objects, I insist, stand in a certain constant and curious relation to your mind whenever you are thinking about them, a relation that we often miss because it is so familiar. What is this relation? Such an object, while you think about it, need not be, as popular thought often supposes it to be, the *cause* of your thoughts concerning it. Thus, when you think about Cromwell's character, Cromwell's character is not just now *causing* any ideas in you—is not, so to speak, doing anything to you. Cromwell is dead, and after life's fitful fever his character is a very inactive thing. Not as the *cause,* but as the *object* of your thought is Cromwell present to you. Even so, if you choose now to think of the moment of your death, that moment is somewhere off there in the future, and you can make it your object, but it is not now an active cause of your ideas. The moment of your death has no present physical existence at all, and just now causes nothing. So, too, with the mountains on the other side of the moon. When you make them the object of your thought, they remain indifferent to you. They do not affect you. You never saw them. But all the same you can think about them.

Yet this thinking *about* things is, after all, a very curious relation in which to stand to things. In order to think *about* a thing, it is *not* enough that I should have an idea in me that merely resembles that thing. This last is a very important observation. I repeat, it is *not* enough that I should merely have an idea in me that resembles the thing whereof I think. I have, for instance, in me the idea of a pain. Another man has a pain just like mine. Say we both have toothache; or have both burned our fingertips in the same way. Now, my idea of pain is just like the pain in him, but I am not on that account necessarily thinking about *his* pain, merely because what I am thinking about, namely my own pain, resembles his pain. No; to think about an object you must not merely have an idea that resembles the object, but you must *mean* to have your idea resemble that object. Stated in other form, to think of an object you must consciously aim at that object, you must pick out that object, you must already in some measure possess that object enough, namely, to identify it as what you mean. But how can you *mean*, how can you *aim at*, how can you *possess*, how can you *pick out*, how can you *identify* what is not already present in essence to your own hidden self? Here is surely a deep question. When you aim at yonder object, be it the mountains on the moon or the day of your death, you really say, "I, as my real self, as my larger self, as my complete consciousness, already in deepest truth possess that object, have it, own it, identify it. And that, and that alone, makes it possible for me in my transient, my individual, my momentary personality, to mean yonder object, to inquire about it, to be partly aware of it and partly ignorant of it." You can not mean what is utterly foreign to you. You mean an object, you assert about it, you talk about it, yes, you doubt or wonder about it, you admit your private and individual ignorance about it, only in so far as your larger self, your deeper personality, your total of normal consciousness already *has* that object. Your momentary and private wonder, ignorance, inquiry, or assertion, about the object, implies, asserts, presupposes, that your total self is in full and immediate possession of the object. This, in fact, is the very nature of that curious relation of a thought to an object which we are now considering. The self that is doubting or asserting, or that is even feeling its private ignorance about an object, and that still, even in consequence of all this, is *meaning*, is *aiming at* such object, is in essence identical with the self for which this object exists in its complete and consciously known truth.

So paradoxical seems this final assertion of idealism that I cannot hope in one moment to make it very plain to you. It is a difficult topic, about which I have elsewhere printed a very lengthy research,[2] where-with I cannot here trouble you. But what I intend by thus saying that the self which thinks about an object, which really, even in the midst of the blindest ignorance and doubt concerning its object still means the object—that this self is identical with the deeper self which possesses and truly knows the object—what I intend hereby I can best illustrate by simple cases taken from your own experience. You are in doubt, say, about a name that you have forgotten, or about a thought that you just had, but that has now escaped you. As you hunt for the name or the lost idea, you are all the while sure that you mean just one particular name or idea and no other. But you do not yet know what name or idea this is. You try, and reject name after name. You query, "Was this what I was thinking of, or this?" But after searching, you before long find the name or the idea, and now at once you *recognize* it. "Oh, that," you say, "was what I meant all along, only—I didn't know what I meant." Did you know? Yes, in one sense you knew all the while—that is, your deeper self, your true consciousness knew. It was your momentary self that did not know. But when you found the long-sought name, recalled the lost idea, you recognized it at once, because it was all the while your own, because you, the true and larger self, who owned the name or the idea and were aware of what it was, now were seen to include the smaller and momentary self that sought the name or tried to recall the thought. Your deeper consciousness of the lost idea was all the while there. In fact, did you not presuppose this when you sought the lost idea? How can I mean a name, or an idea, unless I in truth am the self who knows the name, who possesses the idea? In hunting for the name or the lost idea, I am hunting for my own thought. Well, just so I know nothing about the far-off stars in detail, but in so far as I mean the far-off stars at all, as I speak of them, I am identical with that remote and deep thought of my own that already knows the stars. When I study the stars, I am trying to find out what I really mean by them. To be sure, only experience can tell me, but that is because only experience can bring me into relation with my larger self. The escape from the prison of the inner self is simply the fact that the inner self is through and through an appeal to a larger self. The self that inquires, either inquires without meaning, or if it has a meaning, this meaning exists in and for the larger self that knows.

Here is a suggestion of what I mean by Synthetic Idealism. No truth, I repeat, is more familiar. That I am always meaning to inquire into objects beyond me, what clearer fact could be mentioned? That only in case it is already I who, in deeper truth, in my real and hidden

---

[2] See *The Religious Aspect of Philosophy*, Boston, 1885, Chap 11, "The Possibility of Error," pp. 384–435.

thought, *know* the lost object yonder, the object whose nature I seek to comprehend, that only in this case I can truly *mean* the thing yonder—this, as we must assert, is involved in the very idea of *meaning*. That is the logical analysis of it. You can mean what your deeper self knows; you cannot mean what your deeper self does not know. To be sure, the complete illustration of this most critical insight of idealism belongs elsewhere. Few see the familiar. Nothing is more common than for people to think that they mean objects that have nothing to do with themselves. Kant it was, who, despite his things in themselves, first showed us that nobody really means an object, really knows it, or doubts it, or aims at it, unless he does so by aiming at a truth that is present to his own larger self. Except for the unity of my true self, taught Kant, I have no objects. And so it makes no difference whether I know a thing or am in doubt about it. So long as I really *mean* it, that is enough. The self that *means* the object is identical with the larger self that possesses the object, just as when you seek the lost idea you are already in essence with the self that possesses the lost idea.

In this way I suggest to you the proof which a rigid analysis of the logic of our most commonplace thought would give for the doctrine that in the world there is but *one* Self, and that it is *his* world which we all alike are truly meaning, whether we talk of one another or of Cromwell's character or of the fixed stars or of the far-off æons of the future. The relation of my thought to its object has, I insist, this curious character, that *unless* the thought and its object are parts of one larger thought, I cannot even be *meaning* that object yonder, cannot be in error about it, cannot even doubt its existence. You, for instance, are part of one larger self with me, or else I cannot even be meaning to address you as outer beings. You are part of one larger self along with the most mysterious or most remote fact of nature, along with the moon, and all the hosts of heaven, along with all truth and all beauty. Else could you not even intend to speak of such objects beyond you. For whatever you speak of you will find that your world is meant by you as just your world. Talk of the unknowable, and it forthwith becomes your unknowable, your problem, whose solution, unless the problem be a mere nonsense question, your larger self must own and be aware of. The deepest problem of life is, "What is this deeper self?" And the only answer is, *It is the self that knows in unity all truth.* This, I insist, is no hypothesis. It is actually the presupposition of your deepest doubt. And that is why I say: Everything finite is more or less obscure, dark, doubtful. Only the Infinite Self, the problem-solver, the complete thinker, the one who knows what we mean even when we are most confused and ignorant, the one who includes us, who has the world present to himself in unity, before whom all past and future truth, all distant and dark truth is clear in one eternal moment, to whom far and forgot is near, who thinks the whole of nature, and in whom are all things, the Logos, the world-possessor—only his existence, I say, is perfectly sure.

Yet I must not state the outcome thus confidently without a little more analysis and exemplification. Let us put the whole matter in a slightly different way. When a man believes that he knows any truth about a fact beyond his present and momentary thought, what is the position, with reference to that fact, which he gives himself? We must first answer, He believes that one who really knew his, the thinker's, thought, and compared it with the fact yonder, would perceive the agreement between the two. Is this *all*, however, that the believer holds to be true of his own thought? No, not so, for he holds not only that his thought, as it is, agrees with *some* fact outside his present self (as my thought, for instance, of my toothache may agree with the fact yonder called my neighbor's toothache), but also that his thought agrees with the fact with which it *meant* to agree. To *mean* to agree, however, with a specific fact beyond my present self, involves such a relation to that fact that if I could somehow come directly into the presence of the fact itself, could somehow absorb it into my present consciousness, I should become immediately aware of it as the fact that I all along had meant. Our previous examples have been intended to bring clearly before us this curious and in fact unique character of the relation called *meaning* an object of our thought. To return, then, to our supposed believer: he believes that he *knows* some fact beyond his present consciousness. This involves, as we have now seen, the assertion that he believes himself to stand in such an actual relation to the fact yonder that were it in, instead of out of his present consciousness, he would recognize it both as the object *meant* by his present thought, and also as in agreement therewith; and it is all this which, as he believes, an immediate observer of his own thought and of the object—that is, an observer who should include our believer's present self, and the fact yonder, and who should reflect on their relations—would find as the real relation. Observe, however, that only by *reflection* would this higher observer find out that real relation. Nothing but Reflective Self-consciousness could discover it. To believe that you know anything beyond your present and momentary self is, therefore, to believe that you do stand in such a relation to truth as only a larger and reflectively observant self, that included you and your object, could render intelligible. Or once more, so to believe is essentially to appeal confidently to a possible larger self for approval. But now to say, I know a truth, and yet to say, This larger self to whom I appeal is appealed to only as to a possible self, that need not be real—all this involves just the absurdity against which our whole idealistic analysis has been directed in case of all the sorts of fact and truth in the world. To believe, is to say, I stand in a *real* relation to truth, a relation which transcends wholly my present momentary self; and this real relation is of such a curious nature that only a larger inclusive self which consciously reflected upon my meaning and consciously possessed the object that I mean, could know or grasp the reality of the relation. If, however, this *relation* is a real one, it must, like the colors, the sounds, and all the other things of which we spoke before be real *for* somebody. Bare possibilities are nothing. Really possible things are already in some sense real. If, then, my relation to the truth, this complex relation of meaning an object and conforming to it, when the object, although at this moment meant by me, is not now present to my momentary thought—if this relation is genuine, and yet is such as only a possible larger self could render intelligible, then my possible larger self must be real in order that my momentary self should in fact possess the truth in question. Or, in briefest form, The relation of conforming one's thought to an outer object meant by this thought is a relation which only a Reflective Larger Self could grasp or find real. If the relation is real, the larger self is real, too.

So much, then, for the case when one believes that one has grasped a truth beyond the moment. But now for the case when one is actually in *error* about some object of his momentary and finite thought. Error is the actual failure to agree, not with any fact taken at random, but with just the fact that one had meant to agree with. Under what circumstances, then, is error possible? Only in case one's real thought, by virtue of its meaning, does transcend his own momentary and in so far ignorant self. As the true believer, meaning the truth that he believes, must be in real relation thereto, even so the blunderer, really meaning, as he does, the fact yonder, in order that he should be able even to blunder about it, must be, in so far, in the same real relation to truth as the true believer. His error lies in missing that conformity with the meant object at which he aimed. None the less, however, did he really mean and really aim; and, therefore, is he in error, because his real and larger self finds him to be so. True thinking and false thinking alike involve, then, the same fundamental conditions, in so far as both are carried on in moments; and in so far as, in both cases, the false moment and the true are such by virtue of being organic parts of a larger, critical, reflective, and so conscious self.

To sum up so far: Of no object do I speak either falsely or truly, unless I mean that object. Never do I mean an object, unless I stand in such relation thereto that were the object in this conscious moment, and immediately present to me, I should myself recognize it as completing and fulfilling my present and momentary meaning. The relation of meaning an object is thus one that only conscious reflection can define, or observe, or constitute. No merely *foreign* observer, no external test, could decide upon what is meant at any moment. Therefore, when what is meant is outside of the moment which means, only a Self inclusive of the moment and its object could complete, and so confirm or refute, the opinion that the moment contains. Really to mean an object, then, whether in case of true opinion or in case of false opinion, involves the real possibility of such a reflective test of one's meaning from the point of view of a larger self. But to say, My relation to the object is such that a reflective larger self, and *only* such a reflective and inclusive self, could see that I meant the object, is to assert a fact, a relation, an existent truth in the world, that either is a truth for nobody, or is a truth for an actual reflective self, inclusive of the moment, and critical of its meaning. Our whole idealistic analysis, however, from the beginning of this discussion, has been to the effect that facts must be facts for somebody, and cannot be facts for nobody, and that *bare* possibilities are really impossible. Hence whoever believes, whether truly or falsely, about objects beyond the moment of his belief, is an organic part of a reflective and conscious larger self that has those objects immediately present to itself, and has them in organic relation with the erring or truthful momentary self that believes.

Belief, true and false, having been examined, the case of doubt follows at once. To doubt about objects beyond my momentary self is to admit the "possibility of error" as to such objects. Error would involve my inclusion in a larger self that has directly present to it the object meant by me as I doubt. Truth would involve the same inclusion. The inclusion itself, then, is, so far, no object of rational doubt. To doubt the inclusion would be merely to doubt whether I meant anything at all beyond the moment, and not to doubt as to my particular knowledge about the *nature* of some object beyond, when once the object had been supposed to be meant. Doubt presupposes then, whenever it is a definite doubt, the real possibility, and so, in the last analysis, the reality of the normal self-consciousness that possesses the object concerning which one doubts. But if, passing to the extreme of skepticism, and stating one's most despairing and most uncompromising doubt, one so far confines himself to the prison of the inner life as to doubt whether one ever does mean any object beyond the moment at all, there comes the final consideration that in doubting one's power to transcend the moment, one has already transcended the moment, just as we found in following Hegel's analysis. To say, It is impossible to mean any object beyond this moment of my thought, and the moment is for itself "the measure of all things," is at all events to give a meaning to the words *this moment*. And *this moment* means something only in opposition to *other* moments. Yes, even in saying *this moment*, I have already left this moment, and am meaning and speaking of a past moment. Moreover, to deny that one can mean an object "beyond the moment" is already to give a meaning to the phrase *beyond the moment*, and then to deny that anything is meant to fall within the scope of this meaning. In every case, then, one must transcend by one's meaning the moment to which one is confined by one's finitude.

Flee where we will, then, the net of the larger Self ensnares us. We are lost and imprisoned in the thickets of its tangled labyrinth. The moments are not at all in themselves, for as moments they have no meaning; they exist only in relation to the beyond. The larger Self alone is, and they are by reason of it, organic parts of it. They perish, but it remains; they have truth or error only in its overshadowing presence.

And now, as to the unity of this Self. Can there be many such organic selves, mutually separate unities of moments and of the objects that these moments mean? Nay, were there *many* such, would not their manifoldness be a truth? Their relations, would not these be real? Their distinct places in the world-order, would not these things be objects of possible true or false thoughts? If so, must not there be once more the inclusive real Self for whom these truths were true, these separate selves interrelated, and their variety absorbed in the organism of its rational meaning?

There is, then, at last, but one Self, organically, reflectively, consciously inclusive of all the selves, and so of all truth. I have called this self, Logos, problem-solver, all-knower. Consider, then, last of all, his relation to problems. In the previous lecture we doubted many things; we questioned the whole seeming world of the outer order; we wondered as to space and time, as to nature and evolution, as to the beginning and the end of things. Now he who wonders is like him who doubts. Has his wonder any rationality about it? Does he *mean* anything by his doubt? Then the truth that he means, and about which he wonders, has its real constitution. As wonderer, he in the moment possesses not this solving truth; he appeals to the Self who can solve. That Self must possess the solution just as surely as the problem has a meaning. The real nature of space and time, the real beginning of things, where matter was at any point of time in the past, what is to become of the world's energy: these are matters of truth, and truth is necessarily present to the Self as in one all-comprehending self-completed moment, beyond which is naught, within which is the world.

The world, then, is such stuff as ideas are made of. Thought possesses all things. But the world is not unreal. It extends infinitely beyond our private consciousness, because it is the world of a universal mind. What facts it is to contain only experience can inform us. There is no magic that can anticipate the work of science. Absolutely the *only* thing sure from the first about this world, however, is that it is intelligent, rational, orderly, essentially comprehensible, so that all its problems are somewhere solved, all its darkest mysteries are known to the supreme Self. This Self infinitely and reflectively transcends our consciousness, and therefore, since it includes us, it is at the very least a person, and more definitely conscious than we are; for what it possesses is self-reflecting knowledge, and what is knowledge aware of itself, but consciousness? Beyond the seeming wreck and chaos of our finite problems, its eternal insight dwells, therefore, in absolute and supreme majesty. Yet it is not far from every one of us. There is no least or most transient thought that flits through a child's mind, or that troubles with the faintest line of care a maiden's face, and that still does not contain and embody something of this divine Logos.

THE PHILOSOPHY OF LOYALTY [3]

Lecture 3

LOYALTY TO LOYALTY

The two foregoing lectures have been devoted to defending the thesis that loyalty is, for the loyal individual himself, a supreme good, whatever be, for the world in general, the worth of his cause. . . .

We have deliberately declined, so far, to consider what the causes are to which men ought to be loyal. To turn to this task is the next step in our philosophy of loyalty.

Your first impression may well be that the task in question is endlessly complex. In our opening lecture we defined indeed some general characteristics which a cause must possess in order to be a fitting object of loyalty. A cause, we said, is a possible object of loyalty only in case it is such as to join many persons into the unity of a single life. Such a cause, we said, must therefore be at once personal, and, for one who defines personality from a purely human point of view, superpersonal. Our initial illustrations of possible causes were; first, a friendship which unites several friends into some unity of friendly life; secondly, a family, whose unity binds its members' lives together; and, thirdly, the state, in so far as it is no mere collection of separate citizens, but such a unity as that to which the devoted patriot is loyal.

[3] Josiah Royce, *The Philosophy of Loyalty*. New York: Macmillan, 1908.

As we saw, such illustrations could be vastly extended. All stable social relations may give rise to causes that may call forth loyalty.

Now, it is obvious that nobody can be equally and directly loyal to all of the countless actual social causes that exist. It is obvious also that many causes which conform to our general definition of a possible cause may appear to any given person to be hateful and evil causes, to which he is justly opposed. A robber band, a family engaged in a murderous feud, a pirate crew, a savage tribe, a Highland robber clan of the old days—these might constitute causes to which somebody has been, or is, profoundly loyal. Men have loved such causes devotedly, have served them for a lifetime. Yet most of us would easily agree in thinking such causes unworthy of anybody's loyalty. Moreover, different loyalties may obviously stand in mutual conflict, whenever their causes are opposed. Family feuds are embittered by the very strength of the loyalty of both sides. My country, if I am the patriot inflamed by the war spirit, seems an absolutely worthy cause; but my enemy's country usually seems hateful to me just because of my own loyalty; and therefore even my individual enemy may be hated because of the supposed baseness of his cause. War songs call the individual enemy evil names just because he possesses the very personal quality that, in our own loyal fellow countrymen, we most admire. "No refuge could save the hireling and slave." Our enemy, as you see, is a slave, because he serves his cause so obediently. Yet just such service we call, in our own country's heroes, the worthiest devotion.

Meanwhile, in the foregoing account of loyalty as a spiritual good to the loyal man, we have insisted that true loyalty, being a willing devotion of the self to its cause, involves some element of autonomous choice. Tradition has usually held that a man ought to be loyal to just that cause which his social station determines for him. Common sense generally says, that if you were born in your country, and still live there, you ought to be loyal to that country, and to that country only, hating the enemies across the border whenever a declaration of war requires you to hate them. But we have declared that true loyalty includes some element of free choice. Hence our own account seems still further to have complicated the theory of loyalty. For in answering in our last lecture the ethical individualists who objected to loyalty, we have ourselves deliberately given to loyalty an individualistic coloring. And if our view be right, and if tradition be wrong, so much the more difficult appears to be the task of defining wherein consists that which makes a cause worthy of loyalty for a given man, since tradition alone is for us an insufficient guide.

To sum up, then, our apparent difficulties, they are these: Loyalty is a good for the loyal man; but it may be mischievous for those whom his cause assails. Conflicting loyalties may mean general social disturbances; and the fact that loyalty is good for the loyal does not of itself decide whose cause is right when various causes stand opposed to one another. And if, in accordance with our own argument in the foregoing lecture, we declare that the best form of loyalty, for the loyal individual, is the one that he freely chooses for himself, so much the greater seems to be the complication of the moral world, and so much the more numerous become the chances that the loyalties of various people will conflict with one another.

In order to overcome such difficulties, now that they have arisen in our way, and in order to discover a principle whereby one may be guided in choosing a right object for his loyalty, we must steadfastly bear in mind that, when we declared loyalty to be a supreme good for the loyal man himself, we were not speaking of a good that can come to a few men only—to heroes or to saints of an especially exalted mental type. As we expressly said, the mightiest and the humblest members of any social order can be morally equal in the exemplification of loyalty. Whenever I myself begin to look about my own community to single out those people whom I know to be, in the sense of our definition, especially loyal to their various causes, I always find, amongst the most exemplary cases of loyalty, a few indeed of the most prominent members of the community, whom your minds and mine must at once single out because their public services and their willing sacrifices have made their loyalty to their chosen causes a matter of common report and of easy observation. But my own mind also chooses some of the plainest and obscurest of the people whom I chance to know, the most straightforward and simpleminded of folk, whose loyalty is even all the more sure to me because I can certainly affirm that they, at least, cannot be making any mere display of loyalty in order that they should be seen of men. Nobody knows of their loyalty except those who are in more or less direct touch with them; and these usually appreciate this loyalty too little. You, all of you, similarly know plain and wholly obscure men and women, of whom the world has never heard, and is not worthy, but who have possessed and who have proved in the presence of you who have chanced to observe them, a loyalty to their chosen causes which was not indeed expressed in martial deeds, but which was quite as genuine a loyalty as that of a Samurai, or as that of Arnold von Winkelried when he rushed upon the Austrian spears. As for the ordinary expressions of loyalty, not at critical moments and in the heroic instants that come to the plainest lives, but in daily business, we are all aware how the letter carrier and the housemaid may live, and often do live, when they choose, as complete a daily life of steadfast loyalty as could any knight or king. Some of us certainly know precisely such truly great personal embodiments of loyalty in those who are, in the world's ill-judging eyes, the little ones of the community.

Now these facts, I insist, show that loyalty is in any case no aristocratic gift of the few. It is, indeed, too rare a possession today in our own American social order; but that defect is due to the state of our present moral education. We as a nation, I fear, have been forgetting loyalty. We have been neglecting to cultivate it in our social order. We have been making light of it. We have not been training ourselves for it. Hence we, indeed, often sadly miss it in our social environment. But all sound human beings are made for it and can learn to possess it and to profit by it. And it is an essentially accessible and practical virtue for everybody.

This being true, let us next note that all the complications which we just reported are obviously due, in the main, to the fact that, as loyal men at present are, their various causes, and so their various loyalties, are viewed by them as standing in mutual, sometimes in deadly conflict. In general, as is plain if somebody's loyalty to a given cause, as for instance to a family, or to a state, so expresses itself as to involve a feud with a neighbor's family, or a warlike assault upon a foreign state, the result is obviously an evil; and at least part of the reason why it is an evil is that, by reason of the feud or the war, a certain good, namely, the enemy's loyalty, together with the enemy's opportunity to be loyal, is assailed, is thwarted, is endangered, is, perhaps, altogether destroyed. If the loyalty of A is a good for him, and if the loyalty of B is a good for him, then a feud between A and B, founded upon a mutual conflict between the causes that they serve, obviously involves this evil, namely, that each of the combatants assails, and perhaps may altogether destroy, precisely what we have seen to be the best spiritual possession of the other, namely, his chance to have a cause and to be loyal to a cause. The militant loyalty, indeed, also assails, in such a case, the enemy's physical comfort and well-being, his property, his life; and herein, of course, militant loyalty does evil to the enemy. But if each man's having and serving a cause is his best good, the worst of the evils of a feud is the resulting attack, not upon the enemy's comfort or his health or his property or his life, but upon the most precious of his possessions, his loyalty itself.

If loyalty is a supreme good, the mutually destructive conflict of loyalties is in general a supreme evil. If loyalty is a good for all sorts and conditions of men, the war of man against man has been especially mischievous, not so much because it has hurt, maimed, impoverished, or slain men, as because it has so often robbed the defeated of their causes, of their opportunities to be loyal, and sometimes of their very spirit of loyalty.

If, then, we look over the field of human life to see where good and evil have most clustered, we see that the best in human life is its loyalty; while the worst is whatever has tended to make loyalty impossible, or to destroy it when present, or to rob it of its own while it still survives. And of all things that thus have warred with loyalty, the bitterest woe of humanity has been that so often it is the loyal themselves who have thus blindly and eagerly gone about to wound and to slay the loyalty of their brethren. The spirit of loyalty has been misused to make men commit sin against this very spirit, holy as it is. For such a sin is precisely what any wanton conflict of loyalties means. Where such a conflict occurs, the best, namely, loyalty, is used as an instrument in order to compass the worst, namely, the destruction of loyalty.

It is true, then, that some causes are good, while some are evil. But the test of good and evil in the causes to which men are loyal is now definable in terms which we can greatly simplify in view of the foregoing considerations.

If, namely, I find a cause, and this cause fascinates me, and I give myself over to its service, I in so far attain what, for me, if my loyalty is complete, is a supreme good. But my cause, by our own definition, is a social cause, which binds many into the unity of one service. My cause, therefore, gives me of necessity fellow servants, who with me share this loyalty, and to whom this loyalty, if complete, is also a supreme good. So far, then, in being loyal myself, I not only get but give good; for I help to sustain, in each of my fellow servants, his own loyalty, and so I help him to secure his own supreme good. In so far, then, my loyalty to my cause is also a loyalty to my fellow's loyalty. But now suppose that my cause, like the family in a feud, or like the pirate ship, or like the aggressively warlike nation, lives by the destruction of the loyalty of other families, or of its own community, or of other communities. Then, indeed, I get a good for myself and for my fellow servants by our common loyalty; but I war against this very spirit of loyalty as it appears in our opponent's loyalty to his own cause.

And so, a cause is good, not only for me, but for mankind, in so far as it is essentially a *loyalty to loyalty*, that is, is an aid and a furtherance of loyalty in my fellows. It is an evil cause in so far as, despite the loyalty that it arouses in me, it is destructive of loyalty in the world of my fellows. My cause is, indeed, always such as to involve some loyalty to loyalty, because, if I am loyal to any cause at all, I have fellow servants whose loyalty mine supports. But in so far as my cause is a predatory cause, which lives by overthrowing the loyalties of others, it is an evil cause, because it involves disloyalty to the very cause of loyalty itself.

In view of these considerations, we are now able still further to simplify our problem by laying stress upon one more of those very features which seemed, but a moment since, to complicate the matter so hopelessly. Loyalty, as we have defined it, is the willing devotion of a self to a cause. In answering the ethical individualists, we have insisted that all of the higher types of loyalty involve autonomous choice. The cause that is to appeal to me at all must indeed have some elemental fascination for me. It must stir me, arouse me, please me, and in the end possess me. Moreover, it must, indeed, be set before me by my social order as a possible, a practically significant, a living cause, which binds many selves in the unity of one life. But, nevertheless, if I am really awake to the significance of my own moral choices, I must be in the position of accepting this cause, as the Speaker of the House, in the incident that I have narrated, had freely accepted his Speakership. My cause cannot be merely forced upon me. It is I who make it my own. It is I who willingly say: "I have no eyes to see nor tongue to speak save as this cause shall command." However much the cause may seem to be assigned to me by my social station, I must co-operate in the choice of the cause, before the act of loyalty is complete.

Since this is the case, since my loyalty never is my mere fate, but is always also my choice, I can of course determine my loyalty, at least to some extent, by the consideration of the actual good and ill which my proposed cause does to mankind. And since I now have the main criterion of the good and ill of causes before me, I can define a principle of choice which may so guide me that my loyalty shall become a good, not merely to myself, but to mankind.

This principle is now obvious. I may state it thus: In so far as it lies in your power, so choose your cause and so serve it, that, by reason of your choice and of your service, there shall be more loyalty in the world rather than less. And, in fact, so choose and so serve your individual cause as to secure thereby the greatest possible increase of loyalty amongst men. More briefly: *In choosing and in serving the cause to which you are to be loyal, be, in any case, loyal to loyalty.*

This precept, I say, will express how one should guide his choice of a cause, in so far as he considers not merely his own supreme good, but that of mankind. That such autonomous choice is possible, tends, as we now see, not to complicate, but to simplify our moral situation. For if you regard men's loyalty as their fate, if you think that a man must be loyal simply to the cause which tradition sets before him, without any power to direct his own moral attention, then indeed the conflict of loyalties seems an insoluble problem; so that, if men find themselves loyally involved in feuds, there is no way out. But if, indeed, choice plays a part—a genuine even if limited part—in directing the individual's choice of the cause to which he is to be loyal, then indeed this choice may be so directed that loyalty to the universal loyalty of all mankind shall be furthered by the actual choices which each enlightened loyal person makes when he selects his cause.

At the close of our first discussion we supposed the question to be asked, Where, in all our complex and distracted modern world, in which at present cause wars with cause, shall we find a cause that is certainly worthy of our loyalty? This question, at this very moment, has received in our discussion an answer which you may feel to be so far provisional—perhaps unpractical—but which you ought to regard as, at least in principle, somewhat simple and true to human nature. Loyalty is a good, a supreme good. If I myself could but find a worthy cause, and serve it as the Speaker served the House, having neither eyes to see nor tongue to speak save as that cause should command, then my highest human good, in so far as I am indeed an active being, would be mine. But this very good of loyalty is no peculiar privilege of mine; nor is it good only for me. It is a universally human good. For it is simply the finding of a harmony of the self and the world—such a harmony as alone can content any human being.

In these lectures I do not found my argument upon some remote ideal. I found my case upon taking our poor passionate human nature just as we find it. This "eager anxious being" of ours, as Gray calls it, is a being that we can find only in social ties, and that we, nevertheless, can never fulfill without a vigorous self-assertion. We are by nature proud, untamed, restless, insatiable in our private self-will. We are also imitative, plastic, and in bitter need of ties. We profoundly want both to rule and to be ruled. We must be each of us at the center of his own active world, and yet each of us longs to be in harmony with the very outermost heavens that encompass, with the lofty orderliness of their movements, all our restless doings. The stars fascinate us, and yet we also want to keep our own feet upon our solid human earth. Our fellows, meanwhile, overwhelm us with the might of their customs, and we in turn are inflamed with the naturally unquenchable longing that they should somehow listen to the cries of our every individual desire.

Now this divided being of ours demands reconciliation with itself; it is one long struggle for unity. Its inner and outer realms are naturally at war. Yet it wills both realms. It wants them to become one. Such unity, however, only loyalty furnishes to us; loyalty, which finds the inner self intensified and exalted even by the very act of outward looking and of upward looking, of service and obedience; loyalty, which knows its eyes and its tongue to be never so much and so proudly its own as when it earnestly insists that it can neither see nor speak except as the cause demands; loyalty, which is most full of life at the instant when it is most ready to become weary, or even to perish in the act of devotion to its own. Such loyalty unites private passion and outward conformity in one life. This is the very essence of loyalty. Now, loyalty has these characters in any man who is loyal. Its emotions vary, indeed, endlessly with the temperaments of its adherents; but to them all it brings the active peace of that rest in a painful life—that rest such as we found the mystic, Meister Eckhart, fully ready to prize.

Loyalty, then, is a good for all men. And it is in any man just as much a true good as my loyalty could be in me. And so, then, if indeed I seek a cause, a worthy cause, what cause could be more worthy than the cause of loyalty to loyalty; that is, the cause of making loyalty prosper amongst men? If I could serve that cause in a sustained and effective life, if some practical work for the furtherance of universal human loyalty could become to me what the House was to the Speaker, then indeed my own life-task would be found; and I could then be assured at every instant of the worth of my cause by virtue of the very good that I personally found in its service.

Here would be for me not only a unity of inner and outer, but a unity with the unity of all human life. What I sought for myself I should then be explicitly seeking for my whole world. All men would be my fellow servants of my cause. In principle I should be opposed to no man's loyalty. I should be opposed only to men's blindness in their loyalty, I should contend only against that tragic disloyalty to loyalty which the feuds of humanity now exemplify. I should preach to all others, I should strive to practice myself, that active mutual furtherance of universal loyalty which is what humanity obviously most needs, if indeed loyalty, just as the willing devotion of a self to a cause, is a supreme good.

And since all who are human are as capable of loyalty as they are of reason, since the plainest and the humblest can be as true-hearted as the great, I should nowhere miss the human material for my task. I should know, meanwhile, that if indeed loyalty, unlike the "mercy" of Portia's speech, is not always mightiest in the mightiest, it certainly, like mercy, becomes the throned monarch better than his crown. So that I should be sure of this good of loyalty as something worthy to be carried, so far as I could carry it, to everybody, lofty or humble.

Thus surely it would be humane and reasonable for me to define my cause to myself—if only I could be assured that there is indeed some practical way of making loyalty to loyalty the actual cause of my life. Our question therefore becomes this: Is there a practical way of serving the universal human cause of loyalty to loyalty? And if there is such a way, what is it? Can we see how personally so to act that we bring loyalty on earth to a fuller fruition, to a wider range of efficacy, to a more effective sovereignty over the lives of men? If so, then indeed we can see how to work for the cause of the genuine kingdom of heaven. . . .

Yet herewith we have only begun to indicate how the cause of loyalty to loyalty may be made a cause that one can practically, efficaciously, and constantly serve. Loyalty, namely, is not a matter merely of today or of yesterday. The loyal have existed since civilization began. And, even so, loyalty to loyalty is not a novel undertaking. It began to be effective from the time when first people could make and keep a temporary truce during a war, and when first strangers were regarded as protected by the gods, and when first the duties of hospitality were recognized. The way to be loyal to loyalty is therefore laid down in precisely the rational portion of the conventional morality which human experience has worked out.

Herewith we approach a thesis which is central in my whole philosophy of loyalty. I announced that thesis in other words in the opening lecture. My thesis is that *all those duties which we have learned to recognize as the fundamental duties of the civilized man, the duties that every man owes to every man, are to be rightly interpreted as special instances of loyalty to loyalty.* In other words, all the recognized virtues can be defined in terms of our concept of loyalty. And this is why I assert that, when rightly interpreted, loyalty is the whole duty of man.

For consider the best-known facts as to the indirect influence of certain forms of loyal conduct. When I speak the truth, my act is directly an act of loyalty to the personal tie which then and there binds me to the man to whom I consent to speak. My special cause is, in such a case, constituted by this tie. My fellow and I are linked in a certain unity—the unity of some transaction which involves our speech one to another. To be ready to speak the truth to my fellow is to have, just then, no eye to see and no tongue to speak save as this willingly accepted tie demands. In so far, then, speaking the truth is a special instance of loyalty. But whoever speaks the truth, thereby does what he then can do to help everybody to speak the truth. For he acts so as to further the general confidence of man in man. How far such indirect influence may extend, no man can predict.

Precisely so, in the commercial world, honesty in business is a service, not merely and not mainly to the others who are parties to the single transaction in which at any one time this faithfulness is shown. The single act of business fidelity is an act of loyalty to that general confidence of man in man upon which the whole fabric of business rests. On the contrary, the unfaithful financier whose disloyalty is the final deed that lets loose the avalanche of a panic, has done far more harm to general public confidence than he could possibly do to those whom his act directly assails. Honesty, then, is owed not merely and not even mainly to those with whom we directly deal when we do honest acts; it is owed to mankind at large, and it benefits the community and the general cause of commercial loyalty.

Such a remark is in itself a commonplace; but it serves to make concrete my general thesis that every form of dutiful action is a case of loyalty to loyalty. For what holds thus of truthfulness and of commercial honesty holds, I assert, of every form of dutiful action. Each such form is a special means for being, by a concrete deed, loyal to loyalty.

We have sought for the worthy cause; and we have found it. This simplest possible of considerations serves to turn the chaotic mass of separate precepts of which our ordinary conventional moral code consists into a system unified by the one spirit of universal loyalty. By your individual deed you indeed cannot save the world, but you can at any moment do what in you lies to further the cause which both for you and for the human world constitutes the supreme good, namely, the cause of universal loyalty. Herein consists your entire duty.

Review in the light of this simple consideration, the usually recognized range of human duties. How easily they group themselves about the one principle: *Be loyal to loyalty.*

Have I, for instance, duties to myself? Yes, precisely in so far as I have the duty to be actively loyal at all. For loyalty needs not only a willing but also an effective servant. My duty to myself is, then, the duty to provide my cause with one who is strong enough and skillful enough to be effective according to my own natural powers. The care of health, self-cultivation, self-control, spiritual power—these are all to be morally estimated with reference to the one principle that, since I have no eyes to see or tongue to speak save as the cause commands, I will be as worthy an instrument of the cause as can be made, by my own efforts, out of the poor material which my scrap of human nature provides. The highest personal cultivation for which I have time is thus required by our principle. But self-cultivation which is not related to loyalty is worthless.

Have I private and personal rights, which I ought to assert? Yes, precisely in so far as my private powers and possessions are held in trust for the cause, and are, upon occasion, to be defended for the sake of the cause. My rights are morally the outcome of my loyalty. It is my right to protect my service, to maintain my office, and to keep my own merely in order that I may use my own as the cause commands. But rights which are not determined by my loyalty are vain pretense.

As to my duties to my neighbors, these are defined by a well-known tradition in terms of two principles: justice and benevolence. These two principles are mere aspects of our one principle. Justice means, in general, fidelity to human ties in so far as they are ties. Justice thus concerns itself with what may be called the mere forms in which loyalty expresses itself. Justice, therefore, is simply one aspect of loyalty—the more formal and abstract side of loyal life. If you are just, you are decisive in your choice of your personal cause, you are faithful to the loyal decision once made, you keep your promise, you speak the truth, you respect the loyal ties of all other men, and you contend with other men only in so far as the defense of your own cause, in the interest of loyalty to the universal cause of loyalty, makes such contest against aggression unavoidable. All these types of activity, within the limits that loyalty determines, are demanded if you are to be loyal to loyalty. Our principle thus at once requires them, and enables us to define their range of application. But justice, without loyalty, is a vicious formalism.

Benevolence, on the other hand, is that aspect of loyalty which directly concerns itself with your influence upon the inner life of human beings who enjoy, who suffer, and whose private good is to be affected by your deeds. Since no personal good that your fellow can possess is superior to his own loyalty, your own loyalty to loyalty is itself a supremely benevolent type of activity. And since your fellow man is an instrument for the furtherance of the cause of universal loyalty, his welfare also concerns you, in so far as, if you help him to a more efficient life, you make him better able to be loyal. Thus benevolence is an inevitable attendant of loyalty. And the spirit of loyalty to loyalty enables us to define wherein consists a wise benevolence. Benevolence without loyalty is a dangerous sentimentalism. Thus viewed, then, loyalty to universal loyalty is indeed the fulfillment of the whole law.

Lecture 7

LOYALTY, TRUTH, AND REALITY

In closing my last lecture I said that whatever trains us in the arts of loyalty enables us to enter into a world of spiritual truth. These words were intended to indicate that the loyal life has another aspect than the one hitherto most emphasized in these lectures. Our foregoing account has been deliberately one-sided. We have been discussing the moral life as if one could define a plan of conduct without implying more about man's place in the real universe than we have yet made explicit in these lectures. Hence our discussion, so far, is open to obvious objections. . . .

What must be true about the universe if even loyalty itself is a genuine good, and not a merely inevitable human illusion?

Well, loyalty is a service of causes. A cause, if it really is what our definition requires, links various human lives into the unity of one life. Therefore, if loyalty has any basis in truth, human lives can be linked in some genuine spiritual unity. Is such unity a fact, or is our belief in our causes a mere point of view, a pathetic fallacy? Surely, if any man, however loyal, discovers that his cause is a dream, and that men remain as a fact sundered beings, not really linked by genuine spiritual ties, how can that man remain loyal? Perhaps his supreme good indeed lies in believing that such unities are real. But if this belief turns out to be an illusion, and if a man detects the illusion, can he any longer get the good out of loyalty?

And as for even this personal good that is to be got out of loyalty, we have all along seen that such good comes to a loyal man's mind in a very paradoxical way. A loyal man gets good, but since he gets it by believing that his cause has a real existence outside of his private self, and is of itself a good thing, he gets the fascination of loyalty not as a private delight of his own, but as a fulfillment of himself through self-surrender to an externally existing good—through a willing abandonment of the seeking of his own delight. And so the loyal man's good is essentially an anticipation of a good that he regards as not his own but as existent in the cause. The cause, however, is itself no one fellow man, and no mere collection of fellow men. It is a family, a country, a church, or is such a rational union of many human minds and wills as we have in mind when we speak of a science or an art. Now, can such causes contain any good which is not simply a collection of separate human experiences of pleasure or of satisfaction? Thus, then, both the reality and the good of a loyal man's cause must be objects of the loyal man's belief in order that he should be able to get the experience of loyalty. And if his loyalty is indeed well founded, there must be unities of spiritual life in the universe such that no one man ever, by himself, experiences these unities as facts of his own consciousness. And these higher unities of life must possess a degree and a type of goodness—a genuine value, such that no one man, and no mere collection of men, can ever exhaustively experience this goodness, or become personally possessed of this value.

How paradoxical a world, then, must the real world be, if the faith of the loyal is indeed well founded! A spiritual unity of life, which transcends the individual experience of any man, must be real. For loyalty, as we have seen, is a service of causes that, from the human point of view, appear superpersonal. Loyalty holds these unities to be good. If loyalty is right, the real goodness of these causes is never completely manifested to any one man, or to any mere collection of men. Such goodness, then, if completely experienced at all, must be experienced upon some higher level of consciousness than any one human being ever reaches. If loyalty is right, social causes, social organizations, friendships, families, countries, yes, humanity, as you see, must have the sort of unity of consciousness which individual human persons fragmentarily get, but must have this unity upon a higher level than that of our ordinary human individuality.

Some such view, I say, must be held if we are to regard loyalty as in the end anything more than a convenient illusion. Loyalty has its metaphysical aspect. It is an effort to conceive human life in an essentially superhuman way, to view our social organizations as actual personal unities of consciousness, unities wherein there exists an actual experience of that good which, in our loyalty, we only partially apprehend. If the loyalty of the lovers is indeed well founded in fact, then they, as separate individuals, do not constitute the whole truth. Their spiritual union also has a personal, a conscious existence, upon a higher than human level. An analogous unity of consciousness, a unity superhuman in grade, but intimately bound up with, and inclusive of, our apparently separate personalities, must exist, if loyalty is well founded, wherever a real cause wins the true devotion of ourselves. Grant such an hypothesis, and then loyalty becomes no pathetic serving of a myth. The good which our causes possess, then, also becomes a concrete fact for an experience of a higher than human level. That union of self-sacrifice with self-assertion which loyalty expresses, becomes a consciousness of our genuine relations to a higher social unity of consciousness in which we all have our being. For from this point of view we are, and we have our worth, by virtue of our relation to a consciousness of a type superior to the human type. And meanwhile the good of our loyalty is itself a perfectly concrete good, a good which is present to that higher experience, wherein our cause is viewed in its truth, as a genuine unity of life. And because of this fact we can straightforwardly say: We are loyal not for the sake of the good that we privately get out of loyalty, but for the sake of the good that the cause —this higher unity of experience—gets out of this loyalty. Yet our loyalty gives us what is, after all, our supreme good, for it defines our true position in the world of that social will wherein we live and move and have our being.

I doubt not that such a view of human life—such an assertion that the social will is a concrete entity, just as real as we are, and of still a higher grade of reality than ourselves—will seem to many of you mythical enough. Yet thus to view the unity of human life is, after all, a common tendency of the loyal. That fact I have illustrated in every lecture of this course. That such a view need not be mythical, that truth and reality can be conceived only in such terms as these, that our philosophy of loyalty is a rational part of a philosophy which must view the whole world as one unity of consciousness, wherein countless lesser unities are synthesized—this is my general philosophical thesis. . . .

BIBLIOGRAPHY

ROYCE, Josiah, *The Religious Aspect of Philosophy: A Critique of the Basis of Conduct and of Faith.* Boston: Houghton Mifflin, 1885.

———— *The Spirit of Modern Philosophy.* Boston: Houghton Mifflin, 1892.

———— *The Conception of God: A Philosophical Discussion Concerning the Nature of the Divine Idea as a Demonstrable Reality.* Co-author with G. H. Howison, J. LeConte, and S. E. Mezes. New York: Macmillan Co., 1897.

———— *Studies of Good and Evil.* New York: D. Appleton, 1898.

———— *The Conception of Immortality.* Boston: Houghton Mifflin, 1900.

———— *The World and the Individual.* Gifford Lectures. New York: Macmillan, 1900–1901, 2 vols.

———— *Outlines of Psychology.* New York: Macmillan, 1903.

———— *The Philosophy of Loyalty.* New York: Macmillan Co., 1908.

———— *Race Questions, Provincialism, and Other American Problems.* New York: Macmillan Co., 1908.

———— *William James and Other Essays in the Philosophy of Life.* New York: Macmillan Co., 1911.

———— *The Sources of Religious Insight.* New York: Charles Scribner's Sons, 1912.

———— "The Principles of Logic," *Encyclopaedia of the Philosophical Sciences*, Vol. I, from the German by B. Ethel Meyer. London: Macmillan Co., 1913.

———— *The Problem of Christianity.* New York: Macmillan Co., 1913, 2 vols.

———— *War and Insurance.* New York: Macmillan Co., 1914.

———— *Lectures on Modern Idealism.* New Haven: Yale U. Press, 1919.

———— *Fugitive Essays*, with an Introduction by J. Lowenberg. Cambridge: Harvard U. Press, 1925.

———— *The Social Philosophy of Josiah Royce.* Selections ed. by S. G. Brown. Syracuse: Syracuse U. Press, 1950.

———— *Logical Essays*, ed. by Daniel S. Robinson. Dubuque, Iowa: Wm. C. Brown, 1951.

———— *The Religious Philosophy of Josiah Royce.* Selections ed. by S. G. Brown. Syracuse, Syracuse U. Press, 1952.

COSTELLO, Harry T., ed., *Josiah Royce's Seminar, 1913–1914, as Recorded in the Notebooks of Harry T. Costello.* New Brunswick: Rutgers U. Press, 1963.

COTTON, James Harry, *Royce on the Human Self*. Cambridge: Harvard U. Press, 1954.

CREIGHTON, J. E., ed., *Papers in Honor of Josiah Royce on His Sixtieth Birthday*. New York: Longmans, Green, 1916. Contains a Bibliography of Royce's writings.

Journal of Philosophy, Vol. LIII (Feb. 2, 1956). Special Royce issue.

LOEWENBERG, J., *Royce's Synoptic Vision*. Pub. for the Dept. of Philosophy of Johns Hopkins U., 1955.

MARCEL, Gabriel, *Royce's Metaphysics*, trans. by Virginia and Gordon Ringer. Chicago: H. Regnery, 1956.

SANTAYANA, George, *Character and Opinion in the United States: with Reminiscences of William James and Josiah Royce and Academic Life in America*. New York: Charles Scribner's Sons, 1920.

SMITH, John Edwin, *Royce's Social Infinite, The Community of Interpretation*. New York: Liberal Arts Press, 1950.

PART SIX

Evolution and Darwinism
(1859-1900)

John Fiske

[1842–1901]

The publication of Charles Darwin's theory of evolution had important repercussions in the intellectual life of America. Although evolutionary ideas had been advocated throughout the nineteenth century and even earlier, it was Darwin who provided sufficient empirical evidence to make the theory highly plausible. The controversy that his thought stimulated in Europe had its reverberations here. John Fiske, as a young man of twenty, studied the synthetic philosophy of Herbert Spencer, who had attempted to extend the implications of Darwinism throughout the universe. As a result, Fiske became a leading exponent of Darwin and Spencer in the United States.

In *Outlines of Cosmic Philosophy*, portions of which are here reproduced, Fiske attempted to construct a cosmic philosophy or a "theory of the universe" in conformity with scientific method (see especially "The Question Stated"). Fiske adopted Spencer's general "Law of Evolution," which he claimed applied to all the processes of nature, including the intellectual and moral evolution of man. Fiske's account of the evolution of morality and society is especially interesting, and a large extract from Fiske's chapter, "Genesis of Man, Morally," is here reprinted. Fiske related the development of moral sympathy to the prolonged period of human infancy and dependency. His theory was able, he thought, to reconcile both utilitarianism and Kantianism in ethics. Fiske further maintained that Auguste Comte's Positivism pointed to a truly scientific account of all social change; however, Fiske was careful to show that his own position did not involve positivism, atheism or materialism. Instead, he defended a form of "cosmic theism," which he claimed went beyond Spencer's agnosticism while avoiding anthropomorphism.

Born Edmund Fisk Green in Hartford, Connecticut, he changed his name to John Fiske. He was graduated from Harvard in 1862, and later studied for the bar. Fiske was a man of letters, a popular lecturer, an author of books on history. His style was lucid, his method synoptic. Among his best known works are *Darwinism and Other Essays* (1879), *Excursions of an Evolutionist* (1884), *Through Nature to God* (1899), and *A Century of Science and Other Essays* (1902). Unlike Spencer, Fiske was not primarily interested in liberal, social, and political reform. Although his cosmic system did not gain widespread acceptance, Fiske helped to make evolution palatable, and in this regard to pave the way for the newer philosophical and scientific attitudes which were shortly to prevail in American thought.

OUTLINES OF COSMIC PHILOSOPHY

Based on the Doctrine of Evolution,
with Criticisms on the Positive Philosophy

THE QUESTION STATED [1]

We . . . are prepared to begin the work of constructing a theory of the universe out of the elements which science can furnish. . . . In undertaking this task, there are two opposite courses, either of which we might pursue, though with differing degrees and kinds of success. On the one hand, we might begin with a survey of the concrete sciences; and having ascertained the most general truths respectively formulated by astronomy, geology, biology, psychology, and sociology, we might interpret all these truths in common by merging them all in a single widest generalization concerning the concrete universe as a whole; and lastly, through an analysis of this widest generalization we might seek the ultimate axiom by which the validity of our conclusions is certified. Or, on the other hand, we might begin by searching directly for this ultimate axiom; and having found it, we might proceed to deduce from it that widest generalization which interprets the most general truths severally formulated by the concrete sciences; and finally, by the help of these universal principles, we might perhaps succeed in eliciting sundry generalizations concerning particular groups of concrete phenomena which might otherwise escape our scrutiny.

The latter, or synthetic method of procedure, is much better adapted for our present purpose than the former, or analytic method. Indeed the mass of phenomena with which we are required to deal is so vast and so heterogeneous, the various generalizations which we are required to interpret in common are apparently so little related to one another, that it may well be doubted if the appliances of simple induction and analysis would ever suffice to bring us within sight of our prescribed goal. The history of scientific discovery affords numerous illustrations—and nowhere more convincingly than in the sublime chapter which tells the triumph of the Newtonian astronomy—of the comparative helplessness of mere induction where the phenomena to be explained are numerous and complicated. A simple tabulation and analysis of the planetary movements would never have disclosed, even to Newton's penetrating gaze, the law of dynamics to which those movements conform. But in these complicated cases, where induction

[1] Cambridge Riverside Press (1902), Part I, Chap. 11, Vol. II, pp. 117–21.

has remained hopelessly embarrassed, the most brilliant success has often resulted from the adoption of a hypothesis by which the phenomena have been deductively interpreted, and which has been uniformly corroborated by subsequent inductions. The essential requisite in such an hypothesis is that it must have been framed in rigorous conformity to the requirements of the objective method. It must be based upon properties of matter or principles of dynamics that have previously been established or fully confirmed by induction; it must appeal to no unknown agency, nor invoke any unknown attribute of matter or motion; and it must admit ultimately of inductive verification. Such a hypothesis, in short, is admissible only when it contains no unverifiable element. And of hypotheses framed in accordance with these rigorous requirements, the surest mark of genuineness is usually that they are not only uniformly verified by the phenomena which first suggested them, but also help us to the detection of other relations among phenomena which would otherwise have remained hidden from us.

In conformity, then, to these requirements of scientific method, our course is clearly marked out for us. We have first to search, among truths already indisputably established, for that ultimate truth which must underlie our synthesis of scientific truths. We have next to show how the widest generalization which has yet been reached concerning the concrete universe as a whole, may be proved to follow, as an inevitable corollary, from this ultimate truth. This widest generalization will thus appear, in the light of our demonstration, as a legitimate hypothesis, which we may verify by showing that the widest generalizations severally obtainable in the concrete sciences are included in it and receive their common interpretation from it. Throughout the earlier part of this special verification, in which we shall be called upon to survey the truths furnished respectively by astronomy, geology, biology, and psychology, I shall follow closely in the footsteps of Mr. Spencer, who has already elaborately illustrated these truths in the light of the Doctrine of Evolution. When we arrive at sociology—still following Mr. Spencer's guidance, but venturing into a region which he has as yet but cursorily and fragmentarily surveyed for us—I shall endeavor to show that our main hypothesis presents the strongest indications of its genuineness by affording a brilliant interpretation of sundry social phenomena never before grouped together under a general law. This interpretation I shall then seek further to verify by showing how it includes and justifies whatever is defensible in the generalizations which such writers as Comte and Buckle have obtained from an inductive survey of the facts of human history. Finally I shall apply our central hypothesis to the special problem of the Origin of Man, and show how, from its marvelous success in dealing with the difficult questions of intellectual and moral progressiveness, the doctrine of evolution must be pronounced to have sustained the severest test of verification which our present scientific resources enable us to apply upon this great scale. With this most significant and interesting inquiry, our synthesis of scientific doctrines will be completed. Such ultimate questions as must inevitably be suggested on our route—questions concerning the relations of the Doctrine of Evolution to religion and ethics—will be considered, with the help of the general principles then at our command, in the corollaries which are to follow. . . .

THE LAW OF EVOLUTION [2]

. . . Let us begin by briefly summing up the results already obtained. It has been shown that the coexistence of antagonist forces throughout the knowable universe necessitates a universal rhythm of motion; and that in proportion to the number of forces anywhere concerned in producing a given set of motions, the resulting rhythms are complex. It has been further shown that, save where the rhythms are absolutely simple—a case which is never actually realized—there must occur a redistribution of matter and motion as the result of each rhythm. It next appeared that such a redistribution involves on the one hand an integration of matter, which implies a concomitant dissipation of motion, and on the other hand a distintegration of matter, which implies a concomitant absorption of motion. The former process, which results in the acquirement of an individual existence by sensible objects, has been named Evolution—the latter process, which results in the loss of individual existence by sensible objects, has been named Dissolution. And we saw it to be a corollary from the universality of rhythm that, while these two antagonist processes must ever be going on simultaneously, there must be an alternation of epochs during which now the former and now the latter is predominant. In conclusion, it was barely hinted that these two fundamental modes of redistribution must give rise, in the majority of cases, to second redistributions, which it is the business of a scientific philosophy to define and formulate.

Now, as we are about to start upon a long and complicated inquiry, the proper treatment of which must task our utmost resources of exposition, it will be desirable at the outset to disencumber ourselves of all such luggage as we are not absolutely obliged to take along with us. We shall therefore, for the present, leave the process of Dissolution entirely out of the account, or shall refer to it only incidentally, in cases where such a reference may assist in the elucidation of the

[2] Part II, Chap. 4, Vol. II, pp. 206–41 (selected).

counter-process. In the following chapter we shall have occasion to treat of Dissolution in some detail as exemplified in the probable future distintegration of our planetary system; at present we are concerned only with Evolution, which we have already seen to consist in the integration of matter and concomitant dissipation of motion, but which, as we shall presently see, implies in most cases much more than this. Let us first point out the conditions under which the secondary redistributions attending Evolution take place; and let us then proceed to point out the common characteristics of these secondary changes.

Obviously in speaking of secondary redistributions that go on while a body is integrating its matter and losing its motion, we refer to redistributions among the parts of the body and among the relative motions of the parts—or, in other words, to alterations in structure and function going on within the body. Now the ease with which such redistributions are effected, and the ease with which they are maintained, must depend alike, though in precisely opposite ways, upon the amount of motion retained by the integrating body. The greater the amount of retained motion, the more easily will internal redistributions be affected. The smaller the amount of retained motion, the more easily will such redistributions be rendered permanent. . . .

. . . Having shown that Evolution is always and primarily an integration of matter attended by a dissipation of motion; and having shown that under certain conditions, most completely realized by organic bodies, certain secondary but equally important phenomena of structural rearrangement may be expected to accompany this fundamental process; we must next show what these secondary phenomena are.

The exposition will be rendered clearer by the preliminary explanation of four technical terms, which will continually recur, and which must be thoroughly understood before any further step can be taken toward comprehending the Law of Evolution. These terms are neither obscure in themselves, nor newly coined, but because we shall henceforth employ them in a strict and special sense, they require careful definition.

I. An object is said to be *homogeneous* when each of its parts is like every other part. An illustration is not easy to find, since perfect homogeneity is not known to exist. But there is such a thing as relative homogeneity; and we say that a piece of gold is homogeneous as compared with a piece of wood; or that a wooden ball is homogeneous as compared with an orange.

II. An object is said to be *heterogeneous* when its parts do not all resemble one another. All known objects are more or less heterogeneous. But, relatively speaking, a tree is said to be heterogeneous as compared with the seed from which it has sprung; and an orange is heterogeneous as compared with a wooden ball.

III. *Differentiation* is the arising of an unlikeness between any two of the units which go to make up an aggregate. It is the process through which objects increase in heterogeneity. A piece of cast iron before it is exposed to the air is relatively homogeneous. But when, by exposure to the air, it has acquired a coating of ferric oxide, or iron-rust, it is relatively heterogeneous. The units composing its outside are unlike the units composing its inside; or, in other words, its outside is differentiated from its inside.

IV. The term *integration* we have already partly defined as the concentration of the material units which go to make up any aggregate. But a complete definition must recognize the fact that, along with the integration of wholes, there goes on (in all cases in which structural complexity is attained) an integration of parts. This secondary integration may be defined as the segregation, or grouping together, of those units of a heterogeneous aggregate which resemble one another. A good example is afforded by crystallization. The particles of the crystallizing substance, which resemble each other, and which do not resemble the particles of the solvent fluid, gradually unite to form the crystal, which is thus said to be *integrated* from the solution. Integration is also seen in the rising of cream upon the surface of a dish of milk, and in the frothy collection of carbonic acid bubbles covering a newly filled glass of ale.

Obviously as it is through differentiation that an aggregate increases in heterogeneity, so it is through integration that an aggregate increases in definiteness, of structure and function. But there is still another way in which integration is exemplified. Along with increasing heterogeneity and definiteness of structure and function, the evolution of an aggregate is marked by the increasing subordination of the various functions, with their structures, to the requirements of the general functional activity of the aggregate. In other words, along with growing specialization of parts, there is a growing co-operation of parts, and an ever-increasing mutual dependence among parts. An illustration is furnished by the contrasted facts, that a slightly evolved animal, like a common earthworm, may be cut in two without destroying the life of either part; while a highly evolved animal, like a dog, is destroyed if a single artery is severed, or if any one of the viscera is prevented from discharging its peculiar functions. This third kind of integration is the process through which an evolving aggregate increases in *coherence*. And with this, our definition of the factors which concur in the process of evolution is complete.

We are now prepared to show inductively that wherever, as in organic aggregates, the conditions permit: the integration of matter and concomitant dissipation of motion, which primarily constitutes Evolution, is attended by a continuous change from indefinite, incoherent homogeneity to definite, coherent heterogeneity of structure and function, through successive differentiations and integrations. . . .

Embracing now in one general view the various kinds of transformation exemplified in the present chapter, we find that our survey of organic development completely justifies Mr. Spencer's technical statement: "Evolution is an integration of matter and concomitant dissipation of motion, during which the matter passes from an indefinite, incoherent homogeneity to a definite, coherent heterogeneity; and during which the retained motion undergoes a parallel transformation." [3] . . .

GENESIS OF MAN, MORALLY [4]

There are two things, said Kant, which fill me with awe because of their sublimity—the starry heavens above us, and the moral law within us. From the modern point of view there is interest as well as instruction to be found in the implied antithesis. While in the study of the stellar universe we contemplate the process of evolution on a scale so vast that reason and imagination are alike baffled in the effort to trace out its real significance, and we are overpowered by the sense of the infinity that surrounds us; on the other hand, in the study of the moral sense we contemplate the last and noblest product of evolution which we can ever know, the attribute latest to be unfolded in the development of psychical life, and by the possession of which we have indeed become as gods—knowing the good and the evil. The theorems of astronomy and the theorems of ethics present to us the process of evolution in its extremes of extension and of intension respectively. For although upon other worlds far out in space there may be modes of existence immeasurably transcending humanity, yet these must remain unknowable by us. And while this possibility should be allowed its due weight in restraining us from the vain endeavor to formulate the infinite and eternal Sustainer of the universe in terms of our own human nature, as if the highest symbols intelligible to us were in reality the highest symbols, nevertheless it can in no way influence or modify our science. To us the development of the noblest of human attributes must ever remain the last term in the stupendous series of cosmic changes, of which the development of planetary systems is the first term. And our special synthesis of the phenomena of cosmic evolution, which began by seeking to explain the genesis of the earth and

[3] *First Principles*, p. 396.
[4] Part II, Chap. 22, Vol. IV, pp. 104–52.

its companion worlds, will be fitly concluded when we have offered a
theory of the genesis of those psychical activities whose end is to secure
to mankind the most perfect fullness of life upon this earth, which is
its dwelling place.

The great philosopher whose remark has suggested these reflections
would not, however, have been ready to assent to the interpretation
here given. Though Kant was one of the chief pioneers of the Doctrine
of Evolution, having been the first to propose and to elaborate in
detail the theory of the nebular origin of planetary systems, yet the
conception of a continuous development of life in all its modes,
physical and psychical, was not sufficiently advanced, in Kant's day,
to be adopted into philosophy. Hence in his treatment of the mind,
as regards both intelligence and emotion, Kant took what may be
called a statical view of the subject; and finding in the adult civilized
mind, upon the study of which his systems of psychology and ethics
were founded, a number of organized moral intuitions and an organized moral sense, which urges men to seek the right and to shun the
wrong irrespective of utilitarian considerations of pleasure and pain,
he proceeded to deal with these moral intuitions and this moral sense
as if they were ultimate facts, incapable of being analyzed into simpler
emotional elements. Now, as the following exposition may look like a
defense of utilitarianism, it being really my intention to show that utilitarianism in the deepest and widest sense is the ethical philosophy
imperatively required by the facts, it is well to state, at the outset,
that the existence of a moral sense and moral intuitions in civilized
man is fully granted. It is admitted that civilized man possesses a complex group of emotions, leading him to seek the right and avoid the
wrong, without any reference to considerations of utility—and I disagree entirely with those utilitarian disciples of Locke, who would
apparently refer these ethical emotions to the organization of experiences of pleasure and pain in the case of each individual. So long as
the subject is contemplated from a statical point of view, so long as
individual experience is studied without reference to ancestral experience, the follower of Kant can always hold his ground against the
follower of Locke, in ethics as well as in psychology. When the
Kantian asserts that the intuitions of right and wrong, as well as the
intuitions of time and space, are independent of experience, he occupies a position which is impregnable, so long as the organization of
experiences through successive generations is left out of the discussion.
But already, on two occasions of supreme importance, we have found
the Doctrine of Evolution leading us to a common ground upon which
the disciples of Kant and the disciples of Locke can dwell in peace
together. We have seen that the experience test and the inconceiv-
ability test of truth are, when deeply considered, but the obverse faces

of the same thing. We have seen that there is a standpoint from which the experience theory and the intuition theory of knowledge may be regarded as mutually supplementing each other. We shall presently see, in like manner, that the so-called doctrine of utilitarianism and the doctrine of moral intuitions are by no means so incompatible with one another as may at first appear. As soon as we begin to study the subject dynamically, everything is shown in a new light. Admitting the truth of the Kantian position, that there exists in us a moral sense for analyzing which our individual experience does not afford the requisite data, and which must therefore be regarded as ultimate for each individual, it is nevertheless open to us to inquire into the emotional antecedents of this organized moral sense as exhibited in ancestral types of psychical life. The inquiry will result in the conviction that the moral sense is not ultimate, but derivative, and that it has been built up out of slowly organized experiences of pleasures and pains.

But before we can proceed directly upon the course thus marked out, it is necessary that we should determine what are meant by pleasures and pains. What are the common characteristics, on the one hand, of the states of consciousness which we call pleasures, and, on the other hand, of the states of consciousness which we call pains? According to Sir William Hamilton, "pleasure is a reflex of the spontaneous and unimpeded exertion of a power of whose energy we are conscious; pain is a reflex of the overstrained or repressed exertion of such a power." That this theory, which is nearly identical with that of Aristotle, is inadequate to account for all the phenomena of pleasure and pain, has been, I think, conclusively proved by Mr. Mill. With its complete adequacy, however, we need not now concern ourselves; as we shall presently see that a different though somewhat allied statement will much better express the facts in the case. Hamilton's statement, however inadequate, is illustrated by a number of truths which for our present purpose are of importance. A large proportion of our painful states of consciousness are attendant upon the inaction, or what Hamilton less accurately calls the "repressed exertion," of certain organic functions. According to the character of the functions in question, these painful states are known as cravings or yearnings. Inaction of the alimentary canal, and that molecular inaction due to deficiency of water in the system, are attended by feelings of hunger and thirst, which vary from slight discomfort to intense agony according as the inaction is prolonged. Of kindred character are the acquired cravings for tobacco, alcohol, and other narcotics. Inaction of the muscles causes great discomfort in children who are compelled to sit still, and grown persons feel similar annoyance when the enforced stillness is long enough kept up. Prisoners kept in dark cells soon feel an intense craving for light, which in time becomes scarcely less intolerable than raging hunger. A similar explanation suffices for the emotional yearnings involved in homesickness, ennui, deprivation of the approval of our fellow creatures, or in separation from our favorite pursuits. All these painful states are due to the enforced inaction of certain feelings, social or aesthetic. And in similar wise, as Mr. Spencer observes, the bitter grief attendant upon the death of a friend results from the ideal representation of a future in which certain groups of habitual emotions must remain inactive or unsatisfied by outward expression.

The objection may be made that all this is but an elaborate way of saying that certain pains result from the deprivation of certain pleasures. But since such an objection, in its very statement, recognizes that certain kinds of unimpeded activity, physical or psychical, are pleasures, it need not disturb us, or lead us to underestimate the value of Hamilton's suggestion. Let us note next that excessive action of any function, equally with deficient action, is attended by pain. Local pain results from intensified sensations of heat, light, sound, or pressure; and though it may be in some cases true, as Mr. Spencer asserts, that sweet tastes are not rendered positively disagreeable by any degree of intensity,[5] the alleged fact seems quite contrary to my own experience, and to that of several other persons whom I have questioned. Other local pains, as in inflammation and sundry other forms of disease, are apparently due to increased molecular activity in the parts affected. And the feelings of pain or discomfort, both local and systemic, attendant upon overexercise, overeating, or excessive use of a narcotic, are to be similarly explained.

Thus we may say that pleasure, generally speaking, is "the concomitant of an activity which is neither too small nor too great," and we get at the significance of the Epicurean maxim, μηδὲν ἄγαν. But this doctrine, as already hinted, is by no means complete. For, as Mr. Mill and Mr. Spencer ask, "What constitutes a medium activity? What determines that lower limit of pleasurable action below which there is craving, and that higher limit of pleasurable action above which there is pain?" And furthermore, how happen there to be certain feelings (as among tastes and odors) which are disagreeable in all degrees of intensity, and others that are agreeable in all degrees of intensity? The answer, as Mr. Spencer shows, is to be sought in the study of the past conditions under which feelings have been evolved.

If the tentacles of a polyp are rudely struck by some passing or approaching body, the whole polyp contracts violently in such a manner as to throw itself slightly out of the way; but if a fragment of assimilable food, floating by, happens to touch one of the tentacles gently, the tentacle grasps it and draws it slowly down to the polyp's

[5] Spencer, *Principles of Psychology*, Vol. I, p. 276.

digestive sac. Now, between these contrasted actions there is no such psychical difference as accompanies the similarly contrasted human actions of taking food and ducking the head to avoid a blow; for the polyp's contractions, being simply reflex actions of the lowest sort, are unattended by states of consciousness, either agreeable or disagreeable. Nevertheless, there is one respect in which the two cases perfectly agree. In both cases there is a seeking of that which is beneficial to the organism, and a shunning of that which is injurious. And while, in the case of the polyp, there is no conscious pleasure or pain, we may fairly surmise that, as soon as any animal's psychical life becomes sufficiently complex to be attended by distinct states of consciousness, the presence of that which is beneficial is accompanied by a pleasurable feeling which leads to the seeking of it, while the presence of that which is injurious is accompanied by a painful feeling which leads to the shunning of it. Our surmise is strengthened as we reconsider the human actions lately enumerated, and observe that the abnormal activity of a function, either in deficiency or in excess, is injurious, while the normal activity of a function in balance with its companion functions is beneficial. As Mr. Spencer says, "In a mutually dependent set of organs having a consensus of functions, the very existence of a special organ having its special function implies that the absence of its function must cause disturbance of the consensus—implies, too, that its function may be raised to an excess which must cause disturbance of the consensus—implies, therefore, that maintenance of the consensus goes along with a medium degree of its function." In accordance with this view, we may note that hunger and thirst are feelings attendant upon a kind of functional inaction which is harmful, and even fatal if prolonged; that inaction or excessive action of the muscles is injurious as well as painful; that the intense heat and cold, and the violent pressure, which cause distress, will also cause more or less injury, and may cause death; that the discomfort following repletion and narcosis is the concomitant of a state of things which, if kept up, must end in dyspepsia, or other forms of disease, entailing usually a permanent lowering of nutrition; and that the intense sounds and lights which distress the ear and eye also tend to produce deafness and blindness. And in like manner, the enforced inaction of the social and aesthetic feelings, which is attended by mental discomfort, is also attended in the long run by a diminution of the fullness and completeness of psychical life, which in extreme cases may result in consumption, insanity, or narcotic craving.

It would seem, therefore, that the class of cases upon which Hamilton relied will justify an interpretation much deeper than the one which he proposed for them. They will apparently justify us in asserting that pleasure is a state of consciousness accompanying modes of activity which tend to increase the fullness of life of an organism, while pain is a state of consciousness accompanying modes of activity which tend to diminish the fullness of life. . . .

We are now prepared to deal with the phenomena of right and wrong, and to notice how they become distinguished from the phenomena of pleasure and pain. Though the foregoing discussion forms the basis for a general doctrine of morality, it is nevertheless an inadequate basis, until properly supplemented. The existence of a moral sense has purposely been as far as possible unrecognized—for I believe that in dealing with these complex subjects, little can be accomplished, save on the plan of separately cornering the various elements in the problem, and flooring them one by one. Any philosophy of ethics, therefore, which might be founded upon the preceding analysis, could be nothing more than a theory of hedonism, recognizing no other incentive to proper action than the pleasing of one's self. By one of the innumerable tricks which the misuse of current words plays with the understanding, the so-called utilitarian theory has been, and still is, not unfrequently identified with this kind of hedonistic philosophy, which is in truth its very antipodes. The error is much like that involved in the accusation of fatalism, commonly hurled at those who maintain the obvious and harmless assertion that moral actions conform to law. But the difference, comprising the entire difference between the noblest self-sacrifice and the meanest self-fondling, is as follows: In our theory of pleasure and pain, which if taken as ultimate would be hedonism, the well-being of the community has been as far as possible omitted from the account. Wherever I have introduced references to social phenomena, I have considered them only in their effects upon the fullness of life of the individual. In dealing with the incentives to action in a race of brute animals, the foregoing considerations would be sufficient. But in the so-called utilitarian theory as it is now to be expounded, the well-being of the community, even when incompatible with that of the individual, is the all-important consideration. While the actions deemed pleasurable are those which conduce to the fullness of life of the individual, the actions deemed right are those which conduce to the fullness of life of the community. And while the actions deemed painful are those which detract from the fullness of life of the individual, the actions deemed wrong are those which detract from the fullness of life of the community. According to utilitarianism, therefore, as here expounded, the conduct approved as moral is the disinterested service of the community, and the conduct stigmatized as immoral is the selfish preference of individual interests to those of the community. And bearing in mind that the community, which primevally comprised only the little tribe, has by long-continued social integration come to comprise the entire human race, we have the ultimate theorem of the utilitarian philosophy, as properly understood, that actions morally right are those which are beneficial to humanity, while actions morally wrong are those which are detrimental to humanity.

Are we to maintain, then, that when we approve of certain actions, we do so because we consciously and deliberately reason out, in each particular case, the conclusion that these actions are beneficial to mankind? By no means. Not only is it that the highest science cannot always enable us to say surely of a given action that it is useful to mankind, but it is also that we do not stop to apply science to the matter at all. We approve of certain actions and disapprove of certain actions quite instinctively. We shrink from stealing or lying as we shrink from burning our fingers; and we no more stop to frame the theorem that stealing and lying, if universally practiced, must entail social dissolution and a reversion to primeval barbarism, than we stop to frame the theorem that frequent burning of the fingers must entail an incapacity for efficient manual operations. In short, there is in our psychical structure a moral sense which is as quickly and directly hurt by wrongdoing or the idea of wrongdoing as our tactile sense is hurt by stinging.

Shall we then maintain, as a corollary from the Doctrine of Evolution, that our moral sense is due to the organic registration, through countless ages, of deliberate inferences that some actions benefit humanity, while others injure it? Shall we say that the primeval savage began by reasoning his way to the conclusion that if treachery were to be generally allowed within the limits of the tribe, then the tribe must succumb in the struggle for existence to other tribes in which treachery was forbidden; and that, by a gradual organization of such inductions from experience, our moral sense has slowly arisen? This position is no more tenable than the other. Mr. Richard Hutton and Mr. St. George Mivart would seem to have attributed to Mr. Spencer some such doctrine. But Mr. Spencer is too profound a thinker to ignore so completely the conditions under which permanent emotional states are generated. Our moral sense has arisen in no such way. But to understand the way in which it has arisen, we must recur to our fundamental problem, and seek for the conditions which first enabled social evolution, as distinguished from organic evolution, to start upon its career.

It is now time to propose an answer to the question, already twice suggested and partly answered, How did social evolution originate? Starting from the researches of Sir Henry Maine, which are supported by those of Messrs. Tylor, M'Lennan, and Lubbock, we have come to the conclusion that it originated when families, temporarily organized among all the higher gregarious mammals, became, in the case of the highest mammal, permanently organized. Starting from the deductions of Mr. Wallace, we have seen reason for believing that civilization originated when, in the highest mammal, variations in intelligence became so much more important than variations in physical structure that they began to be seized upon by natural selection to the relative exclusion of the latter. In the permanent family we have the germ of society. In the response to outer relations by psychical changes, which almost completely subordinate physical changes, we have the germ of civilization. Let us now take a step in advance of previous speculation,[6] and see what can be done by combining these two theorems, so that the permanent organization of families and the complex intelligence of the highest mammal will appear in their causal relations to each other.

Many mammals are gregarious, and gregariousness implies incipient power of combination and of mutual protection. But gregariousness differs from sociality by the absence of definitive family relationships, except during the brief and intermittent periods in which there are helpless offspring to be protected. Now it might be maintained that the complex intelligence of the highest mammal led him vaguely to recognize the advantage of associating in more and more permanent groups for the sake of mutual protection. From this point of view Mr. Darwin argues that men were originally a race of weak and mild creatures like chimpanzees, and not a race of strong and ferocious creatures like gorillas, and were accordingly forced to combine because unable to defend themselves singly. It is undeniable that man is, relatively to his size, a weak animal; and there is much value in Mr. Darwin's suggestion, in so far as it goes, to explain the origin of gregariousness among those primates who were the ancestors of man. Nevertheless it can hardly be said to explain sociality as distinguished from gregariousness. It may also be argued that the superior sagacity even of the lowest savage makes him quite a formidable antagonist to animals much more powerful than himself. Besides, the study of savage life brings out results at variance with the notion of man's primitive gentleness. A strong case might be made in support of the statement that uncivilized man is an extremely ferocious animal, and that among savage races, which certainly differ very notably in natural ferocity of disposition, the most ferocious tribes are often the most likely to be-

[6] The latest writer upon these subjects is inclined to give up the problem as insoluble. "I at least find it difficult to conceive of men at all like the present men, unless existing in something like families, that is, in groups avowedly connected, at least on the mother's side, and probably always with a vestige of connection, more or less, on the father's side, and unless these groups were, like many animals, gregarious, under a leader more or less fixed. It is almost beyond imagination how man, as we know man, could by any sort of process have gained this step in civilization." Bagehot, *Physics and Politics*, p. 136.—F.

come dominant and assist social integration by subduing other tribes. The earliest annals of the highest of human races, the Aryan, certainly bear witness to extreme ferocity, checked and determined in its direction by a moral sense further developed than that of savages. While recognizing, therefore, the value of Mr. Darwin's suggestion, so far as it goes, I believe that the true explanation lies much further beneath the surface.

It will be remembered that, in treating of the parallel evolution of the mind and the nervous system, it was shown that the increase of intelligence in complexity and speciality involves a lengthening of the period during which the nervous connections involved in ordinary adjustments are becoming organized. Even if the physical interpretation there given should turn out to be inadequate, the fact remains undeniable that while the nervous connections accompanying a simple intelligence are already organized at birth, the nervous connections accompanying a complex intelligence are chiefly organized after birth. Thus there arise the phenomena of infancy, which are nonexistent among those animals whose psychical actions are purely reflex and instinctive. Infancy, psychologically considered, is the period during which the nerve connections and correlative ideal associations necessary for self-maintenance are becoming permanently established. Now this period, which only begins to exist when the intelligence is considerably complex, becomes longer and longer as the intelligence increases in complexity. In the human race it is much longer than in any other race of mammals, and it is much longer in the civilized man than in the savage.[7] Indeed among the educated classes of civilized society, its average duration may be said to be rather more than a quarter of a century, since during all this time those who are to live by brainwork are simply acquiring the capacity to do so, and are usually supported upon the products of parental labor.

It need not be said that, on the general theory of evolution, the passage from the short infancy of other primates to the relatively long infancy witnessed among the lowest contemporary savages cannot have been a sudden one.[8] But a special reason may be assigned why nature, which never makes long jumps, must have been incapable of making

[7] Possibly there may be a kindred implication in the fact that women attain maturity earlier than men.—F.

[8] In this connection it is interesting to observe that the phenomena of infancy seem to be decidedly more marked in the anthropoid apes than in other nonhuman primates. At the age of one month the orangutan begins to learn to walk, holding on to convenient objects of support, like a human infant. Up to this time it lies on its back, tossing about and examining its hands and feet. A monkey at the same age has reached maturity, so far as locomotion and prehension are concerned. See Mr. Wallace's interesting experience with an infant orangutan in his *Malay Archipelago,* Vol. I, pp. 68–71.—F.

this particular jump. Throughout the animal kingdom the period of infancy is correlated with feelings of parental affection, sometimes confined to the mother, but often shared by the father, as in the case of animals which mate. Where, as among the lower animals, there is no infancy, there is no parental affection. Where the infancy is very short, the parental feeling, though intense while it lasts, presently disappears, and the offspring cease to be distinguished from strangers of the same species. And in general the duration of the feelings which ensure the protection of the offspring is determined by the duration of the infancy. The agency of natural selection in maintaining this balance is too obvious to need illustration. Hence, if long infancies could have suddenly come into existence among a primitive race of apelike men, the race would have quickly perished from inadequate persistence of the parental affections. The prolongation must therefore have been gradual, and the same increase of intelligence to which it was due must also have prolonged the correlative parental feelings, by associating them more and more with anticipations and memories. The concluding phases of this long change may be witnessed in the course of civilization. Our parental affections now endure through life —and while their fundamental instinct is perhaps no stronger than in savages, they are, nevertheless, far more effectively powerful, owing to our far greater power of remembering the past and anticipating the future.

I believe we have now reached a very thorough and satisfactory explanation of the change from gregariousness to sociality. . . .

As already shown in describing the chief characteristics of the evolution of society, the primary cause which has developed sympathy at the expense of the egoistic instincts has been the continued integration of communities, originally mere tribes or clans, into social aggregates of higher and higher orders of complexity. For by this long-continued process the opportunities for the exercise of the altruistic feelings have been necessarily increased in number and frequency of occurrence, while the occasions requiring the exercise of the antisocial feelings have become less frequent, so that the former set of feelings have become strengthened by use, while the latter have become relatively weakened by disuse. Along with this direct and obvious effect of social integration, another effect has been wrought, indirect and less obvious. A high development of sympathy cannot be secured without a high development of representativeness, so closely interrelated are our intellectual and moral natures. A very feeble faculty of imagining objects and relations not present to sense must necessitate an absence of active sympathetic emotion, save in its crudest form. It is a familiar fact that many men are cruel, in word or deed, because they are incapable of adequately representing to themselves the pain, physical or mental, of which they are the cause. The validity of such an interpretation is confirmed by the fact that even where there is a very high representative capacity, the lack of the requisite elements of personal experience will prevent the rise of sympathetic feeling. Thus it is notoriously difficult for strong and healthy people to enter into the feelings of those who are weak and nervous. These facts show that the development of sympathy is largely determined by the development of the representative faculty and by increasing width and variety of experience. With the simplest form of sympathy, such as the painful thrill felt on seeing someone in a dangerous position, contrast such a complex sentiment as the sense of injustice, and it becomes evident that the latter feeling differs from the former mainly in degree and quantity of representativeness. In the former case there is a representation of the injury or death impending over some person immediately in sight; and it is the shrinking from this detriment to the fullness of life of another person which constitutes the sympathetic feeling. In the latter case—supposing, for example, the kind of injustice in question to be that against which English-speaking people have made provision in habeas corpus acts—there is the sympathetic excitement of that highly representative egoistic sentiment known as the love of personal freedom. At first a mere recalcitration against whatever impedes the free action of the limbs, this egoistic feeling has, through increased power of representation, developed into a dislike and dread of whatever possible combination of circumstances may in any way, however remotely, interfere with the fullest legitimate exercise of all the functions of physical and psychical life. To have this complex feeling sympathetically excited for persons whom one has never seen, and who are perhaps yet unborn—and still more, to be so far possessed by this highly generalized and impersonal sympathy as to risk one's own liberty and life in efforts to avert the possible evils which are the objects of its dread—implies a power of representing absent relations such as has yet been acquired by only two or three of the most highly gifted families of mankind. And manifestly the sentiments which respond to the notions of justice and injustice in the abstract are still more remotely representative, still more highly generalized, and still more thoroughly disengaged from the consideration of concrete instances of pleasure and pain.

To this expansion of the power of sympathetically representing feelings detached from the incidents of particular cases, until the sphere of its exercise has become even wider than the human race, and includes all sentient existence, is due our instinctive abhorrence of actions which the organically registered experience of mankind has associated with pain and evil, and our instinctive approval of actions similarly associated with pleasure and increased fullness of life. It is not that, as in intellectual progress, there has been a registration of inferences, at first conscious, but finally automatic; but it is that there has been a registration of feelings respectively awakened by pleasure-giving and pain-giving actions. And just as men's intellectual conceptions of the causes of phenomena become more and more impersonal as they are extended over wider and wider groups of phenomena, generating at last an abstract conception of Universal Cause, so free from the element of personality that to less cultivated minds it seems atheistic; so in like manner, as the sympathetic feelings are extended over wider and wider areas, no longer needing the stimulus of present pains and pleasures to call them forth, they generate at last an abstract moral sense, so free from the element of personality that to grosser minds it is unintelligible. The savage cannot understand the justice which he sees among Europeans, and the mercy of the white man is ascribed by him to imbecility or fear. To him some personal end seems necessary as an incentive to action. But the philanthropist finds an adequate incentive in the contemplation of injustice in the abstract.

Thus the ethical theories, as well as the psychology, of the schools of Hume and Kant, appear to be reconciled in the deeper synthesis rendered possible by the theory of evolution. On the one hand, it is a corollary from the laws of life that actions desired by the individual and approved by the community must in the long run be those which tend to heighten the life respectively of the individual and of the community. And on the other hand, it is equally true that there is a highly complex feeling, the product of a slow emotional evolution, which prompts us to certain lines of conduct irrespective of any conscious estimate of pleasures or utilities. . . .

. . . In asserting that we possess an instinctive and inherited moral sense, it is not meant that we possess, anterior to education and experience, an organic preference for certain particular good actions, and an organic repugnance to certain particular bad actions. We do not inherit a horror of stealing, any more than the Hindu inherits the horror of killing cattle. We simply inherit a feeling which leads us, when we are told that stealing is wrong, to shun it, without needing to be taught that it is detrimental to society. . . .

. . . In no department of inquiry is the truth and grandeur of the Doctrine of Evolution more magnificently illustrated than in the province of ethics. . . .

COSMIC THEISM [9]

. . . Although the construction of a theology, or science of Deity, is a task which exceeds the powers of human intelligence, there is nevertheless one supreme important theorem in which science and religion find their permanent reconciliation, and by the assertion of

[9] Part III, Chap. 3, Vol. IV, pp. 232–38.

which the mind is brought into a positive attitude of faith with reference to the Inscrutable Power manifested in the universe. The outcome of the present argument is not atheism or positivism, but a phase of theism which is higher and purer, because relatively truer, than the anthropomorphic phase defended by theologians.

This all-important theorem in which science and religion are reconciled is neither more nor less than the theorem which alone gives complete expression to the truth that all knowledge is relative. In the first chapter of this work it was elaborately proved that as soon as we attempt to frame any hypothesis whatever concerning the Absolute, or that which exists out of relation to our consciousness, we are instantly checkmated by alternative impossibilities of thought, and when we seek to learn why this is so, we are taught by a psychologic analysis that, from the very organization of our minds, and by reason of the very process by which intelligence has been evolved, we can form no cognition into which there do not enter the elements of *likeness, difference,* and *relation*—so that the Absolute, as presenting none of these elements, is utterly and forever unknowable. Translating this conclusion into more familiar language, we found it to mean, first, "that the Deity, in so far as absolute and infinite, is inscrutable by us, and that every hypothesis of ours concerning its nature and attributes can serve only to illustrate our mental impotence," and, secondly, "that the universe in itself is likewise inscrutable; that the vast synthesis of forces without us, which in manifold contact with us is from infancy till the close of life continually arousing us to perceptive activity, can never be known by us as it exists objectively, but only as it affects our consciousness."

These are the closely allied conclusions which were reached in our opening discussion. But since such abstruse theorems need to be taken one by one into the mind, and allowed one after the other to dwell there for a while, in order to be duly comprehended, it did not then seem desirable to encumber the exposition with any reference to the third statement in which these two are made to unite; nor, indeed, would it have been possible to illustrate adequately this third statement until we had defined our position in relation to the questions of phenomenality, of causation and deanthropomorphization, of the persistence of force, and of the evolution of the phenomenal world. But now, having obtained definite conclusions upon these points, we are at last enabled to present the case as a whole. Having seen that in certain senses the Deity and the Cosmos are alike inscrutable, let us now see if there is any sense in which it may be legitimately said that the Unknowable contained in our first theorem is identical with the Unknowable contained in our second theorem.

Upon what grounds did we assert the unknowableness of Deity? We were driven to the conclusion that Deity is unknowable, because that which exists independently of intelligence and out of relation to it, which presents neither *likeness, difference,* nor *relation,* cannot be cognized. Now, by precisely the same process, we were driven to the conclusion that the Cosmos is unknowable, only in so far as it is absolute. It is only as existing independently of our intelligence and out of relation to it, that we can predicate unknowableness of the Cosmos. As manifested to our intelligence, the Cosmos is the world of phenomena—the realm of the knowable. We know stars and planets, we know the surface of our earth, we know life and mind in their various manifestations, individual and social. But as we have seen, this vast aggregate of phenomena exists as such only in relation to our intelligence. Its *esse* is *percipi.* To this extent we have gone with Berkeley. But underlying this aggregate of phenomena, to whose extension we know no limit in space or time, we have found ourselves compelled to postulate an Absolute Reality—a Something whose existence does not depend on the presence of a percipient mind, which existed before the genesis of intelligence, and would continue to exist though all intelligence were to vanish from the scene. Without making such a postulate, we concluded that it would be impossible to frame any theory whatever, either of subjective or of objective phenomena. Thus the theorem of the relativity of knowledge, when fully expressed, asserts that there exists a Something, of which all phenomena, as presented in consciousness, are manifestations, but concerning which we can know nothing save through its manifestations.

. . . There exists a Power, to which no limit in time or space is conceivable, of which all phenomena, as presented in consciousness, are manifestations, but which we can know only through these manifestations. Here is a formula legitimately obtained by the employment of scientific methods, as the last result of a subjective analysis on the one hand, and of an objective analysis on the other hand. Yet this formula, which presents itself as the final outcome of a purely scientific inquiry, expresses also the fundamental truth of theism—the truth by which religious feeling is justified. The existence of God—the supreme truth asserted alike by Christianity and by inferior historic religions—is asserted with equal emphasis by that Cosmic philosophy which seeks its data in science alone. . . .

BIBLIOGRAPHY

FISKE, John, *The Writings of John Fiske.* Boston: Riverside Press, 1902, 24 vols.

_____ *Outlines of Cosmic Philosophy Based on the Doctrine of Evolution:*

With Criticisms on the Positive Philosophy. Boston: Houghton Mifflin, 1874.

——— *A Century of Science and Other Essays.* Boston: Houghton Mifflin, 1899.

——— *Excursions of an Evolutionist.* Boston: Houghton Mifflin, 1884.

——— *Through Nature to God.* Boston: Houghton Mifflin, 1899.

——— *Darwinism and Other Essays.* Boston: Houghton Mifflin, 1879.

——— *The Letters of John Fiske,* ed. by Ethel F. Fisk. New York: Macmillan Co., 1940.

BERMAN, Milton, *John Fiske: The Evolution of a Popularizer.* Cambridge: Harvard U. Press, 1961.

CLARK, John Spencer, *The Life and Letters of John Fiske.* Boston: Houghton Mifflin, 1917, 2 vols.

PANILL, H. Burnell, *The Religious Faith of John Fiske.* Durham, N.C.: Duke U. Press, 1957.

ROYCE, Josiah, "John Fiske as a Thinker." *Harvard Graduates Magazine,* Vol. X (1901–02), pp. 23–33.

WIENER, Philip, *Evolution and the Founders of Pragmatism.* Cambridge: Harvard U. Press, 1949. Chap. on Fiske.

Chauncey Wright

[1830–1875]

"If the power of analytic intellect pure and simple could suffice, the name of Chauncey Wright would assuredly be as famous as it is now obscure"[1]—so wrote William James of his friend and colleague. Wright never published a systematic work in philosophy, except for a few scattered articles and reviews in the *North American Review*, the *New York Evening Post*, and the *Nation*. He did not hold any regular academic position, except a year at Harvard in mathematical physics in 1874, just prior to his death. Yet James' judgment of Wright's keen critical ability was shared by others who knew him at Cambridge. Wright was born in Northampton, attended Harvard College, worked for many years as a mathematician in astronomy, and later became recording secretary of the American Academy of Arts and Sciences. Wright's main contributions to American philosophy probably can be traced to his membership in the Metaphysical Club, a small group of men—including William James, Charles Peirce, John Fiske, and Oliver Wendell Holmes, Jr.—who gathered for philosophical discussion in and about Cambridge. Peirce called Wright the "strongest member" of the group and "our boxing master." His influence on those about him was Socratic, in the sense that it was the spoken

rather than the written word which was the true mark of his talent.

Wright was a firm defender of Darwin's theory of evolution, which he thought a model of scientific explanation. The influence of Darwin on Wright's thought can be seen in his essay, *Evolution by Natural Selection* (1877). But Wright was also a critic of attempts to go beyond evolution as a scientific hypothesis, or to convert Darwinism into a theistic interpretation of the universe (such as Fiske's). Thus, he attacked grandiose metaphysical and teleological speculations. Wright suggested instead as possible the doctrine of "tychism," which attributed the evolution of the universe to "cosmic weather," not to final causes. This idea is put forward by Wright in his essay, *The Limits of Natural Selection* (1870). Wright's longest essay, *Evolution of Self-Consciousness* (1873), although often obscure in style and allusion, is highly suggestive, and a portion is reproduced below. Here Wright attempts to give an account of self-consciousness in terms of evolution from natural biological capacities. This essay is also suggestive of James' later doctrine of "pure experience" in which there is no sharp dualism between subject and object. What is especially interesting is Wright's anticipation of many of Peirce's and Mead's ideas

[1] *Collected Essays and Reviews*, New York: Longmans, Green, 1920, p. 20.

concerning the development of "mind" out of sign behavior and language.

In Wright's writings one finds ideas that were later to become central to pragmatism and positivism. He holds, for instance, a form of the principle of verifiability—ideas are to be tested by sensory observation— and of the principle of pragmatism— hypotheses are confirmed by reference to consequences. He emphasizes the need for ridding metaphysics of linguistic confusion, and he defends scientific objectivity in knowledge. Wright was influenced by Mill, Whewell, Bacon, and Comte; but he went beyond them by giving a decided experimental bent to empiricism. In Wright's *A Fragment on Cause and Effect* (1873), reprinted below, and in the opening pages of his *The Philosophy of Herbert Spencer* (1865), which is here entitled *On Science*, we find a powerful, early statement of the philosophy of experimentalism.

EVOLUTION BY NATURAL SELECTION [2]

The physical problem, proposed independently and almost simultaneously near the beginning of this century by three eminent men of genius, Goethe, Geoffroy St. Hilaire, and the elder Darwin, *how* animals and plants came to have the structures and habits that characterize them as distinct species, this question which was proposed in place of the teleological inquiry, *why* they were so produced, has now fairly become a simple question for scientific investigation. There is no longer any doubt that this effect was by some natural process, and was not by a formless creative fiat. Moreover, there scarcely remains any doubt that this natural process connects the living forms of the present with very different forms in the past; and that this connection is properly described in general terms as "descent with modification." The question has thus become narrowed down to the inquiry, What is the nature of this modification, or what are the causes and the modes of action by which such modifications have been effected?

This is a great step in scientific progress. So long as a doubt remained about the fact that such modifications have been effected, and that present living forms are the results of them, the inquiry, how they were effected, belonged to the region of profitless speculation— profitless except for this, that speculative minds, boldly laying aside doubts which perplex and impede others, and anticipating their solution, have often in the history of science, by preparing a way for further progress, greatly facilitated their actual solution. Difficulties

[2] From the *North American Review*, July, 1872. Reprinted in *Philosophical Discussion*, ed. by C. E. Norton, New York: Henry Holt, 1877, pp. 168–71.

and questions lying beyond such doubts—walls to scale after outworks and ditches are passed—do not inspire the cautious with courage. And so the scientific world waited, though prepared with ample force of evidence, and hesitated to take the step which would bring it face to face with the questions of the present and the future. Darwin's *Origin of Species*, by marshaling and largely reinforcing the evidences of evolution, and by candidly estimating the opposing evidence, and still more by pointing out a way to the solution of the greatest difficulty, gave the signal and the word of encouragement which effected a movement that had long been impending.

The "that," the fact of evolution, may be regarded as established. The "how," the theory or explanation of it, is the problem immediately before us. Its solution will require many years of patient investigation, and much discussion may be anticipated, which will doubtless sometimes degenerate into acrimonious disputes, more especially in the immediate future, while what may be called the dialectics of the subject are being developed, and while the bearings and the limits of views and questions are being determined, and conceptions and definitions and kinds of arguments appropriate to the discussion, are the subjects on which it is necessary to come to a common understanding. It is highly desirable that this discussion should be as free as possible from mere personalities, and there is strong hope that it may be kept so through the manners and methods of procedure established by means of the experience which the history of modern science affords. That it is impossible, however, to avoid errors of this sort altogether, is evident from the provocations experienced and keenly felt by some of the noblest of modern students of science in the establishment of theories in modern astronomy, and of theories in geology, to which may now be added the theory of evolution. That the further discussion of rival hypotheses on the causes and modes of evolution will profit by these older examples may be hoped, since there have grown up general methods of investigation and discussion, which prescribe limits and precautions for hypothesis and inference, and establish rules for the conduct of debate on scientific subjects, that have been of the greatest value to the progress of science, and will, if faithfully observed, doubtless direct the present discussion to a successful issue.

These methods are analogous in their purposes to the general rules in courts of law, and constitute the principles of method in experimental philosophy, or in philosophy founded on the sciences of observation. They serve to protect an investigation, by demanding that it shall be allowed on certain pretty strict conditions (in the conduct of experiments and observations, and in the formation and verification of hypotheses) to proceed without hindrance from prejudice for any existing doctrine or opinion. An investigation may thus start from the simplest basis of experience, and, for this purpose, may waive, yet without denying, any presumption or conclusion held in existing theories or doctrines. Again, these rules protect an investigation from a one-sided criticism or ex parte judgment, since they demand of the criticism or judgment the same judicial attitude that is demanded of the investigation. Advocacy, and especially the sort that is of essential value in courts of law, where two advocates are set against each other, each with the duty of presenting only what can be said for his own side, and where the same judge and jury are bound to hear both, is singularly out of place in a scientific discussion, unless in oral debate before the tribunal of a scientific society. Moreover, there are no burdens of proof in science. Such advocacy in a published work claiming scientific consideration is almost an offense against the proprieties of such discussions. To collect together in one place all that can be said for an hypothesis, and in another all that can be said against it, is at best a clumsy and inconvenient method of discussion, the natural results of which may best be seen in the present condition of theological and religious doctrines. These practical considerations are of the utmost importance for the attainment of the end of scientific pursuit; which is not to arrive at decisions or judgments that are probably true, but is the discovery of the real truths of nature, for which science can afford to wait, and for which suspended judgments are the soundest substitutes.

No work of science, ancient or modern, dealing with problematic views and doctrines, has more completely conformed to these principles, or more fully justified them by its success, than the *Origin of Species*. For its real or principal success has been in convincing nearly all naturalists, a majority of whom, at least, were still unconvinced, of the truth of the theory of evolution; and this has resulted from its obvious fairness and spirit of caution almost as much as from the preponderance of the evidences for the theory when thus presented. And the very same qualities of spirit and method governed the leading and more strictly original design of the work, which cannot, however, yet be said to be a complete success, namely, the *explanation* of evolution by natural selection. That Mr. Darwin himself is fully convinced of the truth of this explanation is sufficiently evident. He holds that natural selection is the principal or leading cause in determining the changes and diversities of species, though not the only cause of the development of their characters. Conspicuously at the close of the Introduction in the first edition of the work, and in all subsequent editions, occur these words: "I am convinced that Natural Selection has been the most important, but not the exclusive, means of modification." That the work is not a merely dialectical performance is clear; and it is equally clear that in proportion to the strength of the author's conviction is his solicitude to give full and just weight to all valid objections to it. In this respect the work stands in marked contrast to much that has been written on the subject and in reply to it. . . .

EVOLUTION OF SELF-CONSCIOUSNESS [3]

It has come to be understood, and very generally allowed, that the conception of the origin of man as an animal race, as well as the origin of individual men within it, in accordance with the continuity of organic development maintained in the theory of evolution, does not involve any very serious difficulties, or difficulties so great as are presented by any other hypothesis of this origin, not excepting that of "special creation"; if that can be properly called a hypothesis, which is, in fact, a resumption of all the difficulties of natural explanation, assuming them to be insuperable and summarizing them under a single positive name. Yet in this evolution, the birth of self-consciousness is still thought by many to be a step not following from antecedent conditions in "nature," except in an incidental manner, or in so far only as "natural" antecedents have prepared the way for the "supernatural" advent of the self-conscious soul. . . .

. . . A sketch only is attempted in this essay of some of the results of . . . an examination into the psychological conditions, or antecedents, of the phenomena of self-consciousness; an examination which does not aim at diminishing, on the one hand, the real contrasts of mental powers in men and animals, nor at avoiding difficulties, on the other, by magnifying them beyond the reach of comparison.

The terms "science" and "scientific" have come, in modern times, to have so wide a range of application, and so vague a meaning, that (like many other terms, not only in common speech, but also in philosophy and in various branches of learning, which have come down to us through varying usages) they would oppose great difficulties to any attempts at defining them by genus and difference, or otherwise than by enumerating the branches of knowledge and the facts, or relations of the facts, to which usage has affixed them as names. Precision in proper definition being then impossible, it is yet possible to give to these terms so general a meaning as to cover all the knowledge to which they are usually applied, and still to exclude much besides. As the terms thus defined coincide with what I propose to show as the character of the knowledge peculiar to men, or which distinguishes the

[3] From the *North American Review*, April, 1873. Reprinted in *Philosophical Discussions*, pp. 199–266.

minds of men from those of other animals, I will begin with this definition. In science and in scientific facts there is implied a conscious purpose of including particular facts under general facts, and the less general under the more general ones. Science, in the modern use of the term, consists, essentially, of a knowledge of things and events either as effects of general causes, or as instances of general classes, rules, or laws; or even as isolated facts of which the class, law, rule, or cause is sought. The conscious purpose of arriving at general facts and at an adequate statement of them in language, or of bringing particular facts under explicit general ones, determines for any knowledge a scientific character.

Many of our knowledges and judgments from experience in practical matters are not so reduced, or sought to be reduced, to explicit principles, or have not a theoretical form, since the major premises, or general principles, of our judgments are not consciously generalized by us in forms of speech. Even matters not strictly practical, or which would be merely theoretical in their bearing on conduct, if reduced to a scientific form, like many of the judgments of common sense, for example, are not consciously referred by us to explicit principles, though derived, like science, from experience, and even from special kinds of experience, like that of a man of business or that of a professional adept. We are often led by being conscious of a sign of anything to believe in the existence of the thing itself, either past, present, or prospective, without having any distinct and general apprehension of the connection of the sign and thing, or any recognition of the sign under the general character of a sign. Not only are the judgments of common sense in men, both the inherited and acquired ones, devoid of heads, or major premises (such as "All men are mortal"), in deductive inference, and devoid also of distinctly remembered details of experience in the inferences of induction, but it is highly probable that this is all but exclusively the character of the knowledges and judgments of the lower animals. Language, strictly so-called, which some of these animals also have, or signs *purposely used* for communication, is not only required for scientific knowledge, but a second step of generalization is needed, and is made through reflection, by which this use of a sign is itself made an object of attention, and the sign is recognized in its general relations to what it signifies, and to what it has signified in the past, and will signify in the future. It is highly improbable that such a knowledge of knowledge, or such a *re*-cognition, belongs in any considerable, or effective, degree to even the most intelligent of the lower animals, or even to the lowest of the human race. This is what is properly meant by being "rational," or being a "rational animal." It is what I have preferred to call "scientific" knowledge; since the growing vagueness and breadth of application common to all ill-comprehended words (like "Positivism" in recent times) have given to "scientific" the meaning probably attached at first to "rational." This knowledge comes from reflecting on what we know in the common-sense, or semi-instinctive form, or making what we know a field of renewed research, observation, and analysis in the generalization of major premises. The line of distinction between such results of reflection, or between scientific knowledge and the common-sense form of knowledge, is not simply the dividing line between the minds of men and those of other animals; but is that which divides the knowledge produced by outward attention from that which is further produced by reflective attention. The former, throughout a considerable range of the higher intelligent animals, involves veritable judgments of a complex sort. It involves combinations of minor premises leading to conclusions through implicit major premises in the enthymematic reasonings, commonly employed in inferences from signs, and likelihoods, as in prognostications of the weather, or in orientations with many animals. This knowledge belongs both to men and to the animals next to men in intelligence, though in unequal degrees.

So far as logicians are correct in regarding an enthymeme as a reasoning, independently of its statement in words; or in regarding as a rational process the passing from such a sign as the human nature of Socrates to the inference that he will die, through the data of experience concerning the mortality of other men—data which are neither distinctly remembered in detail nor generalized explicitly in the formula, "all men are mortal," but are effective only in making mortality a more or less clearly understood part of the human nature, that is, in making it one of the attributes suggested by the name "man," yet not separated from the essential attributes by the contrasts of subject and attributes in real predication—so far, I say, as this can be regarded as a reasoning, or a rational process, so far observation shows that the more intelligent dumb animals reason, or are rational. But this involves great vagueness or want of that precision in the use of signs which the antitheses of essential and accidental attributes and that of proper predication secure. There is little or no evidence to show that the animals which learn, to some extent, to comprehend human speech have an analytical comprehension of real general propositions, or of propositions in which both subject and predicate are general terms and differ in meaning. A merely verbal general proposition, declaring only the equivalence of two general names, might be comprehended by such minds, if it could be made of sufficient interest to attract their attention. But this is extremely doubtful, and it would not be as a *proposition*, with its contrasts of essential and added elements of conception, that it would be comprehended. It would be, in effect, only repeating in succession two general names of the same class of objects. Such minds could, doubtless, comprehend a single class of objects, or an indefinite number of resembling things by several names; that is, several signs of such a class would recall it to their thoughts, or revive a representative image of it; and they would thus be aware of the equivalence of these signs; but they would not attach precision of meaning and different degrees of generality to them, or regard one name as the name or sign of another name; as when we define a triangle to be a rectilinear figure, and a figure of three sides.

Only one degree of generality is, however, essential to inference from signs, or in enthymematic reasoning. Moreover, language in its relation to thought does not consist exclusively of spoken, or written, or imagined words, but of signs in general, and, essentially, of internal images or successions of images, which are the representative imaginations of objects and their relations; imaginations which severally stand for each and all of the particular objects or relations of a *kind*. Such are the visual imaginations called up by spoken or written concrete general names of visible objects, as "dog" or "tree"; which are vague and feeble as images, but effective as notative, directive, or guiding elements in thought. These are the internal signs of things and events, and are instruments of thought in judgment and reasoning, not only with dumb animals but also with men, in whom they are supplemented, rather than supplanted, by names. But being of feeble intensity, and little under the influence of distinct attention or control of the will, compared to actual perceptions and to the voluntary movements of utterance and gesture, their nature has been but dimly understood even by metaphysicians, who are still divided into two schools in logic—the conceptualists and the nominalists. The "concepts" of the former are really composed of these vague and feeble notative images, or groups of images, to which clearness and distinctness of attention are given by their associations with outward (usually vocal) signs. Hence a second degree of observation and generalization upon these images, as objects in reflective thought, cannot be readily realized independently of what would be the results of such observations, namely, their associations with outward signs. Even in the most intelligent dumb animal they are probably so feeble that they cannot be associated with outward signs in such a manner as to make these distinctly appear as substitutes, or signs equivalent to them.

So far as images act in governing trains of thought and reasoning, they act as signs; but, with reference to the more vivid outward signs, they are, in the animal mind, merged in the things signified, like stars in the light of the sun. Hence, language, in its narrower sense, as the instrument of reflective thought, appears to depend directly on the intensity of significant, or representative, images; since the power to attend to these and intensify them still further, at the same time that an equivalent outward sign is an object of attention, would appear to depend solely on the relative intensities of the two states, or on the relations of intensity in perception and imagination, or in original and revived impressions. The direct power of attention to intensify a revived impression in imagination does not appear to be different in kind from the power of attention in perception, or in outward impressions generally. But this direct power would be obviously aided by the indirect action of attention when fixed by an outward sign, provided attention could be directed to both at the same time; as a single glance may comprehend in one field of view the moon or the brighter planets and the sun, since the moon or planet is not hidden like the stars, by the glare of day.

As soon, then, as the progress of animal intelligence through an extension of the range in its powers of memory, or in revived impressions, together with a corresponding increase in the vividness of these impressions, has reached a certain point (a progress in itself useful, and therefore likely to be secured in some part of nature, as one among its numerous grounds of selection, or lines of advantage), it becomes possible for such an intelligence to fix its attention on a vivid outward sign, without losing sight of, or dropping out of distinct attention, an image or revived impression; which latter would only serve, in case of its spontaneous revival in imagination, as a sign of the same thing or the same event. Whether the vivid outward sign be a real object or event, of which the revived image is the counterpart, or whether it be a sign in a stricter meaning of the term—that is, some action, figure, or utterance, associated either naturally or artificially with all similar objects or events, and, consequently, with the revived and representative image of them—whatever the character of this outward sign may be, provided the representative image, or inward sign, still retains, in distinct consciousness, its power as such, then the outward sign may be consciously recognized as a substitute for the inward one, and a consciousness of simultaneous internal and external suggestion, or significance, might be realized; and the contrast of thoughts and things, at least in their power of suggesting that of which they may be coincident signs, could, for the first time, be perceptible. This would plant the germ of the distinctively human form of self-consciousness. . . .

When a thought, or an outward expression acts in an animal's mind or in a man's in the capacity of a sign, it carries forward the movements of a train, and directs attention away from itself to what it signifies or suggests; and consciousness is concentrated on the latter. But being sufficiently vivid in itself to engage distinct attention, it determines a new kind of action, and a new faculty of observation, of which the cerebral hemispheres appear to be the organs. From the action of these, in their more essential powers in memory and imagination, the objects or materials of reflection are also derived. Reflection would thus be, not what most metaphysicians appear to regard it, a fundamentally new faculty in man, as elementary and primordial as memory itself, or the power of abstractive attention, or the function of signs and representative images in generalization; but it would be determined in its contrasts with other mental faculties by the nature of its objects. On its subjective side it would be composed of the same mental faculties—namely, memory, attention, abstraction—as those which are employed in the primary use of the senses. It would be engaged upon what these senses have furnished to memory; but would act as independently of any orders of grouping and succession presented by them, as the several senses themselves do of one another. To this extent, reflection is a distinct faculty, and though, perhaps, not peculiar to man, is in him so prominent and marked in its effects on the development of the individual mind, that it may be regarded as his most essential and elementary mental distinction in kind. For differences of degrees in causes may make differences of kinds in effects. . . .

The outward physical aids of reflective thought, in the articulating powers of the voice, do not appear to have been firmly implanted, with the new faculty of self-consciousness, among the instincts of human nature; and this, at first sight, might seem to afford an argument against the acquisition by a natural process of any form of instinct, since vocal language has probably existed as long as any useful or effective exercise or reflection in men. That the faculty which uses the voice in language should be inherited, while its chief instrument is still the result of external training in an art, or that language should be "half instinct and half art," would, indeed, on second thought, be a paradox on any other hypothesis but that of natural selection. But this is an economical process, and effects no more than what is needed. If the instinctive part in language is sufficient to prompt the invention and the exercise of the art,[4] then the inheritance of instinctive powers of articulation would be superfluous, and would not be effected by selection; but would only come in the form of inherited effects of habit—the form in which the different degrees of aptitude for the education of the voice appear to exist in different races of men. Natural selection would not effect anything, indeed, for men which art and intelligence could, and really do, effect —such as clothing their backs in cold climates with hair or fur— since this could be quite superfluous under the furs of other animals with which art has already clothed them. The more instinctive language

[4] In the origin of the languages of civilized peoples, the distinction between powers of tradition, or *external inheritance,* and proper invention in art becomes a very important one, as will be shown farther on.—W.

of gestures appears also to have only indirect relations to real service-
ableness, or to the grounds of natural selection, and to depend on the
inherited effects of habit, and on universal principles of mental and
physiological action.[5]

The language of gestures may, however, have been sufficient for
the realization of the faculty of self-consciousness in all that the
metaphysician regards as essential to it. The primitive man might, by
pointing to himself in a meditative attitude, have expressed in effect
to himself and others the "I think," which was to be, in the regard of
many of his remote descendants, the distinguishing mark, the outward
emblem, of his essential separation from his nearest kindred and
progenitors, of his metaphysical distinction from all other animals.
This consciousness and expression would more naturally have been
a source of proud satisfaction to the primitive men themselves, just
as children among us glory most in their first imperfect command of
their unfolding powers, or even in accomplishments of a unique and
individual character when first acquired. To the civilized man of the
present time, there is more to be proud of in the immeasurable consequences of this faculty, and in what was evolved through the continued subsequent exercise of it, especially through its outward
artificial instruments in language—consequences not involved in the
bare faculty itself. As being the prerequisite condition of these uses
and inventions, it would, if of an ultimate and underived nature, be
worthy the distinction, which, in case it is referable to latent natures
in pre-existing faculties, must be accorded to them in their higher
degrees. And if these faculties are common to all the more intelligent
animals, and are, by superior degrees only, made capable of higher
functions, or effects of a new and different kind (as longer fins enable
a fish to fly), then the main qualitative distinction of the human race
is to be sought for in these effects, and chiefly in the invention and use
of artificial language.

This invention was, doubtless, at first made by men from social
motives, for the purpose of making known to one another, by means
of arbitrarily associated and voluntary signs, the wishes, thoughts, or
intentions clearly determined upon in their imaginations. Even now,
children invent words, or, rather, attribute meanings to the sounds
they can command, when they are unable to enunciate the words of
the mother tongue which they desire for the purposes of communication. It is, perhaps, improper to speak of this stage of language as
determined by conscious invention through a recognized motive, and
for a *purpose* in the subjective sense of this word. It is enough for a
purpose (in its objective sense) to be served, or for a service to be

[5] See Darwin's *Expression of the Emotions in Man and Animals.*—W.

done, by such arbitrary associations between internal and external language, or thought and speech, however these ties may, in the first instance, be brought about. The intention and the invention become, however, conscious acts in reflection when the secondary motives to the use of language begin to exert influence, and perhaps before the latter have begun to be reflectively known, or recognized, and while they are still acting as they would in a merely animal mind. These motives are the needs and desires (or, rather, the use and importance) of making our thoughts clearer to ourselves, and not merely of communicating them to others. Uncertainty, or perplexity from failures of memory or understanding, render the mnemonic uses of vivid external and voluntary signs the agents of important services to reflective thought, when these signs are already possessed, to some extent, for the purposes of communication. These two uses of language—the social, and the meditative or mnemonic—carried to only a slight development, would afford the means of recognizing their own values, as well as the character of the inventions of which languages would be seen to consist. Invention in its true sense, as a reflective process, would then act with more energy in extending the range of language.

Command of language is a much more efficient command of thought in reflective processes than that which is implied in the simplest form of self-consciousness. It involves a command of memory to a certain degree. Already a mental power, usually accounted a simple one, and certainly not involved in "I think," or only in its outward consequences, has been developed in the power of the will over thought. Voluntary memory, or reminiscence, is especially aided by command of language. This is a tentative process, essentially similar to that of a search for a lost or missing external object. Trials are made in it to revive a missing mental image, or train of images, by means of words; and, on the other hand, to revive a missing name by means of mental images, or even by other words. It is not certain that this power is an exclusively human one, as is generally believed, except in respect to the high degree of proficiency attained by men in its use. It does not appear impossible that an intelligent dog may be aided by its attention, purposely directed to spontaneous memories, in recalling a missing fact, such as the locality of a buried bone.

In the earlier developments of language, and while it is still most subject to the caprices and facilities of individual wills (as in the nursery), the character of it as an invention, or system of inventions, is, doubtless, more clearly apparent than it afterwards becomes, when a third function of language rises into prominence. Traditions, by means of language, and customs, fixed by its conservative power, tend, in turn, to give fixity to the conventions of speech; and the customs and associations of language itself begin to prescribe rules for its inventions, or to set limits to their arbitrary adoption. Individual wills lose their power to decree changes in language; and, indeed, at no time are individual wills unlimited agents in this process. Consent given on grounds not always consciously determining it, but common to the many minds which adopt proposals or obey decrees in the inventions of words, is always essential to the establishment or alteration of a language. But as soon as a language has become too extensive to be the possible invention of any single mind, and is mainly a tradition, it must appear to the barbarian's imagination to have a will of its own; or, rather, sounds and meanings must appear naturally bound together, and to be the fixed names and expressions of wills in things. And later, when complex grammatical forms and abstract substantive names have found their way into languages, they must appear like the very laws and properties of nature itself, which nothing but magical powers could alter; though magic, with its power over the will, might still be equal to the miracle. Without this power, not even a sovereign's will could oppose the authority of language in its own domain. Even magic had failed when an emperor could not alter the gender of a noun. Education had become the imperial power, and schoolmasters were its prime ministers.

From this point in the development of language, its separations into the *varieties* of dialects, the divergences of these into *species*, or distinct languages, and the affinities of them as grouped by the glossologist into *genera* of languages, present precise parallels to the developments and relations in the organic world which the theory of natural selection supposes. It has been objected [6] to the completeness of these parallels that the process of development in languages is still under the control of men's wills. Though an individual will may have but little influence on it, yet the general consent to a proposed change is still a voluntary action, or is composed of voluntary actions on the part of the many, and hence is essentially different from the choice in natural selection, when acting within its proper province. To this objection it may be replied, that a general consent to a change, or even an assent to the reasons for it, does not really constitute a voluntary act in respect to the whole language itself; since it does not involve in itself any intention on the part of the many to change the language. Moreover, the conscious intention of effecting a change on the part of the individual author, or speaker, is not the agent by which the change is effected; or is only an incidental cause, no more essential to the process than the causes which produce variations are to the process of natural selection in species. . . .

---

[6] See article on "Schleicher and the Physical Theory of Language," in Professor W. D. Whitney's *Oriental and Linguistic Studies.*—W.

ON CAUSE AND EFFECT [7]

"Thought is a secretion of the brain" was the announcement of a distinguished naturalist and physiologist, which excited strong aversion to those studies and views of nature which could thus degrade, as it appeared to do, the dignity of so important a function of life. What was probably meant, however, by the saying, is the physiological truth that the brain is the organ of thought in a manner analogous to that in which a gland is the organ of secretions, or a muscle of contractions, or the heart and vascular system of circulations. Thought no more resembles a secretion, however, than this resembles a contraction, or than either of these resembles the movements and effects of circulation; not so much, indeed, as these three resemble each other; yet, like all these three kinds of action, it is dependent, as physiological investigations show, on the intimate structure and vital activity of a special tissue, and its living arrangements and special changes in the brain. It is altogether likely that this is what was meant, and all that was meant, by the somewhat sinister and disagreeable observation that "thought is a secretion of the brain." Men of science sometimes resort to paradoxes, figures of speech, concrete ways of stating truths in science, which those who are ignorant of the science and its real ground of evidence, but imagine that they can judge of its conclusions, are almost sure to misunderstand. Irony is not a more dangerous figure than such a use of comparisons and illustrative figures of speech. Men of science are supposed, except by other men of science, to be literal and exact, and unlike poets, in all their utterances, and when, as Professor Carl Vogt did in the present instance, they seek to impress the imagination by a comparison or figure which is made at the expense of sentiment, their expositions are almost sure to be misconceived, not only by those who are ignorant of their science and its grounds of inference, but even by the more sentimental and unreflective student of the science. What these persons seem to have supposed to be meant is not that thought and its expression are allotted to the brain as a secretion is to a gland, but that thought is a function in life which, as function, is of no more worth or dignity than the functions of the kidneys or of a cutaneous gland. It is altogether probable, however, that a certain feeling of impatience or contempt for the sentimental shallowness which could so misinterpret a scientific comparison, and confound it with moral or practical considerations is a real motive prompting to the utterance of shocking paradoxes, in

[7] From "A Fragment on Cause and Effect," 1873. Reprinted in *Philosophical Discussion*, pp. 406–13.

disregard alike of the practical effect and of scientific clearness and discrimination in the communications of truth. Native common sense is too apt to be coarse and barbarous in its manners, and too inconsiderate of weakness.

We will not venture to say that this was the case with the distinguished biologist whose words have been the cause of so much scandal. The metaphysical doctrine of materialism so often charged against or imputed to such scientific thinkers is, in fact, a doctrine quite foreign to science, quite out of its range. It belongs, so far as it is intelligible, to the sphere of sentiment, moral feeling and practical principles. A thinker is properly called a materialist when he concludes that his appetites and passions and actions, having material objects and results for their motives, are those most worthy of serious consideration. This does not imply that he believes that natures so different as thoughts, sensations, bodies liquid and solid and their movements, are all fundamentally of the same nature or are natures some of which are derived from certain other more fundamental ones among them: the spiritual from the material ones. It does not imply the opinion that thought is constituted of motions or liquids, does not even imply that the materialist thinker believes in, or knows anything about, the truth that actual thinking depends, phenomenally, on the tissues, structures and conditions of an organ, as intimately as the liquid secretions and the internal and external movements of a living body do. Scientific doctrines and investigations are exclusively concerned with connections in phenomena which are susceptible of demonstration by inductive observation, and independent of diversities or resemblances in their hidden natures, or of any question about their metaphysical derivation, or dependence.

That like produces like, and that an effect must resemble its cause are shallow scholastic conceptions, hasty blunders of generalization, which science repudiates: and with them it repudiates the scholastic classification or distinction of material and spiritual which depended on these conceptions, or supposed that a cause conferred its nature on its effect, or that the conditions of a cause by the combination of their natures constituted the nature of the effect. This, in a sense— in an identical or tautological sense—is indeed true; but from this true, though identical sense, a false and mischievous one was generalized, and still continues to corrupt and misinterpret the results of scientific observation.

In discovering anything to be the cause of something else we have added to our knowledge of the nature of the first thing. We have included in our conception of this thing the attribute of its producing, or being the cause of, the second. If now this attribute of it be the most prominent quality of it in our regard, as it is in contemplating a cause qua cause, the effect may, in an identical sense, be said to be constituted by its cause. In this view all the other attributes of the cause are subordinated to the attribute of producing a defined effect, or are regarded as accidental or nonessential attributes, and this is the view of the elementary relations in geometry and mathematics generally which abstraction produces, and is the source of the semblance of demonstrative certainty, and objective necessity which mathematical theorems have. But when science discovers, by induction or empirically, a new cause, the thing previously known by other attributes, to which is now added the attribute of producing a given or defined effect, has nothing in its essential or previously defining attributes at all resembling, implying or constituting its effect, and its newly discovered attribute of producing this effect remains among the added, subordinate or accidental attributes of such a cause. In its essence it does not imply, suggest or resemble its effect, and in this case the assertion that the nature of the cause determines or defines the nature of its effect, is clearly seen, so far as it is true, to be an identical proposition, meaning only that the production of the defined effect is a part, and a subordinate part, of the nature of a thing. The definition of the effect is added to that of the thing which is its cause, at least while we are contemplating this as the cause of the defined effect, and it is only by refunding to the effect what we have thus borrowed from it that we arrive at the metaphysician's mathematical conception of causation, the transference of the nature of one thing, that is, the cause, to another thing, its effect. In mathematics the elements of demonstration are so selected, by abstraction, and their definition so determined that this transference of nature is what is ostensibly done; though it is no more really done than in inferring consequents from antecedents, or effects from causes in so-called empirical science. In all cases where this appears to be the character of the connection of antecedent and consequent, or cause and effect, the transference of the nature of the cause to its effect, is only a restoration to the effect of natures borrowed from it, or into which it is resolvable by analysis. This fact is observed especially in mathematical inference, since such inference is always from a complex antecedent, or from the combination of a number of conditions, of which the aggregate is not known, named or defined by any attributes other than those which by the analysis and recombinations of mathematical demonstrations are shown to depend on the most obvious and elementary truths of our experience of measured quantities. The protasis of a geometrical theorem by the aid of geometrical constructions previously shown, or, when ultimate, simply assumed to be legitimate, is resolved into conditions which, recombined, are the apodosis or conclusion of the proposition. These conditions may be used to define the natures of both the antecedent or reason, and the consequent, and by this means their natures become identical. And both are analyzed ultimately in the course of a series of demonstrations into a few axioms, and these axiomatic truths implied in a few definitions. But not only in the mathematical, but also in the so-called empirical discovery of the connections of antecedent and consequent, or cause and effect, the antecedent or cause is almost always a combination of conditions, or a concurrence of things, relations and events, the definition of which in their aggregate, in merely logical consideration, may as well be the effect which follows, provided this is sufficient for defining it, as be anything else; since this aggregate of conditions is not usually denoted by a single name, the connotation of which would define its nature. Yet for practical and scientific purposes this aggregate is best defined by the enumeration of the conditions that compose it, to which observation adds the fact, or nature, that it will whenever it exists be followed by a given or defined effect. In this case the conditions which constitute the cause do not constitute the effect. They are simply followed by the effect, whose nature is wholly unlike that of its cause, or is like and is implied in its cause only so far as the capacity of producing it may be thought of identically as a part of the nature of its cause. Thus a stone, or any body denser (1) than the air, left unsupported (2) above (3) the surface of the earth, will fall (4) to it, is a proposition in so-called empirical science, in which the conditions (1) (2) (3) form an aggregate to which if we add as a part of its nature the result (4), that is, add the unconditional *tendency* to fall inferred from facts of observation, then the fall is a necessary consequence of the nature of its antecedent conditions, and it is like or is implied in this nature, quite as truly as any mathematical consequence is necessary, or is implied in mathematical protases of causes or antecedents. But ordinarily physical philosophers are not so anxious to make a scholastic show of demonstration as to surreptitiously add (4) to the group of conditions (1) (2) and (3) so as to make out their proof on the maxims that like produces like, or that effects resemble or partake of the nature of their causes. These maxims are really no more true of abstract reasonings in the elementary demonstrations of geometry; but the aim of these elementary reasonings justifies the procedures which give apparent countenance to their maxims.

Other and real illustrations vaguely related to these apparent ones are given in the organic world, in the phenomena of assimilation and reproduction. Tissues turn nutriment into substances of the same kind as their own. Offspring resemble their parents. These facts, together with the geometrical principle of Sufficient Reason, appeared to be sufficient grounds with scholastic philosophers for generalizing the identity of natures in real causes and effects. But, in fact, the very opposite is true. Elementary relations of antecedence and consequence are always those of unlikeness. A simple nature or phenomenon A is invariably followed by, or joined with, another different one B. Weight in a body manifested to us primarily by pressure, or in the tension of our muscles through the statical muscular sense, is a simple nature not resembling or implying at all the downward movement which always follows it when isolated or freed from other forces or conditions that are of a nature to produce an opposite effect, namely, an elastic movement, or bearing upward, and are as unlike this effect as weight is unlike the movement of falling. So in the elements of geometry the quality straightness and that of minimum length—duration or effort in traversing a line—are antecedent and consequent, or else concomitant qualities which are essentially different in their natures, but so intimately joined in all experience and in our conceptive powers, that they seem to be different aspects of one and the same nature. Yet the fully adequate and constructive definition of straight lines as a sort, of which only one can be drawn between two given points, does not imply that this is the shortest that can be drawn, or the one soonest and easiest traversed. This constructive definition joined to the meaning of the word inclosure gives what is often regarded as an axiom, the more complex proposition, that two straight lines cannot enclose a space. Starting with these and other constructive definitions, with the most general axioms of quantity, and with postulates of construction, and combining them into more and more complex relations of magnitudes in extension, we arrive at geometrical theorems in which the protasis states the least possible that is essential as the cause, or reason, and the apodosis, or conclusion, defines succinctly the consequent, or effect; theorems in which the connections of these two terms is far from obvious, but is nevertheless necessary, at least in the abstract, or on the supposition of precise, real definition and construction. Reason and consequent imply one the other, or the nature of a cause determines that of its effect, because one is analyzed into relations already determined from fundamental propositions, and these relations serve to define, or constitute the other. It is not true in general that the effect is like its cause, or has a nature determined by that of its cause, but it is true that like causes produce like effects. Parents may be said with tolerable correctness to be the causes of their offspring resembling them, and hence, in this case, the causes produce effects like themselves; yet it is more correct to say that the offspring resemble their parents, because both are products, though successive ones, of similar real causes and processes, some of which in nowise resemble or transfer their natures to their effects. Some implements and agents of the useful arts likewise are used to make precisely similar implements and agents, as a blacksmith's hammer to produce a similar hammer, or fire to kindle another one, or to reproduce the easily ignited substances with which fires are kindled; yet in these cases the agent that produces its like is not the whole of the cause of production. The blacksmith's forge and anvil and his arm and sight are concauses or conditions of this reproduction: and the nature of these does not re-appear in the effect, unless, as we have said, there is added to the conception of the aggregate of conditions, namely, to the conception of the iron, forge, welding hammer, arm and sight combined, also the fact that these will produce an effect resembling one of its conditions. So in organic reproduction, the plant produces seed similar not to itself but to the seed from which it grew, and the new seed grows into a similar plant: and in this alternation in which the immediate cause really produces effects unlike itself there are many subordinate conditions and processes the similarity of which in the parent and offspring makes them similar through successive effects of similar causes, which are not of the same nature as their effect. It is only because one condition or element of the cause (the one which resembles its effect) is singled out and, in accordance with the practical usage of common language, is called the cause, on account of its prominence or conspicuousness, that it is at all proper to speak of the parent organism as the cause of the production of its offspring. The existence of the parent organism is a condition *sine qua non* of the production of its offspring, but there are other conditions equally indispensable, the natures of which in themselves are in nowise reproduced in the effects.

ON SCIENCE [8]

Why the inductive and mathematical sciences, after their first rapid development at the culmination of Greek civilization, advanced so slowly for two thousand years—and why in the following two hundred years a knowledge of natural and mathematical science has accumulated, which so vastly exceeds all that was previously known that these sciences may be justly regarded as the products of our own times—are questions which have interested the modern philosopher not less than the objects with which these sciences are more immediately conversant. Was it in the employment of a new method of research, or in the exercise of greater virtue in the use of old methods, that this singular modern phenomenon had its origin? Was the long period one of arrested development, and is the modern era one of a normal growth? Or should we ascribe the characteristics of both periods to so-called historical accidents—to the influence of conjunctions in circumstances of which no explanation is possible, save in the omnipotence and wisdom of a guiding Providence?

[8] From "The Philosophy of Herbert Spencer," *North American Review,* 1865. Reprinted in *Philosophical Discussions,* pp. 43–54.

The explanation which has become commonplace, that the ancients employed deduction chiefly in their scientific inquiries, while the moderns employ induction, proves to be too narrow, and fails upon close examination to point with sufficient distinctness the contrast that is evident between ancient and modern scientific doctrines and inquiries. For all knowledge is founded on observation, and proceeds from this by analysis and synthesis, by synthesis and analysis, by induction and deduction, and if possible by verification, or by new appeals to observation under the guidance of deduction—by steps which are indeed correlative parts of one method; and the ancient sciences afford examples of every one of these methods, or parts of the one complete method, which have been generalized from the examples of science.

A failure to employ or to employ adequately any one of these partial methods, an imperfection in the arts and resources of observation and experiment, carelessness in observation, neglect of relevant facts, vagueness and carelessness in reasoning, and the failure to draw the consequences of theory and test them by appeal to experiment and observation—these are the faults which cause all failures to ascertain truth, whether among the ancients or the moderns; but this statement does not explain why the modern is possessed of a greater virtue, and by what means he attained to his superiority. Much less does it explain the sudden growth of science in recent times.

The attempt to discover the explanation of this phenomenon in the antithesis of "facts" and "theories" or "facts" and "ideas"—in the neglect among the ancients of the former, and their too exclusive attention to the latter—proves also to be too narrow, as well as open to the charge of vagueness. For, in the first place, the antithesis is not complete. Facts and theories are not co-ordinate species. Theories, if true, are facts—a particular class of facts indeed, generally complex ones, but still facts. Facts, on the other hand, even in the narrowest signification of the word, if they be at all complex, and if a logical connection subsists between their constituents, have all the positive attributes of theories.

Nevertheless, this distinction, however inadequate it may be to explain the source of true method in science, is well founded, and connotes an important character in true method. A fact is a proposition of which the verification by an appeal to the primary sources of our knowledge or to experience is direct and simple. A theory, on the other hand, if true, has all the characteristics of a fact, except that its verification is possible only by indirect, remote, and difficult means. To convert theories into facts is to add *simple verification*, and the theory thus acquires the full characteristics of a fact. When Pascal caused the Torricellian tube to be carried up the Puy de Dôme, and thus showed that the mercurial column was sustained by the weight of the atmosphere, he brought the theory of atmospheric pressure nearly down to the level of a fact of observation. But even in this most remarkable instance of scientific discovery theory was not wholly reduced to fact, since the verification, though easy, was not entirely simple, and was incomplete until further observations showed that the quantity of the fall in the Torricellian tube agreed with deductions from the combined theories of atmospherical pressure and elasticity. In the same way the theory of universal gravitation fails to become a fact in the proper sense of this word, however complete its verification, because this verification is not simple and direct, or through the immediate activity of our perceptive powers.

Modern science deals then no less with theories than with facts, but always as much as possible with the verification of theories—if not to make them facts by simple verification through experiment and observation, at least to prove their truth by indirect verification.

The distinction of fact and theory thus yields an important principle, of which M. Comte and his followers have made much account. It is in the employment of verification, they say, and in the possibility of it, that the superiority of modern inductive research consists; and it is because the ancients did not, or could not, verify their theories, that they made such insignificant progress in science. It is indisputable that verification is essential to the completeness of scientific method; but there is still room for debate as to what constitutes verification in the various departments of philosophical inquiry. So long as the philosophy of method fails to give a complete inventory of our primary sources of knowledge, and cannot decide authoritatively what are the origins of first truths, or the truths of observation, so long will it remain uncertain what is a legitimate appeal to observation, or what is a real verification. The Platonists or the rationalists may equally with the empiricists claim verification for their theories; for do they not appeal to the reason for confirmation of deductions from their theories, which they regard as founded on observation of what the reason reveals to them?

The positivists' principle of verification comes, then, only to this—that, inasmuch as mankind are nearly unanimous about the testimony and trustworthiness of their senses, but are divided about the validity of all other kinds of authority, which they in a word call the reason, or internal sense, therefore verification by the senses produces absolute conviction, while verification by the reason settles nothing, but is liable to the same uncertainty which attends the primary appeals to this authority for the data of speculative knowledge.

But not only does the so-called metaphysical philosophy employ a species of verification by appealing to the testimony of reason, consciousness, or internal sense; but the ancient physical sciences afford examples of the confirmation of theory by observation proper. The Ptolemaic system of astronomy was an instance of the employment of every one of the partial steps of true method; and the theory of epicycles not only sought to represent the facts of observation, but also by the prediction of astronomical phenomena to verify the truth of its representation. Modern astronomy does not proceed otherwise, except that its theories represent a much greater number of facts of observation, and are confirmed by much more efficient experimental tests.

The difference, then, between ancient and modern science is not truly characterized by any of the several explanations which have been proposed. The explanation, however, which, in our opinion, comes nearest to the true solution, and yet fails to designate the real point of difference, is that which the positivists find in the distinction between "objective method" and "subjective method." The objective method is verification by sensuous tests, tests of sensible experience—a deduction from theory of consequences, of which we may have sensible experiences if they be true. The subjective method, on the other hand, appeals to the tests of internal evidence, tests of reason, and the data of self-consciousness. But whatever be the origin of the theories of science, whether from a systematic examination of empirical facts by conscious induction, or from the natural biases of the mind, the so-called intuitions of reason, in other words what seems probable without a distinct survey of our experiences—whatever the origin, real or ideal, the *value* of these theories can only be tested, say the positivists, by an appeal to sensible experience, by deductions from them of consequences which we can confirm by the undoubted testimony of the senses. Thus, while ideal or transcendental elements are admitted into scientific researches, though in themselves insusceptible of simple verification, they must still show credentials from the senses, either by affording from themselves consequences capable of sensuous verification, or by yielding such consequences in conjunction with ideas which by themselves are verifiable.

It is undoubtedly true that one of the leading traits of modern scientific research is this reduction of ideas to the tests of experience. The systematic development of ideas through induction from the first and simplest facts of observation, is by no means so obvious a characteristic. Inductions are still performed for the most part unconsciously and unsystematically. Ideas are developed by the sagacity of the expert, rather than by the systematic procedures of the philosopher. But when and however ideas are developed, science cares nothing, for it is only by subsequent tests of sensible experience that ideas are admitted into the pandects of science.

It is of no consequence to scientific astronomy whence the theory of gravitation arose; whether as an induction from the theories of attractions and the law of radiations, or from the rational simplicity of this law itself, as the most natural supposition which could be made.

Science asks no questions about the ontological pedigree or a priori character of a theory, but is content to judge it by its performance; and it is thus that a knowledge of nature, having all the certainty which the senses are competent to inspire, has been attained—a knowledge which maintains a strict neutrality toward all philosophical systems, and concerns itself not at all with the genesis or a priori grounds of ideas.

This mode of philosophizing is not, however, exclusively found in modern scientific research. Ptolemy claimed for his epicycles only that "they saved the appearances"; and he might have said, with as much propriety as Newton, *"Hypotheses non fingo,"* for it was the aim of his research to represent abstractly, and by the most general formulas, the characteristics of the movements of the planets—an aim which modern astronomy, with a much simpler hypothesis, and with immensely increased facilities, still pursues.

We find, therefore, that while moderns follow a true method of investigation with greater facilities and greater fidelity than the ancients, and with a clearer apprehension of its elements and conditions, yet that no new discoveries in method have been made, and no general sources of truth have been pointed out, which were not patent and known to the ancients; and we have so far failed to discover any solution to the problem with which we began. We have seen that it was not by the employment of a new method of research, but in the exercise of greater virtue in the use of old methods, that modern scientific researches have succeeded. But whence this greater virtue? What vivifying, energizing influence awakened the sixteenth century to the movement, which has continued down to the present day to engross, and even to create, the energies of philosophic thought in the study of natural phenomena? Obviously some interest was awakened which had before been powerless, or had influenced only men of rare and extraordinary genius, or else some opposing interest had ceased to exercise a preponderating influence.

We have now arrived at a new order of inquiries. We ask no longer what are the differences of *method* between ancient and modern scientific researches, but we seek the difference in the *motives* which actuated the philosophic inquiries of the two periods. We seek for the interests which in modern times have so powerfully drawn men of all orders of intelligence to the pursuit of science, and to an observance of the conditions requisite for its successful prosecution. We do not inquire what course has led to successful answers in science, but what motives have prompted the pertinent questions.

In place of the positivists' phraseology, that the ancients followed "the subjective method," or appealed for the verification of their theories to natural beliefs, while the moderns follow "the objective

method," or appeal to new and independent experimental evidence—
if we substitute the word "motive" for "method," we have the terms
of one of the conclusions on which we wish to insist. But these require
explanation.

By a subjective motive we mean one having its origin in natural
universal human interests and emotions, which existed before philosophy was born, which continue to exist in the maturity of philosophy,
and determine the character of an important and by no means defunct
order of human speculations. By an objective motive we mean one
having an empirical origin, arising in the course of an inquiry; springing from interests which are defined by what we already know, and
not by what we have always felt—interests which depend on acquired
knowledge, and not on natural desires and emotions. Among the latter
we must include the natural desire for knowledge, or the primitive,
undisciplined sentiment of curiosity. This becomes an objective
motive when it ceases to be associated with our fears, our respects,
our aspirations—our emotional nature; when it ceases to prompt questions as to what relates to our personal destiny, our ambitions, our
moral worth; when it ceases to have man, his personal and social
nature, as its central and controlling objects. A curiosity which is
determined chiefly or solely by the felt imperfections of knowledge
as such, and without reference to the uses this knowledge may subserve, is prompted by what we call an objective motive.

A spirit of inquiry which is freed from the influence of our active
powers, and the interests that gave birth to theological and metaphysical philosophies—which yields passively and easily to the direction of objective motives, to the felt imperfections of knowledge as
such—is necessarily, at all times, a weak feeling; and before a body
of systematic, well-digested, and well-ascertained scientific truth had
been generated, could hardly have had any persistent influence on the
direction of inquiry.

The motives to theological and metaphysical speculation exist from
the beginning of civilized human life in the active emotional nature
of man. Curiosity as a love of the marvelous, or as a love of facts—new
facts, prized because they are new and stimulating—also dates back
of civilized life. These motives find play in human nature, as it
emerges from a semi-animal state; but they also persist and determine
the growth of the human mind in its most advanced development.

The questions of philosophy proper are human desires and fears
and aspirations—human emotions—taking an intellectual form. Science
follows, but does not supersede, this philosophy. The three phases
which the positivists assign to the development of the human mind—
the Theological, the Metaphysical, and the Positive or Scientific—are
not in reality successive, except in their beginnings. They coexist in

all the highest developments of civilization and mental activity. They coexisted in the golden age of Greek civilization, in the intense mental activity of the Middle Ages. They move on together in this marvelous modern era. But until this latest epoch positive science was always the inferior philosophy—hardly a distinct philosophy at all—not yet born. But at the beginning of the modern era its gestation was completed. A body of knowledge existed, sufficiently extensive, coherent, and varied, to bear within it a life of its own—an independent life— which was able to collect to itself, by its own determinations, the materials of a continued, new, and ever-increasing mental activity— an activity determined solely by an objective curiosity, or by curiosity in its purest, fullest, and highest energy.

We are probably indebted to the few men of scientific genius who lived during the slow advancement of modern civilization for the foundation of this culture—for the accumulation of the knowledge requisite for this subsequent growth. These men were doubtless, for the most part, the products of their own time and civilization, as indeed all great men have been, but still originators, by concentrating and making productive the energies, tendencies, and knowledges which, but for them, would have remained inert and unfruitful. It is to such men, born at long intervals in the slow progress of civilization, each carrying forward a little the work of his predecessor, that we probably owe our modern science, rather than to the influence of any single mind, like Bacon, who was, like his predecessors, but the lens which collected the light of his times—who prophesied rather than inaugurated the new era. And we owe science to the combined energies of individual men of genius, rather than to any tendency to progress inherent in civilization.

We find, then, the explanation of the modern development of science in the accumulation of a body of certified knowledge, sufficiently extensive to engage and discipline a rational scientific curiosity, and stimulate it to act independently of other motives. It is doubtless true that other motives have influenced this development, and especially that motives of material utility have had a powerful effect in stimulating inquiry. Ancient schools of philosophy despised narrow material utilities, the servile arts, and sought no instruction in what moderns dignify by the name of useful arts; but modern science finds in the requirements of the material arts the safest guide to exact knowledge. A theory which is utilized receives the highest possible certificate of truth. Navigation by the aid of astronomical tables, the magnetic telegraph, the innumerable utilities of mechanical and chemical science, are constant and perfect tests of scientific theories, and afford the standard of certitude, which science has been able to apply so extensively in its interpretations of natural phenomena.

But the motives proper to science, though purified by their dissociation from the subjective determinations and tendencies, which gave an anthropomorphic and teleological character to ancient views of nature, are not the only legitimate motives to philosophical inquiry. There is another curiosity purified by its association with the nobler sentiments—with wonder, admiration, veneration—and with the interests of our moral and aesthetical natures. This curiosity is the motive to philosophy proper. "Wonder is a highly philosophical affection," says Plato's Socrates; "Indeed, there is no other principle of philosophy but this."

Curiosity determined by natural sentiments and emotions—subjective curiosity—is the cause of a culture coextensive with civilization, long preceding the growth of science, and constituting all that is peculiar to civilized life except the material arts. However meanly the conclusions of theological and metaphysical speculations may appear, when tried by the objective standard of science, they too have their superiorities, by the test of which science becomes in turn insignificant. Unverified conclusions, vague ideas, crude fancies, they may be, but they certainly are the products of activities which constitute more of human happiness and human worth than the narrow material standards of science have been able to measure.

Philosophy proper should be classed with the religions and with the fine arts, and estimated rather by the dignity of its motives, and the value it directs us to, than by the value of its own attainments. To condemn this pursuit because it fails to accomplish what science does, would be to condemn that which has formed in human nature habits, ideas, and associations on which all that is best in us depends—would warrant the condemnation of science itself, since science scarcely existed at all for two thousand years of civilization, and represented as a distinct department during this period only the interests of the servile arts. The objects of philosophy were those which the religious ideas and emotions of man presented to his speculative curiosity. These motives, though proper to philosophy, also gave direction to inquiries in physics and astronomy. The fine arts sprang from the same interests, and persisted through the conservative power of religious interests in a development to which the modern world offers no parallel. We have no styles in art, no persistently pursued efforts for perfection in beauty, because we are not held to the conditions of this perfection by the religious motives which directed ancient art. The growth of theology and metaphysics is less vigorous now for the same reason. Theology was philosophy developed in the interests of religion or of religious feeling, and metaphysics was cultivated in the interests of theology. Both aimed at truth; both were determined by the same love of simplicity and unity in knowledge which determines all search after truth; but neither cared for simple truth alone. When pursued for the truth of fact alone, they both degenerate into affectation and emptiness. We do not omit the skeptical philosophies of antiquity from this description, because they were not held independently of the religious interests of the orthodox philosophy, but in opposition to them or in criticism of them.

Theology and Metaphysics failed to apply a correct method and to arrive at certain results, not because philosophers were ignorant of method, but because the object-matters of their research were not questions of sensible experience—were not mere questions of facts of which the mind is the passive recipient through the senses. Their aim was to *prove* truth, not to discover it—to reduce opinions and ideas which had the warrant of religious associations to the simplicity and consistency of truth; and when ideas and opinions have this warrant, it does not require the verification of the senses to make the conclusions of philosophy acceptable and true to the religious instincts. To educe conclusions acceptable to these instincts and in opposition to no known truth—in other words, to free religious beliefs from contradictions and to give them consistency—was the aspiration and the devoted service of philosophy.

Philosophy has in fact three phases instead of two. For as theology was a speculation prosecuted in the interest of religious feeling, and metaphysics a speculation in defense or criticism of the doctrines of theology, so Criticism or Critical Philosophy is an examination of metaphysical conclusions. But the latter is properly, in its motives, a scientific speculation. Such is the true logical order of philosophy proper, though all these phases may and do coexist in history.

It is the opinion of many modern thinkers, besides the so-called positivists, or avowed followers of M. Comte, that science, as we have defined it, or truth pursued simply in the interests of a rational curiosity, and for the mental discipline and the material utilities of its processes and conclusions, will hereafter occupy more and more the attention of mankind, to the exclusion of the older philosophy. It is also the opinion of these thinkers, that this is not to be regretted, but rather welcomed as a step forward in the advancement of human welfare and civilization; that the pursuit of science and its utilities is capable of inspiring as great and earnest a devotion as those which religious interests have inspired, and which have hitherto determined the destinies of mankind and given form to human thought, and one vastly more beneficent.

Whatever foundations there are for these opinions, it is certain that the claims of science, as a new power in the world, to the regard of thoughtful and earnest men, are receiving a renewed and more candid attention. Through its recent progress, many of the questions which have hitherto remained in the arena of metaphysical disputation are brought forward in new forms and under new auspices. Scientific investigations promise to throw a flood of light on subjects which have interested mankind since the beginning of speculation—subjects related to universal human interests. History, society, laws, and morality —all are claimed as topics with which scientific methods are competent to deal. Scientific solutions are proposed to all the questions of philosophy which scientific illumination may not show to have their origin in metaphysical hallucination. . . .

BIBLIOGRAPHY

WRIGHT, Chauncey, *Philosophical Discussions*, with a Biographical Sketch of the Author by Charles Eliot Norton. New York: Henry Holt, 1877.

_____ *The Philosophical Writings, Representative Selections*, edited with an Introduction by Edward H. Madden. New York: Liberal Arts Press, 1958.

_____ *Letters of Chauncey Wright: With Some Account of His Life*, ed. by J. B. Thayer. Cambridge, 1878.

FISKE, John, "Chauncey Wright," *Darwinism and Other Essays*. New ed., Boston: Houghton Mifflin, 1888, pp. 79–110.

JAMES, William, "Chauncey Wright," *Collected Essays and Reviews*. New York: Longmans, Green, 1920, pp. 20–25.

KENNEDY, Gail, "The Pragmatic Naturalism of Chauncey Wright," *Studies in the History of Ideas*. New York: Columbia U. Press, 1935, Vol. III, pp. 477–503.

MADDEN, Edward H., *Chauncey Wright and the Foundations of Pragmatism*. Seattle: U. of Washington Press, 1963.

PERRY, Ralph Barton, "Chauncey Wright," *The Thought and Character of William James*. Boston: Little, Brown, 1935, Chap. 31.

WIENER, Philip, "Chauncey Wright's Defense of Darwin and the Neutrality of Science." *Journal of the History of Ideas*, Vol. VI (1945), pp. 19–45.

_____ "Chauncey Wright, Defender of Darwin and Precursor of Pragmatism," *Evolution and the Founders of Pragmatism*. Cambridge: Harvard U. Press, 1949, pp. 31–69.

John Dewey

[1859–1952]

John Dewey bridges two centuries. His birth in 1859 coincides with the publication of Darwin's *Origin of Species*, and he was able to observe the impact of Darwinism on thought in America. Many observers, both disciples and critics, consider Dewey to have been the most influential philosopher in twentieth-century America. A pragmatist and instrumentalist, Dewey was a leading advocate of naturalistic humanism. His numerous writings dealt with logic, epistemology, philosophy of science, ethics, theory of value and valuation, aesthetics, education, political and social theory, philosophy of religion, and metaphysics.

Dewey was born in Burlington, Vermont. He studied at the University of Vermont, and took his Ph.D. in 1884 at the newly founded Johns Hopkins University. He taught at the Universities of Michigan, Minnesota, Chicago, and, in his later and most influential years, at Columbia University. Dewey carried his philosophical activities far beyond the confines of the learned journals and books to the public place of ideas and actions. The range of his involvement in public affairs was great: he was considered a leader of liberalism and progressive education in America.

Dewey's thought is the product of an early involvement with neo-Hegelianism, the Darwinian theory of evolution, the pragmatism of Charles Peirce (and Chauncey Wright), and behavioral psychology. The following article, *Darwin's Influence Upon Philosophy* (1909), contains Dewey's own appraisal of Darwinism and its effect on religion, morals, and philosophy, of the biological interpretation of ideas, and of the resulting destruction of "absolutes." A fuller treatment of Dewey's philosophy is given in the companion volume, *American Philosophy in the Twentieth Century*.

DARWIN'S INFLUENCE UPON PHILOSOPHY [1]

I

That the publication of the *Origin of Species* marked an epoch in the development of the natural sciences is well known to the layman. That the combination of the very words origin and species embodied

[1] One of a course of lectures on "Charles Darwin and His Influence on Science" given at Columbia University in 1909. It was first published in *The Popular Science Monthly*, Vol. LXXV (July, 1909), pp. 90–98, and is reprinted in the present volume with the permission of the editors of *The Popular Science Monthly* and Mrs. John Dewey.

an intellectual revolt and introduced a new intellectual temper is easily overlooked by the expert. The conceptions that had reigned in the philosophy of nature and knowledge for two thousand years, the conceptions that had become the familiar furniture of the mind, rested on the assumption of the superiority of the fixed and final; they rested upon treating change and origin as signs of defect and unreality. In laying hands upon the sacred ark of absolute permanency, in treating the forms that had been regarded as types of fixity and perfection as originating and passing away, the *Origin of Species* introduced a mode of thinking that in the end was bound to transform the logic of knowledge, and hence the treatment of morals, politics and religion.

No wonder then that the publication of Darwin's book, a half century ago, precipitated a crisis. The true nature of the controversy is easily concealed from us, however, by the theological clamor that attended it. The vivid and popular features of the anti-Darwinian row tended to leave the impression that the issue was between science on one side and theology on the other. Such was not the case—the issue lay primarily within science itself, as Darwin himself early recognized. The theological outcry he discounted from the start, hardly noticing it save as it bore upon the "feelings of his female relatives." But for two decades before final publication he contemplated the possibility of being put down by his scientific peers as a fool or as crazy; and he set, as the measure of his success, the degree in which he should affect three men of science: Lyell in geology, Hooker in botany and Huxley in zoology.

Religious considerations lent fervor to the controversy, but they did not provoke it. Intellectually, religious emotions are not creative but conservative. They attach themselves readily to the current view of the world and consecrate it. They steep and dye intellectual fabrics in the seething vat of emotions; they do not form their warp and woof. There is not, I think, an instance of any large idea about the world being independently generated by religion. However much the ideas that rose up like armed men against Darwinism owed their intensity to religious associations, their origin and meaning are to be sought elsewhere.

II

Few words in our language foreshorten intellectual history as does the word species. The Greeks in initiating the intellectual life of Europe, were impressed by characteristic traits of the life of plants and animals; so impressed indeed that they made these traits the key to defining nature and to explaining mind and society. And truly, life is so wonderful that a seemingly successful reading of its mystery might well lead men to believe that the key to the secrets of heaven and earth was in their hands. The Greek rendering of this mystery, the Greek formulation of the aim and standard of knowledge, was in the course of time embodied in the word species and controlled philosophy for two thousand years. To understand the intellectual face-about expressed in the phrase "Origin of species," we must, then, understand the long dominant idea against which it was a protest.

Consider how men were impressed by the facts of life. Their eyes fell upon certain things slight in bulk, and frail in structure. To every appearance, these perceived things were inert and passive. Suddenly, under certain circumstances, these things—henceforth known as seeds or eggs or germs—begin to change, to change rapidly in size, form and qualities. Rapid and extensive changes occur, however, in many things—as when wood is touched by fire. But the changes in the living thing are orderly; they are cumulative; they tend constantly in one direction; they do not, like other changes, destroy or consume, or pass fruitless into wandering flux; they realize and fulfill. Each successive stage, no matter how unlike its predecessor, preserves its net effect and also prepares the way for a fuller activity on the part of its successor. In living beings changes do not happen as they seem to elsewhere, any which way; the earlier changes are regulated in view of later results. This progressive organization does not cease till there is achieved a true final term, a τελὸς, a complete, perfected end. This final form exercises in turn a plenitude of functions, not the least noteworthy of which is production of germs like those from which it took its own origin, germs capable of the same cycle of self-fulfilling activity.

But the whole miraculous tale is not yet told. The same drama is enacted to the same destiny in countless myriads of individuals so sundered in time, so severed in place, that they have no opportunity for mutual consultation and no means of interaction. As an old writer quaintly said, "things of the same kind go through the same formalities"—celebrate, as it were, the same ceremonial rites.

This formal activity which operates throughout a series of changes and holds them to a single course; that subordinates their aimless flux to its own perfect manifestation; which, leaping the boundaries of space and time, keeps individuals in spite of their being distant in space and remote in time to a uniform type of structure and function: this principle seemed to give insight into the very nature of reality itself. To it Aristotle gave the name εἶδος. This term the scholastics translated as *species*.

The force of this term was deepened by its application to everything in the universe that observes order in flux and manifests constancy through change. From the casual drift of daily weather, through the uneven recurrence of seasons and unequal return of seed time and harvest, up to the majestic sweep of the heavens—the image of eternity in time—and from this to the unchanging pure and contemplative intelligence beyond nature lies one unbroken fulfillment of ends.

Nature, as a whole, is a progressive realization of purpose strictly comparable to the realization of purpose in any single plant or animal.

The conception of εἶδος, species, the fixed form and final cause, was the central principle of knowledge as well as of nature. Upon it rested the logic of science. Change as change is mere flux and lapse; it insults intelligence. Genuinely to know is to grasp a permanent end that realizes itself through changes, holding them thereby within the metes and bounds of fixed truth. Completely to know is to relate all special forms to their one single end and good: pure contemplative intelligence. Since, however, the scene of nature which directly confronts us is in change, nature as directly and practically experienced cannot satisfy the conditions of knowledge. Human experience is also in flux, and hence the instrumentalities of sense perception and of inference based upon observation are condemned in advance. Science is compelled to aim at realities lying behind and beyond the processes of nature, and to carry on its search for these realities by means of rational forms transcending ordinary modes of perception and inference.

There are, indeed, but two alternative courses. We must either find the appropriate objects and organs of knowledge in the mutual interactions of changing things; or else, to escape the infection of change, we *must* seek them in some transcendent and supernal region. The human mind, deliberately as it were, exhausted the logic of the changeless, the final and the transcendent, before it essayed adventure on the pathless wastes of generation and transformation. We dispose all too easily of the efforts of the schoolmen to interpret nature and mind in terms of real essences, hidden forms and occult faculties, forgetful of the seriousness and dignity of the ideas that lay behind. We dispose of them by laughing at the famous gentleman who accounted for the fact that opium put people to sleep on the ground it had a dormitive faculty. But the doctrine, held in our own day, that knowledge of the plant that yields the poppy consists in referring the peculiarities of an individual to a type, to a universal form, a doctrine so firmly established that any other method of knowing was conceived to be unphilosophical and unscientific, was a survival of precisely the same logic. This identity of conception in the scholastic and anti-Darwinian theory may well suggest greater sympathy for what has become unfamiliar and greater humility regarding the further unfamiliarities that history has in store.

Darwin was not, of course, the first to question the classic philosophy of nature and of knowledge. The beginnings of the revolution are in the physical science of the sixteenth and seventeenth centuries. When Galileo said: "It is my opinion that the earth is very noble and admirable by reason of so many and so different alterations and generations which are incessantly made therein," he expressed the changed temper that was coming over the world; the transfer of interest from the permanent to the changing. When Descartes said: "The nature of physical things is much more easily conceived when they are beheld coming gradually into existence, than when they are only considered as produced at once in a finished and perfect state," the modern world became self-conscious of the logic that was henceforth to control it, the logic of which Darwin's *Origin of Species* is the latest scientific achievement. Without the methods of Copernicus, Kepler, Galileo and their successors in astronomy, physics and chemistry, Darwin would have been helpless in the organic sciences. But prior to Darwin the impact of the new scientific method upon life, mind and politics, had been arrested for the most part, because between these ideal or moral interests and the inorganic world there intervened the kingdom of plants and animals. The gates of the garden of life were barred to the new ideas while only through this garden was there access to mind and politics. The influence of Darwin upon philosophy resides in his having freed the new logic for application to mind and morals by conquering the phenomena of life. When he said of species what Galileo had said of the earth, *e pur se muove*, he emancipated once for all genetic and experimental ideas as an organon of asking questions and looking for explanations in philosophy.

III

The exact bearings upon philosophy of the new logical outlook are, of course, as yet, uncertain and inchoate. We live in the twilight of intellectual transition. One must add the rashness of the prophet to the stubbornness of the partisan to venture a systematic exposition of the influence upon philosophy of the Darwinian method. At best, we can but inquire as to its general bearing—the effect upon mental temper and complexion, upon that body of half-conscious, half-instinctive intellectual aversions and preferences which determine, after all, our more deliberate intellectual enterprises. In this vaguer inquiry there happens to exist as a kind of touchstone one problem of great historic significance that has also been much discussed in Darwinian literature. I refer to the old problem of design versus chance, mind versus matter, as the causal explanation, first and final, of things.

As we have already seen, the classic notion of species carried with it the idea of purpose. In all living forms, a specific type is present directing the earlier stages of growth to the realization of its own perfection. Since this purposive regulative principle is not visible to the senses, it follows that it must be an ideal or rational force. Since, however, the perfect form is gradually approximated through the sensible changes, it also follows that in and through a sensible realm a rational ideal force is working out its own ultimate manifestation. These two inferences were extended to nature: (1) She does nothing in vain; but all for an ulterior purpose. (2) Within natural sensible events there is therefore contained a spiritual causal force, which as spiritual escapes perception, but is apprehended by an enlightened reason. (3) The manifestation of this principle brings about a sub-ordination of matter and sense to its own realization, and this ultimate fulfillment is the goal of nature and of man. The design argument thus operated in two directions. Purposefulness accounted for the intelligibility of nature and the possibility of science, while the abso-lute or cosmic character of this purposefulness gave sanction and worth to the moral and religious endeavors of man. Science was underpinned and morals authorized by one and the same principle, and their mutual agreement was eternally guaranteed.

This philosophy remained, in spite of skeptical and polemic out-bursts, the official and the regnant philosophy of Europe for over two thousand years. The expulsion of fixed first and final causes from astronomy, physics and chemistry had indeed given the doctrine some-thing of a shock. But, on the other hand, increased acquaintance with the details of plant and animal life made a counterbalance, and per-haps even strengthened the argument from design. The marvelous adaptations of organisms to their environment, of organs to the or-ganism, of unlike parts of a complex organ—like the eye—to the organ itself; the foreshadowing by lower forms of the higher; the preparation in earlier stages of growth for organs that only later had their func-tioning—these things were increasingly recognized with the progress of botany, zoology, paleontology and embryology. Together they added such prestige to the design argument that by the late eighteenth cen-tury it was, as proved by the sciences of organic life, the central point of theistic and idealistic philosophy.

The Darwinian principle of natural selection cut straight under this philosophy. If all organic adaptations are due simply to constant varia-tion and the elimination of those variations that are harmful in the struggle for existence which is brought about by excessive reproduc-tion, there is no call for a prior intelligent causal force to plan and preordain them. Hostile critics charged Darwin with materialism and with making chance the cause of the universe.

Some naturalists, like Asa Gray, favored the Darwinian principle and attempted to reconcile it with design. Gray held to what may be called design on the installment plan. If we conceive the "stream of variations" to be itself intended, we may suppose that each successive variation was designed from the first to be selected. In that case, varia-tion, struggle and selection simply define the mechanism of "secondary causes" through which the "first cause" acts; and the doctrine of design is none the worse off because we know more of its *modus operandi*.

Darwin could not accept this mediating proposal. He admits, or rather he asserts, that it is "impossible to conceive this immense and wonderful universe including man with his capacity of looking far backward and far into futurity as the result of blind chance or necessity." [2] But nevertheless he holds that since variations are in useless as well as useful directions, and since the latter are sifted out simply by the stress of the conditions of struggle for existence, the design argument as applied to living beings is unjustifiable; and its lack of support there deprives it of scientific value as applied to nature in general. If the variations of the pigeon, which under artificial selection give the pouter pigeon, are not preordained for the sake of the breeder, by what logic do we argue that variations resulting in natural species are predesigned? [3]

IV

So much for some of the more obvious facts of the discussion of design versus chance as causal principles of nature and of life as a whole. We brought up this discussion, you recall, as a crucial instance. What does our touchstone indicate as to the bearing of Darwinian ideas upon philosophy? In the first place, the new logic outlaws, flanks, dismisses—what you will—one type of problem and substitutes for it another type. Philosophy forswears inquiry after absolute origins and absolute finalities in order to explore specific values and the specific conditions that generate them.

Darwin concluded that the impossibility of assigning the world to chance as a whole and to design in its parts indicated the insolubility of the question. Two radically different reasons, however, may be given as to why a problem is insoluble. One reason is that the problem is too high for intelligence; the other is that the question in its very asking makes assumptions that render the question meaningless. The latter alternative is unerringly pointed to in the celebrated case of design versus chance. Once admit that the sole verifiable or fruitful object of knowledge is the particular set of changes that generate the object of study, together with the consequences that further flow from it, and no intelligible question can be asked about what, by assumption, lies outside. To assert—as is often asserted—that specific values of particular truths, social bonds and forms of beauty, if they can be shown to be generated by concretely knowable conditions, are meaningless and in vain; to assert that they are justified only when they and their particular causes and effects have all at once been gathered up into some inclusive first cause and some exhaustive final goal, is intellectual atavism. Such argumentation is reversion to the logic that explained the extinction of fire by water through the formal essence of aqueousness and the quenching of thirst by water through the final

[2] *Life and Letters*, Vol. I., p. 282; cf. 285.—D.

[3] *Life and Letters*, Vol. II., pp. 146, 170, 245; Vol. I., 283–84. See also the closing portion of his "Variations of Animals and Plants under Domestication."—D.

cause of aqueousness. Whether used in the case of the special event or in that of life as a whole, such logic only abstracts some aspect of the existing course of events in order to reduplicate it as a petrified eternal principle by which to explain the very changes of which it is the formalization.

When Henry Sidgwick casually remarked in a letter that as he grew older his interest in what or who made the world was altered into interest in what kind of a world it is anyway, his voicing of a common experience of our own day illustrates also the nature of that intellectual transformation effected by the Darwinian logic. Interest shifts from the wholesale essence back of special changes to the question of how these special changes serve and defeat concrete purposes; shifts from an intelligence that shaped things once for all, to the particular intelligences which things are even now shaping; shifts from an ultimate goal of good to the direct increments of justice and happiness that intelligent administration of existent conditions may beget and that present carelessness or stupidity will destroy or forego.

In the second place, the classic type of logic inevitably set philosophy upon proving that life *must* really have certain qualities and values—no matter how experience presents the matter—because of some remote cause and eventual goal, while the logic of the new science frees philosophy from this apologetic habit and temper. The duty of wholesale justification inevitably accompanies all thinking that makes the meaning of special occurrences depend upon something that lies once and for all behind them. The habit of derogating from present meanings and uses prevents our looking the facts of experience in the face; it prevents serious acknowledgment of the evils they present and serious concern with the goods they promise but do not yet fulfill. It turns thought to the business of finding a wholesale transcendent remedy for the one and guarantee for the other. One is reminded of the way many moralists and theologians greeted Herbert Spencer's recognition of an unknowable energy from which welled up the phenomenal physical processes without and the conscious operations without. Merely because Spencer labeled his unknowable energy "God," this faded piece of metaphysical goods was greeted as an important and grateful concession to the reality of the spiritual realm. Were it not for the deep hold of the habit of seeking justification for ideal values in the remote and transcendent, surely this reference of them to an unknowable absolute would be despised in behalf of the daily demonstrations of experience that knowable energies are daily generating about us precious values.

The displacing of this wholesale type of philosophy will doubtless not arrive by sheer logical disproof, but rather by growing recognition of its futility. Were it a thousand times true that opium produces sleep because of its dormitive energy, the inducing of sleep in the tired and the recovery to waking life of the poisoned, would not be thereby one least step forwarded. And were it a thousand times dialectically demonstrated that life as a whole is regulated by a transcendent principle to a final inclusive goal, truth and error, health and disease, good and evil, hope and fear in the concrete would remain none the less just what and where they now are. To improve our education, to ameliorate our manners, to advance our politics, we must have recourse to specific conditions of generation.

Finally, the new logic introduces responsibility into the intellectual life. To idealize and rationalize the universe at large is after all a confession of inability to master the courses of things that specifically concern us. As long as mankind suffered from this impotency, naturally it shifted a burden of responsibility which it could not carry over to the more competent shoulders of the transcendent cause. But if insight into specific conditions of value and into specific consequences of ideas is possible, philosophy must in time become a method of locating and interpreting the more serious of the conflicts that occur in life, and a method of projecting ways for dealing with them: a method of moral and political diagnosis and prognosis.

The claim to formulate a priori the legislative constitution of the universe is by its nature a claim that may lead into elaborate dialectic developments. But it is also one which removes these very conclusions from subjection to experimental test, for, by definition, these results make no differences in the detailed course of events. But a philosophy that humbles its pretensions to the work of projecting hypotheses for the education and conduct of mind, individual and social, is thereby subjected to test by the way in which the ideas it propounds work out in practice. In having modesty forced upon it, philosophy also acquires responsibility.

Doubtless I may seem to have violated the implied promise of my earlier remarks and to have turned both prophet and partisan. But in anticipating the direction of the transformations in philosophy to be wrought by the Darwinian genetic and experimental logic, I do not profess to speak for any changes save those wrought in those who yield themselves consciously or unconsciously to this logic. No one can fairly deny that at present there are evident two effects of the Darwinian mode of thinking. On the one hand, there are making many sincere and vital efforts to revise our traditional philosophic conceptions in accordance with its demands. On the other hand, there is as definitely a recrudescence of absolutistic philosophies; an assertion of a type of philosophic knowing distinct from that of the sciences, which opens to us another kind of reality from that to which the sciences give access; an appeal through experience to something that radically transcends experiences. This reaction affects popular creeds and religious movements as well as technical philosophies. In other words, the very conquest of the biological sciences by the new ideas has led many to effect a more explicit and rigid separation of philosophy from science.

Old ideas give way slowly; for they are more than abstract logical forms and categories. They are habits, predispositions, deeply engrained attitudes of aversion and preference. Moreover, the conviction persists—though history shows it to be a hallucination—that all the questions that the human mind has asked are questions that can be answered in terms of the alternatives that the questions themselves present. But, in fact, intellectual progress usually occurs through sheer abandonment of such questions, together with both of the alternatives they assume—an abandonment that results from decreasing vitality and interest in their point of view. We do not solve them: we get over them. Old questions are solved by disappearing, evaporating, while new questions corresponding to the changed attitude of endeavor and preference take their place. Doubtless the greatest dissolvent of old questions, the greatest precipitant of new methods, new intentions, new problems, is the one effected by the scientific revolution completed in the *Origin of Species*.

BIBLIOGRAPHY

DEWEY, John, *The Influence of Darwin on Philosophy and Other Essays in Contemporary Thought*. New York: Henry Holt & Co., 1910.

——— *Democracy and Education*. New York: Macmillan Co., 1916.

——— *Essays in Experimental Logic*. Chicago: U. of Chicago Press, 1916.

——— *Reconstruction in Philosophy*. New York: Henry Holt & Co., 1920.

——— *Human Nature and Conduct: An Introduction to Social Psychology*. New York: Henry Holt & Co., 1922.

——— *Experience and Nature*. Chicago: Open Court Pub. Co., 1925.

——— *The Quest for Certainty*. New York: Minton, Balch, 1929.

——— *Individualism, Old and New*. New York: Minton, Balch, 1930.

——— *Philosophy and Civilization*. New York: Minton, Balch, 1931.

——— *How We Think*, rev. ed. Boston: D. C. Heath, 1933.

——— *A Common Faith*. New Haven: Yale U. Press, 1934.

——— *Art as Experience*. New York: Minton, Balch, 1934.

——— *Liberalism and Social Action*. New York: G. P. Putnam's Sons, 1935.

——— *Logic: The Theory of Inquiry*. New York: Henry Holt & Co., 1938.

——— *Freedom and Culture*. New York: G. P. Putnam's Sons, 1939.

——— *Theory of Valuation*. Chicago: The U. of Chicago Press, 1939.

——— *Education To-day*, ed. by Joseph Ratner. New York: G. P. Putnam's Sons, 1940.

——— *Problems of Men*. New York: Philosophical Library, 1946.

——— and James H. Tufts, *Ethics*. New York: Henry Holt & Co., 1908.

——— and Arthur F. Bentley, *Knowing and the Known*. Boston: Beacon Press, 1949.

BLEWETT, John, ed., *John Dewey: His Thought and Influence*. New York: Fordham U. Press, 1960.

CLAYTON, Alfred S., ed., *John Dewey in Perspective: Three Papers in Honor of John Dewey*. Bloomington: Indiana U. School of Ed. Bull., Vol. XXXVI (1960).

CROSSER, Paul K., *The Nihilism of John Dewey*. New York: Philosophical Library, 1955.

EDMAN, Irwin, ed., *John Dewey, His Contribution to the American Tradition*. Indianapolis: Bobbs-Merrill, 1955.

Essays in Honor of John Dewey, on the Occasion of His Seventieth Birthday. New York: Henry Holt, 1929.

FELDMAN, William Taft, *The Philosophy of John Dewey: A Critical Analysis*. Baltimore: Johns Hopkins Press, 1934.

GEIGER, George, *John Dewey in Perspective*. New York: Oxford U. Press, 1958.

HENDEL, Charles W., ed., *John Dewey and the Experimental Spirit in Philosophy*. New York: Liberal Arts Press, 1959.

HOOK, Sidney, *John Dewey: An Intellectual Portrait*. New York: John Day, 1939.

———— ed., *John Dewey: Philosopher of Science and Freedom*. New York: Dial Press, 1950.

HOWARD, Delton T., *John Dewey's Logical Theory*. New York: Longmans, Green & Co., 1918.

John Dewey, The Man and His Philosophy; Addresses Delivered in New York in Celebration of His Seventieth Birthday. Cambridge: Harvard U. Press, 1930.

LAMONT, Corliss, ed., *Dialogue on John Dewey*. New York: Horizon Press, 1959.

LEVITT, Morton, *Freud and Dewey on the Nature of Man*. New York: Philosophical Library, 1960.

MEAD, George Herbert, "The Philosophy of John Dewey." *International Journal of Ethics*, Vol. XLVI (1935), pp. 64–81.

NATHANSON, Jerome, *John Dewey: The Reconstruction of the Democratic Life*. New York: Charles Scribner's Sons, 1951.

RATNER, Sidney, *The Philosopher of the Common Man. Essays in Honor of John Dewey to Celebrate His Eightieth Birthday*. New York: G. P. Putnam's Sons, 1940.

SANTAYANA, George, "Dewey's Naturalistic Metaphysics." *Obiter Scripta*. New York: Charles Scribner's Sons, 1936.

SCHILPP, Paul A., ed., *The Philosophy of John Dewey*. Evanston, Ill.: Northwestern U. Press, 1939.

THAYER, H. S., *The Logic of Pragmatism: An Examination of John Dewey's Logic*. New York: Humanities Press, 1952.

THOMAS, Milton H., ed., *John Dewey, A Centennial Bibliography*. Chicago: U. of Chicago Press, 1962.

WHITE, Morton G., *The Origin of Dewey's Instrumentalism*. New York: Columbia U. Press, 1943.

WOLSTEIN, Benjamin, *Experience and Valuation: A Study in John Dewey's Naturalism*. New York, 1949.

General Bibliography [1]

REFERENCE WORKS

ANDERSON, Paul Russell, and FISCH, Max Harold, *Philosophy in America, From the Puritans to James, With Representative Selections.* New York: Appleton-Century, 1939.

BEARD, Charles A. and Mary R., *The American Spirit, a Study of the Idea of Civilization in the United States.* New York: Macmillan Co., 1942.

Biblioteca Americana: A Dictionary of Books Relating to America, from its Discovery to the Present Time. New York: Bibliographical Society of America, 1868–1936, 29 vols.

BLAU, Joseph L., ed., *American Philosophic Addresses, 1700–1900.* New York: Columbia U. Press, 1946.

_____ *Men and Movements in American Philosophy.* New York: Prentice-Hall, 1952.

COHEN, Morris R., *American Thought, A Critical Sketch,* ed. by Felix S. Cohen, Glencoe, Ill.: The Free Press, 1954.

CURTI, Merle, *The Growth of American Thought,* 2nd ed. New York: Harper, 1950.

Dictionary of American Biography, ed. by Allen Johnson. New York: Charles Scribner's Sons, 1928–37, 20 vols.

Dictionary of Philosophy and Psychology, ed. by J.M. Baldwin. New York: Macmillan Co., 1901–05, 3 vols.

Encyclopedia of Philosophy, ed. by Paul Edwards. 10 vols. New York: Macmillan Co., forthcoming. Articles on American Philosophy.

GETTELL, R.D., *History of American Political Thought.* New York: Century Co., 1929.

JACOBSON, J. Mark, *The Development of American Political Thought.* New York: Appleton-Century, 1932.

JONES, Adam LeRoy, *Early American Philosophers.* New York: Macmillan Co., 1898.

MAYER, Frederick, *A History of American Thought—An Introduction.* Dubuque, Iowa: Wm. C. Brown, 1951.

MERRIAM, Charles E., *A History of American Political Theories.* New York: Macmillan Co., 1903.

MUELDER, Walter G., SEARS, Laurence, SCHLABACH, Anne V., *The Development of American Philosophy, A Book of Readings,* 2nd ed. Boston: Houghton Mifflin, 1960.

PARRINGTON, V.L., *Main Currents in American Thought.* New York: Harcourt Brace, 1927–30, 3 vols.

---

[1] This General Bibliography contains books not listed in the separate Bibliographies for each author.

PERRY, Ralph B., *Characteristically American*. New York: A.A. Knopf, 1949.

PERSONS, Stow, *American Minds, A History of Ideas*. New York: Henry Holt, 1958.

RILEY, I.W., *American Thought from Puritanism to Pragmatism and Beyond*. New York: Henry Holt, 1915; 2nd ed., 1923.

ROGERS, A.K., *English and American Philosophy Since 1800*. New York: Macmillan Co., 1922.

SANTAYANA, George, *Character and Opinion in the United States*. New York: Charles Scribner's Sons, 1920.

SCHNEIDER, Herbert W., *A History of American Philosophy*. New York: Columbia U. Press, 1946; rev. ed., 1963.

TAYLOR, Walter F., *A History of American Letters*. Atlanta: American Book Co., 1936.

TOWNSEND, H.G., *Philosophical Ideas in the United States*. New York: American Book Co., 1934.

TRENT, William P., ERSKINE, J., SHERMAN, Stuart P., VAN DOREN, Carl, eds., *The Cambridge History of American Literature*. New York: G.P. Putnam's Sons, 1917–21, 4 vols.

WARFEL, H.R., GABRIEL, R.H., and WILLIAMS, S.T., *The American Mind*. New York: American Book Co., 1947, 2 vols.

WERKMEISTER, W.H., *A History of Philosophical Ideas in America*. New York: Ronald Press, 1949.

PART ONE: THE COLONIAL PERIOD

BOORSTIN, Daniel J., *The Americans, The Colonial Experience*. New York: Random House, 1958.

COVEY, Cyclone, *The American Pilgrimage. The Roots of American History, Religion and Culture*. New York: Collier Books, 1961.

FISKE, John, *The Beginnings of New England; or, The Puritan Theocracy in Its Relations to Civil and Religious Liberty*. Boston: Houghton Mifflin, 1889.

FOSTER, F.H., *A Genetic History of the New England Theology*. Chicago: U. of Chicago Press, 1907.

GAUSTAD, Edwin Scott, *The Great Awakening in New England*. New York: Harpers, 1957.

HAROUTUNIAN, Joseph, *Piety versus Moralism, The Passing of the New England Theology*. New York: Henry Holt, 1932.

JONES, Adam LeRoy, *Early American Philosophers*. New York: Macmillan Co., 1898; F. Ungar, 1958.

MILLER, Perry, *The New England Mind: The Seventeenth Century*. New York: Macmillan Co., 1939; Cambridge: Harvard U. Press, 1945.

———— *The New England Mind: From Colony to Province*. Cambridge: Harvard U. Press, 1953.

———— *Errand into the Wilderness*. Cambridge: Harvard U. Press, 1956.

MORISON, Samuel Eliot, *The Puritan Pronaos. Studies in the Intellectual Life of New England in the Seventeenth Century*. New York: N.Y.U. Press, 1936. Reissued as *The Intellectual Life of Colonial New England*, 1956.

NEWLIN, Claude M., *Philosophy and Religion in Colonial America*. New York: Philosophical Library, 1962.

OSGOOD, Herbert L., "The Political Ideas of the Puritans." *Political Science Quarterly*, Vol. VI (1891), pp. 1–28, 201–31.

SCHNEIDER, Herbert W., *The Puritan Mind*. New York: Henry Holt, 1930.

SIMPSON, Alan, *Puritanism in Old and New England*. Chicago: U. of Chicago Press, 1955.

WALLER, George M., ed., *Puritanism in Early America*. Boston: D.C. Heath, 1950.

PART TWO: REASON AND REVOLUTION

BALDWIN, Alice M., *The New England Clergy and the American Revolution*. Durham, N.C.: Duke U. Press, 1928.

BARLOW, Joel, *The Political Writings*, New York, 1796.

BEARD, Charles A., *Economic Origins of Jeffersonian Democracy*. New York: Macmillan Co., 1915.

BECKER, Carl L., *The Heavenly City of Eighteenth Century Philosophers*. New York: Harcourt, Brace, 1922.

BOORSTIN, Daniel Joseph, *The Lost World of Thomas Jefferson*. New York: Henry Holt, 1948.

CAIRNS, John, *Unbelief in the Eighteenth Century*. New York: Harper, 1881.

FAY, Bernard, *The Revolutionary Spirit in France and America. A Study of Moral and Intellectual Relations Between France and the United States at the End of the Eighteenth Century*. New York: Harcourt, Brace, 1927.

HIBBEN, John G., *The Philosophy of the Enlightenment*. New York: Charles Scribner's Sons, 1910.

KOCH, G. Adolf, *Republican Religion. The American Revolution and the Cult of Reason*. New York: Henry Holt, 1933.

KRAUS, Michael, *The Atlantic Civilization. Eighteenth Century Origins*. Ithaca: Cornell U. Press, 1949.

MACIVER, R.M., "The Philosophical Background of the Constitution." *Journal of Social Philosophy*, Vol. III (1937–38), pp. 201–09.

MORAIS, Herbert M., *Deism in Eighteenth Century America*. New York: Columbia U. Press, 1934.

OSGOOD, Herbert L., *The American Colonies in the Eighteenth Century*. New York: Columbia U. Press, 1924, 4 vols.

PERRY, Ralph Barton, *Puritanism and Democracy*. New York: Vanguard, 1944.

RILEY, I.W., *American Philosophy. The Early Schools*. New York: Dodd, Mead, 1907.

SAVELLE, Max, *Seeds of Liberty. The Genesis of the American Mind*. New York: A.A. Knopf, 1948.

TYLER, Moses Coit, *The Literary History of the American Revolution, 1763–1783*. New York: G.P. Putnam's Sons, 1897.

WILTSE, Charles M., *The Jeffersonian Tradition in American Democracy*. Chapel Hill: U. of N.C. Press, 1939.

WRIGHT, B.F., Jr., *American Interpretations of Natural Law: A Study in the History of Political Thought*. Cambridge: Harvard U. Press, 1931.

WRIGHT, Charles Conrad, *The Beginnings of Unitarianism in America.* Boston: Beacon Press, 1955.

PART THREE: CONSERVATISM IN POLITICAL THEORY AND PHILOSOPHY

A. SOUTHERN RACIAL ARISTOCRACY

BLEDSOE, Albert Taylor, *An Essay on Liberty and Slavery,* Philadelphia, 1856.

BLAU, Joseph, ed., *Social Theories of Jacksonian Democracy. Representative Writings of the Period, 1825–1850.* New York: Hafner Publ. Co., 1947.

BURGESS, John W., *The Middle Period,* New York, 1897.

CHANNING, William Ellery, *Slavery.* Boston, 1835.

CRAVEN, Avery, *The Coming of the Civil War,* 2nd ed. Chicago: U. of Chicago Press, 1957.

EATON, Clement, *Freedom of Thought in the Old South.* Durham: Duke U. Press, 1940.

GETTELL, Raymond G., *History of American Political Thought.* New York: Appleton, 1928; 2nd ed., 1953.

JENKINS, William Sumner, *Pro-Slavery Thought in the Old South.* Chapel Hill: U. of N. C. Press, 1935.

LIEBER, Francis, *On Civil Liberty and Self-Government.* Philadelphia, 1853.

SCHLESINGER, Arthur M., Jr., *The Age of Jackson.* Boston: Little, Brown, 1946.

SMITH, Wilson, *Professors and Public Ethics: Studies of Northern Moral Philosophers Before the Civil War.* Ithaca: Cornell U. Press, 1956.

THORP, W., CURTI, M., and BAKER, C., *American Issues.* New York: Lippincott, 1941. See "The Southern Cause, 1800–1860"; rev. ed., 1955.

WARD, John William, *Andrew Jackson. Symbol for an Age.* New York: Oxford U. Press, 1955.

B. ACADEMIC PHILOSOPHY: SCOTTISH REALISM

BOWEN, Francis, *Treatise on Logic: or, The Laws of Pure Thought: Comprising both the Aristotelic and Hamiltonian Analysis of Logical Terms.* Cambridge, 1865.

––––––– *On the Application of Metaphysical and Ethical Science to the Evidences of Religion.* Boston: Little, Brown, 1849.

HAVEN, Joseph, *Mental Philosophy: Including the Intellect, Sensibilities and Will.* Boston, 1857.

––––––– *Moral Philosophy: Including Theoretical and Practical Ethics.* Boston, 1857.

––––––– *Studies in Philosophy and Theology.* Andover, Mass., 1869.

PORTER, Noah, *The Human Intellect; with an Introduction Upon Psychology and Soul.* New York: Scribner's Sons, 1868; abridged ed., 1871.

———— *The Elements of Moral Science: Theoretical and Practical.* New York: Scribner's Sons, 1885; first ed., 1835.

SMITH, Samuel Stanhope, *An Essay on the Causes of the Variety of Complexion and Figure in the Human Species.* New Brunswick, N.J., 1787; 2nd ed., 1810.

———— *The Lectures, Corrected and Improved, Which Have Been Delivered for a Series of Years in the College of New Jersey; on the Subjects of Moral and Political Philosophy.* Trenton, N.J., 1812, 2 vols.

———— *A Comprehensive View of the Leading and Most Important Principles of Natural and Revealed Religion, etc.* New Brunswick, N.J., 1815.

TYLER, Samuel, *A Discourse of the Baconian Philosophy.* Maryland, 1844.

WITHERSPOON, John, *Lectures on Moral Philosophy,* ed. by V.L. Collins. Princeton: Princeton U. Press, 1912.

PART FOUR: TRANSCENDENTALISM

ALLEN, Gay Wilson, *Walt Whitman Handbook.* Chicago: Packard and Co., 1946.

BROOKS, Van Wyck, *The Flowering of New England.* Boston: Houghton Mifflin, 1938.

CHARVAT, William, *The Origins of American Critical Thought, 1810–1835.* Philadelphia: U. of Pennsylvania Press, 1936.

CHRISTY, Arthur, *The Orient in American Transcendentalism.* New York: Columbia U. Press, 1932.

COMMAGER, Henry Steele, *Theodore Parker.* Boston: Little, Brown, 1936.

DIRKS, John E., *The Critical Theology of Theodore Parker.* New York: Columbia U. Press, 1948.

ELLIS, Charles Mayo, *An Essay on Transcendentalism (1842),* ed. by Walter Harding. Gainsville, Fla.: Scholars Facsimile and Reprints, 1954.

FAUSSET, Hugh L'Anson, *Walt Whitman: Poet of Democracy.* New Haven: Yale U. Press, 1942.

FROTHINGHAM, Octavius, *Transcendentalism in New England.* New York: G.P. Putnam's Sons, 1880; reprinted, Harper, 1959.

GODDARD, H.C., *Studies in New England Transcendentalism.* New York: Columbia U. Press, 1908.

HUTCHINSON, William R., *The Transcendentalist Ministers.* New Haven: Yale U. Press, 1959.

MATTHIESSEN, F.O., *American Renaissance.* New York: Oxford U. Press, 1941.

MILLER, Perry, *The Transcendentalists. An Anthology.* Cambridge: Harvard U. Press, 1950.

MUMFORD, Lewis, *The Golden Day.* New York: Boni & Liveright, 1926.

NICOLSON, Marjorie H., "James Marsh and the Vermont Transcendentalists." *Philosophical Review,* Vol. XXXIV (1925), pp. 28–50.

SHEPARD, Odell, *Pedlar's Progress: The Life of Bronson Alcott.* Boston: Little, Brown, 1937.

SMITH, H. Shelton, "Was Theodore Parker a Transcendentalist?" *New England Quarterly,* Vol. XXIII (1950), pp. 351–64.

STOVALL, Floyd, *Walt Whitman: Representative Selections, with Introduction, Bibliography and Notes*, rev. ed. New York: American Book Co., 1939.

WRIGHT, Conrad, *The Beginnings of Unitarianism in America*. Boston: Star King Press, 1955.

PART FIVE: SPECULATIVE AND ABSOLUTE IDEALISM [2]

ARMSTRONG, A.C., Jr., "Philosophy in the United States." *Educational Review*, Vol. X (1895), pp. 1–11.

BOWNE, Borden Parker, *Philosophy of Theism*. New York: Harper, 1887.

———— *Metaphysics*. New York: American Book Co., 1882.

———— *Personalism*. Boston: Houghton Mifflin, 1908.

———— *Theory of Thought and Knowledge*. New York: Harpers, 1897.

BROKMEYER, Henry C., *A Mechanic's Diary*. Washington, D.C., 1910.

BRIGHTMAN, E.S., "Personalism and the Influence of Bowne." *Proceedings of the Sixth Intl. Congress of Philosophy*. New York: Longmans, Green, 1927.

BUCKMAN, John W., and STRATTON, George Malcolm, eds., *G. Holmes Howison, Philosopher and Teacher; a Selection from His Writings with a Biographical Sketch*. Berkeley, Cal., 1934.

DAVIDSON, Thomas, *The Philosophical System of Antonio Resmini-Serbati*. New York, 1882.

———— *The Education of the Wage-Earners*. Boston, 1904.

FRÁNKQUIZ, Ventura J.A., *Borden Parker Bowne's Treatment of the Problem of Change and Identity*. Puerto Rico: The U. of Puerto Rico Bull., 1942.

HALL, G. Stanley, "Philosophy in the United States." *Mind*, Vol. IV (1879), pp. 89–105.

HOWISON, George H., *The Limits of Evolution and Other Essays*. New York: Macmillan Co., 1901, 1905.

———— *The Conception of God: A Philosophic Discussion Concerning the Nature of the Divine Idea as a Demonstrable Reality*, with J. LeConte, S.E. Meyers and J. Royce. New York: Macmillan Co., 1897.

LADD, George Trumbull, *Philosophy of Mind; An Essay in the Metaphysics of Psychology*. New York: Scribner's Sons, 1895.

———— *Philosophy of Knowledge: An Inquiry into the Nature, Limits, and Validity of Human Cognitive Faculty*. New York: Scribner's Sons, 1897.

LEWIS, Taylor, "Two Schools of Philosophy." *American Theological Review*, Vol. IV (1862), pp. 102–34.

MCCONNELL, F.J., *Borden Parker Bowne*. New York: Abingdon Press, 1929.

MUIRHEAD, J.H., "How Hegel Came to America." *Philosophical Review*, Vol. XXXVII (1928), pp. 226–40.

RAND, Benjamin, "Philosophical Instruction in Harvard University from 1636 to 1906." Part II, *Harvard Graduates' Magazine*, Vol. XXXVII (1929), pp. 291–311.

---

[2] A more extensive bibliography on latter-day idealism appears in the companion volume, *American Philosophy in the Twentieth Century*.

ROGERS, Arthur K., *English and American Philosophy Since 1800.* New York: Macmillan Co., 1922.

SNIDER, Denton J., *Will and Its World: Psychical and Ethical.* St. Louis, 1899.

———— *Social Institutions in Their Origin, Growth and Interconnection: Psychologically Treated.* St. Louis, 1901.

———— *Cosmos and Diocosmos; The Processes of Nature Psychologically Treated.* St. Louis, 1909.

WARREN, Austin, "The Concord School of Philosophy." *New England Quarterly,* Vol. II (1929), pp. 199–233.

PART SIX: EVOLUTION AND DARWINISM

ABBOTT, Francis Ellington, *Scientific Theism; or, Organic Scientific Philosophy.* Boston, 1885.

———— *The Syllogistic Philosophy; or, Prolegomena to Science.* Boston, 1890, 2 vols.

ADAMS, Henry, *The Education of Henry Adams* (1906). Boston: Houghton Mifflin, 1918.

AGASSIZ, Louis, *An Essay on Classification.* London, 1859.

———— "Evolution and Permanence of Type." *Atlantic Monthly,* Vol. XXXIII (1874), pp. 92–101.

DRAPER, John W., *Evolution; Its Origin, Progress, and Consequences.* New York, 1877.

GRAY, Asa, "Darwin and His Reviewers." *Atlantic Monthly,* Vol. VI (1860), pp. 406–25.

HOFSTADER, Richard, *Social Darwinism in American Thought—1865–1915.* Philadelphia: U. of Penn. Press, 1944; rev. ed., Boston: Beacon Press, 1955.

LOWENBERG, Bert J., "The Reaction of American Scientists to Darwin." *American Historical Review,* Vol. XXXVIII (1932–33), pp. 657–70.

———— "Darwinism Comes to America, 1859–1900." *Mississippi Valley Historical Review,* Vol. XXVIII (1941), pp. 339–68.

PERSONS, Stow, ed., *Evolutionary Thought in America.* New Haven: Yale U. Press, 1950.

RATNER, Sidney, "Evolution and the Rise of the Scientific Spirit in America." *Philosophy of Science,* Vol. III (1936), pp. 104–22.

ROBERTS, Windsor Hall, *The Reaction of American Protestant Churches to the Darwinian Philosophy, 1860–1900.* Dissertation. Chicago: U. of Chicago History Dept., 1938.

WIENER, Philip, *Evolution and the Founders of Pragmatism.* Cambridge: Harvard U. Press, 1949.

WILLIAMS, C.M., *A Review of the Systems of Ethics Founded on the Theory of Evolution.* New York, 1893.

WHITE, Andrew D., *History of the Warfare Between Science and Theology.* New York, 1896.

YOUMANS, Edward L., *Herbert Spencer on the Americans and the Americans on Herbert Spencer.* New York, 1883.

Index of Authors and Selections